Dear Dean:

Best Wishes,

Pomdhito Shinder

April 2, 2001

LEADING JAPAN

The Role of the Prime Minister

TOMOHITO SHINODA

PRAEGER

Westport, Connecticut
London

Library of Congress Cataloging-in-Publication Data

Shinoda, Tomohito, 1960–
    Leading Japan : the role of the prime minister / Tomohito Shinoda.
      p. cm.
    Includes bibliographical references and index.
    ISBN 0–275–96994–0 (alk. paper)
    1. Prime ministers—Japan. 2. Executive power—Japan. 3. Japan—Politics and
government—1945– I. Title.
    JQ1640.S55   2000
    352.23'0952—dc21   00–022886

British Library Cataloguing in Publication Data is available.

Library of Congress Catalog Card Number: 00–022886
ISBN: 0–275–96994–0

First published in 2000

Praeger Publishers, 88 Post Road West, Westport, CT 06881
An imprint of Greenwood Publishing Group, Inc.
www.praeger.com

Printed in the United States of America

The paper used in this book complies with the
Permanent Paper Standard issued by the National
Information Standards Organization (Z39.48–1984).

10 9 8 7 6 5 4 3 2 1

To Dr. Nakayama Sohei

Contents

Tables and Figures

Preface

In the 1990s, the Japanese political scene witnessed a series of drastic changes, including the end of the 38-year-long reign of the Liberal Democratic Party (LDP), the establishment of the LDP-Socialist coalition government, the formation of the minority government led by LDP president Hashimoto Ryûtarô, LDP's reemergence as a majority in the lower house, LDP's loss in the 1998 upper house election and Hashimoto's resignation, and the establishment of the Obuchi Keizô administration. While these rapid changes perhaps provided embarrassment to the so-called revisionists who assert that Japan can never change, they offered excitement to many Japan scholars, and at the same time headaches to those of us trying to finish a book on current Japanese politics: I have spent the past several years constantly revising my draft to keep up with the current situation.

These changes not only have provided different political environments surrounding the Japanese prime minister but also have significantly increased public interest in his political leadership. Whereas interest has increased, however, understanding has fallen far behind. There are very few academic works in any language totally dedicated to describing the leadership role of the Japanese prime minister. Lack of literature and understanding is not unique to Japan's leadership, of course. As James MacGregor Burns describes, "Leadership is one of the most observed and least understood phenomena on earth."[1] Although people recognize the central role of a national leader, the scholarship on the president, the prime minister, or the chancellor lags far behind scholarship on other areas of political science.

For Japan, there are biographies of individual prime ministers in separate books or series of books written mostly by journalists closely associated to one personality. The focus of these studies, however, is the life and career of a particular prime minister, not the function of the office of the prime minister; nor do they offer comparison of one with another. Neither systematic nor analytical, these studies are often biased as a result of an author's friendship with an individual politician. Literature devoted solely to the role of the prime minister in policy making did not exist in either the Japanese or English until just recently.

One of the most important reasons for this lack of literature is access to information sources. There is no official record of cabinet meetings. Information on what the prime minister does and who influences cabinet decisions is kept very much in a black box. Only journalists who have special access through a personal network can obtain behind-the-scene accounts.

Fortunately, I had the opportunity to talk to the former assistants to most of the LDP prime ministers from the Tanaka Kakuei administration (1972–74) to the Hashimoto Ryûtarô administration (1996–98). I was also very fortunate to interview two former prime ministers, Hosokawa Morihiro and Murayama Tomiichi. Their comments helped me learn from their firsthand knowledge and experiences and their involvement in the policy process. If readers feel that this work is unique and concrete, it is owed to their invaluable and lively comments.

The completion of this study would not have been possible without the support of many individuals and institutions. I am particularly indebted to George R. Packard, who has guided me through my academic and professional career for the past fifteen years. Without him, this work would not have even begun. I would also like to thank Arthur J. Alexander, Hans-Georg Betz, Michael Green, Ronald Morse, Nathaniel B. Thayer, and Daniel H. Unger for their useful comments. I am also thankful to the Foundation of International Education, which financially supported part of this study.

I am grateful to those who granted me audience and for their invaluable comments—in particular to the two prime ministers, to the former assistants to the prime minister under the administrations of Tanaka Kakuei to Hashimoto Ryûtarô, and to those who were involved in the administrative and tax reforms dealt with in the case studies of this book: Asakura Kôji, Fukuda Yasuo, Gotôda Masaharu, Hamaoka Takashi, Handa Yoshihiro, Hirose Katsusada, Hosokawa Morihiro, Katô Hiroshi, Kannari Yoji, Kitazawa Hideo, Konaga Keiichi, Kumon Shumpei, Matoba Junzô, Miyawaki Raisuke, Mizuno Masaru, Moroi Ken, Murayama Tatsuo, Murayama Tomiichi, Nagatomi Yûichirô, Nakamura Keiichirô, Namikawa Shino, Okano Tadashi, Saka Atsuo, Watanabe Hiroshi, and Yamanaka Sadanori. I am especially grateful to Hosokawa Morihiro, Murayama Tomiichi and Gotôda Masaharu, who graciously gave of their time for an interview, and to Miyawaki Raisuke, who generously spent considerable time in relating personal experiences at the Prime Minister's Office. I use this preface to advise that the comments from all these interviews were the principal source for this study.

My sincere gratitude goes to Kimura Tarô, Kimura Kazuko, and Aizawa Mami, who helped in arranging interviews and in finding useful books in Tokyo, invaluable assistance to an author who lived in Washington. I am also most appreciative to my parents and in-laws for their encouragement. My wife, Gretchen, played a crucial role in the inception and development of this book. In addition to her unlimited moral support, she gave me numerous insightful comments and provided expert editing. Without her, I could not have completed this work. My daughter, Erika, was born during this book project. She brought new meaning to my life and motivation to finish this project.

Finally, I dedicate this work to Nakayama Sohei, a Japanese senior business leader who has guided me in both my professional and my personal life and generously introduced me to the people I interviewed for this study. I cannot thank him enough for his contributions to this work and to my life.

A NOTE ON CONVENTIONS

Japanese words and personal names are romanized according to the modified Hepburn system. Macron marks are used for long vowels. Japanese personal names are normally presented in the Japanese order—family name first and given name second. Exceptions to these rules are Tokyo (which should be *Tôkyô*) and Japanese scholars whose English-language publications give the author's name in Western order. Most figures are given in yen and not translated into U.S. dollars, as the yen-dollar exchange has fluctuated since the collapse of the Bretton Woods system in the early 1970s. A dollar value has been between 79 and 360 yen.

NOTE

1. James MacGregor Burns, *Leadership* (New York: Harper Torchbooks, 1978), p. 2.

Introduction

Japan's politics is often compared to a *mikoshi*, or a miniature shrine carried by many people in a Japanese festival. Nobody knows who controls it: Many people with differing ideas are involved, and it moves right and left, somehow eventually moving in a certain direction. A powerful leader can control the direction by manipulating the participants. A leader without a strong power base within his own party must acquire public support to give pressure to the participants. Without strong leadership, however, the participants lose the direction, in the end going nowhere.

In the Pulitzer Prize–winning work *Leadership*, James MacGregor Burns describes leadership as an aspect and special form of power, whose two essential ingredients are motive and resources.[1] As Burns maintains, "The two are interrelated. Lacking motive, resource diminishes; lacking resource, motive lies idle. Lacking either one, power collapses."[2]

An effective political leader can share his motive with his followers to achieve policy goals. Burns defines "the ultimate test" of leadership as "the realization of intended, real change that meets people's enduring needs."[3] Since policy goals such as administrative and tax reforms, described in this study, can fit into this definition, the motive for the prime minister is clear. What resources, then, are available to prime ministers, and which do they apply to achieve their policy goals? What factors make the difference between success and failure? The purpose of this study is to provide answers to these questions. The study first identifies the sources of power available to Japanese prime ministers. Whatever sources of power the prime minister has, they are wasted unless he actually utilizes them to successfully achieve his policy goals. Second, this study shows how prime ministers use political and personal resources to achieve policy goals, and it proves that the prime minister can make a difference in policy development, an aspect largely ignored.

Numerous political resources appear to be available to a Japanese prime minister. As head of a cabinet vested with executive power, the prime minister is at the top of the executive branch. He leads the political party or a coalition of parties that hold the majority seats in the powerful lower house (the House of Representatives). The prime minister handles both administrative and political affairs as the leader of the government and the ruling party or coalition.

In spite of his many responsibilities and authorities, the Japanese prime minister is often considered weak. Lack of leadership is a recurring theme in many analyses of Japanese politics. Reinforcing the power of the prime minister was one of the three major focuses in administrative reform efforts under the Hashimoto Ryûtarô administration. Japan scholars have long argued that political leaders depend on Japan's strong bureaucracy for the formulation and execution of policies. Some even argue that the bureaucracy is so strong that political leaders, including the prime minister, have a limited role in policy making. Karel van Wolferen, for example, describes the Japanese policy-making mechanism as "The System," which is made up of elites in the political, bureaucratic, and business world who as a unit somehow make decisions. According to Wolferen, Japan's system has no political center and thus no political leadership.[4]

Many Japan scholars have emphasized the role of LDP politicians in dealing with specific issues and have concluded that the relative power of the LDP vis-à-vis the bureaucracy has increased. This argument does not support a strong prime-ministerial theme. Instead, it describes the decentralization of political power within the Liberal Democratic Party or the division of power among members with a specific policy interest. The issue-specific sectionalism within the party and within the government has eroded the ability of the prime minister to lead under an LDP-led government.

Although academic literature on the role of the bureaucracy and the ruling party is abundant, the prime minister's function in policy making has been largely neglected until recently. The first systematic study on the prime minister by Hayao argues that the leadership of the prime minister is crippled by the selection process of the LDP presidency, by intra- and interparty politics, by the subgovernment, and by the small size of the prime minister's support staff. Kenji Hayao uses Nakasone's educational reform effort as well as his tax reform proposal as case studies, with both efforts ending in failure. Focusing on the ineffectual aspects of the prime minister's power, Hayao successfully illustrates the constraints that can block the prime minister in the exercise of leadership.[5] Although Hayao also argues that the prime minister can have an important impact on policy, he fails to offer examples.[6]

In contrast, this study presents both successful and unsuccessful case studies to prove the author's theses: The prime minister plays a crucial role in the policy-making process by utilizing a combination of various sources of power to exercise leadership. This study identifies the sources of power available to Japanese prime ministers—some from legal authorities, and others from informal sources. Is the institution of the prime minister weak, or do political constraints block the prime minister from achieving policy goals? An examination of each source of power enables a determination of the limitations the prime minister faces and the resources that are at his disposal to enable him to be an effective national leader. Three case studies provide examples of how different prime ministers have either failed or succeeded in applying their political resources.

In search for appropriate case studies of "prime-ministerial policy," I came across four categories of issues after the interviews with former assistants to the prime ministers. First are those that require the prime minister to coordinate conflicting interests inherent in ministerial sectionalism. Major economic issues and administrative and tax reforms emphasized in this study fall in this category. Second are issues that require international consideration. There are many cases in which the government needs to put priority on foreign relations over domestic interests. In fact, the prime minister often shows his leadership on security issues most effectively and most free-handedly. The third category involves cases that question the basic ideology of the nation. Frequent discussion of the revision of the Japanese Constitution and Nakasone's visit to Yasukuni Shrine, a shrine that memorializes war criminals of World War II, are examples of this category. Fourth are issues on which the prime minister chooses to impose his political will. Tanaka Kakuei's plan for restructuring the Japanese archipelago and Nakasone's educational reform fall in this category.

Major economic and government reform policies were chosen as case studies of this work for several reasons. The popularity of the prime minister depends in good measure on the nation's economic condition. Every prime minister, therefore, must deal with economic issues. His leadership is required to stimulate the economy in the recession and to control prices in times of inflation. Major economic reforms usually involve most agencies of the executive branch. Administrative reform is another category of policy that involves many, if not all, ministries and agencies. Any major reform in the government organization meets some opposition from somewhere. In the cases of tax and administrative reforms, the involvement of the prime minister is required in order to coordinate among the conflicting interests of different agencies.

With case studies on fiscal and tax reform, Junko Kato wrote *The Problem of Bureaucratic Rationality*.[7] In the book, Kato argues that tax reform under the Takeshita administration was achieved largely by the skillful maneuvering of Ministry of Finance officials to persuade legislators. The author's view on the issue is different. There is no doubt that the role of bureaucrats was important. They served as scenario writers and played an important role behind the scenes. However, it is the political actors who played on the stage. Whereas some faithfully followed the prepared scenario, others ignored it. The prime ministers served as producers who decided the general casting as well as the lead actor in the play. This study demonstrates that the national leader plays a pivotal role in unsuccessful and successful efforts to introduce administrative and tax reforms.

OUTLINE

The study begins with Part I, which explains the political environment surrounding the prime minister. The prime minister is chosen by a majority of the Diet, but this support is not necessarily assured throughout his term. Chapter 1 presents an analytical framework for the prime minister's role in Japan's decision making. Under this framework, there exist two dimensions of fraction within the government and the ruling party that the prime minister faces—intraparty factionalism and issue-specific sectionalism.

Although Japan had a single-majority government led by the LDP for nearly 40 years, the ruling party was a loose coalition of five to eight different intraparty factions—inner-party groups formed not for ideological reasons but to achieve the premiership for their leader. To become and remain a prime minister, a faction leader needed to retain at least a majority of the party supporting him while maintaining overall party harmony. Therefore, he was politically forced to form a cabinet with members from factions not his own and over whom he had little control.

The prime minister under the coalition governments dealt, not with factions within one party but with different parties in a coalition. Maintaining coalition harmony was similar to handling factions in the ruling party. The same dynamics, though more along ideological lines than political ambitions, were present and are even more volatile. Diverse loyalties weakened the cabinet's unity and thus its control over individual ministries.

The individual government ministries have their own interests and industries to protect. Civil servants in the bureaucracy spend almost their entire career in a single ministry, and their loyalty to home ministries is very strong. They tend to put ministerial interest over national interest, and this sectionalism has often been a major obstacle to the prime minister's achievement of his policy goals. His leadership is seen in his will and ability to overcome these two fractions.

Chapter 2 analyzes the prime ministership after 1993 when the 38-year-long reign of the LDP's single-party control ended. The newly elected non-LDP prime minister, Hosokawa Morihiro, led a fragile eight-party coalition government. As his power base within the coalition parties was weak, he at least tried to centralize the decision-making process by establishing a new policy organ. This centralized system worked in several cases, but it was criticized for its aristocratic nature.

The Socialist prime minister Murayama Tomiichi, who led the LDP-Socialist-*Sakigake* coalition government, introduced a decentralized decision-making system under which three coalition parties discussed policy issues to reach consensus. This system continued even under the LDP prime minister, Hashimoto Ryûtarô. After the 1996 general election, however, LDP members became dominant in the decentralized system, creating a situation similar to that of the pre-1993 period.

Part II is devoted to explaining the prime minister's sources of power by presenting examples for each category. In Chapter 3, the institutional power sources of the prime minister are addressed. Obvious examples are the legal authorities given by the Constitution, the Cabinet Law, and other laws. The four major sources of institutional power discussed in this chapter are the authority granted as head of the cabinet; the authority to appoint and dismiss cabinet members; the authority to dissolve the lower house; and the ability to draw upon staff support from the Cabinet Secretariat. This chapter argues that the prime minister's legal authority has been surprisingly limited. In order for the prime minister to effectively exercise his role as head of the cabinet, he must utilize informal sources of power.

Chapter 4 focuses on the informal sources of power. Having the powers of the presidency of the ruling party has been a major political resource that supplements the prime minister's limited legal authority. The effectiveness of his party-leader status, however, depends on his power base within the party. In general, leaders of large factions have enjoyed a more secure power base within the party, while those who lead smaller factions depend on other personal sources of power. Personal sources come from the prime minister's own experience, from his expertise, and from his personality.[8] What shape this type of power takes depends, of course, on the nature of the individual prime minister and the political environment of the nation at the time. Personal power can be derived from his professional reputation among fellow politicians, business leaders, and the media, as well as from his public support, which increasingly influences the power base of national leaders. Popularity levels depend on the overall status of the country. For example, popular support for the cabinet is generally higher when the economy is in good condition. Even so, an unexpected political scandal involving the ruling party can lower popular trust of the political system, thus lowering the popularity of the prime minister.

Part III of this study is a chronological analysis of major reform efforts by five different prime ministers. The detailed and descriptive case studies support the author's view that the prime minister plays a critical role in the policy-making process. The three case studies presented in the second half of this study—two examining administrative reform and the other tax reform attempts—demonstrate that the reforms had broad implications for most government agencies. The prime minister is the only political figure with the authority to coordinate agreements among the various agencies and the members of the ruling party to create the political environment necessary for reforms to be effective.

The case studies illustrate how four different prime ministers handled major reform. The first case study, found in Chapter 5, illustrates efforts toward administrative reform undertaken by Suzuki Zenkô in the first half of the 1980s. When Suzuki lost intraparty support, he resigned before achieving his administrative reforms. Backed by public support, Nakasone Yasuhiro successfully pushed through major administrative reforms by defeating the sectional resistance of the bureaucracy and other LDP members.

The second case study in Chapter 6 describes how Nakasone failed and Takeshita succeeded in introducing a consumption tax. Under the case of administrative reform, Nakasone failed to obtain public support, and sectionalism defeated his tax reform attempt in 1987. Takeshita Noboru, in contrast, successfully contained sectionalism by effectively utilizing his political resources, including those available to him as leader of the largest LDP faction, by calling on his strong ties with the opposition parties and by exercising his control over the bureaucracy. Takesita's extraordinary skill in political maneuvering within his own party and within the government made this unpopular tax possible.

Chapter 7 analyzes the recent Hashimoto Ryûtarô's efforts in administrative reform in 1996–98. This time, the focus of administrative reform shifted to reform of the national bureaucracy largely as a result of bureaucratic scandals. With the limited internal sources of power, Hashimoto actively sought public support. Everything fell apart, however, after the cabinet reshuffling of September 1997 when Hashimoto appointed to the cabinet a man with a criminal record for taking a bribe. As his popularity rating dropped dramatically, LDP's *zoku* members took the opportunity to attack the prime minister's administrative reform. The final report for Hashimoto's administrative reform was a major setback for the interim report.

Chapter 8—the conclusion—presents an overview of this study. Even with the two dimensions of fraction within the government and the ruling party, a Japanese prime minister can be an effective leader. Some prime ministers successfully contain fractions by effectively utilizing power to achieve policy objectives. This chapter presents four leadership styles of postwar prime ministers. It finishes with an exploration of institutional changes that resulted with the 1994 electoral changes the 1999 Diet and government reform, and the 1999 administrative reform laws, which would affect the leadership of the Japanese prime minister.

NOTES

1. James MacGregor Burns, *Leadership* (New York: Harper Torchbooks, 1978), pp. 12–17.

2. Ibid., p. 12.

3. Ibid., p. 461.

4. Karel G. van Wolferen, *The Enigma of Japanese Power* (New York: Alfred A. Knopf, 1989). See also Karel G. van Wolferen, "The Japan Problem," *Foreign Affairs* 65 (winter 1987): pp. 288–303.

5. Kenji Hayao, "The Japanese Prime Minister and Public Policy" (Ph.D. dissertation, University of Michigan, 1990). See also Kenji Hayao, *The Japanese Prime Minister and Public Policy* (Pittsburgh: University of Pittsburgh Press, 1993).

6. Ibid., especially chapter 8, pp. 238–57.

7. Junko Kato, *The Problem of Bureaucratic Rationality: Tax Politics in Japan* (Princeton: Princeton University Press, 1994).

8. The author owes insights for this categorization to former chief cabinet secretary Gotôda Masaharu, who explained the function of the prime minister.

Part I

Political Environments Surrounding the Prime Minister

Chapter 1

Two Dimensions of Fraction: An Analytical Framework

As in many parliamentary democratic nations, the Japanese prime minister is the central political figure that runs the government. He is elected by an elected parliament, the Diet. The prime minister selects the cabinet, and the cabinet has executive power. Collectively, it is responsible to the Diet. The lower house of the Diet, the House of Representatives, can remove the prime minister and his cabinet by a vote of no-confidence. Similarly, the prime minister can dissolve the lower house when he wishes.

This institutional setting of the Japanese prime minister is similar to that found in Great Britain, the mother country of the parliamentary system. His institutional power is stronger than that in continental European countries, such as France, Germany, and Italy, where the prime minister shares authority with an elected president.

The postwar Japanese prime minister is institutionally much stronger than his prewar predecessors. Under the prewar Meiji Constitution of 1889, the Emperor was clearly the head of state who held national sovereign and executive power. The prime minister and his cabinet were to assist the Emperor in administering the government.

In 1885, four years before the promulgation of the Meiji Constitution, Japan's cabinet system originated with the creation of the post of prime minister. It is interesting that this Constitution made no specific mention of the prime minister's position. All ministers were legally equal, and all were appointed by the Emperor; the prime minister was head of the cabinet, but he was only *primus inter pares*, or first among equals.[1] His actual control over the cabinet was quite limited. Article 55 of the Meiji Constitution instructed each minister to directly advise the Emperor. Furthermore, because the cabinet operated under the rule of unanimity, each member in effect held veto power over decisions made in the cabinet. Disagreement over decisions within the cabinet often ended with the resignation of the entire cabinet.

The cabinet was not the only advisory group to the Emperor. The Privy Council existed outside the cabinet's jurisdiction, and when instructed by the Emperor, it deliberated "upon the important matters of State." In addition, the Ministry of Imperial Household assisted the Emperor in an advisory role in policy matters. The authority to command the military belonged to the Emperor. This authority enabled the military to act independently from the civilian cabinet in the name of the Emperor's Right of Supreme Command, and the military led the nation into a military state in the prewar and wartime periods.

Today's Shôwa Constitution, promulgated in 1947, specifically defines the role of the prime minister: He is head of the cabinet, which is vested with all executive powers. The Emperor is reduced to a symbol of state, and the Ministry of Imperial Household is an agency under the Prime Minister's Office. The primary intent of the designers of the new Constitution, executed under the auspices of American Occupation authorities, was clear: to shift sovereignty from the Emperor to the people. This emphasis is reflected in an institutional setting surrounding the prime minister that is stricter than its counterpart in other parliamentary countries.

In order to transform Japan into a representative parliamentary democracy, the founders of the Constitution gave the legislature supremacy over the executive.[2] The Diet is defined not only as the sole legislative body but also as the highest institution of the government. The prime minister must be a Diet member when he is elected by his peers in the Diet. He must select at least one-half of his cabinet ministers from among Diet members. In running the government, the prime minister and his cabinet are responsible to the Diet and ultimately to the people.

These formal institutions define the status of the Japanese prime minister, but his actual role has been further shaped by postwar political and institutional developments. This chapter focuses on two major developments that helped to determine the role of the prime minister and the Japanese political scene. First, the rise of civil servants in each government agency during the immediate postwar period developed an issue-specific sectionalism within the government. Sectionalism further strengthened in the 1970s when members of the ruling party joined in sectional interests. Second, during the Liberal Democratic Party's long reign, the prime minister was a party leadership position before it was a government post because the president of the majority party automatically became premier. However, the party was a loose coalition of intraparty factions. Because faction members wanted to see their leader become the prime minister, their loyalty to the party president was limited. To remain prime minister, he needed to maintain support from a majority of the party, which meant that he had to appease other factions to maintain party harmony. These two dimensions of fractions within the government and the ruling party have eroded the central role of the prime minister.

ISSUE-SPECIFIC SECTIONALISM

Although the prime minister is the central figure in the government, because of time constraints and other limitations he cannot micro-manage the many different issues he must deal with. Because of his central role in the larger political scene, most of his day-to-day administrative actions are handled by ministries and government agencies. Although the indirectly elected prime minister and his cabinet hold all the executive power, the nonelected civil servants in the bureaucracy play an influential role in policy making in Japanese politics.

Ironically, it was the American Occupation authorities—which emphasized the popular sovereign and the supremacy of the legislature when drafting the current Constitution—that helped the Japanese bureaucracy gain power, vis-à-vis the legislative branch, in actual policy-making procedures.[3] The Occupation authorities, or the Supreme Commander for the Allied Powers (SCAP), decided to maintain the Japanese bureaucratic institutions and to administer the Occupation indirectly through them. The Occupation planners originally intended to have a government directly administered by the U.S. military. But because of the sudden, unconditional surrender of Japan, they decided to use the existing government institutions to achieve the immediate and enormous task of governing an entire nation. As the Occupation reforms proved to be successful and popular, the Japanese bureaucrats viewed them as their achievements.

The Occupation authorities conducted a widescale purge that removed or excluded more than 200,000 people from public office. Many incumbent legislators became targets of the purge, which thus effectively eliminated from the political parties most of the experienced politicians. Of the legislators elected in the first postwar general election of April 1946, more than 80 percent (381) were newly elected. These inexperienced legislators had to rely completely on the bureaucracy in formulating legislation. The Diet was no more than a rubber stamp for legislation submitted by the bureaucracy. The ideal of legislative supremacy over the executive, held by the American reformers, was far from reality. After the Allies left, the bureaucrats continued to administer government programs developed under the Occupation. As a result, the bureaucracy became the primary political beneficiary in Japanese society in the immediate postwar period.

The bureaucracy did not escape from Occupation reforms, however. The hardest hit government agency was the prewar Home Ministry, the most prestigious and powerful agency under the Meiji Constitution. In the Occupation authorities' view, the ministry "represented the heart and center of the internal administrative bureaucracy and exercised the controls which reached down through regional, prefectural, city, town, and village governments and to the ward offices and neighborhood association system to enter, influence and restrict every phase of every man, woman and child in Japan."[4] About 60 percent of the Home Ministry's high officials were purged, and its administrative authorities were divided among the new Ministries of Construction, Labor, Health and Welfare, and Home Affairs, and the Police Agency. However, the purge did not cut deeply into the civil service of other ministries, where less than 20 percent of civil servants were removed, except in the Foreign Ministry, where about 30 percent were purged.[5] Overall, the purge helped bring new, younger officials to power in the government and had little negative impact on the efficiency of the bureaucracy, which promoted postwar reforms.

In the area of economic policy making, the relative power of the bureaucracy increased while its major rivals lost power. The Imperial Army and Navy, instrumental in prewar industrial policy making, were abolished. The influential *zaibatsu*, privately owned business empires, were dissolved into small business organizations, and many business leaders were purged. In contrast, under the controlled economy during the Occupation period, the power of the economic bureaucrats in the Ministry of Finance (MOF) and the Ministry of International Trade and Industry (MITI) grew as they implemented a wide range of economic policies. After the Occupation, the economic ministries retained "the emergency controls that they could effectively use, while endeavoring to dismantle other Occupation reforms that threatened to reduce or restrict their powers."[6]

The experience of the Occupation helped strengthen sectionalism among the ministries and agencies in the Japanese government. The Occupation authorities were a bureaucratic organization staffed by U.S. Army officials. Individual sections of SCAP competed with each other to achieve reforms. American reformers began to cooperate with Japanese counterparts in specific areas such as fiscal austerity, civil liberties, local sanitation, highway construction, democratization of the elementary and high school curricula, and revitalization of newspapers. Sometimes this cross-national alliance jointly fought its superior in the Japanese government and the American Occupation.[7] Although the cabinet was collectively responsible for overall administrative actions, the individual ministries grew in power in actual decision making during the Occupation.

The individual ministries maintained their power after the Occupation authorities left Japan. Today, each ministry is staffed by a group of highly competent elite bureaucrats who have strong loyalty to their ministry. The majority of these bureaucrats are graduates of top national universities—most of them are from the Universities of Tokyo and Kyoto—who have passed a highly competitive entrance examination for civil service. Although there are occasional interagency personnel exchange programs, the career patterns of the bureaucrats are dominated by service in a single ministry.[8] This strengthens their loyalty to their ministry and also promotes sectionalism in the various agencies.

Throughout their careers, elite bureaucrats learn to design, draft, and implement legislation in the jurisdiction of their ministries. Their major interest is to protect their ministry's interests and expand its authority, and thus they tend to put their ministerial interest over national interest. In the postwar era, individual ministries have created their own jurisdiction and empowered themselves through various laws. The Ministry of International Trade and Industry, for example, worked to have a multitude of functions assigned to it by 175 separate laws as of April 2000. Knowledge of the complicated network of laws has proved a great asset to the elite bureaucrats who can cite various legal restrictions to block the policy initiatives of other political actors. Such sectionalism backed by expertise often becomes a major obstacle for the prime minister and his cabinet in initiating major policies.

Although ministries are technically subordinate to the cabinet, bureaucrats are responsible only to their ministers. Because Japan's postwar ruling party has reshuffled the cabinet almost once a year, an individual serving as minister generally has little time to accumulate the experience and knowledge necessary to become influential in actual decision making within his ministry. Given this lack of experience and expertise, many ministers have had to rely completely on the civil servants in their ministry. All their official statements in the Diet are prepared in advance by career bureaucrats. Before the 1999 Diet reform (see Chapter 8), when ministers could not answer the questions of other Diet members, the high-level bureaucratic officials answered them on behalf of the minister. This differed from the situation in the British Parliament, where nonelected government officials cannot attend a session. The Japanese system has allowed even incompetent ruling party members to be appointed as cabinet members, and this has over the long run weakened the influence of the minister vis-à-vis civil servants.

A top civil service official, the administrative vice minister, is in charge of coordinating the activities of the various branches of the ministry, preparing ministerial decisions, and supervising their implementation, just like the British Permanent Secretary. Although the minister holds appointive authority, the appointments of the vice minister as well as other positions are almost always decided within the bureaucracy, with the minister rubber-stamping the decision.[9] During his short tenure, the minister more often than not represents the interest of the ministry vis-à-vis the cabinet and the ruling party. As minister, an elected legislator has an excellent opportunity to build personal relationships with the bureaucracy and related industries. Unlike in France, in Japan the minister does not have elite bureaucrats who serve as his private advisors and watchdogs. In order to gain trust and administrative assistance from elite bureaucrats, the minister is expected to be loyal to his ministry, which makes it difficult for the prime minister to coordinate conflicting interests in the cabinet.

These developments support the bureaucratic supremacy or the power elite model, which perhaps is the most popular among the explanations of the Japanese policy-making process. In this model, there are characteristically three actors: bureaucracy, politicians, and business and other interest groups. Sometimes, this is portrayed as the "iron triangle" model. Although supporters of this view markedly disagree on which actor is the most powerful among the three, the bureaucracy is often described as pivotal.[10] Karel van Wolferen describes the Japanese power elite model as "The System," with a submissive middle class. The so-called system in Japan does not and need not have political leadership, according to Wolferen's account. The system, constituted by elites in the political, bureaucratic and business world, as a unity somehow makes

Table 1.1
The LDP's Policy Subcommittees

Policy Subcommittees	
1. Prime Minister's Office	10. Agriculture and Forestry
2. Home Affairs	11. Fisheries
3. National Defense	12. Commerce and Industry
4. Judicial Affairs	13. Transportation
5. Foreign Affairs	14. Communication
6. Finance	15. Construction
7. Education	16. Science and Technology
8. Social Affairs	17. Environment
9. Labor	

decisions. Everybody within tries to preserve the system. A similar monolithic view of Japanese society is suggested by the popular phrase "Japan, Inc."[11] In this view, Japan is described as a country where the intimate tie between government and industries dominates decision making in industrial and other related policies.

A corporatist argument is a variation of this power elite model. A typical argument is presented by T. J. Pempel and Keiichi Tsunekawa.[12] According to Pempel and Tsunekawa, policies were made between the government and peak organizations with hierarchical orders such as *Keidanren* (the Federation of Economic Organizations) and the National Association of Agricultural Cooperatives. Whereas in European corporatist societies labor organizations act as a peak group, in Japanese policy making they are not active participants.

This power elite view is often criticized as oversimplified. The critics emphasize that Japan's elites do not constitute a single solid entity. Many Japan scholars focus on the power shift and argue for the pluralist model, as a gradual structural change took place during the long reign of the LDP.[13] Some LDP Diet members accumulated knowledge and experience in specific policy areas and became identified as *zoku*, or policy tribes.

These *zoku* members formed subgovernments based in the LDPs Policy Research Council (PRC, or *Seichô-kai*) (see Table 1.1). The LDP had 17 *bukai* or subcommittees and more than 30 research commissions. Commissions were designed to deal with broader issues rather than specific legislation; *bukai*, in contrast, were set up corresponding to administrative ministries and used by the LDP to influence policy decision and budget making in each policy area. Those who earned the *zoku* label became the ultimate arbiters of political power in a specific issue and increased their influence vis-à-vis bureaucrats in the same policy field. As a result, they became instrumental in policy making.

The power shift from the bureaucracy to the LDP policy committees became more evident after the two oil shocks of the 1970s. In the rapid growth that characterized the 1950s and 1960s, government revenue increased significantly each year. A majority of policy decisions involved the allocation of extra revenues to different programs. After the oil shocks, however, lower economic growth slowed down government revenue increases and thus decreased the money available to these programs. With funds limited, bureaucratic officials became more dependent on the mediation and political decisions of the ruling party members when reallocating funds among administrative programs.[14] It became part of the official process for bureaucrats to seek approval from the relevant *zoku* members before submitting budget proposals and other policy initiatives to the cabinet. The prime minister delegated considerable policy-making power in specific issues to these specialists within the party organization while he concentrated on broader issues.

While LDP *zoku* members increased their influence and became a major actor in the "iron triangle," the bureaucracy continued to play a pivotal role in drafting legislative proposals.[15] Because LDP headquarters had only a limited staff, LDP members could not turn to their party's policy staff for extra help, as could their German counterparts. With a limited personal staff (officially only two staffers for each Diet member prior to 1993, three thereafter), LDP members did not command the resources necessary to draft legislation by themselves, as did many in the U.S. Congress. The LDP had to continue to rely substantially on the bureaucracy in the policy making of specific issues.

The increase of the LDP's policy-making influence did not correspondingly increase the power of the prime minister or the LDP cabinet members. On the contrary, the cabinet's central executive role declined with the emergence of bureaucratic sectionalism into the party organization. Many specific policy issues were handled by *zoku* members and ministries not only outside the Diet but also often beyond the reach of the cabinet. When a prime minister tried to introduce a major policy change not desired by one ministry, *zoku* members and their related ministry countered with an issue-specific alliance to thwart such a change. In a broader issue that might involve several ministries, the members will form a smaller "iron triangle" in each policy arena, and these triangles compete with each other for their sectoral interests. With the growth of *zoku* members' influences, the prime minister and his cabinet faced stronger sectionalism, which had to be overcome in order to pursue policies initiated by the prime minister.[16]

The situation changed under the non-LDP coalition government of eight political groups led by Hosokawa Morihiro (1993–94). He introduced a more centralized decision-making organ. As more elaborately explained in Chapter 2, however, this centralized system did not last long. Prime Minister Murayama Tomiichi (1994–96), who was critical of the autocratic nature of the system, introduced a decentralized decision-making system with issue-specific project teams and committees. While the coalition parties—the LDP, the Socialist Party, and *Sakigake*—tried to reach consensus under the Murayama government, LDP *zoku* members regained a stage to become politically active. This eventually returned the system to something akin to the pre-1993 situation.

"Defeating the sectionalism of the bureaucracy and their patron LDP members is the biggest challenge the prime minister faces," states Gotôda Masaharu, who served as chief cabinet secretary to Prime Minister Nakasone Yasuhiro. Gotôda explains the role of the prime minister in policy making as follows:

Today, many issues are so complicated and intertwined that there are very few issues which can be handled by a single ministry. The related ministries, therefore, talk and negotiate with each other. As each ministry has its own interests to protect, however, problems are often stuck in gridlock. Sectionalism makes it very difficult for the government to handle issues especially when they require urgency. This is where the prime minister is required to exercise his leadership.[17]

This view is shared by other former assistants to prime ministers. Miyawaki Raisuke, who served as a senior assistant to Prime Minister Nakasone Yasuhiro, defines the leadership of prime ministers as "to crush the walls of the 'Vertical Administration.' . . . Otherwise, they can do nothing during their tenure."[18]

FACTION POLITICS

Besides issue-specific sectionalism, prime ministers have faced another kind of fraction within the ruling party. Although the prime minister represents a majority of the lower house, he does not necessarily have solid support from that majority. The prime minister always faces potential challenges from members of other groups who make up the majority—intraparty factions in a single party majority—and who seek to replace him with their leader if given the chance. When the prime minister's public support drastically drops or he makes a serious mistake, such challenges surface. Factions or other parties of a coalition with their own strong candidates openly seek to oust the current prime minister, and conflicts arise within the ruling party or coalition. In these cases, the loyalty of members in the ruling body usually belongs to the group rather than to the prime minister.

The party control of the prime minister significantly weakened in the mid-1970s. From the LDP's inception in 1955 through the end of the Tanaka Kakuei administration in 1974, LDP presidents appointed a member of their own faction or a close associate to the post of secretary general (the number two position within the party in charge of day-to-day party affairs) in order to better control the party.[19] However, this concentration of power within the same faction created unequal treatment of factions in terms of campaign and financial support. Party leaders perceived that Prime Minister Tanaka had gone too far in doling out money to pro-Tanaka members in his faction as well as in other factions, increasing interfactional conflicts. Seeking to ease factional fighting, they determined that the selection of the secretary general should come from a faction other than that of the LDP president.[20] Ironically, under the three successive administrations of Miki Takeo (1974–76), Fukuda Takeo (1976–78), and Ôhira

Masayoshi (1978–80), the prime minister's weaker party control exacerbated factional conflicts. Intraparty fights forced Miki and Fukuda out of office and drove Ôhira to excessive fatigue, which eventually led to his death. The LDP prime ministers thus found themselves having to delegate much of the authority over day-to-day party affairs to a secretary general not necessarily loyal to them and over whom they had limited control. As noted, this change was intended to facilitate party harmony, but in practice it weakened the prime minister's control.

The birth of the new non-LDP coalition government in August 1993 underscored the volatility of LDP unity, a volatility that had existed just under the surface for a long time. The Liberal Democratic Party was originally formed by combining various conservative political groups, some with their roots in prewar political parties. Therefore, from its start the LDP had been highly fractional with several intraparty factions, each with its own leader and different political goals. During the long LDP reign, the prime ministership was rotated among the major factions, all of which were constantly competing with each other. This rotation was not only inevitable but also justifiable because factions could effectively provide necessary alternatives for the leadership position.[21] Interfactional competition, however, often led to disharmony or friction within the ruling party and forced several prime ministers out of office; it also led to the breakup of the LDP and the end of its 38-year reign.

Factions within the LDP were not formed for ideological reasons. Their primary goal was to make their leader the prime minister.[22] Despite the high cost of supporting faction members, faction leaders maintained their factions in order to become prime minister one day. In the words of Watanabe Tsuneo: "To become the prime minister, [an LDP politician] must become 'the boss' of a faction. Becoming 'the boss' of a faction means to be on the short list of the [LDP] presidential candidates."[23] Being a faction leader was considered necessary to becoming LDP president. During the LDP reign between 1955 and 1993, with two extreme exceptions in the waning years of the LDP's reign,[24] every president who automatically became the prime minister was a faction leader.

Because no faction alone had enough members or votes to secure the prime ministership for the faction's leader, the factions had to cooperate and form coalitions to challenge other intraparty coalitions. The faction leader who successfully formed a coalition of a majority of the LDP Diet members won the LDP presidential race and thus acquired the premiership. The prime minister then had to maintain that support to be an effective leader.

Maintaining intraparty support for policy objectives was more difficult when a prime minister's leadership was openly challenged. Kishi Nobusuke faced strong opposition from the anti-Kishi faction within the party during the policy process to revise the U.S.–Japan Security Pact in 1960. One of the anti-Kishi faction leaders repeatedly demanded that Kishi resign once the bill was passed. Kishi sacrificed his premiership to secure support for the security revision within the ruling party and resigned after its passage. Later he stated how unfortunate it was for a political leader to be forced to spend much more energy on party affairs than on conducting his task as prime minister.[25] Kishi is not the only leader forced to sacrifice his post to achieve a policy goal. Prime Minister Hatoyama Ichirô, for example, resigned because of factional pressure right after he successfully normalized relations with the Soviet Union in 1956.

Some structural factors enhanced the rise of intraparty factions in the ruling party. The LDP's lack of central control over election finances and campaigns increased each candidate's reliance on his faction rather than on the party. Since the size of the candidate's faction was a vital source of power within the ruling party, factions competed in recruiting new candidates and supported reelection campaigns of existing members. Furthermore, the old "middle-size" electoral system of the lower house (until 1994) with three to five seats in each electoral district encouraged multiple candidates from a single party. Because LDP candidates shared a similar voting base, the competition among them was usually more fierce than the competition with candidates from opposition parties.

LDP factions took over the political party's other functions besides campaign support. Although the appointive authority belonged to the prime minister, who also held the party presidency, factions served as a channel to allocate not only cabinet posts but also subcabinet seats, Diet committee chairmanships, and party posts. Factions were also a central source of information for their members. Each faction had representatives in the cabinet, the Diet, and the party policy committees. These representatives briefed other faction members on current events. The faction representatives, in turn, served as channels through which members could voice their opinions on government and party decisions.

The development of factions may well stem from Japan's cultural heritage as an agrarian society, a theory offered by a former government official who had dealt closely with LDP politicians as vice minister of agriculture, forestry, and fishery. Not much more than a century ago, 90 percent of the Japanese were farmers. For farmers to grow their rice and other crops, securing the supply of water and cooperation from others during the harvest seasons was crucial. Hierarchy was established in the farming society so leaders could fairly distribute water to farmers without causing unnecessary conflicts. The community as a whole supported this hierarchy, knowing that it was needed for their survival. "This mentality is still alive in the Japanese society," argues a former government official. According to him, the most visible example of the enduring farming mentality is found in the factions of political parties. "Instead of water, politicians distribute money and positions through the factions."[26] This theory coincides with the fact that LDP members call their factions *mura*, or villages. Factions became the communities that LDP politicians had to join in order to survive, just as the farmer had to participate in and rely on his village.

Although several LDP diet members did not belong to any faction even under the LDP-led government, as a consequence they faced little chance of becoming a cabinet member. Furthermore, they also needed to have an exceptionally strong supporting body to be reelected. Most LDP members, like other Japanese, felt

more comfortable having a community, or a faction, with which to closely identify themselves.

According to sociologist Nakane Chie, factions within political parties are the
product of the characteristics of a Japanese society that puts more emphasis on
vertical relations, such as leader-follower and superior-junior, than on horizontal
relations among colleagues. In Nakane's view, Japanese communities are usually
organized in a pyramidal hierarchy of ranks that consists of many personal,
person-to-person relationships between superiors and juniors, the basis of most
relationships in Japan. Japanese leaders, therefore, are directly supported by
subleaders who themselves have their own followers.[27] Formal, institutional
group organizations are often eroded and subsumed by the unity of subgroups
with traditional values. Nakane's description of the way the Japanese organize
themselves fits perfectly with the structure of Japanese political parties, with a
formal party leader and members grouped into factions. As Prime Minister Ôhira
Masayoshi once said, "When there are three politicians, there will be at least
two factions." As long as this cultural heritage remains, factionalism within
Japanese political parties will continue.

Factionalism is not unique to the Japanese political system, of course. Although their forms and functions vary depending on political institutions and
environments, factions exist in the politics of many democratic states. Generally,
factionalism is weaker in nations with a single-seat electoral system, such as
Great Britain, where party affiliation is the dominant factor in elections. In contrast hand, nations like Italy that until recently had an electoral system of proportional representation and multimember districts with preference voting—
which urged voters of a particular party to vote for specific candidates—have
developed strong factionalism.[28]

As party leader of the majority party, the British prime minister has stronger
control over the ruling party than the Japanese counterpart. Of course, chief
colleagues of the British prime minister have their followers, and factions do
exist within British political parties. This limits politically the prime minister's
authority to form his or her own cabinet. As G. W. Jones describes, "His [or
her] cabinet must represent a cross-section of opinion in the party and contain
the main faction leaders."[29] Factions in Britain are not, however, as highly institutionalized as those in Japan or Italy. The prime minister remains the "monopoly supplier" of cabinet posts and "can exploit this monopoly position to
influence the behavior of backbenchers who want to be ministers and of ministers who want to be promoted and not to be dismissed."[30] The British prime
minister, therefore, has strong control over the cabinet and thus over the government through his ministers. This differs from the case of Japan, where LDP
faction leaders—or party leaders in a coalition government—play instrumental
roles in cabinet formations, and where the cabinet members act as factional
representatives rather than as cabinet representatives to their own factions.

In terms of strong factionalism within the ruling party, Giovanni Sartori, a scholar on comparative political parties, describes the governmental system in Japan and Italy as having "a similarity verging on twinship."[31] In both countries, factionalism had been highly developed within the long-term dominant ruling party, and this had presented tremendous difficulties to the national leaders. The problems faced by Japanese and Italian prime ministers are evident in the length of their tenures. In the postwar period, both Japan and Italy had a few dozen individuals holding this office. This number is extremely high compared to 12 different individuals in Great Britain and 7 chancellors in West Germany during the same period. Although the term of office for the Japanese prime minister is equal to that for lower house members—four years unless the house is dissolved—Japan has had a new national leader, on average, every two and one-half years in the postwar period (see Table 1.2). This short tenure has been partly because of the two-year term limit of the LDP presidency,[32] but its primary reason has been pressure from the other LDP factions whose leaders were waiting in line for election to the office.

In July 1993, however, two groups within the LDP joined the opposition parties in disapproval of the LDP government and forced Prime Minister Miyazawa Kiichi out of office. In a subsequent general election, while three new conservative parties gained a significant number of lower house seats, the LDP did not achieve enough seats to form a majority in the lower house. The new conservative parties, with the help of long-established opposition parties, formed a non-LDP coalition government. This coalition of eight political groups, which together held 260 of the 511 lower house seats, chose a joint candidate for prime minister, Hosokawa Morihiro. Although Hosokawa successfully passed a political reform package, his administration's top priority issue, maintaining the coalition, was not an easy task. In March 1993, for example, the prime minister's attempt to reshuffle his cabinet was blocked by the opposition of several parties in the coalition. After eight months of reign when the Diet operation faced gridlock as a result of his own financial scandal, Hosokawa suddenly announced his resignation, which led to the establishment of a minority coalition government led by Hata Tsutomu. The Hata cabinet lasted only two months without achieving any major policy goal.

After Hata, Murayama Tomiichi led a new coalition government of the LDP, the Socialist Party, and *Sakigake*. As leader of the second largest party in the coalition and without any experience of government position, Murayama needed to consult with the LDP. After Murayama resigned, LDP president Hashimoto Ryûtarô took over the office. Hashimoto was careful about maintaining the same coalition framework, and he closely consulted with the other two coalition parties. Because political views and objectives differ party by party, the Japanese prime minister faced a volatile situation similar to that in Italian politics.

Under the Hashimoto administration, the LDP regained a majority in the lower house to run the government single-handedly. The traditional framework of LDP factions, however, faced a critical change. The new electoral rules,

Table 1.2
Postwar Prime Ministers: Terms of Office

Higashikuni Naruhiko (NP)		8/17/45 - 10/9/45	54 days
Shidehara Kijûrô	(JPP)	10/9/45 - 5/22/46	226
Yoshida Shigeru	(JLP)*	5/22/46 - 5/24/47	368
Katayama Tetsu	(JSP)**	5/24/47 - 3/10/48	292
Ashida Hitoshi	(DP)**	3/10/48 - 10/19/48	220
Yoshida Shigeru	(DLP/LP)	10/19/48 - 12/10/54	2,248
Hatoyama Ichirô	(LP/LDP)	12/10/54 - 12/23/56	745
Ishibashi Tanzan	(LDP)	12/23/56 - 2/25/57	65
Kishi Nobusuke	(LDP)	2/25/57 - 7/19/60	1,241
Ikeda Hayato	(LDP)	7/19/60 - 11/9/64	1,575
Satô Eisaku	(LDP)	11/9/64 - 7/7/72	2,798
Tanaka Kakuei	(LDP)	7/7/72 - 12/9/74	886
Miki Takeo	(LDP)	12/9/74 - 12/24/76	747
Fukuda Takeo	(LDP)	12/24/76 - 12/7/78	714
Ôhira Masayoshi	(LDP)	12/7/78 - 6/12/80***	576
Suzuki Zenkô	(LDP)	7/17/80 - 11/27/82	864
Nakasone Yasuhiro	(LDP)	11/27/82 - 11/6/87	1,806
Takeshita Noboru	(LDP)	11/6/87 - 6/2/89	576
Uno Sôsuke	(LDP)	6/2/89 - 8/8/89	69
Kaifu Toshiki	(LDP)	8/8/89 - 11/5/91	818
Miyazawa Kiichi	(LDP)	11/5/91 - 8/6/93	644
Hosokawa Morihiro	(JNP)****	8/6/93 - 4/28/94	265
Hata Tsutomu	(RP)*****	4/28/94 - 6/29/94	63
Murayama Tomiichi	(JSP)	6/29/94 - 1/11/96	561
Hashimoto Ryûtarô	(LDP)	1/11/96 - 7/30/98	932
Obuchi Keizô	(LDP)	7/30/98 - 4/5/00	616
Mori Yoshirô	(LDP)	4/5/00 -	

NP—No party affiliation. JPP—Japan Progressive Party. JLP—Japan Liberal Party. JSP—Japan Socialist Party. DP—Democratic Party. DLP—Democratic Liberal Party. LP—Liberal Party. LDP—Liberal Democratic Party (formed on 11/15/55). JNP—Japan New Party. RP—Renewal Party.

*Coalition with the JPP.

**Coalition of the JSP, the DP, and the National Cooperative Party.

***After Ôhira's death, Itô Masayoshi served as acting prime minister for 35 days.

****Coalition of the Japan Socialist Party, the Renewal Party, *Kômeitô*, the Japan New Party, *Sakigake* Party, the Democratic Socialist Party, the United Social Democratic Party, and the Democratic Reform Federation.

*****Coalition of the Renewal Party, *Kômeitô*, the Japan New Party, the Democratic Socialist Party, the Liberal Party, *Kaikaku no Kai*, and the Democratic Reform Federation.

introduced under the non-LDP Hosokawa government, weakened functions of LDP factions, leading to their reorganization. The single-seat electoral system for the lower house eliminated the competition among LDP candidates, weakening the need for campaign support from the factions. The introduction of the proportional representative system for the lower house and the injection of public funds strengthened the functions of the LDP leadership. As a result, especially the secretary general, who is in charge of making the list of candidate ranking and allocating funds, gained new power within the party. Election campaigns became more centrally controlled within the LDP.

Although the LDP continued to play a major role in the process of post allocations under the Hashimoto and Obuchî Keizô cabinets, factional control over its members weakened. In the 1998 LDP presidential race, for example, the Obuchi faction could not stop faction member and former chief cabinet secretary Kajiyama Seiroku from challenging the faction leader. In the voting, most factions failed to force all their members to vote for the candidate of factional choice. As the power of the party leadership increased, there emerged a division between the pro-leadership group and the anti-leadership group across the traditional factions, creating new factionalism within the LDP.

SUMMARY

The Japanese political system has developed somewhat differently from the plans of the founders of the Constitution. In order to emphasize popular sovereignty, the Constitution defines the Diet as the highest body in the government, an institution meant to provide legislative supremacy over the executive. The Diet elects the prime minister, who selects his cabinet, a group endowed with executive powers to administer the civil service in the bureaucracy. However, the immediate postwar experience gave advantages to the civil servants of individual ministries in policy making. The individual ministries implemented many important postwar policies to reform Japan with divisions of the American Occupation authorities. Most experienced legislators were removed from the Diet in the purge, and the power of the Diet was limited.

The postwar experience has developed an efficient bureaucracy with strong sectionalism among various ministries and agencies. The cabinet is the only political institution that has the authority to coordinate conflicting sectional interests. Because ministers tend to represent their ministry, the prime minister must be head of the cabinet to combat sectionalism. Whether he can successfully coordinate sectional interests depends upon his control over his cabinet.

Even under a single majority government such as the LDP-led government, the prime minister's control over the cabinet is almost as limited as that of the Italian prime minister in Italy's coalition government. Under the LDP, a majority of the cabinet members belonged to factions within the ruling party over which the prime minister had little control. This is distinct from Great Britain, where the prime minister as leader of the ruling party holds relatively strong control over the cabinet. The British prime minister manages to control the strong civil service through his ministers. In the 1970s in Japan, issue-specific sectionalism further strengthened as the power of the LDP *zoku* members increased in support of sectional interests. Strong sectionalism within the civil service and factionalism within the ruling parties combined to erode the role of the prime minister and his cabinet as a coordinator among various ministries.

The prime minister faces two types of fractions: the issue-specific sectionalism that is strictly policy oriented; and the factionalism that involves political struggles within the ruling party or coalition. If the issue-specific sectionalism is a vertical axis, the intraparty factionalism within the party is a horizontal axis. If

Figure 1.1
Conceptual Framework of the Prime Minister

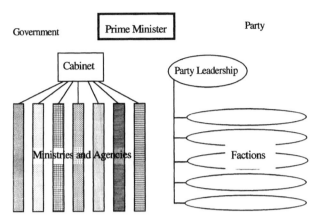

the prime minister's leadership is weak, members of the ruling party can split either horizontally or vertically. When the prime minister becomes a lame duck because of low popularity or the ending of his term, factional conflicts are more likely to increase, and the party will show a horizontal split. If the prime minister's policy is politically controversial, there will be a vertical split among ruling party members and government agencies. Whereas effective leaders can persuade the party and the government, ineffective, weak prime ministers lose in their battle with two dimensions of fractions within the party and the government.

The two dimensions of fractions under the LDP government—issue-specific sectionalism and intraparty factionalism—are illustrated in Figures 1.1 and 1.2. Between the establishment of the LDP in 1955 and the early 1970s, when the influence of the LDP *zoku* members was limited, the prime minister faced two separate fractions (Figure 1.1): sectionalism among civil servants within the government (the left side), and intraparty factionalism based on political ambitions within the LDP (the right side). The prime minister controlled the party by placing his faction member at the post of secretary general.

During the period between the mid-1970s and 1993 when the LDP lost control over the government, two major changes occurred in this political structure that affected the prime minister's relationship with these two fractions. First, because the LDP secretary general no longer belonged to the prime minister's faction, the prime minister's control over day-to-day party affairs weakened. Second, the issue-specific *zoku* groups formed among the factions within the LDP. The *zoku* groups often acted as the allies of their client agencies, which shared the same policy interests. As a result, the prime minister had to face issue-specific sectionalism from within the ruling party and from within the government. In this study, the role of the prime minister in policy making is defined as the

Figure 1.2
Conceptual Framework with Strong *Zoku*

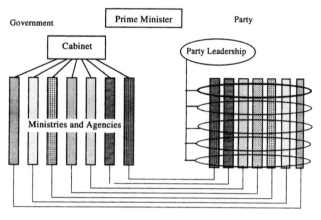

Issue-specific politico-administrative alliance

execution of political leadership while confronting the issue-specific sectional interests of the bureaucracy and *zoku* LDP members and intraparty factionalism.

The non-LDP coalition governments under Hosokawa and Hata faced a situation similar to that which confronted the LDP between 1955 and the early 1970s. Most LDP *zoku* members did not have the same degree of influence until they regained their political influence under the Hashimoto administration. Instead of intraparty factionalism, the national leader under the coalition governments faced partisanship among the government parties within the coalition. Because political ideas and ideologies varied among the parties, the coalition governments were more fragile in terms of unity and faced even stronger fractions among their members than the LDP-led government had to face. The leadership of the prime minister depended substantially on his ability and that of his assistants to maintain the unity of the coalition—whether a coalition of factions or a coalition of parties. The next chapter treats the political changes after 1993 to which different prime ministers responded in different ways.

NOTES

1. Article 55 reads, "The respective Ministers shall give their advice to the Emperor and be responsible for it." The Emperor held all the governing authority, including the administrative authority, while being assisted by his ministers.

2. For a discussion of the intent of the American Occupation authority, see Government Section, Supreme Commander for the Allied Powers, *Political Reorientation of Japan* (Washington, D.C.: U.S. Government Printing Office, 1949), pp. 82–118.

3. The classic study on this view is Tsuji Kiyoaki, *Shinban Nihon Kanryôsei no*

Kenkyû [New edition, study on the Japanese Bureaucracy system] (Tokyo Daigaku Shuppan-kai, 1969).

4. Government Section, Supreme Commander for the Allied Powers, *Political Reorientation of Japan*, p. 128.

5. Ibid., p. 29.

6. John O. Haley, "Consensual Governance: A Study of Law, Culture, and the Political Economy of Postwar Japan," in *The Political Economy of Japan*, vol. 3, *Cultural and Social Dynamics*, ed. Shumpei Kumon and Henry Rosovsky (Stanford, California: Stanford University Press, 1992), p. 52.

7. T. J. Pempel, "Organizing for Efficiency: The Higher Civil Service in Japan," in *Bureaucrats and Policy Making: A Comparative Overview*, ed. Ezra N. Suleiman (New York: Holms and Meier, 1984), p. 96.

8. See Bradley M. Richardson and Scott C. Flanagan, *Politics in Japan* (Boston: Little, Brown, 1984), p. 344.

9. Early 1994, MITI minister Kumagai Hiroshi forced a bureau director to resign, and this became big news because political intervention in bureaucratic placement is extremely unusual.

10. Tsuji Kiyoaki, *Shinban Nihon Kanryôsei no Kenkyû*. Tsuji argues that the bureaucracy is the only national institute that maintained influence under the American Occupation force. The bureaucracy with support by General Headquarters could exercise relatively strong power vis-à-vis the Diet and had established itself as pivotal in decision making.

11. This frequently used term first appeared in a study of U.S. Commerce Department. Eugene J. Kaplan, *Japan: The Government-Business Relationship* (Washington, D.C.: Department of Commerce, 1972).

12. T. J. Pempel and Keiichi Tsunekawa, "Corporatism without Labor?: The Japanese Anomaly," in Phillippe C. and Lehmbruch Schumitter, eds., *Trend toward Corporatist Intermediation* (London: Sage Publications, 1979), pp. 231–69.

13. Gerald Curtis argues that the big business influence has declined. Gerald Curtis, "Big Business and Political Influence," in Ezra F. Vogel, ed., *Modern Japanese Organization and Decision-Making* (Berkeley and Los Angeles: University of California Press, 1975), p 60. Satô Seizaburô and Matsuzaki Tetsuhisa argue that Japan's peak associations are limited to specific issues such as the Japan Doctors Association and *Nôkyô*. *Keidanren* and *Sôhyô* are not peak organizations but loose umbrella organizations. Mesocorporatism, a loose, industry-specific corporatism, can be applied to the Japanese system. Satô Seizaburô and Matsuzaki Tetsuhisa, *Jimintô Seiken* [The LDP administrations] (Tokyo: Chuô Kôron, 1986), pp. 163, 167.

14. See Nakamura Akira, "Jiyûminshutô no Yottsu no Kao" [The four faces of LDP], in *Nihon no Seisaku Karei: Jimintô, Yatô, Kanryô* [Japanese policy making: The LDP, the opposition parties, and the bureaucracy], ed. Nakamura Akira and Takeshita Yuzuru (Tokyo: Azusa Shuppan, 1984), pp. 3–63.

15. Almost all supporters of the pluralistic perspective recognize the limitations and conditionality. Haruhiro Fukui, for example, states, "Several cases show that those groups which the elite model dismisses as powerless and inconsequential do in fact contribute significantly to important policy." Although Fukui refuses to make a clear choice of the pluralist model over the power elite model, he recognizes the importance of LDP members and the opposition parties in the policy making. Haruhiro Fukui, "Studies in Poli-

cymaking: Review of the Literature," in *Policymaking in Contemporary Japan*, ed. T. J. Pempel (Ithaca: Cornell University Press, 1977), p. 42.

Based on the "comparative historical structure," Inoguchi Takashi describes the Japanese system as "bureaucracy-led mass-inclusionary pluralism." Inoguchi views that the strong bureaucracy, which is sensitive to the preference of the people, adds the pluralistic perspective to the policy-making process. Inoguchi Takashi, *Gendai Nihon Seiji Keizai no Kôzu* [The composition of contemporary Japanese political economy] (Tokyo: Tôyô Keizai Shinpô 1983).

The pluralism with a strong bureaucracy is also expressed by Muramatsu Michio and Ellis S. Krause in their term "the patterned pluralism." They view Japan as a strong state with its own interests and an institutionalized accommodation with pluralistic elements. In this system, LDP politicians act as mediators between the bureaucracy and interest groups. One-party dominance made the LDP a "catch-all" party and brought this pluralistic integration between the state and the society. Michio Muramatsu and Ellis Krauss, "The Conservative Policy Line and the Development of Patterned Pluralism," in *The Political Economy of Japan*, vol. 1, *The Domestic Transformation*, ed. Kozo Yamamura and Yasukichi Yasuba (Stanford, California: Stanford University Press, 1987), pp. 516–54.

Yet, some scholars like Nakamura Akira and Takeshita Yuzuru emphasized the role of LDP's Policy Research Committee and see its subcommitees as a chore of the policy making. According to their view, the power shift from the bureaucracy to the LDP committee took place after the oil shock. Lower growth brought a significant slowdown to the growth of budget size and made it impossible for the bureaucracy to make a political decision of budget allocation with the limited fund. Nakamura and Takeshita, *Nihon no Seisaku Katei.*

A similar view is expressed by Satô Seizaburô and Matsuzaki Tetsuhisa in their term "compartmentalized pluralism." They agree with Nakamura that the policy process is divided into specific policy areas, but they do not use the term "fragmentalized," which is used to describe American pluralistic representation, which is less patterned. Satô and Matsuzaki view the Japanese system as a more stable, patterned one with a number of issue-specific circles governed cooperatively by the LDP and the bureaucracy. Satô Seizaburô and Matsuzaki Tetsuhisa, *Jimintô Seiken.*

16. Leonard J. Schoppa illustrates how the sectional interest within the LDP effectively blocked a major policy effort of LDP leaders by using Nakasone's educational reform attempt as a case study. In this case study, conservative education *zoku* members successfully blocked the prime minister's initiative by tying up with the conservative Education Ministry. In his conclusion, Schoppa argues that "the rise in *zoku* influence has made it particularly difficult for the party to achieve substantial policy *change*" and that "[the party] has suffered in its ability to achieve policy change that requires leadership from a broader, national perspective." Leonard J. Schoppa, "*Zoku* Power and LDP Power: A Case Study of the *Zoku* Role in Education Policy," *Journal of Japanese Studies* 17, no. 1 (winter 1991): 79–106.

17. Gotôda Masaharu, interview by author, Tokyo, December 18, 1992.

18. Raisuke Miyawaki, "Difference in the Governing Style between Nakasone and Takeshita" (paper presented at the Johns Hopkins University's School of Advanced International Studies, December 3, 1992) Miyawaki was appointed to senior assistant on public affairs to the prime minister, a newly created post at the cabinet secretariat, which

is considered one of the five cabinet councilors with a rank nearly equivalent to a vice ministership in the bureaucratic ladder.

19. Strictly speaking, the first two LDP secretaries general were not chosen from the president's faction. Hatoyama Ichirô picked Kishi Nobusuke, and Ishibashi Tanzan chose Miki Takeo, both leading their own faction. At the early period of the LDP history, however, the division of the faction was not as clear. Kishi and Miki saw Hatoyama and Ishibashi as their bosses.

20. For a discussion of Tanaka's taking advantage of the concentration of power, see Masumi Junnosuke, *Gendai Seiji 1955 nen igo* [Contemporary politics after 1955] (Tokyo: Tokyo Daigaku Shuppan, 1985), pp. 370–72.

21. Arguments for this function of LDP factions, see Haruhiro Fukui, "Japan: Factionalism in a Dominant Party System," in *Faction Politics: Political Parties and Factionalism in Comparative Perspective*, ed. Frank P. Belloni and Dennis C. Beller (Santa Barbara, California: ABC-Clio, 1978), pp. 65–66.

22. Nathaniel B. Thayer, *How the Conservatives Rule Japan* (Princeton: Princeton University Press, 1969), chapters 2 and 4.

About the prewar history of political factions, see Robert Scalapino, *Democracy and the Party Movement in Prewar Japan* (Berkeley: University of California Press, 1953). Yamamoto Shichihei argues that Japan's modern political history is the history of political factions, which started with *Hanbatsu* or factions in the Meiji government based on the politicians' clans. Yamamoto Shichihei, *Habatsu no Kenkyû* [Study on factions] (Tokyo: Bungei Shunjû, 1989).

23. Watanabe Tsunco, *Habatsu to Tatôka Jidai* [Factions and the multiparty era] (Tokyo: Sekka-sha, 1967), p. 142.

24. Uno Sôsuke (1989) and Kaifu Toshiki (1989–91) were chosen without being faction leaders in the wake of political scandals that made other possible candidates ineligible.

25. Yomiuri Shimbun Seiji-bu, ed., *Sôri Daijin* [The prime minister] (Tokyo: Yomiuri Shimbun-sha, 1971; revised in 1972), p. 89.

26. Uchimura Yoshihide, interview by author, Tokyo, April 1989.

27. Chie Nakane, *Human Relations in Japan: Summary Translation of "Tate Shakai no Ningen Kankei"* (Tokyo: Ministry of Foreign Affairs, 1972), pp. 57–84.

28. See Dennis C. Beller and Frank P. Belloni, "Party and Faction: Modes of Political Competition," in Belloni and Beller, ed., *Faction Politics* (Santa Barbara, California: ABC Clio, 1978), pp 432–35.

29. G. W. Jones, "The Prime Minister's Power," in *The British Prime Minister*, ed. Anthony King (Durham, North Carolina: Duke University Press, 1985), p. 209.

30. Anthony King, "The British Prime Ministership in the Age of the Career Politician," *West European Politics* 14 (April 1991): 38.

31. Giovanni Sartori, *Parties and Party Systems: A Framework for Analysis* (Cambridge: Cambridge University Press, 1976), p. 90.

32. Except between 1971 and 1977 when the term of LDP presidency was extended to three years.

Chapter 2

The Prime Ministers after the 1993 Political Change

Since 1993 when the LDP's 38-year-long reign ended, the Japanese political scene witnessed a series of drastic changes: the eight-party, non-LDP coalition led by Hosokawa Morihiro, the short-lived minority government under Hata Tsutomu, and the LDP-Socialist-*Sakigake* coalition governments under the socialist leader Murayama Tomiichi and LDP president Hashimoto Ryûtarô. Under Hashimoto's leadership, the LDP was briefly back in position to run a single-party majority government. Four months after the July 1998 upper house election, however, Prime Minister Obuchi Keizô decided to form another coalition with the Liberal Party (LP) in order to smoothen the Diet operation. In August 1999, the Obuchi government further expanded the coalition to include *Kômeitô*, or the Clean Government Party. In April 2000 after Obuchi unexpectedly resigned due to a stroke, Mori Yoshirô formed a new coalition. These changes created a new political environment affecting Japan's policy-making mechanisms. This chapter examines how the role of the prime minister under the coalition governments has transformed since the marked political change of 1993.

THE HOSOKAWA CABINET

In June 1993, the lower house passed a no-confidence resolution against the LDP government headed by Miyazawa Kiichi (1991–93), effectively putting an end to the LDP's 38-year reign after the July general election. This was followed by the establishment of a non-LDP coalition government in August. The prime minister that emerged was Hosokawa Morihiro (1993–94) of the Japan New Party. He had to tackle difficult political issues, including the conclusion of the General Agreement on Tariffs and Trade (GATT) Uruguay Round and political reform at home while trying to lead an unprecedented coalition of eight political groups with a wide range of conflicting political ideas.[1]

In order to maintain the vulnerable coalition, Hosokawa appointed to cabinet posts the leaders of six other coalition parties.[2] Cabinet members are heavily engaged in their official duties as minister of their ministries and agencies. The coalition government needed a new decision-making mechanism outside the cabinet in order to coordinate policies among the parties, which had an immediate need to work together to run the new government. Hosokawa, therefore, created the Council of Representatives of the Coalition Parties, or *Yotô Daihyôsha Kaigi*. The Council was composed of five members who were the secretaries general (second in command) of the coalition parties: Akamatsu Hirotaka (replaced by Kubo Wataru in September 1993) of the Japan Socialist Party (JSP), Ozawa Ichirô of the Renewal Party, Ichikawa Yûichi of *Kômeitô*, Yonezawa Takashi of the Democratic Socialist Party, and Sonoda Hiroyuki of *Sakigake*. They planned to meet and discuss major political issues to build consensus among the coalition parties. Formal decisions were to be finalized at the Government and Party Executive Council, or *Seifu Yotô Shunô Kaigi*, which was attended by the seven party leaders in the cabinet and the five members of the Representative Council.

One of the reasons why Hosokawa wanted to create this centralized system can be found in his writings before his becoming the premier. Hosokawa had repeatedly warned that the rigidity of the Japanese bureaucracy causes problems in Japanese society, such as the so-called vertical administration or sectionalism within the government.[3] This was not the only reason why the new government introduced a new decision-making system. In an interview with the author, Hosokawa confided about the difficult situation he found himself in. "Under the coalition government with eight different political parties, the centralization of policy making was the only choice. It was impossible to have issue-specific committees."[4]

Under the Council of Representatives, Hosokawa also formed the Policy Adjustment Council to discuss policy matters among the coalition parties. Except for members of the Renewal Party and *Sakigake*, however, the coalition parties had no prior experience running a government. Without the old system that included experienced *zoku* members, bureaucratic officials were able to play an even more important role in the decision-making process than they had been able to under the LDP governments.[5] Major policy issues, however, were brought to the Council of the Representatives, where the coalition parties made political decisions.

The Council soon became a center of the power within the coalition. In the national budget making process, for example, its members attended the official negotiation meeting between each ministry and the Ministry of Finance to oversee the process.[6] Under the LDP government, the top three party executives— the secretary general and the chairmen of the Policy Research Council and the

General Council—held a separate meeting in the budget process to influence the government budget, but they never sat in the negotiation meeting within the government. This centralized decision-making institution shaped Hosokawa's major policy outcomes.

Prime Minister Hosokawa personally placed the highest priority on the conclusion of the GATT Uruguay Round. In his words, "Japan is in the world system, and I thought that we must show leadership by contributing to the successful conclusion of the Uruguay Round."[7] To contribute to the success of the multilateral trade agreement, Japan needed to open up its rice market regardless of strong pressures from politically powerful agricultural interest groups and politicians who represented rural areas.

Consensus for opening the rice market had been building since the Miyazawa administration.[8] As the second largest economy and an export superpower, Japan would not be able to maintain a position for which it would later draw blame as the cause of the Uruguay Round's failure. Years of foreign pressure, especially from the United States, had created a mood favorable to the internationalization of Japan's agricultural market, but political leaders were hesitant to make the final decision—they did not want to invite the wrath of farmers. Hosokawa, who happened to take office during the final round of the agricultural negotiations, had to make and announce a politically risky decision. To do so, he needed to have some degree of consensus at the Council of Representatives. Among the coalition parties at the Council, Hosokawa's Japan New Party, the Renewal Party, *Kômeitô* and the Democratic Socialist Party supported the prime minister's policy on the rice issue, but the Socialist Party remained reluctant to support it.[9]

After an agreement was reached between Europe and the United States, Hosokawa announced that his government was ready to accept a compromise on the issue of opening Japan's rice market. Strong opposition, as expected, came from the agricultural interests and LDP politicians who took advantage of being in the opposition to blame the Hosokawa government for damaging Japan's agriculture. To make matters worse, Hosokawa was faced with a rebellion that erupted within his fragile eight-party coalition government. The Socialist Party, the biggest among the eight parties, with many members elected from rural agricultural areas, threatened to leave the coalition.

Hosokawa, however, did not yield, knowing that the public was backing him. Every national poll taken in the months just prior to his announcement showed that most Japanese agreed that the time had come to import at least some rice. "It is a role of a leader to present a specified goal. If the goal was right, I believed the people would support me,"[10] said Hosokawa, expressing his feeling during that time. The Socialist Party held a 12-hour meeting to dramatize its opposition. The Socialist representative at the Council of Representatives, Kubo Wataru, went back and forth between the Council and the Socialist Party headquarters negotiating and persuading Socialist members to comply.[11] In the end, the party decided that breaking with the popular prime minister and bearing the blame for the collapse of the world trade system would be much more dangerous politically than protecting rice farmers. Hosokawa had won.

The centralized nature of the coalition government helped Hosokawa's political decision to open the rice market. The policy subcommittee system would have brought agricultural experts a stage to voice their opposition, making it more difficult for the prime minister to reach a final decision. Hosokawa made a pre-dawn announcement on December 14 that Japan must accept rice imports "for our sake and the world's sake."

After this announcement, political and public interest swiftly shifted to a political reform issue—the introduction of a new single-seat electoral system for the lower house. Prime Minister Hosokawa declared that he would stake his political career on achieving this objective. The public, who had been disappointed by the failure of LDP prime ministers Kaifu Toshiki and Miyazawa Kiichi to deliver a similar reform as a result of intraparty conflicts, strongly supported Hosokawa. He received an unprecedented 70 percent public support rating.

Even with this enormous popularity, it was not easy for Hosokawa to pass the political reform bills that were controversial within the political community. Ozawa Ichirô of the Renewal Party and Ichikawa Yûichi of *Kômeitô*, both members of the Council of the Representatives who formed the so-called Ichi-ichi line, took initiative and actively sought consensus among the coalition parties. Although the Council accepted the political reform package, some members of the coalition parties covertly implemented a rebellious plan. On January 21, 1994, the leftist faction of the Japan Socialist Party effectively killed the political reform bills by voting against them in the upper house, thereby breaking the agreement reached among the party leaders at the Council. Negotiations in the joint committee between the upper and lower house representatives broke up. This meant that Hosokawa had only two more days to achieve political reform in the 128th extraordinary session of the Diet.

Prime Minister Hosokawa publicly restated his willingness to sacrifice his post for political reform, and he called for a meeting with President Kôno Yôhei of the opposition LDP. Behind the scenes, Ozawa had lobbied many LDP members for political reform. Some of them expressed their willingness to leave the LDP if their party blocked Hosokawa's political reform package. Ozawa, then, called LDP secretary general Mori Yoshirô to set up the Hosokawa-Kôno meeting. With fear of the possible breakup of the LDP, Mori agreed.[12] In the negotiations with Kôno, Hosokawa accepted the LDP's requests to change the number of electoral districts and to ease the reporting requirements for political finance. An agreement was reached. Although many LDP members opposed the political reform, they did not want to be blamed for blocking bills that were popular with the public. This compromise enabled the Hosokawa coalition government to pass the political reform bills in both the upper and lower houses on January 29, 1994.

While the centralized decision-making mechanism helped Hosokawa's political reform as well as opening of the rice market, it did not work well in the case of his attempt to raise the consumption tax. This tax issue was deeply connected to the negotiations on the U.S.–Japan Economic Framework Talks, which continued during the political reform debate. The talks during their early stages were primarily focused on Japan's macroeconomic policies. Japan was asked to present an "economic stimulus" package in order to increase its imports. The Hosokawa government thought it was possible to introduce a large-scale tax cut that the U.S. government requested if, and only if, an increase in the consumption tax would follow in a few years to make up for the income shortage that would result. Without a future tax increase, the powerful Ministry of Finance would never agree to a tax cut. MOF officials saw this as a great opportunity to raise the 3 percent consumption tax, which they considered very low.

Prime Minister Hosokawa faced a dilemma: Time for a political debate was needed; but if a tax increase were announced, Hosokawa would fall from the political tightrope he was walking at that time in order to achieve the political reform. He decided to keep the tax issue on the back burner until the political reform bills passed in the Diet. The Diet session lasted longer than Hosokawa expected. When the bills passed both the lower and upper houses, it was already less than two weeks before his scheduled meeting with President Clinton on February 11, where he planned to present an economic stimulus package, including that future tax increase.

At the February 1 meeting of the Council of Representatives, Ozawa and Ichikawa introduced the plan to raise the consumption tax from 3 to 7 percent. The representatives took the proposal back to their own parties for review. In the afternoon of the following day, the Socialist leader Murayama Tomiichi visited the prime minister's office to discuss the tax matter with Hosokawa. Murayama, however, was kicked out of the office by Ichikawa, who was trying to eliminate possible opposition.[13] This dramatic incident hardened the attitude of the Socialist Party. Later in the evening when the Council of Representatives met again, the Socialist Party expressed disagreement, and the representatives of the Renewal Party, the Democratic Socialist Party and the Japan New Party–*Sakigake* announced that they would leave the final decision to the prime minister.

At eleven o'clock, an emergency meeting of the Government and Party Executive Council was called. The leaders of *Sakigake*, the Socialist Party, and the Democratic Socialist Party told Hosokawa that they could not support the abrupt announcement of the new tax plan.[14] They complained that there was not enough discussion on this issue. Murayama, for example, told Hosokawa, "It is undemocratic to be forced to answer 'yes' or 'no' in such a short period. . . . We can never accept this."[15] At the end, they left the final decision to the prime minister.

A few hours later, despite the opposition of the three coalition parties, Hosokawa held a press conference and announced the tax package. This sudden announcement met strong criticism from the media and the opposition LDP as well as several of the coalition parties. The Socialist Party demanded the withdrawal of Hosokawa's tax proposal by threatening to leave the coalition. Strong criticism was aimed at Ozawa and Ichikawa, who drove the prime minister to make a hasty decision without building consensus among the coalition parties. Murayama later pinpointed Ozawa in his criticisms of the decision: "A coalition government should be operated in a democratic manner in order to reflect a wider range of opinions. Secretary General Ozawa of the Renewal Party did not understand this at all."[16]

The prime minister who had used public support to achieve his policies did not take much effort to persuade the public over this tax issue. At the press conference, Hosokawa was asked how the government came up with the 7 percent figure. He answered that it was "a ball-park figure." Obviously, he was not deeply involved in the policy-making process. Hosokawa was no longer seen as a leader who enthusiastically communicated national goals to the public. The public was disappointed to see Hosokawa acting like a servant of the very bureaucrats whose clout he pledged to curb.[17] To many, Hosokawa now seemed to be a puppet leader totally controlled by the Ministry of Finance. With public resentment, Hosokawa was forced into a retreat on the tax plan the very next day. Public support for Hosokawa further eroded after this event. In April 1994, Prime Minister Hosokawa suddenly announced his resignation amidst allegations of personal financial impropriety, bringing an abrupt end to a unique period in postwar politics with a centralized decision-making system.

THE MURAYAMA CABINET

As Hosokawa left, Hata Tsutomu of the Renewal Party took over the office in April 1994. The Hata cabinet faced political difficulty from the beginning. On the same day Hata was elected prime minister, four of the eight coalition parties, excluding the Japan Socialist Party, formed a new political group within the Diet. Becoming the largest faction among the coalition parties, the new group would gain political advantages, including the acquisition of the chairmanships of Diet committees that would have gone to the Socialist Party. Upset by this treatment, the Socialist Party broke away from the coalition, leaving the new government in a vulnerable, minority status. The Hata cabinet lasted only two months without achieving any political results except the passing of the 1994 budget.

The LDP, suffering from its opposition party status, contacted the Socialist leader, Murayama Tomiichi, regarding the possibility of a cooperative relationship between the LDP and the Socialist Party. Meanwhile, the Hata government failed to convince the Socialist Party to return to the coalition. Instead, the minority coalition supported as the next premier candidate former prime minister Kaifu, who had defected from the LDP with 34 other members. In the following election in the lower house, an unexpected three-party coalition was formed by the LDP, the Socialist Party, and *Sakigake* to elect Murayama as national leader.

Table 2.1
The Composition of Project Teams under the Murayama Government

Project Team	LDP	Socialist Party	Sakigake
Welfare	9	7	3
Administrative Reform	6	4	2
Tax Reform	10	7	3
Economic Policy	8	5	3
50th Anniversary of WWII	6	4	2
Decentralization of Government Power	5	3	2
Human Rights and Discrimination	3	3	2
New Ainu Act	3	3	2
NPO (Non Profit Organization)	6	3	2
Insurance Market Access to Labor Union	6	3	2
Hanshin Earthquake	12	12	6
Disaster Relief	5	4	3
Minamata Disease	5	3	1
Disclosure of Special Corporations	5	2	2
Religious Corporation	5	3	2
Finance and Security	6	6	2
Forest and Greenery	4	3	1
Housing Loan Companies	10	7	3

The coalition was quickly criticized as a "marriage of convenience." Many Japanese doubted that Japan's new leader would be able to depart from the traditional Socialist stance against the will of many other Socialist members to support the U.S.–Japan alliance and Japan's Self Defense Forces (SDF). Murayama's determination to support the U.S.–Japan security alliance and the SDF arrangement was firm. In July 1994, the Socialist prime minister, breaking from the past, officially declared in the Diet that the Self Defense Forces were constitutional. Two months later, the Socialist Party approved Murayama's position to abandon its traditional goal of unarmed neutrality. This "historical policy shift" of the Socialist Party in effect put an end to the 1955 system, the political framework under which the LDP and the Socialists remained ideologically split as the government and the main opposition party.

As the biggest policy gap between the Socialist Party and the LDP was thus filled, Murayama, who had opposed the undemocratic decision-making process under the Hosokawa and Hata governments, introduced a new process to deal with policy differences within the coalition. He formed 18 different issue-specific project teams for major policy issues where the three government parties could exchange their views and find agreeable solutions. Murayama said to the author in an interview, "Clearly, policy differences existed among the three parties. In many cases, we could not reach an agreement. But through serious discussions, I believe, we developed mutual understanding and trust."[18]

The composition of the 18 project teams was set almost in proportion to the numbers of Diet members affiliated with each party (see Table 2.1). In half of the 18 teams, the number of LDP members equaled that of the Socialist Party and *Sakigake* combined. In three project teams (NPO, Minamata Disease, and Disclosure of Special Corporations), the LDP was overrepresented. In the remaining six teams, the number of the Socialist Party and *Sakigake* members exceeded the number of LDP members.

It is worth noting that no project team was formed to discuss the National Defense Program Outline (approved by the cabinet in November 1995). Murayama knew that the security policy gaps among members of parliament in the coalition parties were still too irreconcilable to permit formulation of concrete defense policies, and intentionally avoided creation of an interparty project team on this issue.

Besides these project teams, Murayama formed a policy coordination committee where the policy committee chairmen of the three coalition parties—Katô Kôichi of the LDP, Sekiyama Nobuyuki of the Socialist Party, and Kan Naoto of *Sakigake*—discussed policy matters in general. Under this committee were subcommittees divided into 19 different fields just like the LDP's issue-specific policy subcommittees, or *bukai*.[19] The old LDP *zoku* members regained their place. In the budge-making process in summer 1994, immediately after the LDP returned to power as a part of the coalition government, *zoku* members started exerting their political influence.

To avoid the LDP's dominance in policy making, the representation of the LDP, the Socialist Party, and *Sakigake* was set at the ratio of 3:2:1. Prime Minister Murayama delegated most of the decision-making power to these project teams and committees, and as a result he was often criticized for not playing a leadership role. Murayama told the author: "This democratic decision-making system takes time. Also, the outcomes are often products of political compromise. I received criticism for the lack of leadership on the Diet floor. But I thought that it was important for the three parties to work hard to reach an agreement in the committees. In cases where they could not reach an agreement, I would make the final decision. I believed this was my role as prime minister."[20] Because the three parties were involved in the decision making, for ministry officials to build consensus within the coalition government became a considerably more time- and energy-consuming process than that under the LDP government.[21]

This system worked quite well in several policy issues. One example is Minamata disease case, which Murayama listed as one of his three major policy achievements, along with the enactment of the A-bomb Victim Aid Law and the World War II comfort women issue. Minamata disease, whose cause was identified as industrial pollution of seawater, drew worldwide concern. Its cause was fully realized in 1959 to be an organomercury compound in wastes discharged into Minamata Bay in Kumamoto Prefecture by a chemical plant owned by a company called Chisso. The company, however, was allowed to continue to dump chemical waste until the closing of the plant in 1969.[22] The issue involving the responsibility of the national government had remained an unsolved political issue through 1995. While the Kumamoto prefectural government and Chisso negotiated with the victims, the national government had refused to take any action over this issue. Murayama told the author:

The Minamata disease was a case which the Socialist Party brought to the Diet so many times under the LDP governments. But the LDP governments always turned it down. After the forty-year time period, many victims passed away and many more had but a short life to live. As prime minister from the Socialist Party, I was determined to solve the problem immediately. Under the Hosokawa government, I proposed to the prime minister from Kumamoto that we act on this issue. Mr. Hosokawa, however, could not do much due to many factors.[23]

Prime Minister Hosokawa tried to tackle the issue, but he met with strong opposition from the bureaucrats of the Ministry of Finance and the Environment Agency, who insisted that the liability to provide full compensation lay on the assailant chemical company.

The Three-Party Project Team on Minamata Disease handled this issue, but its members found a wide gap between the LDP and the Socialist Party over the definition of "victims" at the end of May 1995. Environment *zoku* members of the LDP had been supporting the position of the Environment Agency—to identify victims, the government should accept only medical certificates issued by specified public institutions: In contrast, the Socialist Party demanded that the government also accept those issued by private doctors. To fill the gap, the leaders of the three parties upgraded the status of the project team by appointing the policy committee chairmen (Yamazaki, Sekiyama, and Kan) of the three parties to join three representatives from the original team. On June 21, the new project team reached an agreement that the Kumamoto prefectural government would form a special committee to judge a patient's status based on the medical certificate of both public institutions and private doctors.

The three parties also agreed that the government would recognize its responsibility and express apology to the victims. The national government, however, was still reluctant to take responsibility. In July when Prime Minister Murayama expressed an apology for the government's inability to solve this issue for long time, the top bureaucratic official of the Environment Agency told reporters that Murayama's comment was personal, not representative of the government.

On December 15 after long negotiations over the amount of compensation to the victims, the government announced its final proposal, which was accepted by the organizations of the disease victims. The national and the prefectural governments agreed to provide a 26-billion-yen loan for the chemical company to pay the compensation to the victims. Prime Minister Murayama this time expressed an official apology on behalf of the national government for taking so long to identify the cause of disease and for the delays in taking "appropriate actions." This was a clear case in which the three-party coordination system helped the prime minister against the strong opposition of the bureaucracy and its sponsoring *zoku* members.

When the special interests of the three parties agreed on the direction of policy, however, they constituted an even more powerful lobbying body vis-à-vis the Murayama cabinet than had the LDP *zoku* under the single-party dominance system. Under the LDP government, for example, agricultural *zoku* members always sought a realistic compromise while calling for a higher rice price to protect farmers. In contrast, when the coalition government was planning to reduce the rice price for FY1994, the agricultural interests of the Socialist Party took advantage of being a government party in order to secure electoral bases in rural areas. They insisted on a higher price more stubbornly than did their peers from the LDP. As a result, whereas the rice price was kept at the same level as the previous year, the agricultural subsidy for rice farmers was nearly doubled in July 1994. The media criticized the revival of LDP *zoku* and the emergence of the Socialist *zoku*.

To deal with such criticisms, the policy committee chairmen of the three coalition parties announced their policy on September 7. In order to curb *zoku* activities, the government parties would increase the transparency of their policy process and strengthen anticorruption measures. But this policy had little actual impact on the decision-making process. Agricultural *zoku* members of the three parties pressured the Murayama government to increase the government subsidy to compensate farmers for the opening of Japan's rice market. The Ministry of Finance proposed a total amount of 3.5 trillion yen. Dissatisfied with this figure, *zoku* members threatened to kill the World Trade Organization–related bills that would enable the opening of the rice market unless the number was drastically increased.[24] The Murayama government had to nearly double the amount of agricultural compensation to 6.1 trillion yen. This victory by *zoku* marked their resurgence under the coalition government, and LDP *zoku* members further developed their influence under the following cabinet led by the leader of their own party.

THE HASHIMOTO CABINET

In January 1996, the 71-year-old prime minister exhausted himself in the taxing post and resigned. LDP president and MITI minister Hashimoto Ryûtarô was endorsed by the same coalition to succeed Murayama. Hashimoto promised to maintain the decision-making system comprised of the project teams and committees for policy discussion among the three coalition parties.

The new Hashimoto government had the immediate task of resolving the *jûsen* problem, which involved seven housing loan companies that had gone bankrupt. The Ministry of Finance calculated the total amount of outstanding loans by the seven companies as 13.2 trillion yen and identified about half of the loans as the initial loss. To liquidate these bad loans, creditors had to bear the cost.

The Ministry of Finance drew up its *jûsen* liquidation scheme. In accordance with this scheme, the so-called parent banks, the *jûsen* founding financial institutions, which included city banks, regional banks, life insurers, trust banks, and security firms, agreed to give up their rights to all 3.5-trillion-yen worth of loans to the *jûsen*. Other banks promised to do likewise, accounting for 1.7-trillion-yen worth of loans of the remaining 4.2 trillion yen. The proposal also requested the agricultural financial institutions that had invested 5.5 trillion yen into the housing loan companies to bear 1.1 trillion. This scheme was generous to the agricultural institutions, reflecting their strong political influence. They were asked to cover just 10 percent of their investments, whereas the parent banks gave up 100 percent and the other banks 40 percent of their investments.

The agricultural institutions, however, rejected the MOF request by stating that they were not able to pay that much. They lobbied *zoku* politicians of the LDP and successfully bargained down their payment to less than half of the original request, or 530 billion yen. Agricultural experts in the Socialist Party (by this time, the party had officially changed its name to the Social Democratic Party, or SDP; but it here will be referred as the Socialist Party) also supported the lessening of the burden of the agricultural institutions. With the small amount from the agricultural institutions, the Japanese government rewrote the bail-out plan to use 685 billion yen of public funds from the 1996 fiscal budget. This marked another victory for LDP *zoku* members.

In summer 1996, entering the last year of the lower house's four-year term, election pressure grew among Diet members. Prime Minister Hashimoto and the LDP sought the best timing for an election. Observing the rising popularity of his cabinet in September 1996, Hashimoto dissolved the lower house to call the first election under the new electoral law that introduced single-seat districts. With the new electoral system, LDP candidates, even powerful incumbents, found themselves playing a completely different game. In order to win their seat, they needed to win a higher percentage of the total votes. To many, election pressure was much greater than ever.

In the October 20 general election, the LDP gained 239 seats, up from 211, in the 500-seat lower house. Although the result was generally seen as a victory, the LDP still came up short and was unable to form a majority. Hashimoto approached the two other government parties to maintain the same coalition. However, the election result for these two parties was a disaster: The Socialist Party decreased to 15 seats from a preelection total of 30, and *Sakigake* won only two seats, losing seven. Their participation in the coalition government with the LDP might have been the reason liberal voters withdrew their support. The two parties decided to stay out of the cabinet to maintain their independence while agreeing to support the LDP government to form a majority in the lower house. Thus, the second Hashimoto cabinet started as a minority-led one.

To secure passage of major bills in the Diet, the Hashimoto cabinet tried to maintain the framework of the three-party project teams and policy coordination committees. The Socialist Party and *Sakigake*, however, no longer had enough legislators to maintain the same project team system. They had to reorganize it

Table 2.2

The LDP-SDP-*Sakigake* Project Teams and Commissions under the Second
Hashimoto Cabinet

Project Teams	Policy Coordination Commissions	
1. Hanshin Earthquake Disaster Relief	1. Defense Budget	7. Revision of the Civil Law
2. Decreasing Population	2. Agricultural Policy	8. Electoral System
3. Non-Profit Organization	3. Ethics of Public Officials	9. Okinawa Issues
4. Revision of the Commercial Law	4. Anti-Monopoly Law	10. U.S.-Japan Security Guidelines
5. Establishing New Institution to Oversee Executive Offices	5. Special Corporations Reform	11. Medical Insurance Reform
6. Child Prostitution	6. Tax System	

while reducing membership. As of September 1997, the three parties had six
project teams and 11 policy commissions (see Table 2.2).

As the scale of the three-party committees reduced, so did the significance of
policy coordination among the three parties. LDP subcommittees regained
power. Most of the substantial policy discussions took place within the LDP.
The two other parties were consulted only after discussions were made, in the
words of an LDP politician, "just out of courtesy." Although the LDP theoretically needed approval from the two other parties before introducing legislation
in the Diet, the three-party consultation process became a mere ceremony. The
center of decision making shifted to within the LDP, and decision making within
the ruling party became decentralized as LDP *zoku* members regained their
power.

In running the minority government, Prime Minister Hashimoto began to seek
different partners depending on the nature of the issues on the table. In passing
the 1997 budget bill, Hashimoto used the same three-party coalition framework
to gain support from the Socialist Party and *Sakigake*. Over land-lease agreements for U.S. military bases in Okinawa, however, the Socialist Party refused
to cooperate with the Hashimoto government. The prime minister, in order to
secure the American presence in Okinawa, asked the opposition New Frontier
Party (NFP) for support.

The status of U.S. bases in Okinawa leaped to the center of the political table
with the rape of a Japanese elementary school girl by three U.S. servicemen
stationed in the island prefecture in September 1995. This incident sparked intensified protests and criticisms toward the U.S.–Japan Security Treaty arrangements, which forced the islands, with 1 percent of Japan's land, to provide an
unproportional burden of housing about 75 percent of all U.S. military instal-
lations in Japan and nearly two-thirds of the 47,000 American troops stationed
in the country. To meet Okinawa's requests, Prime Minister Hashimoto negotiated with the Clinton administration to realign and reduce American facilities
in Okinawa. On the occasion of the April 1996 U.S.–Japan summit meeting,
Hashimoto and President William Clinton hailed a plan to reduce 11 U.S. bases
on Okinawa over several years' time. The highlight of the plan was the reversion

of the U.S. Marine Corps's Futenma Air Station, a source of frequent complaints by local residents because of its location in a densely populated area.

This plan, however, did not totally satisfy the people in Okinawa. Some landowners continued their protest and refused to renew their land-lease contracts on which 12 American military facilities were built. Because the renewal process was not expected to be completed by the land-lease expiration date of May 1997, the Hashimoto administration proposed a revision of the 1952 Special Law Governing Land for Armed Forces Stationed in Japan. This revision would give the central government the authority to override opposition from landowners and local governments and renew the leases when those for property within U.S. bases were to expire.

As the Socialist Party refused to cooperate with the government over this revision, Prime Minister Hashimoto contacted NFP president Ozawa Ichirô, knowing that Ozawa strongly believed an American presence in Okinawa was essential for the security of Japan and the Far East. Ozawa promised to support the government's bill, and the *Taiyô* Party, the Democratic Party, and *Sakigake* also agreed to join this coalition to secure the passage of the bill in the Diet in April 1997.

This cooperation between the LDP and the NFP was a major step in the coalition system. Japan's coalition governments since the Hosokawa administration had made agreements among the ruling coalition parties before approaching the opposition parties. Hashimoto's contact with the opposition NFP without a serious effort to come to terms with the Socialist Party was seen as the beginning of a new era, defined by parties forming different coalitions on a policy-by-policy basis.

This political arrangement created a complicated situation for the LDP. Prime Minister Hashimoto did not have a strong power base within his own party. The LDP was split into two groups: one that supported the existing coalition with the Socialists and *Sakigake*, and one that called for a conservative coalition with the NFP. The political contest between the two groups was intensified after the passage of the land-lease bill.

In September 1997, the LDP regained a majority status in the lower house when 12 defectors joined the ruling party, and Hashimoto was reappointed LDP president without an election. The fact remained, however, that he had to run the government on this delicate balance between the two groups within the LDP and with a minority status in the upper house. Although Hashimoto promised to maintain the existing coalition government with the Socialist Party and *Sakigake*, the three-party coalition framework was no longer solid. When the Socialist Party reappointed Doi Takako as chairwoman, and an anticoalition advocator took one of the leadership positions in January 1998,[25] LDP secretary general Katô Kôichi tactically changed the principle of the three-party policy coordination system from a consensual one to one led by majority. The LDP could now introduce legislation without the approval of the Socialist Party and *Sakigake*.[26] This change made it possible for the Socialists to express their opposition without risking a breakup of the three-party coalition framework. The Socialist Party and *Sakigake* were, in effect, no longer involved in the actual decision-making process, and they finally left the coalition government before the July 1998 upper house election. Prime Minister Hashimoto and the LDP hoped to recover a majority in the election.

THE OBUCHI CABINET

In the upper house election, however, the LDP won only 46 seats, leaving it 102 seats of the 252-seat house, 23 short of a majority in the upper house. This historic loss forced Prime Minister Hashimoto to resign and put the LDP and the newly elected premier, Obuchi Keizô, in the difficult position of having to run the government with majority control of only the lower house.

Diet operations were more difficult than expected. In the fall session, the LDP had to team up with different partners to pass important bills. In order to legislate the Financial Renewal Bills, the government party reluctantly adopted the Democratic Party's proposal to gain support from the largest opposition party as well as *Kômeitô* and the Socialist Party. As for the bills for an early reconstruction of the financial system, the LDP forwent teaming up with the Democrats and sought cooperation with the Liberal Party. To pass the budget bills, the LDP had to cut a deal with *Kômeitô* by agreeing to issue consumption coupons to children under 16 and the selected elderly. These tough Diet operations made Prime Minister Obuchi and his cabinet realize the need to form a coalition government in order to secure the passage of the bills to revise the U.S.–Japan Security guideline during the 1999 ordinary Diet session.

Obuchi's choice for partner was Ozawa Ichirô's Liberal Party. It was surprising and reasonable at the same time: surprising in consideration of the strong animosity against Ozawa among LDP members, and reasonable if considering the Liberal Party's policy line on strengthening the U.S.–Japan Security ties. The Liberal Party set several conditions for its participation in the coalition, including the immediate reduction of the number of cabinet ministers, the gradual downsizing of civil servants by 25 percent over ten years, and an end to the government commissioner system, which allowed civil servants to answer questions at the Diet.

Before the coalition was officially formed, the LDP agreed to reduce the number of cabinet posts from 20 to 18, and to form five project teams between the two parties: (1) abolition of the government commissioner system and the introduction of deputy ministers, (2) reduction of the number of Diet seats, (3) basic principle of national security, (4) reorganization of the central government and downsizing of civil servants, and (5) economy and tax system. These project teams produced some concrete policy outcomes. The two parties, for example, agreed on a detailed scheme that would abolish the government commissioner system and on the number of deputy ministers to be introduced. These agreements were incorporated in the Diet reform bills which passed in the Diet on

July 28, 1999. The LDP and the Liberal Party also agreed to reduce 50 of the 200 proportional representation seats in the 500-member lower house. This agreement, however, later met political opposition and was not implemented in the 1999 Diet sessions. For policy discussions on items other than the five areas, the LDP and the LP agreed to hold monthly regular meetings between Obuchi and Ozawa.

While the LDP-LP coalition strengthened the Obuchi government, problems remained. Although the two-party coalition held a secure majority in the lower house, it was still 10 seats short of a majority in the upper house. In order to secure a majority in the upper house, the Obuchi administration sought cooperation from the opposition *Kômeitô*. *Kômeitô* at that time was seeking its new political stance by keeping distance from the largest opposition party, the Democratic Party which lost popular support. Cooperation with the LDP would make the party more politically influential in the actual policy making. *Kômeitô* agreed to cooperate with the LDP-LP coalition government in the Diet operations.

The 145th regular Diet session (January 19–August 13, 1999) was portrayed as the "LDP-LP-*Kômeitô* session." *Kômeitô*'s cooperation was crucial in the passage of politically controversial bills such as the U.S.-Japan Defense Guideline bills, the Flag-anthem bill, and the Anti-organizational Crime bills.[27] In the Diet session, the Obuchi Cabinet was able to pass 110 of the 124 government-sponsored bills under the three-party cooperative framework.[28]

At the end of the Diet session, Prime Minister Obuchi invited *Kômeitô* to officially form a coalition. The policy gap between *Kômeitô* and the Liberal Party was substantial in the fields of welfare and national security. *Kômeitô*, with a strong women subgroup, was traditionally liberal, supporting a larger government welfare program and standing against an increase in the defense budget. On the other hand, the Liberal Party called for Japan's larger role in international politics and a smaller government in welfare programs. Though differences were huge, the biggest gap between the two parties was on electoral reform. The reduction of 50 seats out of the 200 proportional representation seats on which the LDP agreed with the Liberal Party was unacceptable for *Kômeitô*, for, 29 of its 48 lower house members were elected in the proportional representation. In order to form the three-party coalition, the LDP had to renegotiate over electoral reform with the Liberal Party.

Meanwhile, Prime Minister Obuchi faced a presidential election in his own party. In order to retain the office, he had to be reelected as party leader. Two other candidates, former LDP Secretary General Katô Kôichi and former Chairman of LDP Policy Research Council Yamazaki Taku, were both critical of forming a coalition with *Kômeitô* largely due to its relationship with a religious group, *Sôkagakkai*. In the September 20 election, however, Obuchi received 350 of the 514 total votes. Prime Minister Obuchi interpreted his reelection as party approval for the three-party coalition and further accelerated his efforts to conclude an agreement with the Liberal Party and *Kômeitô*.

On October 4, the three parties finally reached an agreement over electoral reform. The parties agreed to submit an electoral reform bill to reduce 20 of the proportional representation seats and postponed the decision over the remaining 30 seats. On the following day, Prime Minister Obuchi formed a new cabinet with one member each from the Liberal Party and *Kômeitô*.[29] For policy coordination, the three-party policy council (*Yotô Sekininsha Kaigi*) was formed with three members from each party.[30] Major policy issues were expected to be brought to this council for building consensus among the three parties. The three-party coalition totaled 356 lower house members (71.2% of the 500 seats) and 143 upper house members (56.7% of the 252 seats). This overwhelming majority made the Obuchi Administration's Diet operation. During the 146th extraordinary session (October 29–December 15, 1999), the Obuchi Cabinet managed to pass all the 74 government sponsored bills.

Downsizing the lower house remained a thorny issue among the three parties. While the electoral reform bill was submitted to the Diet as agreed, the LDP and *Kômeitô* refused to call a vote for the bill during the Diet session. Thus, Liberal Party President Ozawa Ichirô threatened to leave the coalition. The three parties finally reached a compromise that the bill would be called for at the beginning of the following Diet session. In accordance with this compromise, the three parties introduced the electoral reform bill in the 147th ordinary Diet session. The opposition parties, however, refused to attend the Diet session, arguing that the passage of a bill as important as the electoral reform bill should not be determined only by the government parties. Without the presence of all opposition parties in the committee and floor meetings of both houses on February 2, 2000, the three government coalition parties passed the electoral reform bill to reduce 20 proportional representation seats.

The media criticized the Obuchi government for breaking the customary rules of the Diet. Since the early 1970s, the government party had never voted on legislation without the presence of opposition party members. The opposition parties continued to boycott the Diet deliberations and called for an immediate general election. The political climate changed after the Osaka gubernatorial election which was generally regarded as a litmus test for the coming general election. In the February 6 election, Ôta Fusae, a former senior official of the Ministry of International Trade and Industry, who was supported by the three-party government coalition, defeated her two major rivals to become Japan's first female governor. The election result was generally seen as approval for the government coalition. Losing momentum to attack the government, the opposition parties agreed to attend the Diet deliberation. Thus ended the Obuchi government's political crisis.

In March, however, the Obuchi administration faced another political turmoil. The LDP finally gave up on cooperating with Ozawa's Liberal Party in the coming election. The two parties had competing candidates in nearly 30 electoral districts for the forthcoming general election. In seven districts, the incumbents of the two parties would have to battle over one seat. Without any electoral cooperation, being a part of the coalition party would not benefit the Liberal

Party in the election. Ozawa took a gamble. He demanded that the coalition partners, the LDP and *Kômeitô*, immediately legislate the policies the three parties had agreed on in October 1999 when they formed the coalition. These policies included reforms in education, welfare, the tax system, and national security. In Ozawa's calculation, even if the two parties did not accept his demands, he would be able to establish an image as a reformist, which would help in the forthcoming election.

On April 1, Ozawa met with Prime Minister Obuchi and *Kômeitô* leader Kanzaki Takenori. They told Ozawa that they could not accept his demand and that Ozawa's repeated threat to break off the coalition destroyed trust among them. In other words, Obuchi and Kanzaki asked Ozawa to leave the coalition. Once the breakup was decided, it became apparent that the Liberal Party was not a solid entity. More than half of its Diet members saw a political advantage in remaining in the coalition. Twenty-six Liberals broke off from Ozawa to form the new Conservative Party to remain a coalition partner with the LDP and *Kômeitô*. Ozawa's party was left with only 24 Diet members and was out of the coalition.

Several hours after the three-party leaders meeting, a tragedy hit Obuchi. The 62-year-old prime minister suffered a stroke and was hospitalized in a coma. On April 4, the Obuchi Cabinet resigned en masse in accordance with Article 70 of the Constitution that stipulates the cabinet's resignation "when the prime ministerial post is vacant." When LDP Secretary General Mori Yoshirô was elected the 55th prime minister in the Diet, the Obuchi administration officially closed its 616-day history.

SUMMARY

Japan's political changes brought a series of substantial transformations to the political decision-making process since the establishment of the Hosokawa cabinet. The most notable characteristic of Hosokawa's leadership was the centralization of decision-making. He discontinued the issue-specific subcommittee system. In the opening of Japan's rice market, the prime minister made a decision behind the closed doors of the Council of Representatives of the Coalition Parties without disclosing information to the public: He decided to accept the GATT proposal. Similarly, Hosokawa passed the political reform package with a top-down decision-making style after negotiating with the LDP president. The unprecedented high public support successfully contained political opposition and enabled him to achieve these goals.

This centralized decision-making system, however, received heavy criticism. As the Council made a number of policy decisions, Ozawa and Ichikawa, or the so-called Ichi-ichi line, became dominant figures. Other leaders of the coalition parties saw the Council's decision-making process as undemocratic. Ichikawa defends Ozawa and himself by saying, "Everybody became critics probably due to their long experience as opposition party members. . . . Nothing can be achieved by critics. Therefore, we [Ozawa and Ichikawa] had to take action to solve problems."[31]

This centralized policy process turned out be inappropriate for a highly unpopular proposal to raise the tax rate. The nature of the tax policy required political debate where opponents could express their anger about a tax increase. The media criticized that the tax decision was made in an undemocratic process in which a very limited number of policymakers were involved. The public felt betrayed because Hosokawa did not seek their support. Without public support, the prime minister who had boasted his high approval rate had to withdraw the proposal. Hosokawa's credentials and leadership capability were questioned, leading to his resignation.

Murayama, who was critical of the autocratic nature of the Hosokawa government's decision-making style, introduced a decentralized decision-making system with issue-specific project teams and committees. Murayama saw his leadership role as a coordinator in a democratic, bottom-up decision-making process. This system worked in certain policy issues such as Minamata disease. At the same time, it gave LDP *zoku* members a stage to become politically active. New *zoku* from the Socialist Party joined with them, as seen in the case of rice price setting, agricultural subsidies, and the *jûsen* problem, further tilting the power balance between *zoku* and the government.

Hashimoto's leadership style was different from that of Murayama, although he agreed to maintain the same framework of project teams and committees. Hashimoto was able to cut a deal with Ozawa to acquire the NFP's support to pass the land-lease bills of American bases in Okinawa. This incident was reminiscent of Hosokawa's deal with the LDP on political reform. The highly political nature of the two incidents allowed the prime ministers to exercise a top-down style of leadership.

The centralized decision-making system under the Hosokawa administration did not last long. Prime Minister Murayama introduced a decentralized decision-making system among the three coalition parties, and LDP *zoku* members began to regain their influence over policy decision making. When LDP president Hashimoto Ryûtarô succeeded Murayama, LDP *zoku* members established almost the same degree of influence, especially after the LDP recaptured a majority in the lower house in September 1997. With strong *zoku* members, the Japanese prime minister again had to confront the decentralized nature of policy making within the ruling party. Except a temporary deviation during the Hosokawa administration, Japan's decision making surrounding the prime minister reverted to the traditional framework as described in the previous chapter. The goals of the following chapters are to identify the political resources of the prime minister and to illustrate his attempt to exercise leadership to overcome the fractions—and to explain why he sometimes has failed to do so.

NOTES

Although significant additions and revisions were made, this chapter largely relies on my previous study, Tomohito Shinoda, "Japan's Decision Making under the Coalition Governments," *Asian Survey*, July 1998. © 1998 by The Regents of the University of California. Reprinted from *Asian Survey* vol 28, no. 7, pp. 703–23, by permission of The Regents.

1. The eight parties were the Japan Socialist Party, the Renewal Party, *Kômeitô*, the Japan New Party, *Sakigake*, the Democratic Socialist Party, the United Social Democratic Party and the Democratic Reform Federation.

2. Hosokawa appointed Hata Tsutomu of the Renewal Party to the post of deputy prime minister and foreign minister, Yamahana Sadao of the Socialist Party to state minister for political reform, Ishida Kôshirô of *Kômeitô* to director general of the Management and Coordination Agency, Ôuchi Keigo of the Democratic Socialist Party, Takemura Masayoshi of *Sakigake* to chief cabinet secretary, and Eda Satsuki of the United Social Democratic Party to director general of the Science and Technology Agency.

3. Hosokawa Morihiro and Iwakuni Tetsundo, *Hina no Ronri* [The logic of the local community] (Tokyo: Kôbunsha, 1991), especially pp. 10–33.

4. Hosokawa Morihiro, interview by author, November 15, 1996.

5. See Ishihara Nobuo, *Kan Kaku Arubeshi* [how the bureaucrats should be] (Tokyo: Shôgakukan Bunko, 1998), pp. 49–50. Ishihara was the deputy chief cabinet secretary who served under Prime Ministers Takeshita Noboru, Kaifu Toshiki, Miyazawa Kiichi, Hosokawa Morihiro and Murayama Tomiichi. About the formal legislative system under the Hosokawa government, see Minoru Nakano, "The Changing Legislative Process in the Transitional Period," in *Japanese Politics Today: Beyond Karaoke Democracy?*, ed. Purnendra Jain and Takashi Inoguchi (New York: St. Martin's Press, 1997), pp. 45–74.

6. Igarashi Kôzô, *Kantei no Rasen Kaidan* [The spiral staircase of the prime minister's office] (Tokyo: Gyôsei, 1997), pp. 297–99.

7. Hosokawa Morihiro, interview by author, November 15, 1996.

8. See Ishihara Nobuo, *Kantei 2668 nichi* [Twenty-six hundred sixty-eight days at the prime minister's office] (Tokyo: NHK Shuppan, 1995), pp. 100–108.

9. Ibid., pp. 112–13.

10. Hosokawa Morihiro, interview by author, November 15, 1996.

11. Ishihara Nobuo, interview by Mikuriya Takashi and Watanabe Akio in Ishihara Nobuo, *Shushô Kantei no Ketsudan* [The decisions of the prime minister's office] (Tokyo: Chûô Kôron, 1997), p. 153.

12. Mori Yoshirô, interview by Tahara Sôichiro in Tahara Sôichirô, *Atama no Nai Kujira* [A headless whale] (Tokyo: Asahi Shinbun-sha, 1997), pp. 82–86.

13. Takemura Masayoshi, "Renritsu Seikenka no ano 'Fukushizei' tekkai wa Nani wo Monogataruka" [What does the withdrawal of the welfare tax under the coalition government mean], *Bungei Shunjû*, July 1997, pp. 336–38.

14. Ibid.

15. Murayama Tomiichi, "Watashi no Rirekisho" [My personal history], no. 23, *Nihon Keizai Shinbun*, June 27, 1996.

16. Murayama Tomiichi, interview by Kanemori Kazuyuki in Murayama Tomiichi, *Murayama Tomiichi ga Kataru "Tenmei" no 561 nichi* [The destined 561 days by Tomiichi Murayama] (Tokyo: K. K. Best Sellers, 1996), p. 31.

17. Michiyo Nakamoto, "Hosokawa Plan Has Pleased Few and Made Many Unhappy," *Financial Times*, February 4, 1994. See also Paul Blustein, "Japanese Leader Forced to Retreat on Taxes," *Washington Post*, February 5, 1994.

18. Murayama Tomiichi, interview by author, September 13, 1996.

19. The committees were on (1) legal affairs, (2) foreign affairs, (3) finance, (4) education, (5) welfare, (6) agriculture and fishery, (7) industry, (8) transportation, (9) post and communication, (10) labor, (11) construction, (12) local governments, (13) Hokkaido development, (14) cabinet, (15) defense, (16) Okinawa development, (17) science and technology, (18) environment, and (19) budget settlement.

20. Murayama Tomiichi, interview by author, September 13, 1996.

21. Foreign Ministry officials, interview by Fukui Haruhiro, July 4, 1996, and a MITI official, interview by Haruhiro Fukui, July 1, 1996, both quoted in Tomohito Shinoda, "Japan's Political Changes and Their Impacts on U.S.–Japan Relations," in *Redefining the Partnership*, ed. Chihiro Hosaya and Tomohito Shinoda (Lanham, Maryland: University Press of America, 1998), pp. 43–58. Also see Ishihara, *Kan Kakuarubeshi*, pp. 48–50.

22. Manfred Davidmann, "Social Responsibility, Profits and Social Accountability," paper listed on internet at *http://www.demon.co.uk/solbaram/articles/sclrsp.html*.

23. Murayama Tomiichi, interview by author, September 13, 1996.

24. Nihon Keizai Shinbun-sha, ed., *"Renritsu Seiken" no Kenkyû* [Study of coalition governments] (Tokyo: Nihon Keizai Shinbun-sha, 1994), pp. 71–76.

25. Doi reshuffled the party leadership positions and appointed to the Policy Council chairmanship Akiba Tadatoshi, who was known as an advocator for his party to separate from the coalition government.

26. The LDP, for example, introduced the organizational crime bill that was introduced in March 1998 without the approval of the two parties.

27. The Flag-anthem Law legally recognizes the Hinomaru as Japan's National Flag and "Kimigayo" as the national anthem, and the Anti-organizational Crime bills included a legislation to allow law enforcement authorities to wiretap in investigations into organized crime.

28. The rate of enactment was 87 percent, slightly higher than 83 percent in the previous year.

29. Nikai Toshihiro of the Liberal Party was appointed to minister of transportation, and Tuzuki Kunihiro of *Kômeitô* became director-general of the Management and Coordination Agency.

30. The nine members were Kamei Shizuka, Sakurai Shin and Kuze Kimitaka of the LDP, Fujii Hirohisa, Suzuki Toshio and Toda Kuniji of the Liberal Party, and Sakaguchi Tsutomu, Higasa Katsuyuki and Endô Otohiko of *Kômeitô*. They are chairmen, deputy chairman or vice chairman of the policy council of each party.

31. Ichikawa Yûichi, interview by Tahara Sôichiro, *Atama no Nai Kujira*, p. 107.

Part II

The Power of the Prime Minister

Chapter 3

Institutional Sources of Power

As head of the cabinet in which the Constitution vests executive power, the Japanese prime minister leads the executive branch. He remains a member of the Diet and representative of the majority in the legislative branch. Through the cabinet's authority to appoint judges to the supreme court, he has some influence over decisions made in the judiciary branch. The prime minister, therefore, influences all three government branches and seemingly wields enormous power over government operations.

However, the prime minister's direct authority over the executive is surprisingly limited. Although he often gives instructions to the ministries, theoretically he cannot directly control administrative operations. Executive power belongs to the cabinet, and administrative jurisdiction is divided among cabinet members who head administrative agencies. The prime minister controls administrative operations only through the cabinet, which operates under a rule of unanimity.[1]

Political reality further undermines his legal authority. For example, although the Constitution gives the prime minister a free hand in appointing his cabinet members, intraparty politics generally do not allow him to exercise that freedom. Powerful prime ministers, of course, have more freedom in the formation of their cabinet and thus gain control over policy developments.

This chapter focuses on the institutional sources of power available to the prime minister: heading the cabinet; appointing and dismissing cabinet members; and dissolving the Diet. The support provided the prime minister by the Cabinet Secretariat and its effect on his ability to exercise authority will also be discussed. Through concrete cases, each power source is examined, from existing statutory authorities to unwritten authorities established by political tradition or precedent as well as government.

HEADING THE CABINET

The executive power of the prime minister is not precisely defined by the Constitution. It states that executive power is vested in the cabinet (Article 65) and that the prime minister represents the cabinet (Article 72). Article 2 of the Cabinet Law, as well as Article 6 of the Constitution, defines the prime minister as head of the cabinet. This status is supported by his constitutional authority to appoint and dismiss cabinet members (Article 68) and his authority to protect cabinet members from legal actions during their tenure (Article 75).[2] However, his role as a representative and head of the cabinet is ambiguous. For example, Article 72, which defines the job of the prime minister, reads, "The Prime Minister, representing the Cabinet, submits bills, reports on general national affairs and foreign relations to the Diet, and exercises control and supervision over various administrative branches." The wording has created an ongoing debate over whether the prime minister represents the cabinet only when he submits bills or when he conducts all the duties described in the article. This is an important question. If "representing the cabinet" applies only to the submission of bills, the prime minister would have the authority to exercise control and supervision over the executive branch independent from the cabinet. This was indeed the intent of Article 64 in the original English-language draft proposed by the American Occupation authorities.[3] Article 66 of the current Constitution, however, implies limitations to the prime minister's authorities by referring to the cabinet's collective responsibility.[4]

The Cabinet Law more clearly limits the prime minister's executive power. First, Article 5 defines his role as a cabinet representative when he "reports on general national affairs and foreign relations" to the Diet as well as when he submits bills. The statements and actions of the prime minister in the Diet, therefore, are limited by cabinet decisions. Second, according to Article 3, the authority and responsibility of executive power is divided among cabinet members.[5] This provides direct authority over administrative operations to relevant ministers, not the prime minister. The prime minister legally holds direct authority only over the agencies under the Prime Minister's Office, such as the Defense Agency and the National Land Agency. Over most administrative branches, he has indirect authority. The prime minister can block administrative operations with the authority given by Article 8 of the Cabinet Law, but the final decision on operations is decided in cabinet meetings.[6] As Gotôda Masaharu states: "The Prime Minister has no legal authority to control or supervise each minister. Ministers do not receive individual directions from the prime minister unless his direction meets certain conditions.[7]

Even his indirect authority is limited. Article 6 of the Cabinet Law does not allow him to hold executive power independent from decisions made in the cabinet. Thus, he can control or supervise the executive branch only to the extent that he is authorized by the cabinet meeting.[8] In policy making, the prime minister needs to build a consensus among different groups within the ruling party (or parties) to assure a cabinet approval.

This can be problematic, especially in the case of an emergency. The Cabinet Secretariat under the Hashimoto Ryûtarô administration (1996–98) called it the "N6" issue, and explored the possibility of reinforcing the prime minister's authority under the current legal framework. The Administrative Reform Council, an advisory organ to Prime Minister Hashimoto, suggested the cabinet preapprove a package of decisions to authorize the prime minister to act in emergency cases. The Council also recommended the flexible interpretation of the legal restriction of Article 6 in peacetime and urged the government to continue to study this issue. However, these revisions met strong opposition from the Cabinet Legal Bureau, which saw them as a threat to the principle of the collective responsibility of the cabinet. At the end, the revisions were not included in the administrative reform bills, enacted on July 8, 1999.

Presiding over Cabinet Meetings

The cabinet is the highest decision-making institution of the executive branch. It is here that the prime minister officially oversees the operations of administrative agencies. Regular cabinet meetings are usually held twice a week, on Tuesday and Friday.[9] Besides the regular meetings, there are also extraordinary meetings called at the request of members.

Another practice is "cabinet consideration by circular," in which a document is circulated among cabinet members for their signature on a cabinet decision. If no member objects and all the signatures are collected, the item becomes an official cabinet decision. In case of a national emergency, however, the signatures of the prime minister and the relevant minister are sufficient to implement a policy; the signature of the other members are obtained after the fact.

As head of the cabinet, the prime minister theoretically presides over the cabinet meeting. However, his role is unclear. At the meeting, the chief secretary is in charge of proceedings. The prime minister rarely leads discussions. This is completely different from the situation of the British prime minister, who actually chairs cabinet meetings. As chairman, he controls the agenda, speaks at will from the chair, decides who else will speak and in what order, and sums up the debate at the end. He can nudge "collective decision" in a desired direction.[10] The Japanese prime minister, in contrast, does not have such strong control at the meeting.

Cabinet decisions are unanimous, a custom deriving partly from the cabinet's collective responsibility to the Diet cited in Article 66 of the Constitution. Any individual cabinet member has the power to block the prime minister's policy unless that cabinet member is dismissed. When a majority of the cabinet is opposed to his policy, the prime minister can, theoretically, dismiss all the opponents in the cabinet to force a cabinet decision. The political implications of such an action, however, would be so severe that it would be highly unlikely that he would take this step. If a decision were forced through by s'•;h a drastic action, the decision would probably not be approved by the legislative branch. The prime minister's legal authority as head and representative of the cabinet and as president of the cabinet meeting is, therefore, quite limited.[11]

In Japanese politics, actual decisions are rarely made in cabinet meetings, but are made long before the cabinet meetings take place. The agenda for a cabinet meeting is prepared at a subcabinet meeting usually held the day before and attended by the administrative vice ministers, who are top bureaucrats at the administrative ministries. The agenda goes to the cabinet meeting complete with a proposed decision. According to a former cabinet member, the cabinet meeting is where the necessary cabinet members sign official documents, but not where the actual discussions occur.[12] At a cabinet meeting, members seldom speak. Their rare comments are labeled "irregular statements" and are not reflected in the policy outcomes. Although the subcabinet meeting has no legal authority or base for its existence, decisions made at this meeting are seldom repealed by the cabinet.

The powerful subcabinet meeting is chaired by the administrative deputy chief cabinet secretary, who is a political appointee of the prime minister. He also explains the details of the agenda at cabinet meetings. Ishihara Nobuo, who served in this position under seven prime ministers in 1987–95, commented that "it is strange. A cabinet meeting can be held without the prime minister if he designates his proxy, but cannot be held without the administrative deputy chief cabinet secretary."[13]

Critics often describe this subcabinet meeting as evidence of Japan's bureaucratic supremacy. However, most of the subcabinet's recommended decisions have already been made before the issue is presented in the meetings.[14] The Cabinet Secretariat, including the chief cabinet secretary and his deputies who serve the interests of the prime minister, work to build consensus among various agencies and the ruling party long before the issue is taken to the subcabinet meetings. The issues and decisions often originate from the prime minister and his own staff and thus already have the general approval of the cabinet. A former senior assistant to Prime Minister Nakasone explained, "Once an issue reaches the level of the subcabinet meeting, even vice ministers cannot oppose the decision already made."[15]

Cabinet decisions often reflect the interests of the prime minister. He and his staff introduce their idea to the lower ranks in government, and it filters up to the cabinet meeting. In this way, the cabinet decision-making process can be controlled by the prime minister and his political agenda.

Hashimoto's Administrative Reform Council also proposed to institutionalize the policy initiative of the prime minister. Article 4 of the Cabinet Law provides that the prime minister as well as other ministers has authority to propose any issue at cabinet meetings. In actuality, the cabinet rarely initiates policy at its meetings. The proposal of the Council requires the revision of the Law to explicitly clarify the prime minister's authority to propose basic policies, such as foreign and national security policy, and fiscal and economic policy. This revision was included in the administrative reform bills enacted in July 1999 and effective in January 2001.

According to the proponents of this proposal, this legal change would significantly affect the power balance between the prime minister and the bureaucracy. The budget process, for example, would be completely different from the current one characterized by the powerful Ministry of Finance dominating the initial budget-formulating stage. Former deputy chief cabinet secretary Ishihara Nobuo states, "It would demand the prime minister's leadership in basic points such as budget size and priority areas. In actuality, this means that the function of basic policy making regarding the budget would be shifted from the Ministry of Finance to the Cabinet Secretariat."[16] The prime minister's policy initiative would be supported by the Cabinet Secretariat. The reform plan explicitly gives the Secretariat authority to plan and draft basic policies. If these schemes are realized as planned, the prime minister's role in government decision making will be significantly strengthened.

As Chief Spokesperson

The prime minister is the most visible political figure in Japan. His every word is examined and analyzed by journalists and circulated throughout the nation. What the prime minister says, in public or private, can change the course of policy making.

The prime minister makes his policy speech at the opening of the Diet. This action is based on Article 72 of the Constitution, which gives him the authority to report "on general national affairs and foreign relations to the Diet" on behalf of the cabinet. The speech is usually prepared at the Cabinet Councilor's Office in charge of providing clerical support for the cabinet, and it is based on drafts submitted from all the ministries, with consideration given to the prime minister's policy. Ministries lobby hard to the office to have their ideas included in the speech because even a slight mention of their policy area can give them an advantage in budget negotiations with the Ministry of Finance.[17]

The prime minister is required to state his major policy plan in his policy speech; not doing so can prevent the development of his policy. Prime Minister Tanaka Kakuei (1972–74) was unable to pursue his policies because he failed to mention them in his speech to the opening of the Diet. In March 1973, the Liberal Democratic Party's special research committee announced the party's long-term goal of revising the electoral system. Tanaka asked the committee to consider the single-seat electoral system for the lower house. However, he met strong objection from the powerful speaker of the upper house (the House of Councilors), Kôno Kenzô. Kôno told the prime minister that he could not introduce a bill of such importance unless it had been included in his official policy speech. In the end, Tanaka gave up the revision.

Prime Minister Nakasone Yasuhiro (1982–87) was also criticized for failing to mention his policy objectives. In January 1987, when the anti–sales tax movement was building, Nakasone delivered his policy speech to the Diet without explicitly mentioning the sales tax issue. The opposition parties criticized Nakasone's failure to do so and refused to participate in the Diet discussion. This stopped the lower house budget committee procedure for six days and eventually delayed the budget consideration process for a full month. The additional time constraint on the deliberations of the tax reform bills helped kill the legislation.[18]

The occasion for the prime minister to speak on behalf of the government is not limited to policy speeches. He is often asked to address various Diet committees, especially the budget committees of both houses, on official governmental positions. At Diet meetings, the prime minister, on behalf of the cabinet, answers questions from his own party and from opposition parties. Part of this question-and-answer session is often broadcast nationally. This presents a major opportunity for opposition parties to publicly criticize government policies. It also presents an opportunity for a policy under discussion to take a step closer to becoming an official government initiative. If the opposition parties do not present counterarguments to the answers given by the prime minister, this is often interpreted as a "go ahead" sign for the policy.

For example, Prime Minister Kishi Nobusuke (1957–60) told reporters at a Foreign Ministry press conference in May 1957 that Japan would not be in violation of the Constitution if it possessed nuclear weapons. At the upper house floor meeting the next day, a Socialist Party member questioned him about this comment. Kishi said that his administration did not have any plan to possess nuclear weapons, but that it would be possible to have them without violating the Constitution. This interpretation of the Constitution then became official and has never been challenged.[19]

When the opposition parties fail to attack the prime minister for his controversial comment, they may allow him a free hand in promoting the policy. For instance, Prime Minister Satô Eisaku (1964–72), in responding to a Communist Party leader's question in the Diet, said that Japan had two choices: to accept an earlier reversion of Okinawa in which nuclear weapons would remain on the island's U.S. military base; or to insist on upholding the non-nuclear policy even if this would delay the return of the islands. Satô had expected strong opposition to the possible return of the islands with nuclear weapons. However, the opposition parties did not realize that their failure to criticize Satô's answer meant, in effect, giving him the freedom to choose between the two options.[20]

Not only is the prime minister's presentation at each opening Diet session an opportunity to set his political agenda, it is also the time to state the government's political objectives. The Diet has the authority to oversee government actions. The prime minister's statements often become the official voice of the Japanese government unless they are criticized by Diet members and are then withdrawn. Speaking at the Diet as a representative of the cabinet, therefore, has a significant impact on the policy process and the political agenda.

Influence over Government Agencies

The prime minister's impact on the political agenda does not end with his speeches at the Diet. He and his cabinet influence various government agencies. He has the authority to appoint people to positions within government agencies and quasi-government organizations such as public corporations. However, the number of political appointees to ministries is quite limited. A cabinet member can bring one personal assistant to his ministry, who is referred to as the secretary for political affairs (*Seimu Hishokan*). The parliamentary vice minister, who assists the minister and is similar to a British junior minister, is the only other politically appointed post.[21] Other positions within the ministries are occupied by civil servants.

Under the LDP government, the parliamentary vice minister was a relatively junior position for an elected LDP Diet member in his second or third term. The decision-making power of many vice ministers was limited, and they were often referred to as an "appendix of the ministry." However, because the ladder for promotions within the LDP was institutionalized, this was a first and very important step for young LDP members to develop influence in their field.[22] The ties they developed with industries and high-bureaucratic officials could help them influence the decision process within the party where a majority of political decisions were made. Recently under the Hashimoto Ryûtarô administration, the LDP appointed senior politicians in an attempt to strengthen the role of parliamentary vice ministers.

According to Article 17 of the National Administrative Organization Law, the appointments for parliamentary vice ministers are to be decided by the cabinet based on recommendations of the relevant ministers. In actuality, however, the decision involves not only cabinet members but also groups in the ruling party. The appointments of vice ministers, therefore, become important in terms of political considerations within the ruling party. Although the authority of appointing vice ministers legally belongs to the cabinet, this authority is shared with faction or party leaders.

Another significant area of influence lies in the authority of the prime minister and his cabinet to appoint executives of special and public corporations. Among the important appointments is the governor of the Bank of Japan, Japan's central bank. Although the governor is usually chosen from among senior bureaucrats in the bank and the Finance Ministry, the cabinet can theoretically appoint anyone to the post. The appointment authority is one source of influence over the central bank's policy. While the central bank, in principle, has autonomy over monetary policy, it is often subjected to political pressure from the prime minister and the finance minister.[23] This influence is an important tool for the prime minister's economic policies.

Yet another important tool of influence is the power vested in the prime minister and his cabinet to make appointments to—or dismissals from—positions at semiprivate corporations in which the government holds a major portion

of the stocks. These appointments usually go to retired or departing senior bureaucrats. The Nakasone Yasuhiro administration, for example, took advantage
of this authority on several occasions. When the president of Japan National
Railways (JNR) did not support Nakasone's reform efforts, which included the
privatization of JNR, Nakasone forced him to resign. According to Nakasone,
this was a turning point in achieving the politically difficult privatization and
the breakup of the JNR.[24]

The cabinet's appointment authority also extends to the judiciary branch. Although this branch is independent under the Constitution, the Constitution gives
the cabinet the authority to appoint the Chief Justice (Article 6) and the other
judges of the Japanese Supreme Court (Article 79). Although in most cases the
recommendations from the Justice Ministry are considered when the prime minister makes the appointments, the decisive factor in the final decision is often
the prime minister's preference.

The influence of the prime minister and his cabinet over the judiciary branch
is not limited to the appointments to the Supreme Court. It can also affect the
handling of individual law cases. Article 14 of the Public Prosecutor Office Law
authorizes the justice minister to direct the general attorney concerning individual cases, an authority that was exercised in Yoshida Shigeru's administration.
Under the instruction of Prime Minister Yoshida, the justice minister blocked
the arrest of Liberal Party secretary general Satô Eisaku, who was accused of
being involved in the shipbuilding scandal in 1953—a bribery case in which
shipbuilders attempted to influence the government's decision to allocate subsidies for ship construction plans. The public was outraged, and the justice
minister was forced to resign. Not satisfied with his resignation, an affronted
public encouraged the anti-Yoshida faction to break with the Liberal Party,
which ultimately led to the resignation of the Yoshida cabinet. This authority
has not been used since.[25]

The cabinet is vested with legal authorities that significantly affects the legislative branch. The most powerful tool probably is the authority to dissolve the
lower house, a topic to be discussed later in this chapter. There are several other
means of influence, such as the convocation of extraordinary Diet sessions.
Although Article 53 of the Constitution requires the cabinet to convene extraordinary sessions of the Diet at the request of one-fourth or more of either house,
it does not specifically state when the session must open once the request is
made.[26] On June 1, 1970, before the automatic renewal of the U.S.–Japan Security Treaty was to occur on June 22, the opposition parties requested the Diet
to open an extraordinary session. There were 129 lower house cosigners, thus
meeting the required quorum. The Satô cabinet, however, did not open the
session until November.[27] By delaying the convocation past June 22, the cabinet
achieved its policy goal of renewing the U.S.–Japan Security Treaty.

The cabinet has a more direct impact on decision making in the Diet. Article
72 of the Constitution gives the prime minister the authority to submit bills to
the Diet on behalf of the cabinet. Cabinet bills are a major part of the legislative

action in the Diet. According to a study, nearly 70 percent of the bills presented to the Diet have been submitted by the cabinet. As many as 85 percent of cabinet bills passed the Diet, compared with 15 percent for bills submitted by legislators.[28] This enactment ratio underscores the significance of cabinet bills. Because many important bills have a decisive impact on the jurisdiction of more than one ministry, they often require coordination by the Cabinet Secretariat and sometimes the prime minister.

As Chief Diplomat

The prime minister's authority goes beyond domestic affairs. Although he is not constitutionally defined as the head of state, as head of the cabinet he is authorized by Article 73 of the Constitution to conduct foreign affairs. The prime minister represents the nation vis-à-vis foreign nations and attends annual summit meetings as Japan's chief diplomat. The prime minister is given relative freedom in foreign affairs, with the ruling party and the government recognizing his authority. As long as his foreign policy objectives do not conflict with domestic interests, the prime minister, in cooperation with the Ministry of Foreign Affairs, can be an effective leader in dealing with difficult and important foreign issues. Among the postwar prime ministers, Yoshida Shigeru, Hatoyama Ichirô, Kishi Nobusuke, Satô Eisaku, Tanaka Kakuei, and Nakasone Yasuhiro have been especially noteworthy for their foreign policy achievements.

Yoshida Shigeru (1946–47, 1948–54), for example, took full responsibility for the San Francisco Peace Treaty, which relieved Japan from American Occupation in 1952. Yoshida told his finance minister and close advisor Ikeda Hayato not to cosign the treaty, warning that "this issue will cause trouble in the future, so you should not sign it. Only I will sign the treaty and bear full responsibility."[29]

Ikeda recognized Yoshida's pivotal role:

The conclusion of the Peace Treaty and the achievement of independence for Japan, in such a hard time, owes much to Prime Minister Yoshida. He also convinced the American authorities that due to our country's general mood, postwar economic power and other conditions it was impossible for Japan to rearm immediately and thus they could conclude the "Security Treaty" at the same time as the Peace Treaty. I think that his political vision and ability were extraordinary.[30]

An assistant to Ikeda, Miyazawa Kiichi, who later became the prime minister, confirms Yoshida's central role: "As far as I know, Mr. Yoshida never told anyone his intentions [concerning the peace treaty]. Mr. Ikeda advised [Mr. Yoshida] on most of the issues, but [not on diplomatic ones because] he seemed to think that diplomacy was solely the prime minister's area."[31] Once independence was achieved, however, Yoshida's aristocratic leadership style led to a sharp decline in his support within the ruling party and contributed to his ultimate fall from power.

Yoshida's successor, Hatoyama Ichirô (1954–56), also sacrificed his political life over foreign policy issues. In 1955, the Japanese government began to negotiate for the normalization of relations with the Soviet Union. Prime Minister Hatoyama wanted the normalization to include the return of Japanese prisoners-of-war and Soviet approval for Japan's participation in the United Nations. The most controversial issue between the two countries, however, was the return of the Northern Islands. Hatoyama wanted to avoid this issue, but the Yoshida faction, strongly opposed to Hatoyama's strategy, insisted it be included in the negotiations.

Japan's foreign minister visited the Soviet Union to negotiate over the Northern Territory issue and received a Soviet proposal for the return of two of the four islands. Hatoyama refused to agree to the proposal and visited the Soviet Union by himself despite opposition from within the party. In the Soviet Union, Hatoyama successfully reestablished diplomatic relations with the Soviets by issuing a joint statement. He strategically avoided concluding a peace treaty, knowing that to do so the two countries would be forced to deal with the problematic Northern Territory issue. An anti-Hatoyama group within the LDP opposed Hatoyama's handling of the issue. Hatoyama announced his resignation in order to quiet this opposition. His resignation announcement successfully shifted the attention of the LDP members from Japan-Soviet relations to the selection of the next prime minister. Hatoyama, satisfied with his diplomatic achievement, retired from political life.[32]

Kishi Nobusuke (1957–60) also staked his political life on diplomatic issues. During his trip to the United States in June 1957, Kishi met President Dwight Eisenhower and Secretary of State John F. Dulles on the topic of revising the U.S.–Japan Security Treaty of 1952. This unequal treaty had no expiration date or limitation on Japan's commitment, while permitting the United States to use its bases in Japan without restrictions. Kishi told Dulles that the two countries needed to revise the treaty to pursue an equal partnership. The prime minister and the president agreed, and Dulles was to set up a bilateral committee to seek ways of revising the treaty.[33]

As U.S.–China relations worsened over the Taiwan Straits crisis, American interest grew in revising a treaty that would create closer U.S.–Japan relations. In front of the LDP leaders, Kishi stated his determination: "Whatever may occur, I will put through the revision of the security treaty with my own hands." Kishi knew that LDP leaders were opposed to his policy, but that they would support him if he was willing to sacrifice his post after the passage of the treaty revision.[34] In return for his resignation, Kishi received support from the LDP over the revision and acquired the approval of the LDP Executive Council, the highest decision-making body in the party.[35] Kishi appointed himself chief delegate for the mission, and on January 19, 1960, he signed the new security treaty in the United States. Five months later, despite strong popular opposition and violent demonstrations by students, the new treaty was ratified.[36]

Satô Eisaku's (1964–72) major foreign policy achievement was the reversion of Okinawa from American trusteeship to Japan's administration. In August 1965, Satô became the first prime minister to visit Okinawa; and there he stated, "I recognize that the postwar era for our country would not be over without the return of Okinawa."[37] Two years later, Satô brought the issue to the table in a meeting with U.S. president Lyndon B. Johnson. Satô was deeply involved in writing the joint statement, a job usually handled by career diplomats, and successfully inserted the words "within a few years" concerning the timing of the return of Okinawa. These were translated into *ryôsan nen*, meaning two to three years. By setting a concrete deadline, Satô was pushing to resolve the issue.[38]

Bilateral negotiations, however, stopped because of the 1968 U.S. presidential election, and the Japanese government was told to wait until the next year. As Henry Kissinger recalls, "The issue of Okinawa thus was urgent when Nixon assumed office."[39] In June 1969, formal negotiations were reopened, but another issue had heated up in the bilateral relationship—textiles. According to Kissinger, the textile issue was "unconnected with Okinawa but destined to be intimately linked to it" as the "two to three year" deadline was fast approaching.[40]

In November 1969, Prime Minister Satô arrived in Washington, and on the first day of the talks he successfully received Nixon's agreement to remove nuclear weapons from the Okinawan Islands, which was the most thorny issue over the return of Okinawa. However, the U.S. government insisted on linking Okinawa to the textile issue and requested that the Japanese delegation not announce the Okinawa agreement until the economic issues were discussed.[41] On the second day of talks, Prime Minister Satô agreed to take full responsibility for the textile issue.[42] Resolving the issue was not easy for Satô, however. Two successive MITI ministers who wanted to protect the ministry's interests failed to reach an agreement with the U.S. government. In July 1971, one and one-half years after the promised deadline for the reversion, Prime Minister Satô reshuffled his cabinet and appointed Tanaka Kakuei, renowned for his political skill, as MITI minister. Tanaka reopened negotiations with the U.S. government in September and reached an agreement on October 15, 1971. Throughout the negotiations, Satô fully supported Tanaka, suppressing the opposition of the textile industry and its advocates in the ministry.[43]

During Tanaka Kakuei's tenure as prime minister (1972–74), his political skills and leadership were at the forefront in normalizing relations with China. During the LDP presidential race, he had promised the normalization of the bilateral relations to many pro-Peking LDP members in order to build support for his candidacy. On the first day of his administration, Tanaka told a high official at the Foreign Ministry that the cabinet would work on normalizing relations with China and asked him to begin preparation.[44] Within a week, Tanaka had established the Conference on Normalization of China-Japan Relations within the ruling party to enlarge the existing party research committee. The Conference included 249 LDP Diet members, well over half the total membership of 431. With overwhelming intraparty support, even pro-Taiwan right-wing members could no longer easily oppose the trend.

According to the chief cabinet secretary to Tanaka, the prime minister began negotiations with Chou Enlai by stating bluntly: "If these negotiations do not succeed, I will be forced out of office. I would have to dissolve the lower house and hold a general election in which we would lose. I came [to Peking] strongly determined. I might even be killed [by the extreme rightists if we fail]."[45] Chou cooperatively proceeded with the negotiations, and the two countries signed a joint statement to normalize the bilateral relationship in September 1972.

Tanaka's leadership is evident in another foreign policy issue. In 1973, the Japanese government voted for the United Nations Security Council Resolution 242, which supported the self-determination of the Palestinians. Tanaka's action upset the U.S. government, which had voted against the resolution. Secretary of State Henry Kissinger challenged Japan's position when he met Tanaka. Tanaka agreed to change the decision if the U.S. government agreed to be responsible for supplying oil to Japan. When Kissinger replied that his government could not do that, Tanaka told Kissinger that his decision remained firm to vote in favor of the resolution.[46] Tanaka also pointed out that if the American policy toward the Middle East failed, "all the frustrations of the Arab world might fall on Japan."[47] Thereafter, the U.S. government viewed Tanaka as pro-Arab. Tanaka's stance showed his willingness to sacrifice his reputation in the United States.[48]

More recently, Nakasone Yasuhiro (1982–87) displayed his leadership in foreign affairs in the revision of the three arms export principles. The American government had repeatedly asked Japan to share its military technology. When the United States initiated this request in 1980, a Japanese official responded that he would consider the request. Prime Minister Suzuki Zenkô, however, could not act on this issue because of opposition within the government, an opposition based on the principles governing arms exports, which prohibit the export of arms and military-related technology to countries that could be involved in an international conflict or to communist countries.

Soon after Prime Minister Nakasone assumed office following Suzuki, he instructed Chief Cabinet Secretary Gotôda Masaharu to persuade the opposition to come to terms with the need to share this technology with the United States. Gotôda suggested to the new MITI minister that Japan could export military technology to the United States within the framework of the U.S.–Japan Mutual Defense Agreement. The MITI minister, who was in a position to protect domestic technology, agreed to Gotôda's idea, which would limit the transfer only to the United States. At the cabinet meeting on January 14, 1982, Nakasone ruled to make an exception to the arms export principles and to provide Japan's technology to the United States.[49]

Although their degree of interest and involvement in foreign affairs has varied, all Japan's postwar prime ministers have recognized their responsibilities in this area. When a political decision to set priority on an international goal over domestic interests is required, it is the prime minister who must take the lead. Both the ruling party and the government call for this type of initiative. Gotôda summarizes the prime minister's responsibility: The government "needs to make political decisions within the framework of the Constitution, considering external relations. Otherwise, [Japan] cannot survive in this severe international society. Needless to say, such political decisions are made by the prime minister."[50]

Commander in Chief

Along with his role as chief diplomat, the prime minister is also in charge of military operations. Article 7 of the Self Defense Force (SDF) Law states that he is commander in chief of the Self Defense Force on behalf of the cabinet. The prime minister can legally mobilize defense forces in case of an external attack (Article 76) or when the public peace is disturbed (Article 78).

There are two incidents in which cabinet members' opposition blocked the prime minister from using this authority. One occurred during the turmoil over the U.S.–Japan Security Treaty. Student groups surrounded the prime minister's office in an attempt to stop Eisenhower's visit to Tokyo. Prime Minister Kishi privately asked the director of the Defense Agency, Akagi Munenori, about the mobilization of the Self Defense Force based on Article 78 of the SDF Law. Akagi, however, persuaded Kishi not to mobilize the force.[51]

A quarter of a century later, Chief Cabinet Secretary Gotôda Masaharu blocked Prime Minister Nakasone's plan to mobilize the force for international cooperation. When the United States decided to use the U.S. Navy to guard Kuwaiti oil tankers in 1987, Nakasone wanted to send SDF mine sweepers to the Persian Gulf to cooperate with the U.S. effort. Gotôda was opposed to this idea because it would involve Japan in the ongoing war. Gotôda said without hesitation, "I would oppose any plan of the prime minister if it was going against national interests."[52] He told Nakasone that he would not sign a cabinet decision if it were presented at the cabinet meeting. For Nakasone to proceed with the plan, he would be forced to dismiss Gotôda, a step that he was not prepared to take. Nakasone therefore relinquished the plan.[53]

The prime minister's authority to mobilize the Self Defense Force has rarely been exercised except in occasional disaster rescue cases. Recently under the Obuchi Keizô administration, the Self Defense Force was mobilized when two purported fishing boats with suspicious antennas intruded into Japan's territorial waters off Niigata prefecture in March 1999. After the Maritime Safety Agency determined that the boats had fake names, Prime Minister Obuchi ordered the Maritime SDF ships and aircraft to chase them down as a maritime guard activity for the first time in postwar history. Although the SDF ships fired warning shots, the intruders escaped in the direction of North Korea. This incident helped the May 1999 passage of new U.S.–Japan defense guidelines that would give the government more power to act in regional emergencies.

Aside from this exception, the prime ministers have been cautious about mobilizing the Self Defense Force. Even SDF overseas activities in the early 1990s were ordered under an authority other than the prime minister. The SDF mine-sweeping operations conducted after the 1991 Persian Gulf War came under the authority of the general director of the Defense Agency, who cited Article 99 of the SDF Law, which authorizes him to direct mine-sweeping actions. SDF participation in the first peacekeeping operations in Cambodia in 1992–93 were authorized by specific legislation passed in the Diet, not from a direct order from the prime minister. The 1992 United Nations PKO Cooperation Law, passed under the Miyazawa Kiichi administration, requires this legislative process. The law also requires the government to organize a unit for peacekeeping operations separately from the Self Defense Force, even when they recruit SDF staff for it.

In July 1997, Prime Minister Hashimoto Ryûtarô instructed the general director of the Defense Agency to dispatch SDF transport planes to Thailand for preparation to evacuate Japanese nationals in Cambodia. Asian nations, especially China, paid special attention to this first incident of overseas dispatch of SDF airplanes. The Socialist Democratic Party, which was a part of the coalition government with the LDP, opposed the prime minister's action. The Hashimoto government explained that the dispatch was conducted under the Defense Agency director general's authority of SDF use for evacuation of overseas Japanese nationals. This authority was based on Article 100, section 8, of the SDF Law, which was added in the November 1994 revision. The explanation and validation was necessary because the Japanese are very sensitive to allowing the legal authority of the national leader to be used even when necessary.

Although the prime minister may not exercise his authority, being commander in chief is a big responsibility. This became a crucial issue when the coalition of the LDP, the Socialist Party, and *Sakigake* elected Murayama Tomiichi (1994–96) as the national leader. This news caught many Japanese as well as Americans by surprise. Many wondered if Japan's new leader would be able to depart from the traditional Socialist stance against the will of many other Socialist members to support the U.S.–Japan alliance and Japan's Self Defense Forces.

Murayama's determination to support the U.S.–Japan security alliance and the Self Defense Force was firm. Within two weeks of the Naples summit, the Socialist prime minister officially declared in the Diet that the Self Defense Forces were constitutional. There was a strong concern that Murayama's policy shift would split the Socialist Party into two fringe parties and jeopardize the coalition government. The real test came in September 1994 when the Socialists held a national convention. Heated debates ensued, but in the end the party approved the policy shift. Murayama described this process to the author as follows:

The prime minister, who is supreme commander of the Self Defense Force, cannot maintain his office and coalition government while denying the Self Defense Force. I decided to accept the legality of the Self Defense Force as prime minister without consulting the Socialist Party. This turned out right. The party chose to approve my policy, recognizing that I was willing to resign if they did not do so.[54]

This "historical policy shift" of the Socialist Party in effect put an end to the 1955 system, the political framework under which the LDP and the Socialists remained ideologically split as the government and the main opposition party.

MAKING A CABINET

Appointing Cabinet Members

As discussed, executive power rests not with the prime minister but with the cabinet, which means that his effectiveness as a leader depends largely on how much control he has over his own cabinet.

The prime minister's strongest source of influence over the cabinet is the authority to appoint cabinet members and to dismiss them, authority given him by Article 68 of the Constitution. Becoming a cabinet member is probably the first important career goal for most junior members of the ruling party. The Cabinet Law limits the number of cabinet members, excluding the prime minister, to 20. The revision of the law in effect in 2001 further limits it to 14 to 17.[55] Although the cabinet was reshuffled almost once a year during the 38-year LDP reign, achieving a cabinet post was still considered a golden opportunity for about 400 Diet members of the ruling party, and this remains true for those in the coalition government. To a certain degree, cabinet members feel stronger loyalty to the prime minister or to his administration than do other ruling party members. Therefore, this authority is an important political resource for the prime minister. Although the Constitution allows him to choose up to one-half of his cabinet members from outside the Diet, it has been rare today to appoint non-legislators to cabinet positions.[56]

For the prime minister, these appointments are useful tools in achieving his policy and political objectives. With these appointments he can reward the factions or coalition parties as well as the individuals who helped make him prime minister or achieve policy goals. The prime minister cannot advance his policy single-handedly. However excellent his policy, he needs political actors to cooperate with him. The prime minister can also form the cabinet with politically powerful members to achieve his policy objectives.[57] The personal appointment of political actors, therefore, is important in the formulation and execution of policy.

Prime Minister Yoshida Shigeru (1946–47, 1948–54) began the tradition of frequently changing cabinet members. During his tenure of over seven years, Yoshida appointed over 80 people to cabinet positions.[58] He used the appointive authority to reward loyal party members and punish disloyal members. Yoshida's manner of frequently reshuffling his cabinet was carried on by his successors, and this has significantly affected the power structure of Japanese politics. As Watanabe Tsuneo, a politically astute journalist, has observed, Yoshida's frequent reshuffling has lowered the prestige of cabinet positions and weakened the ruling party's control over the bureaucracy.[59]

Although many observers of Japanese politics blame Yoshida for this political custom, Kishi Nobusuke may well be more responsible. Kishi reshuffled his cabinet three times, replacing almost all the cabinet members. Cabinet reshuffling before Kishi was small scale, replacing several members at a time. Kishi observed that Yoshida's manner of removing individual cabinet members created antipathy against the prime minister. After the Yoshida era, the power of the ministers over their ministries further weakened. By reshuffling an entire cabinet, Kishi avoided situations in which cabinet members might lose face. This reshuffling became a tradition under the LDP governments.

After Kishi, cabinet reshuffling became almost an annual event. The political career ladder within the LDP became more institutionalized in the 1970s.[60] Regardless of their ability, almost all the LDP lower house members were entitled to be appointed to the cabinet after their sixth term. It is interesting to note that Yoshida started the mass appointments in order to better control the bureaucracy through ministers loyal to the prime minister. However, in the long term, this tradition has weakened the control of the prime minister over the bureaucracy.

The frequent reshuffling of the cabinet has allowed the prime ministers to change the political environment, often to the benefit of the policy process. The prime minister, however, does not necessarily have a free hand in forming his own cabinet. A prime minister without a strong power base within the ruling party or coalition is unable to appoint freely, but he can build up his power base. Some prime ministers have lost their political influence, thus losing control over the formation of their cabinets. Observing the dynamics of the prime minister making his cabinet lends insight into how his political influence works for him.

Since the inception of the LDP in 1955, its presidents except Kôno Yôhei automatically became the prime minister. The actual selection process was one of the determining factors in the amount of power available to the winner. Prime Minister Fukuda Takeo (1976–78), for example, was selected to the LDP presidency without an election and in the wake of strong campaigning against the incumbent prime minister Miki Takeo. Upon taking office, Fukuda then had to reward the factions that helped him bring down Miki, and he appointed members of the Tanaka faction to several posts in his cabinet. As a result, the Fukuda administration was criticized by the media for being strongly controlled by the Tanaka faction.[61] In his second cabinet, however, Fukuda successfully appointed Tanaka faction members to less powerful cabinet positions.

A similar power shift was seen in the cabinet formation under Prime Minister Miyazawa Kiichi (1991–93). Miyazawa ran for the LDP presidency in October 1991. To gain support from the largest faction led by former prime minister Takeshita Noboru, Miyazawa had to accept that faction's dictates in the selection of his cabinet. One year later, however, largely because of the breakup of the Takeshita faction, he could enjoy a free hand in forming his second cabinet.

Becoming prime minister thus often puts a candidate in political debt to other groups in the ruling party. One way to pay this debt is to share power with those supporters by allocating cabinet positions. This implies, however, that the prime minister's ability to influence and control his first cabinet is limited because that cabinet is made up of individuals loyal to different political leaders. Successful prime ministers increase their control by reshuffling their cabinet as they gain power.

As discussed, although the authority to appoint cabinet members belongs solely to the prime minister under the Constitution, many constraints exist. Following Prime Minister Yoshida Shigeru's era of considerable freedom in making a cabinet, factionalism became stronger. The prime minister now has a less free hand and must appoint cabinet members carefully, considering factional balance and requests from other groups within the ruling party or parties. Obuchi Keizô (1998–2000), for example, was very proud of establishing freedom to appoint four cabinet members in his first cabinet, independent from factional pressures.

Even strong prime ministers cannot totally ignore the cabinet recommendations of other factions. Especially under the coalition governments, prime ministers had to respect the requests of other parties to maintain a fragile alliance. The list of cabinet members shows how much the prime minister owes to other factions or parties. The makeup of a given cabinet, therefore, illustrates how much political power the prime minister has and which faction holds influence over the current administration.

Dismissal of Cabinet Members

Because most cabinet members hold Diet seats and remain leading ruling party members, the political implication of dismissing a member from the cabinet is strong. As Gotôda Masaharu writes, this authority "would also hurt the prime minister" who implements it.[62] Usually the prime minister prefers to accept a "voluntary" resignation rather than dismissing a cabinet member. In September 1997, for example, when Prime Minister Hashimoto Ryûtarô took a bold political gamble by naming Satô Kôkô to the cabinet, the public resented the appointment because of Satô's criminal record in a highly publicized case, the Lockheed scandal, which involved the selection of airplanes for a major Japanese airline. As a result, Satô became the seventy-third cabinet member who voluntarily resigned under the current Constitution.

There have been only three occasions in which a prime minister has exercised the authority of dismissing a cabinet member. This was first exercised in November 1947 by Prime Minister Katayama Tetsu when his agriculture minister, who was trying to organize a new political party, refused to submit his resignation. The second case took place under the Yoshida administration in 1953. His agriculture minister had joined an anti-Yoshida movement and contributed to the passage of a resolution requiring punishment be brought against Yoshida. Outraged, Prime Minister Yoshida Shigeru fired the minister.

A more recent case involves the dismissal of Education Minister Fujio Masayuki by Prime Minister Nakasone. In an interview with the conservative magazine *Bungei Shunjû* (October 1985), Fujio stated that Korea was also responsible for Japan's annexation of Korea in the prewar period because it had been mutually agreed. This was a politically insensitive comment during a delicate time in Japan-Korea relations. Furthermore, this statement was intended to cause trouble for the Nakasone administration. Because Fujio's prior post was LDP's Policy Research Council chairman, his appointment as education minister was widely regarded as a demotion and embarrassed Fujio. Fujio, a strong conservative, was also frustrated by Nakasone's handling of the textbook issue and the Yasukuni Shrine issue, and his statement was made in retaliation.[63] Despite repeated persuasion by several LDP leaders, Fujio refused to resign voluntarily. Nakasone, after meeting with LDP leaders and cabinet members—including Fujio himself—dismissed the education minister.

Fujio's case caused a political stir, but not a turmoil. LDP leaders agreed that Fujio had gone too far and that the dismissal was appropriate. Without such a consensus, the dismissal could have created resentment among LDP leaders toward the prime minister. It is because of this reason that prime ministers hesitate to use their authority of dismissal. That there have been only three incidents in postwar history demonstrates this hesitation. In day-to-day politics, the prime minister has even stricter limitations in exercising his authority to dismiss, as compared to his authority to appoint.

Resignation as Protest

Although the constitutional authority to appoint and dismiss cabinet members is one way for the prime minister to control ruling party members, cabinet members can protest policies of the prime minister by resigning from their cabinet post. The first examples under the LDP administration were the resignations of Ikeda Hayato, Miki Takeo, and Nadao Hirokichi to protest Prime Minister Kishi Nobusuke's actions in December 1958. For Miki, who led the smallest faction in the LDP and thus controlled limited political resources, this stance was an effective way to affect the political situation.

Miki resigned from his cabinet position on two other occasions. In an attempt to emphasize his anti-Satô stance, Miki resigned as foreign minister to run for the LDP presidency against Prime Minister Satô Eisaku in October 1968. Satô was apparently happy to accept Miki's resignation, as Miki had disrupted his efforts to return Okinawa to Japanese administration. Miki again resigned from a cabinet post after the upper house election in July 1974 to protest Prime Minister Tanaka Kakuei's way of running an election campaign widely criticized as "money politics." Fukuda Takeo followed Miki's lead and resigned as finance minister to show his anti-Tanaka standpoint. As Fukuda Takeo observed, these resignations substantially damaged the Tanaka administration.[64]

In summer 1993, three members of the Miyazawa Kiichi cabinet resigned from their posts. Two belonged to the Hata Tsutomu faction that broke off from the LDP in protest against Prime Minister Miyazawa's mishandling of political reform. With the breakoff of this group, the LDP could no longer maintain the majority in the lower house. Upon passage of the no-confidence resolution against the Miyazawa cabinet, the prime minister called a general election. As a result of the July 18 election, the non-LDP political parties formed a coalition that together held 260 seats, more than the majority of the 511 lower house seats. Despite the defeat in the election, Miyazawa did not immediately announce his resignation as LDP president. The minister of posts and telecommunications resigned to add pressure on the prime minister to assume responsibility for the election loss. On July 22, Miyazawa resigned as LDP president.

Maintaining Harmony

Because the cabinet is a group of politicians, each representing a faction of the ruling party, disharmony between factions results in disharmony in the cabinet. Similarly, disagreement among the cabinet members can cause disharmony within the party. The prime minister must maintain harmony both in the cabinet and the party in order to maximize his effectiveness in formulating and executing policy. Careless appointments instantly create resentment.

Some might argue that the prime minister has direct control over the cabinet and thus over administrative operations by choosing cabinet members who agree with him and dismissing those who do not. If he desires, he can legally appoint himself to hold all the ministerial positions.[65] Therefore, he can exercise enormous control over the cabinet and its executive power. This argument is theoretically valid, but it is based on an unrealistic assumption that the prime minister can freely exercise the appointment and dismissal authority without endangering majority support in the Diet, and thus his premiership. In reality, the prime minister does not exercise his only constitutional authority independent from the cabinet and thus free from intraparty political consideration. The prime minister's dismissal of a minister can detrimentally affect party unity. Other ruling party leaders can intentionally heighten the disharmony by resigning, thus weakening the leadership of the prime minister. The prime minister's appointment and dismissal authorities are powerful tools, but they work both ways: They can help him at the same that they can harm him.

DISSOLVING THE DIET

The dissolution of the lower house is the most dramatic action the prime minister can take toward the Diet. The action ends the terms of all the lower house members, both government party members and opposition party members. Once a prime minister announces the lower house's dissolution, a formal request is taken to the Emperor. The Emperor then issues a rescript to the speaker of the lower house, who presents the mandate to the lower house members. When the speaker recites the Imperial rescript to the floor, the lower house fills with excitement and anxiety. Many members shout *Banzai* (a group cheer in celebration). With the reading of the Imperial rescript, all the lower house members are out of public office until reelected.

Dissolution often reshapes Japan's political scene. It can change the balance between the ruling party and the opposition parties. It can change the balance among the factions of the ruling party or coalition. This is a powerful political tool given to the prime minister by the "checks-and-balance" system between the executive and the legislative branches in the democratic Constitution. Whereas a victory in an election strengthens the power of the prime minister, a defeat weakens it and often forces his resignation. Dissolution, therefore, is a critical political decision for the prime minister.

The authority to dissolve the lower house is often referred as an "heirloom sword" or the "trump card" of the prime minister. Today, it is generally held that this authority belongs to the prime minister, the leader of the cabinet, although the authority is not explicitly defined in the Constitution. Article 69 simply states, "If the House of Representatives passes a no-confidence resolution, or rejects a confidence resolution, the cabinet shall resign *en masse*, unless the House of Representatives is dissolved within ten days."

Whether the cabinet can dissolve the lower house without passage of a no-confidence resolution or rejection of a confidence resolution was in question until the mid-1950s. On June 19, 1952, the Diet Joint Legal Committee announced a report that the authority to dissolve the lower house must not be limited to Article 69: Because Article 7 recognizes the cabinet's authority to advise the Emperor to perform matters of state, including dissolution of the lower house, the dissolution based on that article should be legally recognized. Two years later, this interpretation of the Constitution was supported by the Tokyo High Court.[66] The authority to initiate the dissolution of the lower house is now shared by the executive branch. When the cabinet no longer represents the majority of the lower house as a result of political reorganization among the party, or when important new political issues divide the opinions of the house, the cabinet can dissolve the lower house. The cabinet is now equipped with a tool to examine whether or not the representation of the house reflects the latest voices of Japanese voters.

The authority to dissolve the lower house has often been used to benefit the ruling party or the prime minister. At times, the LDP administration has dissolved the lower house to pursue more stable support in the lower house. Some prime ministers have taken this action to strengthen their power bases within the party. Usually, the prime minister's faction has a good chance of increasing its membership in the aftermath of a lower house dissolution and subsequent elections. For example, Nakasone Yasuhiro (1982–87) increased the number of lower house members of his faction from 48 to 64 during his five-year reign. After the 1986 election, his faction grew from the fourth largest to a close second to the Takeshita faction with 70 lower house members. Each prime minister, therefore, would like to have the opportunity to dissolve the lower house at least once during his tenure. Doing so can strengthen his party or faction and provide popular support for his policies.

Including the 2000 general election, the lower house had been dissolved 18 times during 52 years under the current Constitution.[67] The Constitution defines the term of the lower house as four years. However, dissolution takes place so often that the completion of a lower house term is rarely achieved. The only occasion in which the lower house completed its term under the current Constitution was under the weak leadership of Miki Takeo, whose authority was so limited by intraparty politics that he could not dissolve the lower house. Dissolution before a term is completed is thus usually no surprise. In 15 out of the 18 dissolutions, both the ruling party and the opposition parties officially or informally agreed to the dissolution. After the first half of the four-year term passes, both the government and the opposition parties usually start planning for an upcoming election and become active in unofficial campaigning in their home districts. Once the unofficial campaign starts, many candidates hope for an early election date because they have limited campaign funds.

The timing of dissolution is generally planned to benefit the ruling party. To ensure the maximum benefit of the dissolution, a prime minister sometimes leaks misleading information about when an election will be called. This act is generally regarded as politically acceptable and often weakens any opposition. Under the LDP administration, much energy was devoted to planning the timing of an election to maximize the number of voters coming to the polls because high turnout rates generally benefit the ruling party. In many cases, the voting day was set on Sundays or national holidays when more citizens were free to vote. But harvest season, a busy time for pro-LDP farmers, was usually avoided under the LDP-led government, which received majority support from that sector.

Yoshida and Dissolution

Yoshida Shigeru was the first prime minister to utilize the cabinet's authority to initiate dissolution. He dissolved the lower house three times, while failing to do so once. With each dissolution or dissolution attempt, a new precedent was set. The first dissolution under the current Constitution occurred under the strong influence of the American Occupation authorities in December 1948. Despite the strong request from Prime Minister Yoshida, the Government Section of General Headquarters did not allow Yoshida to dissolve the lower house based on Article 7 and instructed the opposition parties to submit a no-confidence resolution on which Yoshida could take action based on Article 69.[68]

With the second dissolution, Yoshida caught many Diet members by surprise: The lower house was dissolved for the first time based on Article 7 before any consensus had been reached. In the third case, Yoshida was forced to dissolve the lower house because of a slip of the tongue. In yet a fourth case, his political power was too weak to exercise this authority. These cases warrant special attention.

The second time Yoshida dissolved the lower house was in August 1952, just one month after the Joint Legal Committee recognized the cabinet's authority to initiate dissolution. By taking this step, Yoshida attempted to overcome the gridlock that characterized the political situation at that time. Anti-Yoshida members in his party had created a policy platform to criticize his economic policy. The dissolution was Yoshida's counterattack of the anti-Yoshida faction within the same party, rather than an attack on opposition parties.[69] Yoshida quietly raised the campaign funds for pro-Yoshida members of the Liberal Party while keeping anti-Yoshida members uninformed in order to catch them off guard. Although a dissolution required the consent of the entire cabinet, Yoshida proceeded with the go-ahead given by only several members of the cabinet, all of whom were closely associated with him.[70] Yoshida's Liberal Party, however, lost over 40 seats in the subsequent election, and the anti-Yoshida movement grew as a result; in other words, his plan backfired.

Yoshida's third case is often referred to as the *Bakayarô* (You idiot) dissolution. At the Budget Committee meeting on February 28, 1953, the prime minister, who was upset by the persistent, offensive questions of a socialist party member, grumbled *Bakayarô*. Although Yoshida immediately apologized for his impolite words, the opposition party submitted a resolution to reprimand the prime minister. The anti-Yoshida faction within Yoshida's own party assisted the passage of the resolution by not attending the voting in the lower house, expecting the passage to force the Yoshida cabinet to resign. Instead, Yoshida dissolved the lower house. In the resulting general election, Yoshida's Liberal Party lost its majority, further weakening Yoshida's control over the Diet.[71]

On November 24, 1954, anti-Yoshida politicians formed a new conservative political party, the Japan Democratic Party. The new party submitted a no-confidence resolution against Yoshida jointly with other opposition parties, and its passage was inevitable. The leaders of the Liberal Party discussed this issue. Whereas Yoshida wanted to dissolve the Diet rather than ask for the resignation of the cabinet, the newly appointed Liberal Party president, Deputy Prime Minister Ogata Taketora, strongly opposed dissolving the lower house. Unable to dismiss Ogata, his own choice to succeed the party presidency, Yoshida had to give up the dissolution attempt.[72]

As a result, Yoshida resigned. But he created the three precedents regarding dissolving the lower house: He tried to use the dissolution to his own benefit; he was forced to dissolve; and he was unable to dissolve. Ironically, Yoshida Shigeru, the prime minister who lobbied hard and won the authority to initiate dissolution, did not enjoy the subsequent election results.

Dissolution after Yoshida

Benefiting from Dissolution

Although Yoshida never benefited from the dissolution process, other prime ministers did enjoy the results of executing the dissolution authority. In 1958, Prime Minister Kishi Nobusuke obtained an agreement from the Japan Socialist Party on an election date before dissolving the lower house. In the three previous elections, the JSP had gained parliamentary seats. When the LDP maintained 287 seats in the subsequent election, losing only 3 seats from the previous lower house, Kishi claimed victory for stopping the expansion of JSP seats.[73]

Ikeda Hayato is another prime minister who was victorious in his use of dissolution. Ikeda dissolved the lower house one month after he announced his economic policy, making it an election issue. Ikeda's policy, with priority placed on the economy, was a departure from postwar politics that had focused on ideological issues. As a result, the LDP won 296 seats. Ikeda increased his power within the party and gained political legitimacy to pursue his policy.

Ikeda's successor, Satô Eisaku, also enjoyed the results of dissolution. In November 1969, he planned for dissolution after successfully finalizing negotiations with the United States on the reversion of Okinawa to Japanese administration. In the following election, the success of the negotiations increased LDP seats from 277 to 288, while decreasing the Socialist seats from 144 to 90.[74] This victory helped Satô to become the LDP president for another term.

Prime Minister Nakasone Yasuhiro successfully used dissolution with a new technique. The technique was to call for a lower house election on the same day as the mandatory date for the upper house election, thus encouraging a high voter turnout. This technique, later called "double election," was first intentionally and successfully used by Prime Minister Nakasone in 1986. As expected, the LDP won over 300 seats in the lower house election.[75] The LDP rewarded Nakasone with an exceptional one-year extension of his LDP presidency because of this victory.[76] Clearly, Nakasone benefited from dissolution.

More recently, Prime Minister Hashimoto Ryûtarô gained momentum by winning an election. In summer 1996, entering the last year of the lower house's four-year term, election pressure grew among Diet members. Hashimoto sought the best timing for an election. Observing the rising popularity of his cabinet in September 1996, he dissolved the lower house to call the first election under the new electoral law, which introduced single-seat districts. In the October 20 general election, the LDP gained 239 seats, up from 211, in the 500-seat lower house. The result was generally seen as a victory. One month after the election, Hashimoto inaugurated the Administrative Reform Council to officially start his efforts to streamline the national government.

Losing from Dissolution

Although a prime minister intends to increase his influence by dissolving the lower house, the results are not always in his favor. When Tanaka Kakuei became prime minister, the term of the lower house had already spanned two years and seven months, long enough to naturally consider dissolution. Many members, both in the opposition parties and in the LDP, expected a general election. Tanaka, returning from his successful trip to Peking to normalize relations with China, did not foresee that the LDP would lose in the election. An election victory would be public support for his major economic policy of restructuring the Japanese archipelago. In November 1972, Tanaka dissolved the lower house, but he lost 13 seats in the election that followed. Confident of victory, Tanaka had issued party endorsements to too many candidates. In many districts, the LDP candidates split the pro-LDP votes and lost. With the loss, Tanaka's economic policy became difficult to carry out.

Issues surrounding Tanaka later forced Prime Minister Nakasone to dissolve the lower house in November 1983, again bringing unfavorable results to the LDP. The issue was the Lockheed scandal. Tanaka was found guilty of receiving money from Lockheed Corporation in return for instructing his transportation minister to direct one of Japan's major airlines to purchase Lockheed planes. This verdict triggered massive media coverage. Justice Minister Hatano Akira said in a magazine interview that the media coverage on the Tanaka trial over the Lockheed scandal violated Tanaka's human rights. He further stated that people should not look for virtue in politicians. The opposition parties criticized the justice minister for his irresponsible statements and demanded that Nakasone dissolve the Diet and call an election. The speakers of both the upper and lower houses joined in this demand. Nakasone said he would comply.

The opposition parties, however, also demanded the consideration of a resolution that would urge Tanaka to resign from his lower house seat. Nakasone refused this demand. If the opposition parties continued to push the issue, he said, he would not dissolve the Diet. The opposition parties gave up. Recognizing that the opposition parties wanted the dissolution badly, Nakasone demanded that they cooperate to pass six bills concerning administrative reform. Although the LDP lost in the election in December 1983, Nakasone had acquired legal authorization to pursue administrative reforms, a pursuit on which he placed the highest priority.[77]

A prime minister may end up with less power as a result of his execution of the dissolution authority. Given a negative result, some prime ministers lose momentum in pursuing their political agenda. As seen in the Nakasone case, however, the prime minister can use the cabinet authority to dissolve the Diet to negotiate with the opposition parties. When the loss of the ruling party is expected, the opposition parties demand that the cabinet call for an election. By sacrificing parliamentary seats, the prime minister may obtain cooperation from the opposition parties.

Forced to Dissolve

The prime minister does not always have the freedom to choose when to dissolve. Pressures created by political scandals and intraparty fights often force the cabinet to dissolve the lower house. Tanaka's Lockheed case, described above, was not the only scandal to trigger dissolution. When the so-called Black Mist scandals—a series of political corruption cases that began in August 1966 with the arrest of an LDP Diet member for blackmailing—came out, the opposition parties blamed the Satô Eisaku cabinet. As the political scandals were revealed one by one, public support for the opposition parties grew. In December 1966, the opposition parties boycotted all the Diet meetings, demanding dissolution. Prime Minister Satô had no choice but to dissolve the lower house.

Intraparty factional fights also force the prime minister to call an election. On one occasion, a group of LDP members joined the opposition parties to overturn an LDP prime minister. When the LDP lost in the October 1979 general election, a number of LDP members demanded Ôhira Masayoshi's resignation just as Prime Minister Miki Takeo resigned to take political responsibility for the LDP loss in the previous election. However, Ôhira refused this demand. The outraged anti-Ôhira factions decided to put forth their own candidate, Fukuda Takeo, in a Diet vote for the premiership against their own party president. This was the first time in Japan's postwar history that the ruling party had more than one candidate for the premiership in the Diet. Although Prime Minister Ôhira managed to win, the split in the party was apparent. Taking advantage of the turmoil within the ruling party, the opposition parties submitted a no-confidence resolution against Ôhira in May 1980. Because the anti-Ôhira LDP factions did not attend the floor voting, the resolution passed the lower house. Ôhira had to call another election in order to keep his cabinet alive.[78]

Policy splits within the ruling party can trigger dissolution. Prime Minister Miyazawa Kiichi publicly promised that he would enact bills leading to political reform in summer 1993, but he was not able to deliver his promise. When the opposition parties submitted a no-confidence resolution in the lower house against the prime minister, they did not have the votes necessary to gain acceptance for the motion. An LDP faction that strongly supported political reform joined them, however, giving them a majority in the house and enabling the no-confidence motion to pass. This forced Miyazawa to call for a general election, eventually leading to the end of the 38-year governance of the Liberal Democratic Party.

While the authority to initiate dissolution is also given to the legislative branch, the opposition parties do not always have the authority because of their minority position in the Diet. When there is enough political pressure stemming from the political scandals of the ruling party, however, the opposition parties can stop the Diet's proceedings without losing public support. This may lead to dissolution of the lower house. Severe intraparty fighting within the ruling party is another leading factor that forces the prime minister to call an election. Factions of the ruling party can act against the prime minister or his policy by joining the opposition parties to pass a no-confidence resolution. The prime minister, who is forced to call an election, soon witnesses the voters' judgment over his administration.

Unable to Dissolve

Some prime ministers have been blocked from dissolving the lower house because of lack of support within the ruling party. In February 1960, Prime Minister Kishi Nobusuke, for example, wanted to dissolve the lower house to seek political legitimacy to pursue the revision of the U.S.–Japan Security Treaty. If voters approved his initiatives, a positive outcome would reveal their support. However, the LDP secretary general who was responsible for party affairs strongly opposed the dissolution because of lack of election funds and the objection by an LDP faction. Forcing LDP members to run an election campaign could create further disharmony within the party and make the security revision more difficult. Kishi had to choose not to dissolve the lower house to maintain political legitimacy for his policy issue rather than to seek support from voters.[79]

Without the intraparty support, publicly popular prime ministers can be blocked from calling an election. In September 1976, Prime Minister Miki Takeo tried to call for an extraordinary session to dissolve the Diet. The Lockheed scandal had been revealed. Miki, who was selected to succeed Tanaka partly because of his clean image, wanted to delve vigorously into the scandal, and he wanted public support for his actions. A victory for the Miki faction and the defeat of the Tanaka faction in a general election would allow him to follow through with this pursuit of the scandal. To dissolve the lower house, however, he needed his cabinet's consent to open an extraordinary Diet session. LDP politicians outside the Miki faction saw his action as self-promoting, and they created an anti-Miki coalition within the ruling party. Fifteen out of the 20 cabinet members who belonged to the coalition strongly opposed the opening of a session to dissolve the lower house. Miki, who was seeking reelection as LDP president, could not order massive dismissal of the opposing cabinet members, and he had to give up on the dissolution.[80]

Miki's successor, Fukuda Takeo, also met strong opposition within the ruling party to his dissolution attempt. Prime Minister Fukuda, facing continual intraparty fighting in attempts to replace him; wanted to increase his power within the party by dissolving the lower house. He could thereby potentially increase the size of his faction, making it difficult to replace him as a leader. Ôhira Masayoshi, who sought to replace Fukuda, began collecting signatures of LDP lower house members opposed to the dissolution. It was not too difficult for Ôhira, who had built the majority intraparty coalition, to collect signatures from 160 LDP lower house members, more than half of the 254 members. This display of disapproval effectively blocked Prime Minister Fukuda from calling an election. Prime ministers who seek only self-promotion have difficulty receiving intraparty support for dissolution.

In fall 1991, Prime Minister Kaifu Toshiki was also unable to dissolve the Diet. After the political reforms bills, the top priority of the Kaifu administration, died, Kaifu wanted to dissolve the lower house. Three LDP factions, seeking to replace Kaifu with their own faction leader, publicly opposed the dissolution, thinking it might help Kaifu's reelection as a party leader. They formed an anti-Kaifu coalition. With the establishment of the coalition, the largest LDP faction led by Takeshita Noboru, which Kaifu had relied on for support, could no longer form a majority within the ruling party, and the faction withdrew its support for Prime Minister Kaifu. Powerless, Kaifu had to abandon dissolution. This incident underscored Kaifu's weakness and accelerated the anti-Kaifu campaign, which led to his resignation.[81]

Dissolving the lower house obviously has a major impact on the political scene. It is a matter of survival for each member of the house. The prime minister, therefore, in order to exercise his dissolution authority needs a general consensus within the ruling party. Without this support, the prime minister is often unable to take this drastic action.

The dissolution authority given to the prime minister is a powerful tool vis-à-vis the legislative branch. Subsequent election results significantly affect the effectiveness of his leadership. When the prime minister is confident of gaining popular support for his policy issue, the authority to dissolve the lower house leads to tremendous leverage in pursuing policies. Because it is such a powerful tool, the prime minister cannot exercise this authority easily. First, he must persuade his own cabinet members. Then, he must convince all LDP factions, including his own. Last, he must have a legitimate reason for the dissolution so that the voters will give him an LDP victory in the subsequent election and thus boost his power.

CABINET SECRETARIAT

The prime minister's time and energy are limited. He must depend on the assistance provided by the Cabinet Secretariat. Article 12 of the Cabinet Law defines the tasks of the Secretariat: "The Cabinet Secretariat is in charge of administrative tasks of the cabinet for overall coordination on important issues relating to cabinet meetings, for other necessary overall coordination to maintain the consistency of the cabinet, and for information gathering over important issues of the cabinet." Although the Secretariat is below the cabinet in the government organizational chart, its actual job is to assist the statutory head, the prime minister, and not necessarily the cabinet as a whole. The effectiveness of the prime minister is affected by the level of competence of the Secretariat.

Although this office, equivalent to the American White House, is important for the missions of the prime minister, its authority is quite limited. In the administrative reform efforts under Prime Minister Hashimoto Ryûtarô, proposals were made to reinforce the power of the Cabinet Secretariat as well as to create a new powerful support organ, the Cabinet Office. The new office, to be created in 2001, would be a part of the cabinet and thus would be located above other ministries and agencies in order to coordinate conflicting interests among different parts of the government.

Chief Cabinet Secretary and His Deputies

The Secretariat's head, the chief cabinet secretary, has the status of a cabinet member.[82] Former chief cabinet secretary Gotôda Masaharu summarizes his job as "to mediate and settle disputes" among various government agencies in the policy-making process.[83] Policy coordination requires political skill, experience, and connections as well as knowledge of the content and implications of specific policies. He must work with other members of the ruling party and the bureaucracy in policy coordination. As Gotôda states, the task depends "on the power balance between the chief cabinet secretary and the relevant ministers of State. Thus it involves competition over their individual political power and character."[84]

Because the prime minister's time and energy are limited, many issues are handled without his involvement, even those that are supposed to require his attention. Ministries often deal with issues within their realm. Gotôda points out: "Although the [officials from] ministries are supposed to bring up important issues relating to other administrative agencies in the cabinet meeting, they may not do so due to jurisdictional conflicts. There are also occasions in which by the time the issue reaches [the cabinet level] there is already no room for discussion when issues are brought up."[85] Finding and presenting such issues to the prime minister is one of the major tasks of the chief cabinet secretary and his support staff.

As discussed in Chapter 1, each special interest area has politicians who specialize in that issue and who are organized into a *zoku* or policy tribe. Under the LDP administrations, the relative power of individual LDP *zoku* members increased. The different *zokus* accelerated sectionalism within the government. Ministries and their patron LDP members tried to maximize their benefit by handling issues without the prime minister's involvement and often even without his knowledge. As a former senior cabinet assistant points out, "The prime minister's involvement and leadership are required to destroy the sectionalism of the ministries."[86] The prime minister counts on his assistants at the Cabinet Secretariat to keep him abreast of sectionalist activities so that he could stop before they picked up steam.

As well as being a policy coordinator, the chief cabinet secretary acts as spokesperson for the prime minister and his cabinet. In a sense, his job is equivalent to that of the U.S. chief of staff and the spokesperson for the White House combined. The chief cabinet secretary, therefore, is involved in the decision-making process for most of the important policy decisions of the prime minister. Even when he is not directly involved, decisions must be reported to him.

To assist in this overwhelming task, the chief cabinet secretary had two deputies, one parliamentary and one administrative. In 1998, the number of parliamentary deputies was increased to two: one from the lower house and the other from the upper house. The parliamentary deputies, usually chosen from the prime minister's faction or party, assists him primarily in matters concerning relations with the ruling party. Although this is a subcabinet position, the post of deputy chief cabinet secretary is often more important in terms of policy making than that of some cabinet positions. This is why senior LDP members with prior cabinet experience were sometimes appointed to the post.[87]

The administrative deputy chief cabinet secretary is also a powerful post because this position acts as the liaison between the prime minister and the bureaucracy. According to an *Asahi Shimbun* survey, Deputy Chief Cabinet Secretary Furukawa Teijirô was the most frequent visitor to Prime Minister Hashimoto's office during year 1997.[88] The post is often called the top position of the entire bureaucracy because it includes the chairmanship of the subcabinet committee attended by the top bureaucrats of all the administrative agencies.

Tanaka Kakuei, for example, appointed a former director of the National Police Agency, Gotôda Masaharu, to this position. Gotôda's skill in handling the bureaucracy was so impressive that Tanaka recruited him as a candidate for the upper house from his faction. Another example of a powerful administrative deputy is Ishihara Nobuo, who served for seven consecutive administrations: the LDP-led administrations of Takeshita Noboru, Uno Sôsuke, Kaifu Toshiki, Miyazawa Kiichi, and the coalition governments led by Hosokawa Morihiro, Hata Tsutomu, and Murayama Tomiichi. This long appointment is quite unusual because prime ministers traditionally make a new appointment to this post when they take office. Ishihara played an important role particularly in the administration of Kaifu Toshiki, who was unprepared to become the nation's leader. The media jokingly reported that the government was run by "Prime Minister Ishihara with assistance from Kaifu Toshiki."

Appointees for this position are usually chosen from officials of the prewar Ministry of Home Affairs (*Naimu-shô*), which was divided after the war into several ministries, including the Ministries of Home Affairs; Health and Welfare; and Labor and the National Police Agency. Senior officials of these agencies are generally considered less partial to ministerial interests and more concerned about the interest of the nation as a whole. According to Gotôda Masaharu, who has also served in this capacity: "[The administrative deputy chief cabinet secretary needs] to conduct operations on the budget, personnel placement and planning impartially, without any personal interest involved. Therefore officials of the Finance Ministry, which has the budget bureau, or officials at the Ministries of International Trade and Industry, Transportation and Foreign Affairs are inappropriate."[89]

Six Cabinet Offices

These three posts, the chief cabinet secretary and his deputies, are the main actors who coordinate the actions of the ruling party or coalition and various ministries with different interests. To assist them are six offices within the Secretariat. The Cabinet Counselor's Office handles the staff work for the cabinet meetings and prepares speech drafts for the prime minister, including his policy speeches given at the opening session of the Diet. The office also acts as a liaison between the cabinet and the Imperial Household when the Cabinet advises the Emperor in matters of state based on Article 7 of the Constitution. Matters of state include the promulgation of laws and orders, the convocation of the Diet, the dissolution of the lower house, and the appointment of cabinet members.

The other five offices are more policy-oriented and work closely with the policy formation and execution by the prime minister. The current structure of the five policy offices is based on the 1986 reorganization of the Cabinet Secretariat.[90]

The Cabinet Councilor's Office on Internal Affairs (*Naikaku Naisei Shingi Shitsu*) is headed by a senior official from the Finance Ministry. This office is responsible for overall coordination for domestic policies, especially economic policies. It assists several Cabinet-level committees, such as the Committee on Economic Affairs. About 10 Cabinet councilors representing various ministries work under the chief of the office along with 40 other councilors who have their main assignment elsewhere in the bureaucracy. This office helps carry out tasks such as environmental issues, the promotion of tourism, countermeasures to drug abuse, and the improvement of facilities for the disabled. It also has administered many private advisory councils for the prime minister, actions requiring interagency coordination.

The Cabinet Councilor's Office on External Affairs (*Naikaku Gaisei Shingi Shitsu*), with a dozen of cabinet councilors, is responsible for handling foreign affairs. Although this office is headed by a career diplomat, the coordination is not limited to operations with the Foreign Ministry. Due to increased international interdependence, for example, coordination with other ministries is essential to deal with global economic problems. This office also copes with key tasks which the prime minister initiates. After the statement by Prime Minister Murayama Tomiichi in August 1995, commemorating the 50th anniversary of WWII, it fostered the "Peace, Friendship and Exchange Initiative" toward Asian nations, and supported the citizens' participation in the activities of the Asian Women's Fund, which was established to cope with the problem of the wartime comfort women. After the 1995 rape of a 12-year-old Okinawan girl by three American marines, this office played a central role to deal with the problem of the U.S. bases in Okinawa to improve the situation.[91]

The Cabinet Public Relations Office (*Naikaku Kôhôkan Shitsu*) was strengthened in its functions by the 1986 reorganization. This office was originally created under the Prime Minister's Office by the Ikeda Hayato administration. After the turmoil over the 1960 revision of the U.S.–Japan Security Treaty, the government realized the need for public relations activities, and in 1973 all public relations activities of the various national government agencies were united in this office. In 1986, the office also began to serve the Cabinet Secretariat by working more closely with the prime minister, and this became the main task of the chief officer, making his task of heading public relations activities for all government agencies secondary. This change was organizationally subtle, but it created a significant difference in the function of the post and actually made it more important. According to a former chief officer, his main task was to provide the prime minister with the raw information the bureaucracy filter system shielded him from and then to make impartial recommendations independent of the interests of the ministry.[92] The chief officer has been invaluable to several prime ministers as one of their true windows to the realities of Japanese society.

Newly created by the 1986 reorganization was the Cabinet Security Affairs Office. It has two basic functions: to handle coordination and administrative tasks related to national defense and to serve as supporting organ to the Security Council of Japan. The Council is composed of the prime minister (chairman) and five Cabinet ministers (the finance minister, the foreign minister, the chief cabinet secretary, the chairman of the National Public Safety Commission, and the director general of the Economic Planning Agency).

This office was set up mainly to overcome the inadequacy of the Cabinet Secretariat in crisis management. Gotôda Masaharu, the chief cabinet secretary of the Nakasone Yasuhiro administration, initiated this office after the KAL 007 incident in 1983. There was strong opposition to its creation, especially from the Foreign Ministry and the Defense Agency, who were afraid that the new office would intervene in their jurisdictions. As a result of this opposition, the jurisdiction of the newly created office was limited to "managing significant emergencies that threaten national security."[93] Thus, the powers of this post remained too weak to aid the government in responding quickly to crisis situations.

Under the Kaifu Toshiki administration, for example, the prime minister failed to identify the Gulf Crisis in 1990 as a "significant emergency." The issue was handled by the Foreign Ministry, not by the Cabinet Security Affairs Office. Given this lack of interagency coordination, the leadership of Kaifu was quite limited, and Japan's crisis response received international criticism.[94] Crises under the government of the Socialist prime minister Murayama Tomiichi, such as the Hanshin earthquake in January 1995 and the Sarin gas attack by an apocalyptic cult named Aum Shinrikyo in March 1995, further emphasized the need to strengthen the crisis management capability of the prime minister's office. The Administrative Reform Council, an advisory organ to Prime Minister Hashimoto Ryûtarô, treated this issue as a first priority and announced its recommendations in May 1997. Responding to the Council's proposal, the Hashimoto government reorganized this office and changed its name to the Cabinet Security Affairs and Crisis Management Office, also creating a vice ministerial position just for crisis management (*Naikaku Kikikanrikan*) in April 1998.

The Cabinet Information Research Office (*Naikaku Jôhô Chôsa Shitsu*) is headed by a career officer of the National Police Agency. This office was known as the Cabinet Research Office before the 1986 reorganization. Although this office is the only national agency comparable to America's CIA or the former

Soviet Republic's KGB, its size and function are quite limited. The Yoshida administration originally established this office to monitor the activities of left-wing groups. Because these groups' activities were closely related to Communist Party actions, the research office was tied to the Foreign Ministry. Today the office continues to gather raw information from the network of police stations across the nation as well as from embassies and consulates throughout the world. The 1986 reorganization added an analysis function to the office. The chief officer regularly briefs the chief cabinet secretary and the prime minister on current affairs. The inner staff of this research office numbers around 100. More than one-half of the budget for this office is spent on outside organizations that conduct specific research projects on behalf of the office.

These five cabinet policy offices are headed by senior bureaucrats who are chosen from ministries with less partial interests: the Ministries of Finance and Foreign Affairs, and the Defense and the National Police Agencies. The chief officers are chosen from officials at the level of bureau general director or higher and who have strong influence over their base ministry. The Administrative Reform Council under the Hashimoto administration, however, criticized the inflexibility of personal appointments to key positions in the Secretariat. The Council recommended that qualified persons be appointed from any agencies within and even without the civil service.

When the five-office system was established, Chief Cabinet Secretary Gotôda Masaharu instructed the five officers to think first of the national interest, not of the interest of their home ministries. One of the five officers recalls:

Officials at the Cabinet Secretariat should change their basic disposition once they enter this office. In the case of the Nakasone cabinet, the prime minister and Chief Cabinet Secretary Gotôda specifically told us that we should work for the cabinet, not for our home ministries. I think all of the five councilors did work for the national interest and not for their ministry's interest. When we had to act hard on other ministries, we could not be soft against our home ministries. I had to be harder on the Ministry of Finance, where I was from, than on other ministries. If I had worked to save my home ministry, I would not have worked effectively.[95]

During the Nakasone administration, the five officers significantly helped the prime minister and the chief cabinet secretary in coordinating policy among the various government agencies. As another of the original five officers recalls: "The first five officers . . . tried as hard as possible to keep [to Mr. Gotôda's instruction]." But he also implies that the system has not continued to work very well under the successive administrations: "Such reforms have not established a solid base [for the operations of the five offices]. . . . The institution does not always function."[96]

Personal Secretaries

In addition to the five cabinet offices, five personal secretaries assist the prime minister in handling day-to-day administrative operations. The Cabinet Law (Article 15) provides legal authority for the prime minister to have three secretaries. Traditionally, the prime minister chooses his close associate for one of these posts: this is usually a long-time personal staffer, a relative, or a press reporter who has followed him for a number of years. This close associate is placed in the role of the secretary for political affairs and is often called the prime minister's chief secretary. The prime minister's four administrative secretaries are appointed from the Ministries of Finance, Foreign Affairs, and International Trade and Industry and from the National Police Agency.

The chief secretary to the prime minister has numerous tasks: He is a liaison between the prime minister and his faction members and sometimes handles the political "dirty work." He acts as liaison to the prime minister's constituency and other supporters. He attends many meetings and ceremonies on behalf of the prime minister. Some powerful chief assistants, such as Kamiwada Yoshihiko, who served with Prime Minister Nakasone, regularly held private briefings for journalists in an effort to develop media understanding of current policies. Prime Minister Hosokawa Morihiro appointed Narita Norihiko, a researcher on comparative politics from the Diet library, as his chief secretary. Since one of the priorities of the Hosokawa government was political reform for introducing a new electoral system, the prime minister needed his academic expertise. Prime Minister Hashimoto Ryûtarô surprised many in the political circle by picking a MITI official, Eda Kenji, as the chief secretary. Eda often played an important role in Hashimoto's governmental reform plans, reflecting the interests of the Ministry of International Trade and Industry.

In the late 1940s Prime Minister Yoshida Shigeru began the tradition of recruiting bureaucrats to assist the prime minister by picking a Foreign Ministry official to serve as personal secretary. The Ikeda Hayato administration, after the 1960 turmoil over the revision of the Security Treaty, saw the importance of public security and added an official from the National Police Agency. Satô Eisaku created another assistant post to handle broad domestic issues, bringing in a bureaucrat from the Ministry of Finance. Tanaka Kakuei also added a MITI official to advise on trade and industrial issues. This five-secretary system, with a chief secretary and four administrative secretaries, has been institutionalized since the Fukuda Takeo administration in 1976.[97]

The four administrative secretaries take shifts in accompanying the prime minister from early morning to evening. If the prime minister does not live in the official residence, the assistant begins his day by picking up the prime minister at his private residence. By the time the secretary reaches the residence, he must be prepared to answer the prime minister's questions on media coverage of political affairs. The assistant carries with him sufficient documents to provide the prime minister with any information he needs. Throughout the day, the secretaries are seen in a continuous briefing session with the prime minister. Most of the secretaries have an amazingly tight schedule. Fukuda Yasuo, a son and former chief secretary of Prime Minister Fukuda Takeo, looks back at his time at the Prime Minister's Office: "The first thing I remember is how busy I was. It was almost suicidal."[98] A foreign service officer who served as the administrative secretary to Prime Minister Nakasone Yasuhiro also describes his near-impossible schedule: "I always got up at 3:30 in the morning to prepare and study for the day, and left home around six, two hours before the prime minister arrived at the office. Now I look back and realize that I have never worked harder in my life."[99]

The four administrative secretaries, as liaisons for the prime minister to the ministries, are also the channels for the ministries to the national leader. One of the most important tasks of the secretaries is to gather and provide information on administrative operations. The four administrative secretaries are connected to their respective agency's information network. The prime minister needs from the ministries they represent constant updates that are most important to his immediate tasks.

The five personal secretaries probably spend more time with the prime minister than with any other government official. Describing how the prime minister conducts his day-to-day business, Prime Minister Miki Takeo stated, "The prime minister moves Japan by playing catch with the secretaries."[100] They deliver messages to the ministries from the prime minister and vice versa and handle almost all the clerical work.

The secretaries' experience at the Cabinet Secretariat is important for their career development; a secretary to the prime minister is on an elite course in the ministries. An often-asked question is where their loyalties lie—with the prime minister or with their home ministry. Hirose Katsusada, a MITI official who served as a secretary to Prime Minister Miyazawa Kiichi, said in an interview: "We cannot deny that some secretaries have strong loyalty to their home ministries. But once we are here at the Prime Minister's Office, we have to, and most of us do, change our thinking."[101]

Some prime ministers wanted to place their own men in the office. Hosokawa Morihiro (1993–94), in order to strengthen the support for his initiatives, created the position of special assistant to the prime minister and appointed Dietman Tanaka Shûsei to the post. Prime Minister Murayama Tomiichi (1994–96) followed suit in order to run the three-party coalition government—the LDP, the Socialists, and *Sakigake*. He chose one representative from each of the three coalition government parties to serve as assistants to the prime minister. Murayama explained to the author the reason for these appointments in an interview: "Before these new positions, there were only three politicians in the Prime Minister's Office. All the policy issues were only brought by bureaucrats. Under such circumstance, I felt that political initiatives were difficult."[102] The new positions, however, were not official. The assistants did not have any legal authority, and their role was limited to acting as a liaison between political parties and the prime minister.

Under the Hashimoto Ryûtarô cabinet, the revision of the Cabinet Law was introduced to allow the prime minister to appoint up to three assistants to officially recognized roles. He filled two out of the three positions by appointing former diplomat Okamoto Yukio the position to handle the U.S. base issue in Okinawa, and former Dietman Mizuno Kiyoshi to deal with administrative reform. The 1999 administrative reform bills raises the maximum appointable number of assistants to five by 2001.

The Proposed Cabinet Office

The support staff of the prime minister is limited in size. The Cabinet Secretariat has a total staff of less than 200, much smaller than that of the White House and less than one-half the size of Britain's Cabinet Office staff. Many observers, including former vice minister of MITI Amaya Naohiro, see the limited support staff as constraining the prime minister.[103]

Reflecting this view, the Administrative Reform Council under the Hashimoto government proposed to create a powerful supporting organ, the Cabinet Office (*Naikakufu*). The new office would be located within the cabinet, and thus ranked above other ministries and agencies. It would support the Cabinet Secretariat in the task of formulating the basic strategy of the cabinet and would be responsible for planning and coordination on matters such as economic and fiscal policy and policy on sciences and technology. The proponents of this idea, including former deputy chief cabinet secretary Ishihara Nobuo, argue that it would be useful as both a planning and coordinating arm and an execution arm for the prime minister and his cabinet.[104] (For further discussion, see chapter 8).

Former chief cabinet secretary Gotôda Masaharu has criticized the creation of the Cabinet Office. As the office's jurisdiction would overlap with that of existing ministries and agencies, he argued, the coordination process would become too complicated.[105] Gotôda emphasizes the role of the prime minister: "What actually matters in ensuring an effective administration is the leadership of the prime minister."[106] Another assistant who worked under Gotôda summarizes the two arguments thus: "A prime minister with a strong will to pursue his policies would spend his time and energy recruiting able officials to form a strong Cabinet Secretariat. His leadership affects the choice of the personnel, thus the effectiveness of the Secretariat."[107] Even when the cabinet is equipped with able staff members, it cannot play an effective coordinating role without political leadership. When the prime minister devotes his time, energy, and political resources in demonstrating his leadership, the cabinet can effectively conduct policy coordination despite its limited size.

SUMMARY

The prime minister is vested with a wide array of institutional sources of power. He is head of the cabinet, which holds executive power. The prime minister represents the cabinet and exercises executive power on its behalf. He has the authority to control and supervise administrative branches. He reports on national and foreign affairs to the Diet and in so doing sets the political agenda for his administration and the legislative branch. He submits the budget and other cabinet bills that become most of the legislation. He acts as representative of and chief diplomat for the nation and is the commander in chief for the Self Defense Force.

The authority of the cabinet is not limited to the executive branch. Based on the authority provided by Article 7 of the Constitution, the cabinet can decide to dissolve the lower house, thus ending the terms of all the legislators in this powerful government organ. Some prime ministers exercised this authority and successfully gained power as a result of the subsequent election. Through the appointment of judges, the prime minister has some control over the judiciary branch. Furthermore, through the justice minister, the prime minister can block the prosecution process.

The prime minister can be a powerful political figure. As leader of the cabinet, he has the legal authority to freely appoint his cabinet members. His almost complete power over the executive authority, however, is based on the assumption that he will utilize his statutory freedom to appoint and dismiss cabinet members to formulate and execute his policies. This assumption is unrealistic, though, because of strong factionalism within the LDP and because of partisanship within the coalition government. No LDP leader could have—nor can any leader of a coalition government—become prime minister without the support of the other factions or parties. Powerful prime ministers can enjoy relative freedom in forming their cabinets, but they cannot totally ignore the factional balance within the cabinet and the requests from other factions of the ruling party. Factionalism prevents a prime minister from exercising his sole authoritative power independently from the cabinet, namely, appointing cabinet members.

Because executive power is vested in the cabinet and not in the prime minister, the effectiveness of the prime minister depends on his control over the cabinet. Cabinet members, though appointed by the prime minister, maintain strong loyalty to their faction or party in the coalition and act as its representatives to the administration. The effectiveness of the prime minister, therefore, depends on his support from other political groups as well as his own group.

There is a large gap between a prime minister's vast potential power over the government and the legal authority given specifically to him. This can potentially create two extreme cases: Whereas a strong prime minister can be dominant, expanding his authority over many areas, a prime minister with weak intraparty support may be powerless to conduct all but the minimum of operations. The limited size of the Secretariat exaggerates this gap.

In short, the legal authority vested in the post of the prime ministership is limited. Whether the prime minister can effectively use his other institutional sources of power depends on his informal sources of power, including his support base within the party, his popularity, his influence over the bureaucracy, and his experience. The following chapter explores informal sources of power.

NOTES

1. Gotôda Masaharu, interview by author, Tokyo, December 18, 1992. See also Gotôda Masaharu, *Naikaku Kanbô Chôkan* [Chief cabinet secretary] (Tokyo: Kôdan-sha, 1989), p. 3.

2. Article 75 reads: "The Ministers of State, during their tenure of office, shall not be subject to legal action without the consent of the Prime Minister. However, the right to take action is not impaired hereby." This was intended to be a safeguard in case the Public Prosecutor's Office attempted to overthrow the existing cabinet.

3. Miyazawa Toshiyoshi, *Nihonkoku Kenpô* [The Japanese Constitution] (Tokyo: Nihon Hyôron-sha, 1955; revised in 1978), pp. 550–56. The first edition of this book includes the American draft. Article 64 of the American draft reads, "The Prime Minister introduces bills on behalf of the Cabinet, reports to the Diet on general affairs of State and the status of foreign relations, and exercises control and supervision over the several executive departments and agencies."

4. Article 66 reads, "The Cabinet, in the exercise of executive power, shall be collectively responsible to the Diet."

5. The Cabinet Law, Article 3, reads, "The Ministers shall divide among themselves administrative affairs and be in charge of their respective shares thereof each as a competent Minister, as provided for by law separately." The National Administrative Organization Law provides the definition of head of ministries. Translation provided in Government Section, Supreme Commander for the Allied Powers, *Political Reorientation of Japan* (Washington, D.C.: U.S. Government Printing Office, 1949), p. 851.

6. The Cabinet Law, Article 8, reads, "The Prime Minister is able to block operations and orders of various administrative branches and to wait for the decision of the Cabinet meeting."

7. Gotôda Masaharu, *Seiji towa Nanika* [What is politics?] (Tokyo: Kôdan-sha, 1988), p. 90.

8. The Cabinet Law, Article 6, reads, "The Prime Minister shall exercise control and supervision over various administrative branches in accordance with the policies to be decided upon after consultation at Cabinet meetings."

9. From April to August, the meetings are held about four times a month on average. Kataoka Hiromitsu, *Naikaku no Kinô to Hosa Kikô* [The function of the cabinet and the supporting organizations] (Tokyo: Seibun-dô, 1982), p. 240.

10. Anthony King, "The British Prime Ministership in the Age of the Career Politician," *West European Politics* 14, no. 2 (April 1991), pp. 32, 34–35.

11. Gotôda presents a pessimistic view of the future role of the prime minister, who will be constrained by these legal limits to authority: "Prime ministers in the past man-

aged to [run the government] due to their own political power, not their institutional authority. I am not necessarily optimistic whether this will work in the future. It is unstable to rely on the personal power of the prime minister as we have been doing. Furthermore, there is no guarantee that we will always get a good prime minister." Gotôda, *Seiji towa Nanika*, pp. 92–93.

12. Fujimoto Takao, *Fujimoto Takao no Daijin Hôkoku* [Report from Minister Fujimoto Takao] (Tokyo: Planet Shuppan, 1989), pp. 74–82.

13. Ishihara Nobuo, *Shushô Kantei no Ketsudan* [The decisions of the prime minister's office] (Tokyo: Chûô Kôron-sha, 1997), pp. 199–201.

14. Murakawa Ichirô, *Nihon no Seisaku Kettei Katei* [Japan's policy-making process] (Tokyo: Gyôsei, 1985), p. 234.

15. Miyawaki Raisuke, interview by author, Washington, D.C., December 9, 1992. If there should be disagreement at the subcabinet meeting, the cabinet member in charge of the issue brings it to the cabinet meeting for discussion. Murakawa, p. 234.

16. Ishihara Nobuo, *Kan Kaku Arubeshi* [How the bureaucrats should be] (Tokyo: Shôgakukan Bunko, 1998), p. 189.

17. Mainichi Shimbun Seiji-bu, ed., *Kenshô Shushô Kantei* [Inspecting the Prime Minister's Office] (Tokyo: Asahi Sonorama, 1988), pp. 133–34.

18. See Maki Tarô, *Nakasone Seiken 1806 nichi* [The Nakasone administration: 1,806 days], vol. 2 (Tokyo: Gyôsei Mondai Kenkyûsho, 1988), pp. 297–313.

19. Kishi Nobusuke, *Kishi Nobusuke Kaisô-roku* [Memoir's of Kishi Nobusuke] (Tokyo: Kôsaido, 1983), pp. 310–11; and Ôhinata Ichirô, *Kishi Seiken 1241 nichi* [The Kishi administration: 1,241 Days] (Tokyo: Gyôsei Mondai Kenkyû-sho, 1985), pp. 70–71.

Japan later signed the nuclear proliferation treaty. Therefore, Japan's possession of nuclear weapons, though constitutional, would become the violation of the treaty.

20. Satô's assistant, Kusuda Minoru, states that this happened partly because the statement came out late at night when many opposition party members and journalists were less vigilant than usual, and partly because the Okinawa issue was creating a volatile atmosphere. Kusuda Minoru, ed., *Satô Seiken: 2797 nichi* [The Satô administration: 2,797 days], vol. 1 (Tokyo: Gyôsei Mondai Kenkyû-sho, 1983), pp. 398–99. Kusuda recalls:

> The prime minister's answer to the questions of JSP chairman Narita would be the basis of the discussion during the Diet session along with his policy speech. It was also the first hurdle to jump over for the Satô administration, which tried to tackle the return of Okinawa. Prime Minister Satô showed the prepared answers to Deputy Prime Minister Kawashima and asked his opinion. Kawashima read quietly and said, "So we will have an election." At this moment the top of the government and the ruling party made the decision. Prior to substantial negotiations with the United States to ask for the return of Okinawa, we were going to attend the sixty-first diet session with the determination to dissolve the lower house if necessary.

Kusuda Minoru, *Shuseki Hishokan: Satô Sôri tono Jûnenkan* [Chief Secretary: Ten years with Prime Minister Satô] (Tokyo: Bungei Shunjû, 1975), pp. 45–46.

21. Until 1999, there was only one parliamentary vice minister in each ministry, except the Ministries of Finance, International Trade and Industry, and Agriculture, Fishery, and Forest, which had two.

22. For the institutionalized system for the ladder within the LDP, see Satô Seizaburô and Matsuzaki Tetsuhisa, *Jimintô Seiken* [The LDP administrations] (Tokyo: Chûô Kôron, 1986), chapter 2. See also Inoguchi Takashi and Iwai Tomoaki, *"Zoku Giin" no*

Kenkyû [Study on "*zoku* members"] (Tokyo: Nihon Keizai Shimbun-sha, 1987), chapters 4 and 5.

23. In August 1960, for example, Prime Minister Ikeda promised to lower interest rates and actually directed the central bank to lower the rate by 1 percent.

24. Nakasone Yasuhiro, *Seiji to Jinsei* [Politics and life] (Tokyo: Kôdan-sha, 1992), p. 305. See also Gotôda, *Naikaku Kanbô Chôkan*, pp. 77–81.

25. Tachibana Takashi, a journalist whose articles led to Tanaka Kakuei's resignation as prime minister, argues that after this incident it became very difficult for the Public Prosecutor's Office to prosecute politicians in power. Tachibana Takashi, "Kensatsu no Kakumo Nagaki Nemuri" [Such a long sleep for the Prosecutor's Office], *Bungei Shunjû* (December 1992), pp. 94–109.

26. Article 53 reads; "The Cabinet may determine to convoke extraordinary sessions of the Diet. When a quarter or more of the total members of either House makes the demand, the Cabinet must determine on such convocation."

27. Yomiuri Shimbun Seiji-bu, ed., *Sôri Daijin* [The prime minister] (Tokyo: Yomiuri Shimbun-sha, 1971; revised in 1972), pp. 57–58.

28. Abe Hitoshi, Shindô Muneyuki, and Kawahito Tadashi, *Gaisetsu Gendai Nihon no Seiji* [Introduction to contemporary Japanese politics] (Tokyo: Tokyo Daigaku Shuppan-kai, 1990), pp. 18–26. For further discussion, see Iwai Tomoaki, *Rippô Katei* [The legislative process] (Tokyo: Tokyo Daigaku Shuppan-kai, 1988), pp. 86–95.

29. Itô Masaya, *Ikeda Hayato Sono Sei to Shi* [Ikeda Hayato: His life and death] (Tokyo: Shiseidô, 1966), p. 69.

30. Ikeda Hayato, *Kinkô Zaisei* [Balanced budget] (Tokyo: Jitsugyô no Nihon-sha, 1952), pp. 293–94.

31. Miyazawa Kiichi, *Sengo Seiji no Shôgen* [Testimony on postwar politics] (Tokyo: Yomiuri Shimbun-sha, 1991), p. 26. See also Miyazawa Kiichi, *Tokyo-Washington no Mitsudan* [The secret conversations between Tokyo and Washington] (Tokyo: Chûkô Bunko, 1999), pp. 45–47.

32. Masumi Junnosuke, *Sengo Seiji 1945–55 nen* [Postwar politics, 1945–55] (Tokyo: Tokyo Daigaku Shuppan, 1983), pp. 445–61. See also Ôhinata Ichirô, *Kishi Seiken*, pp. 28–31, and Ishida Hirohide, *Ishibashi Seiken 71 nichi* [The Ishibashi administration: 71 days] (Tokyo: Gyôsei Mondai Kenkyû-sho, 1985).

33. Kishi Nobusuke, *Kishi Nobusuke Kaisô roku*, pp. 331–33.

34. Ibid., 503–4. See also Ôhinata, *Kishi Seiken*, pp. 210–14.

35. Kishi, *Kishi Nobusuke Kaisô roku*, pp. 508–9; and Ôhinata, *Kishi Seiken*, pp. 214–15.

36. For the details of the protest movements, see George R. Packard, *Protest in Tokyo: The Security Treaty Crisis of 1960* (Princeton: Princeton University Press, 1966).

37. Kusuda, *Shuseki Hishokan*, p. 140.

38. Ibid., pp. 163–64.

39. Henry Kissinger, *White House Years* (Boston: Little, Brown, 1979), p. 326.

40. Kissinger recalls, "American businessmen, legislators, and economic officials were vocal in insisting on some Japanese flexibility on economic matters to smooth the way for American action on Okinawa." Nixon's choice was textiles. Nixon wrote a memorandum to Kissinger: "We have to get something on textile." On his campaign trail in the South, Nixon had promised southern delegates that he would do something for the textile industry, it having been severely damaged by Japanese competition. Ibid., pp. 329–30.

41. Nakano Shirô, "Zecchô no Kageri" [Shadows over the peak], in Kusuda, ed., *Satô Seiken*, pp. 178–79.

42. Kissinger, p. 336. There is a famous story of Satô's statement that deals with mistranslation. Satô reportedly told Nixon in Japanese, *zensho shimasu*, a phrase often interpreted as "I will do something if possible." The diplomat who was interpreting for Satô told Nixon in English, "I will do my best."

43. Ôtake Hideo argues that the successful conclusion was largely due to Satô's leadership. Ôtake Hideo, *Gendai Nihon no Seiji Kenryoku Keizai Kenryoku* [Political power and economic power in contemporary Japan] (Tokyo: San'ichi Shobô, 1979).

44. Nakano, "Zecchô no Kageri," p. 82.

45. Nikaidô Susumu, interview by Suzuki Kenji, in Suzuki Kenji, *Rekidai Sôri Sokkin no Kokuhaku* [Confessions by close associates of the prime ministers] (Tokyo: Mainichi Shimbun-sha, 1991), p. 84.

46. Konaga Keiichi, interview by author, Tokyo, December 14, 1992.

47. Henry Kissinger, *Years of Upheaval* (Boston: Little, Brown, 1982), p. 741.

48. Konaga Keiichi, interview by author, Tokyo, December 14, 1992. See also Nakasone, *Seiji to Jinsei*, pp. 288–92, and Nakano Shirô, *Tanaka Seiken 886 nichi* [The Tanaka administration: 886 days] (Tokyo: Gyôsei Mondai Kenkyû-sho, 1982), pp. 229–30.

49. Gotôda, *Naikaku Kanbô Chôkan*, pp. 30–35. See also Gotôda, *Seiji towa Nanika*, pp. 143–48; and Maki, *Nakasone Seiken*, vol. 1, p. 63.

50. Gotôda, *Seiji towa Nanika*, pp. 147–48.

51. Akagi Munenori, *Imadakara Iu* [I can tell you now], quoted in Kishi Nobusuke, Yatsugi Kazuo, and Itô Takashi, *Kishi Nobusuke no Kaisô* [Memories of Kishi Nobusuke] (Tokyo: Bungei Shunjû, 1981), p. 232.

52. Gotôda Masaharu, interview by author, Tokyo, December 18, 1992.

53. Gotôda, *Naikaku Kanbô Chôkan*, pp. 105–8.

54. Murayama Tomiichi, interview by author, September 13, 1996.

55. The original Cabinet Law of 1947 limited the number to 16. The number was increased to 17 by the 1965 revision, to 18 by the 1966 revision, to 19 by the 1971 revision, and finally to 20 by the 1974 revision. The Administrative Reform Council under the Hashimoto administration proposed to limit the number to between 14 and 17.

56. Prime ministers have appointed business leaders, former bureaucrats, and scholars to their cabinets. Among rare cases in recent LDP cabinets are Nagai Michio to education minister under the Miki administration, Ushiba Nobuhiko to minister for external economic affairs under the Fukuda administration, Ôkita Saburô to foreign minister under the Ôhira administration, and Takahara Sumiko to director general of the Economic Planning Agency under the Kaifu administration. Under the non-LDP Hosokawa administration, two nonpoliticians were appointed to cabinet positions: Akamatsu Yoshiko to the minister of education and Mikazuki Akira to the minister of justice. The Obuchi administration in 1998 drew much media attention by appointing Sakaiya Taichi, a writer and economic critic, to director general of the Economic Planning Agency.

57. See Watanabe Tsuneo, *Tôshu to Seitô: Sono Rîdâshippu no Kenkyû* [Party leaders and political parties: Study on their leadership] (Tokyo: Kôbun-sha, 1961), p. 228.

58. Nathaniel B. Thayer, *How the Conservatives Rule Japan* (Princeton: Princeton University Press, 1969), p. 182.

59. Watanabe, *Tôshu to Seitô*, pp. 87–88.

60. Satô and Matsuzaki, *Jimintô Seiken*, chapter 2.

61. Kiyomiya Ryû, *Fukuda Seiken 714 nichi* [The Fukuda administration: 714 days] (Tokyo: Gyôsei Mondai Kenkyû-sho, 1984), pp. 19–23.

62. Gotôda, *Naikaku Kanbô Chôkan*, p. 3.

63. Nakasone had shifted his conservative stance on those issues in an attempt not to disturb relations with Korea and China. The Nakasone administration received criticism from these two countries when the government approved a Japanese history textbook with rightist view on several issues, including World War II. Prime Minister Nakasone instructed the Education Ministry to rewrite the criticized parts. Also, that year Nakasone did not go to Yasukuni Shrine, although he had gone there and signed his name with the title of prime minister in prior years.

64. Fukuda Takeo, "Watashi no Rirekisho," no. 25, *Nihon Keizai Shimbun* (January 26, 1993). Fukuda recalls: "After the election, I privately met Mr. Miki Takeo. . . . We decided that [it was] the responsibility [of Prime Minister Tanaka] to have created the popular disbelief in politics and that two of us would resign at the same time on October 12, 1983."

65. In 1947, Prime Minister Katayama Tetsu appointed himself to all the ministerial positions until he finally formed a cabinet eight days later.

66. Yomiuri Shimbun Chôsa Kenkyû Honbu, ed., *Nihon no Kokkai* [The Japanese Parliament] (Tokyo: Yomiuri Shimbun-sha, 1988), pp. 96–105. This interpretation was confirmed by the Tokyo High Court on September 22, 1954.

67. There were two elections under the Meiji Constitution in the postwar era. See Watanabe, *Tôshu to Seitô*, p. 179.

68. Ibid., pp. 179–80.

69. Ishida, *Ishibashi Seiken*, pp. 70–74.

70. Watanabe, *Tôshu to Seitô*, pp. 180–82.

71. Fujimoto Kazumi, ed., *Kokkai Kinô Ron: Kokkai no Shikumi to Un'ei* [Arguments for the functional Diet: The mechanism and operation of the Diet] (Tokyo: Hôgaku Shoin, 1990).

72. Ogata reportedly went so far as to say he would rather end his political life than endorse a cabinet decision for dissolution. Although Yoshida considered dismissing Ogata from the cabinet, Ikeda persuaded Yoshida that he should not dismiss his own successor as party president from his cabinet. Miyazawa, *Sengo Seiji no Shôgen*, p. 99.

73. Kishi, *Kishi Nobusuke Kaisôroku*, pp. 418–19.

74. Kusuda, ed., *Satô Seiken*, vol. 2, pp. 94–104.

75. The victory was partly attributable to the efforts of LDP, Takeshita, Miyazawa and Abe. They worked hard in the election position themselves to succeed Nakasone by expanding their factions. As a result, the Abe faction increased from 46 to 56; the Suzuki (Miyazawa's) faction from 51 to 59; the Tanaka (Takeshita's) faction from 67 to 87.

76. Nakasone, referring to the extension of his term, asked LDP general secretary Kanemaru not to add a specific date of termination. Although Kanemaru once agreed with Nakasone, he decided to limit the extension to one year when he met with opposition from young LDP leaders. Maki, *Nakasone Seiken*, vol. 2, p. 231.

77. Gotôda, *Naikaku Kanbô Chôkan*, pp. 48–51. Also see Maki, *Nakasone Seiken*, vol. 2, pp. 197–204.

78. The election was set on the same day as the preset upper house election and became the first double election. During the election campaign, however, Prime Minister Ôhira died from cardiac failure. With the voters' sentiment to mourn the leader's death, as well as the help of a high voting rate, the LDP won 284 seats in the lower house and

69 seats in the upper house, both far above a majority. This victory ended a period of roughly equal strength between the LDP and the opposition party in the Diet. See Kawauchi Issei, *Ôhira Seiken 554 nichi* [The Ôhira administration: 554 days] (Tokyo: Gyôsei Mondai Kenkyû-sho, 1982), pp. 240–43; and Gotôda, *Naikaku Kanbô Chôkan*, pp. 213–14.

79. Kishi, *Kishi Nobusuke Kaisô roku*, p. 534.

80. Miki's personal assistant recalls: "Mr. Miki finally decided that he could not dismiss 15 out of 20 cabinet members whom he himself appointed. Such an action would be a type of fascism. Since Mr. Miki wanted to come back as the prime minister again if he could, he did not want to cause big trouble." Nakamura Keiichirô, interview by author, Tokyo, December 17, 1992. See also Nakamura, *Miki Seiken*, pp. 271–78. Also see Kiyomiya, *Fukuda Seiken*, pp. 66–70.

81. See Morita Minoru, *Seihen: Jimintô Sôsaisen Uramen Antô-shi* [Political upheaval: History of the behind-the-scene battles for the LDP presidency] (Tokyo: Tokuma Shoten, 1991), pp. 143–70; and Nihon Keizai Shimbun-sha, ed., *Dokyumento Seiken Tanjô* [Documentary, the birth of an administration] (Tokyo: Nihon Keizai Shimbun-sha, 1991), pp. 117–202.

A former high government official, who refused to be identified, told the author [Shinoda] in an interview in Tokyo:

> Prime Minister Kaifu did not have any idea how much powerful a political weapon the authority to dissolve the lower house would be for him. To ask voters' voice on political reform was more than an appropriate reason to dissolve the lower house. He could have gained the popular support by dissolving. Gotôda Masaharu and Itô Masayoshi, two senior LDP leaders who were working on the political reform, pressured Kaifu to decide on the dissolution. Kaifu was inclined and publicly announced that he had an "important decision" in mind. Some political commentators suggest that Kaifu would have dissolved if his wife, who was known as the first lady actively involved in political affairs, were in Tokyo instead of London and had encouraged him.

82. The position gained cabinet member status under the Satô administration in 1966. The first chief cabinet secretary with a ministerial status was Aichi Kiichi.

83. Gotôda, *Naikaku Kanbô Chôkan*, p. 3.

84. Ibid., p. 4.

85. Gotôda, *Seiji towa Nanika*, p. 90.

86. Miyawaki Raisuke, interview by the author, Washington, D.C., March 10, 1993.

87. As described in the previous section, Prime Minister Satô Eisaku appointed former chief cabinet secretary Kimura Toshio to this position. Also, Prime Minister Nakasone Yasuhiro appointed a former labor minister, Fujinami Takao, and Prime Minister Takeshita chose a former minister of home affairs, Ozawa Ichirô, both powerful members of their given faction, to this post. Prime Minister Miyazawa Kiichi appointed Kondô Motoji as the deputy chief cabinet secretary directly from the post of minister of agriculture and fishery. Most recently, Prime Minister Hashimoto Ryûtarô selected a former education minister, Yosano Kaoru, to the same post. Hosokawa Morihiro saw the lack of assistance on the political side within the Cabinet Secretariat, and he created a new position of special assistant to the prime minister besides the political deputy.

88. *Asahi Shimbun*, April 15, 1998.

89. Kawaguchi Hiroyuki, *Kanryô Shihai no Kôzô* [The mechanism of bureaucratic control] (Tokyo: Kôdan-sha, 1987), p. 45.

90. Before the 1986 reorganization of the Cabinet Secretariat, it was made up of only three of the now-existing five offices: the Cabinet Councilor's Office, the Cabinet Research Office, and the Cabinet Public Relations Office. In 1985, a subcommittee of the Administrative Reform Promotion Committee, headed by a close advisor to Prime Minister Nakasone, Sejima Ryûzô, issued a recommendation to strengthen the Cabinet Secretariat. Based on this recommendation, the Secretariat was reorganized the following year: The Cabinet Councilor's Office was divided into two, one for domestic affairs and the other for external affairs; the functions of the two other existing offices were enforced; and the Cabinet National Security Office was created.

91. The function of this office is outlined on the web at *http:www.sorifu.go.jp/english/e1-2.html*.

92. Miyawaki Raisuke, a former National Police Agency officer who served as the chief officer of the Cabinet Public Relations Office, states: "The prime minister is isolated from raw information. The information provided for him is filtered through the bureaucracy and modified. Some information, which should reach him, is often blocked by this filtering. My task was to provide raw information, and recommendations based on it, to the prime minister even if it might not be good news for him. Prime Minister Nakasone asked me to see him alone because the information and recommendations I provided sometimes could be against the interests of certain ministries." Miyawaki Raisuke, interview by the author, Washington, D.C., March 10, 1993.

93. The interpretation of the government official's comment at the Diet meeting served to limit the function of this office. In his answer at the Diet, Chief Cabinet Secretary Gotôda specified such emergencies in four categories: (1) highjacks; (2) incidents similar to the Mig 25 exile case; (3) special international emergencies like the KAL 007 case; and (4) large-scale earthquakes. The opposition parties and the existing bureaucratic agencies interpreted this statement as the jurisdiction of the office and not merely as examples of possible emergencies to which the office would respond. Sassa Atsuyuki, *Shin Kiki Kanri no Nouhau* [New know-hows for crisis management] (Tokyo: Bungei Shunjû, 1991), p. 35.

Gotôda Masaharu reveals the opposition of the related agencies, such as the Defense Agency and the Land Agency, in his memoir. Gotôda Masaharu, *Jô to Ri* [Emotion and logics] (Tokyo: Kôdan-sha, 1998), pp. 170–73.

94. See Sassa, *Shin Kiki Kanri no Nouhau*, pp. 17–72.

95. Matoba Junzô, interview by author, Tokyo, December 16, 1992.

96. Sassa, *Shin Kiki Kanri no Nouhau*, p. 180.

97. Ôsuga Mizuo, *Shushô Kantei Konjaku Monogatari* [The prime minister's residence: The past and the present] (Tokyo: Asahi Sonorama, 1995), p. 139.

98. Fukuda Yasuo, interview by author, Tokyo, December 15, 1992.

99. Hasegawa Kazutoshi, "Moto Hishokan Nakasone Yasuhiro wo Kataru III-2" [Former secretary's words on Nakasone Yasuhiro], *Yatchan's* (May 1990), p. 20.

100. Nakamura Keiichirô, interview by author, Tokyo, December 17, 1992.

101. Hirose Katsusada, interview by author, Tokyo, December 15, 1992.

102. Murayama Tomiichi, interview by author, Tokyo, September 13, 1996.

103. Interesting arguments on this point are given by two former governmental officials, Nagatomi Yûichirô and Amaya Naohiro, and are presented in Yamamoto Shichihei, *Habatsu no Kenkyû* [Study on factions] (Tokyo: Bungei Shunjû, 1989), pp. 26–41. See

also Kenji Hayao, "The Japanese Prime Minister and Public Policy" (Ph.D. dissertation, University of Michigan, 1990), chapter 7.

104. The Administrative Reform Council, "Final Report of the Administrative Reform Council," December 3, 1997. Also, Ishihara, *Kan Kaku Arubeshi*, pp. 194–95.

105. Gotôda, *Jô to Ri*, vol. 2, p. 173.

106. Gotôda Masaharu, interview by author, Tokyo, December 18, 1992.

107. Miyawaki Raisuke, interview by author, Washington, D.C., March 10, 1993.

Chapter 4
Informal Sources of Power

The prime minister is equipped with various institutional sources of power over the executive branch and in certain occasions over the legislative and judiciary branches. The extent to which he can utilize this power, however, is often determined by the amount of support he has from the cabinet or from within the ruling party or coalition. In order for a prime minister to effectively exercise his authority to utilize institutional power, he must have support from within and outside the party. How much support he receives from the party, the media, and the public depends largely on his power of a different nature, that deriving from informal sources.

In the current Japanese political system, becoming the prime minister requires substantial credentials as a politician. During several decades of public service, a candidate for prime minister has traditionally had to demonstrate his political skill and ability at various posts in the government, in the party, in the Diet, and within the faction. Even Hosokawa Morihiro, who became the prime minister of the non-LDP coalition government in his first term as a lower house member, would not have been chosen for the post if he had not proven his administrative skill as governor of Kumamoto Prefecture. When people who work with a candidate recognize his ability and efforts, he is allowed to climb the ladder to become a party leader. In the process of reaching that point, he gains a wide variety of skills and experience to become an effective party leader and an effective prime minister.

This chapter addresses two major categories of informal sources of power. The first category is the political resources the prime minister has within the political circle. The most important source of this kind is his status as a party leader. As representative of the majority of the lower house he has the power to form a cabinet, control the executive branch, and influence the legislative branch. Another informal political resource is the prime minister's ability to control the bureaucracy. Japan has a very strong civil service that not only administers government operations but also drafts legislation, implements policies, and interprets existing laws. The prime minister's effectiveness in pursuing his policy depends in good measure on his control over skilled bureaucrats. Still another political resource is the prime minister's ties to the opposition parties. The Japanese Diet does not blindly approve proposed government policies. The prime minister's relationship with opposition parties makes a significant difference in the legislative process.

The second category of informal sources of power stems from outside the political world. One informal resource that has grown increasingly important is popular support. Prime ministers have become extremely sensitive to the reactions of the public and the media in pursuing policies. Several prime ministers were forced to resign because of public resentment. Another type of outside support is the so-called brain trust that provides advice on policy issues. Recently, the brain trust has been institutionalized in the form of advisory councils that not only identify problem areas but also provide feasible remedies. Additional outside support comes from the business community and the United States. Highly visible business leaders respected for their administrative skills and experiences are influential in government policy making. Withdrawal of support from the business community has led to the resignation of several prime ministers. Support from the United States not only enhances the prime minister's image as an international leader but also proves his ability to represent Japan vis-à-vis the global community, and this ability provides leverage in the domestic political scene.

Powerful prime ministers have effectively used a combination of informal sources to supplement their limited legal authority. Some prime ministers enjoy extensive connections and experience inside the political arena that help them become effective leaders. Others, whose experiences as political insiders are limited, must especially depend on outside support in pursuing policies. The informal sources of power that are available and how they are used completely depend on the background and personal character of each prime minister.

SUPPORT FROM WITHIN THE POLITICAL CIRCLE

As Party Leader

The Constitution, which emphasizes popular sovereignty, defines the Diet as "the highest organ of state power" and gives it the authority to appoint a prime minister. This not only assures the party or coalition of parties that control the Diet the ability to appoint its leader to the premiership but also gives the prime minister indisputable legitimacy to run the government.

Even though the prime minister receives support from a majority of the Diet, he does not necessarily maintain solid support throughout his tenure. The ruling party, either the Liberal Democratic Party or the party coalition, has been a loose organization with a high degree of factionalization. Political dynamics among the factions or the political parties can cause friction, and political rivalries and unequal allocation of power can lead to the downfall of a prime minister. Harmony among these groups can, in contrast, lead to a highly successful administration. The extent of control of the party leader depends on his background, his influence within the party, and the political environment.

In the immediate postwar period through the 1950s, political parties were unable to formulate policies. The ruling party, therefore, depended completely on the executive branch for the formulation, drafting, and implementation of legislation. The legislative branch served as little more than a rubber stamp to approve government policies. The prime minister thus controlled administrative operations with relatively little interference from the party.

Furthermore, the LDP, which served as a ruling party for most of the postwar period, gave its leader strong statutory power derived from the party law. In the policy-making process, he is empowered to "take the supreme responsibility" for the party and to "represent and control" it. This means that he has "the power to reject or override whatever executive council decisions he may regard, for his own reasons, as undesirable."[1] During its long reign in the powerful lower house, the LDP relied on strong party discipline, which prohibited party members from voting against party decisions in the Diet. The statutory veto power gave the president the ability to maintain control over ruling party decisions and thus over the Diet.

In actuality, however, the LDP president did not exercise these extensive powers. Although the prime minister was often involved in party decisions, it was rare that he exercised his veto power over any party decision. Instead, he tried to form a party consensus through the LDP secretary general. The power of the LDP secretary general, whose full-time responsibility was to assist the president in party affairs, grew because the president, busy with the tasks of a prime minister, had delegated much of the responsibility of day-to-day party affairs to him.[2] Statutory power was available but not as an effective option. A practical way of achieving party decisions was informal discussion and consensus building.

As discussed in Chapter 1, the 1970s saw the decentralization of power within the ruling party. The prime minister's control over the party decreased because he had to appoint the secretary general from outside of his faction. In the policy side, as the *zoku* members emerged, the prime minister delegated power to make party decisions in specific policy areas to these issue specialists. As the prime minister's control over the party weakened, his status as a faction leader became a vital resource in forming a party consensus. An effective prime minister would mobilize his faction members to persuade other factions and even the opposition parties to form a consensus to support his policies. A member of the Satô faction stated that Prime Minister Satô Eisaku's long reign was largely attributable to the *nemawashi* (Japanese traditional way of building a consensus) skill of Satô himself and his fellow faction members. They actively persuaded people within and outside of the Diet to agree with governmental policies.[3]

Consensus building within the LDP was often more important than receiving support from the opposition party. Prime Minister Miki Takeo, for instance, faced a serious problem because he did not build party consensus. A former assistant to Miki admits, "Mr. Miki was neither good at *nemawashi*, nor fond of doing it."[4] In order to pursue the revision of the Anti-Trust Law in 1975, for example, Miki personally persuaded several key people such as the LDP's Anti-Trust Research Committee chairman, to support the issue. But Miki did not go further and actively seek party consensus. Although the proposal passed the lower house, it met with opposition from the LDP members in the upper house who had not been consulted before the legislation came to the upper house. As a result, the legislation died.[5]

In Japanese politics, it has often been said, "Power exists in number." A prime minister from a large faction has a better chance of building party consensus. Even if his faction is small, however, he can pursue his policy by receiving support from other factions. The largest LDP faction ever, led by Tanaka Kakuei and later by Takeshita Noboru, had long been influential within the party because other factions constantly sought its vote. Support from this faction was crucial for candidates in acquiring the premiership and for the prime minister in executing major policies. At its peak, the Tanaka faction was comprised of more than one-third of the LDP Diet members, and the Takeshita faction of more than one-fourth after separating from the Tanaka umbrella.

The magic number was the equivalent of one-fourth of the LDP membership, according to political journalist Ishikawa Masumi.[6] If the LDP retained more than one-half of the total Diet members, it remained the ruling party. If a coalition of factions was larger than a majority of all LDP Diet members, it could have decisive power over the selection of the prime minister and the execution of major policies. If one faction had a majority within the coalition, that faction controlled the coalition—and thus the party and the government. Through this rule of "a majority of a majority," a faction with more than one-quarter of LDP members could demonstrate strong influence in the political scene. The prime minister's leadership depended on the size of his faction and of the coalition he formed within the ruling party. As Gotôda Masaharu points out: "when the prime minister has a strong support base within the party, his administration is strong. When, however, his support within the party is unstable, he will be a very weak prime minister."[7]

Because the prime minister's legal authority is limited, he has to depend on his status as representative of the majority of the Diet, which gives him the legitimacy to run the government. His effectiveness as a national leader, therefore, depends largely on his support base within the ruling party or coalition. Under both the LDP and the coalition government, the prime minister's control over the ruling party has been relatively weak as a result of the party's loose organization.

Under the LDP, its members largely ran their own election campaigns and tried to build their own voting base through their private organizations, instead of relying on the party organization. Individual LDP members formed factions whose main objective was to put their leader in the premiership. As described in Chapter 1, however, the new electoral rules of 1994 weakened functions of LDP factions while strengthening functions of the LDP leadership, especially the secretary general, who is in charge of making the list of candidate ranking and allocating funds. As the power of the party leadership increased, there emerged a division between the pro-leadership group and the anti-leadership group across the traditional factions. The fact remains that the prime minister's ability to form a consensus within the ruling party or coalition depends on the respect he is accorded by other members, the quality of his leadership skills, and the number of his followers.

Control over the Bureaucracy

As support from within the ruling party is essential for a prime minister to pursue his policy, staff support from the bureaucracy is a must for him to co-ordinate administrative operations. The cabinet and the ruling party depend on the bureaucracy for drafting bills, implementing policies, and interpreting existing laws for administrative operations. As an assistant to two prime ministers argues, "The prime minister cannot achieve anything if bureaucrats do not move."[8] A former MITI vice minister, who also served as an assistant to Prime Minister Tanaka Kakuei, stresses: "Japan has an excellent bureaucratic system. The prime minister's leadership depends on how much he can make the best use of the bureaucracy."[9]

As discussed in Chapter 3, the prime minister does not have direct legal authority to control the bureaucracy. Further weakening his control over the bureaucracy is the fact that the prime minister does not have his own political appointees in the bureaucracy except ministers and vice ministers. "The prime minister's office is isolated and not organically connected to the bureaucracy, which was a big surprise to me," stated the former chief secretary to Prime Minister Satô Eisaku. No system exists in which information from the ministries constantly flows to the prime minister's office. Bureaucrats in each department are responsible to their minister, but they are not directly connected to the prime minister's office.[10]

Each section of the bureaucracy works for its own interests and the industry over which it has administrative jurisdiction. Career bureaucrats change their position every few years. Industries judge the ability of bureaucrats by how much protection and other services they can provide. Bureaucrats, therefore, tend to resist policy changes that negatively affect their clients during their short tenure and that have a "not-in-my-term-of-office" sentiment.

As discussed in Chapter 1, this sectionalism has strengthened since the 1970s as LDP *zoku* members tended to ally with the bureaucracy to protect their related industry. It was the *raison d'être* of *zoku* members, and in return for such protection, the client industry provided them with financial and other assistance. Their political power was questioned if they could not provide such protection. Sectionalism of the bureaucracy, with the support of *zoku* members, was often an obstacle for the prime minister when pursuing major policies that would negatively affect the related industry.

Even when bureaucrats and *zoku* members recognized the need for policy changes, they were hesitant to pursue them if they would damage their industry. At such times the prime minister needed to step in and exercise strong leadership. The prime minister served as a scapegoat to *zoku* members and bureaucrats. They could cite "The Prime Minister's Policy" as the great excuse for them to escape the wrath of their industry. The stronger the prime minister, the more reasonably such excuses could be made. The prime minister's personal involvement, therefore, is very important in persuading bureaucrats, *zoku* members, and their industries to pass new policy.

Powerful prime ministers have found a way to reach and to effectively control the bureaucracy. Their methods, of course, depend on the individual prime minister and the current political environment. Of the 26 postwar prime ministers, including the current Prime Minister Mori Yoshirô, 10 served as bureaucrats prior to entering the political world. Ex-bureaucrat politicians know how the bureaucracy works, enjoy the benefit of a personal network within the bureaucracy, and take advantage of the seniority that bureaucrats highly value.[11] Prime Minister Yoshida Shigeru, an ex-bureaucrat of the Foreign Ministry, realized the advantage of having bureaucrats in his party. In 1948, Yoshida formed a study group on national policies comprised of top bureaucrats, who later became leading LDP members. In the general election the following year, Yoshida brought these senior bureaucrats into his party as newly elected Diet members to improve his party's ability to formulate and execute policies.[12] By utilizing these ex-bureaucrats, Yoshida developed his control over the bureaucracy.

Prime Minister Ikeda Hayato (1960–64) was an expert in economic policy as a former bureaucrat of the Finance Ministry. The expertise enabled him to talk directly with and on the same knowledge level as his bureaucratic allies. Ikeda became so deeply involved in economic policy that he directly instructed his former subordinates at the Finance Ministry without consulting his finance minister. The chief cabinet secretary of the Ikeda cabinet once warned Ikeda: "You appointed each cabinet member with trust. Once you appoint them, you should delegate authority within their jurisdiction, and should not give them detailed instructions unless the matter calls for particular attention."[13] Despite such warning, Ikeda gave direct instructions to pass over the ministers through his personal ties with the bureaucrats regarding his economic policy.

Ikeda's successor, Prime Minister Satô Eisaku (1964–72), another ex-bureaucrat, controlled the bureaucracy through the cabinet's authority of personnel appointment. The cabinet appoints retiring bureaucrats to several hundred positions in public and special corporations or quasi-governmental organizations, where traditionally many go after leaving government—a practice known as "the descendants from heaven." Satô rewarded senior officials who were loyal to him by providing them with good positions after their retirement. This appointment authority of the prime minister is even more important today than it was during Satô's time because an aging Japanese society has made it difficult for bureaucrats to find jobs after leaving the government. Large-size private corporations now have their own problem of aging employees and can no longer afford to hire many ex-bureaucrats.[14] In order to offer more jobs for retiring bureaucrats, the government has created many special organizations, such as foundations, now numbering over 20,000 in Japan.[15] The more difficult it is for retiring bureaucrats to find jobs, the more they rely on the prime minister's appointment authority. This authority has given the prime minister new leverage over the bureaucracy.

Tanaka Kakuei was a good student of Satô. Throughout his political career, Tanaka tried to develop direct contacts with individual bureaucrats. He memorized not only the names but also the backgrounds of all bureaucratic officials at the division director (kachô) level and above. He sent presents to bureaucrats for their and their family members' birthdays and wedding anniversaries. Tanaka kept a large list of bureaucratic officials' office and home telephone numbers at his home. He would often directly not only call senior government officials but also those in posts as low as division director: Calling a division director was unusual for a national leader because the prime minister usually seeks opinions only from bureau directors or their superiors. Lower-ranking officials who received a telephone call from Tanaka felt honored and were willing to work for him. These direct contacts avoided the problems inherent in the bureaucratic hierarchy, including the consumption of time and the possibility of losing control somewhere in the bureaucratic chain of command. Tanaka often made policies over land issues exclusively with bureaucrats without the involvement of relevant ministers.[16] As a result of his direct contact with bureaucrats, the importance of the ministers was lessened.

According to Kent Calder, Tanaka offered three major incentives to bureaucrats.[17] First, he was willing to expand or create public corporations for bureaucrats who joined them after leaving the government and to support a large budget for them. Second, Tanaka supported the political aspirations of top bureaucrats by offering them critical electoral support. Third, he helped policy positions advocated by bureaucrats in the Diet.

With these incentives, Tanaka had strong control over the bureaucracy, including the powerful Finance Ministry in which he had served as minister. In his first cabinet, using these long-term connections, Prime Minister Tanaka intentionally appointed a politically weak politician as finance minister to gain direct control over the ministry. Tanaka was thus able to successfully control the budget planning for his policy for reconstructing the Japanese archipelago. Overwhelmed by the presence and activities of Tanaka, Finance Ministry officials, usually against an excessive expansionary fiscal policy, were left with no real choice but to accept a large increase (24.6 percent increase compared to the previous year) in the government's overall fiscal 1973 budget.

According to Tanaka's assistant, Tanaka's control over the bureaucracy also derived from his professional expertise, especially concerning national land development. In an interview, the assistant stated: "Mr. Tanaka's knowledge on the national land development surpassed that of bureaucrats. With his professional experience as a developer, he had studied the subject from the beginning of his political career in the 1940s. Mr. Tanaka's vision is often cited as a proof of his political leadership, while his expertise is ignored. But vision would not be anything without expertise and hard work which supported it."[18]

Miki Takeo is an example of a prime minister who did not trust the bureaucrats. Miki did not use the drafts prepared by the bureaucracy for his speeches. Miki even occasionally told his secretaries, who were sent by the ministries, that bureaucrats were his enemies.[19] Miki's distrust of the bureaucracy was so strong that even in foreign policy, he tried to conduct his own diplomacy independent of the Foreign Ministry, breaking from tradition. Miki once had a meeting with U.S. president Gerald Ford without any Foreign Ministry official present.[20] He used an interpreter who had extensive connections in Washington as his personal assistant. As Miki's assistant describes: "[Prime Minister Miki] did not have experience as a bureaucrat or even as a salaried worker, and had not developed the skills of using the organization within the organization."[21] With strong public support, Miki successfully pursued the Lockheed scandal case and former prime minister Tanaka Kakuei's involvement in it. However, in economic issues that required assistance from the bureaucracy, he was unsuccessful, as in the case of the revision of the Anti-Trust Law.

Being part of the bureaucracy is not a prerequisite for gaining power or influence over the bureaucracy. A prime minister with weak connections to the bureaucracy can supplement his control by appointing a powerful ex-bureaucrat politician to a cabinet position. An example of this type of prime minister is Nakasone Yasuhiro. Although he briefly served in the bureaucracy, he never served as finance minister or foreign minister, two cabinet positions generally regarded as the most important steps to becoming a national leader. Therefore, his ties with the bureaucracy were limited. To overcome this limitation, Nakasone appointed Gotôda Masaharu, who had served as the deputy chief cabinet secretary, generally regarded as the top bureaucratic position, to handle administrative reforms. The combination of Nakasone and Gotôda may have produced the best ever "one-two punch" in working with the bureaucracy in recent administrations. A former Finance Ministry official who served Nakasone and Gotôda as cabinet councilor for domestic affairs describes their relationship:

I think that Mr. Nakasone and Mr. Gotôda were the best combination of the prime minister and the chief cabinet secretary in postwar political history. Mr. Nakasone presented policy ideas, and Mr. Gotôda followed up on them with his administrative skill. Mr. Gotôda himself used to be a senior bureaucrat and well aware of the bureaucratic system and its limitation. Comparing his style to Japanese *sumô* wrestling, Mr. Gotôda often pushed bureaucrats to the edge of the ring, and pushed even further to the point they almost fell down, and then pulled them back into the ring. Mr. Nakasone, on the other hand, sometimes did not even know where the wrestling ring was. Mr. Gotôda's knowledge, experience and control over the bureaucracy more than supplemented Mr. Nakasone's shortcoming.[22]

These examples demonstrate that under the current Japanese political system, it is essential for the prime minister to use the bureaucracy to formulate and execute policies. All prime ministers have known the importance of the assistance provided by the bureaucracy. Prime Minister Hosokawa Morihiro, for example, had experienced frustrating confrontations with the central government as governor of Kumamoto Prefecture and had strongly criticized bureaucratic red tape. When he took office, he chose deregulation of the central government as a policy priority of his administration. Many bureaucrats worried about the prime minister maintaining his antibureaucracy sentiment as his term proceeded. However, Hosokawa shifted from his confrontational stance with the bureaucracy to a cooperative one. As Hosokawa realized on assuming office, assistance from bureaucrats is vital for the prime minister to run the government.

Relationship with the Opposition Parties

With the support of the bureaucracy, by the time a prime minister's policy is presented at a cabinet meeting, all coordination within the ruling party and among government agencies to promote the policy is usually completed (see Chapter 3). The procedure to pass the prime minister's policy, however, does not stop there. Many times it must be submitted as a cabinet bill and await passage by the legislative branch.

The ruling party's majority in the powerful lower house does not mean an automatic approval in the Diet. About 100 cabinet bills have been submitted in an average year, and their passage rate was about 80 percent.[23] Opposition parties have blocked about one out of five cabinet bills despite their minority position. One of the largest factors in the legislative process, and one that works against the ruling party, is time—time to get a bill through the Diet before the Diet session comes to a close. The short duration of Diet sessions, the two-house system, and the committee system in the Japanese Diet mean that filibusters and time-consuming measures by opposition parties can be effective.[24] Until the late 1960s, however, the LDP often considered and voted on legislation in the Diet even when the opposition parties were not present, in a demonstration of their disapproval. Opposition parties, to block such conduct by the LDP, became physically violent, with violent scenes occasionally occurring in Diet committees and at floor meetings. In some cases, such as with Kishi Nobusuke, political chaos in the Diet even led to the resignation of the prime minister. In the early 1970s; the LDP promised that they would no longer proceed with discussions and voting on legislation without the presence of opposition party members.[25] The filibusters by the opposition thus became more effective, and the opposition parties stopped taking physical measures.

The LDP occasionally ignored its promise and passed measures without the presence of opposition parties, but it was quickly accused of conducting a "tyranny of a majority." Prime ministers, therefore, have taken such a measure only as a last resort. Whether a prime minister takes this forceful step or not depends largely on public support for the legislation. If, on the one hand, the public and the media do not fully support the opposition parties, it is relatively easy for the ruling party to forcefully enact legislation. On the other hand, full public support for the opposition parties' action to block government legislation often results in the ruling party's giving up on its passage.

The Japanese legislative process has adopted a unanimous consent rule in setting legislative schedules for committee and house floor meetings. Political parties that have a sufficient number of seats on each committee can send their representatives as executive members to committee meetings where they decide legislative schedule. Because any executive member possesses veto power over scheduling, the ruling party must spend time and energy to persuade the opposition parties' representatives to follow their scheduling lead. This rule produces additional time constraints and thus works against the ruling party.

These constraints—time, filibusters, and unanimous consent rule—have made the role of the ruling party's Diet liaison post extremely important. The Diet calls on the Committee on Rules and Administration to formally manage legislative operations. The LDP, however, moved the discussion forum with the opposition parties to outside the Diet when the Japan Communist Party, with a strong antigovernment stance, gained enough Diet seats for their representative to serve as an executive committee member in the late 1960s. The role of the LDP Diet policy chairman, who handles the relationship with the opposition parties outside the Diet, therefore, has grown in importance since the 1970s.[26] For this position, LDP prime ministers chose their fellow faction members or someone outside the faction who was close to them.

Although actual operations vis-à-vis the opposition parties were largely delegated to the LDP's secretary general and Diet policy chairman, the ties between the prime minister and the opposition parties helped to smooth Diet operations. Prime Minister Satô Eisaku, for example, at the end of his administration, failed to pass important bills in the Diet mainly because of the lack of communication with the opposition parties. When Tanaka Kakuei was elected to succeed Satô as LDP president, he stated at his first press conference that he would frequently hold meetings with opposition party leaders. Tanaka was proud of his channels to the opposition parties that he had built up as LDP secretary general under the Satô administration. These strong ties with opposition parties were evident in 1972 when Tanaka asked a leader of *Kômeitô* to be a special envoy to deliver Chou Enlai's message from China. His close connection with the opposition parties helped to smooth the way for further development of his China policy, and the normalization of diplomatic relations with China received approval in the Diet.

Takeshita Noboru served as vice chairman of the LDP's Diet Policy Committee for seven consecutive terms before becoming prime minister, and he used this experience in legislative operations during his administration. He not only was close to the Diet liaison members of the opposition parties but also had deep knowledge of the Diet Law and the Diet precedents.[27] This knowledge and ties to the opposition parties helped him to enact the consumption tax bill. (A case study of this significant event is discussed in Chapter 6).

SUPPORT FROM OUTSIDE THE POLITICAL WORLD

Popularity and Public Relations

The popularity of policies, politicians, and the prime minister plays an increasingly important role in Japanese politics. Public prestige alone cannot bring a politician to the post of prime minister, but for a national leader it is "strategically important to his power," as Richard E. Neustadt describes considering the situation of U.S. president.[28] A high degree of popularity helped Prime Minister Nakasone Yasuhiro pursue administrative reforms and maintain his administration for five years despite the relative lack of support from within his own party. Conversely, a low popularity rating has forced out of office even prime ministers who command a stable power base within the ruling party, such as Tanaka Kakuei and Takeshita Noboru.

The popularity of the prime minister affects his support within the party. Similar to the Japan's case, Anthony King explains the relationship between a British prime minister's popularity and his influence:

The greater a prime minister's public prestige—or, more precisely, the greater a prime minister's public prestige is thought to be by his cabinet colleagues—the greater is likely to be his capacity to bend those colleagues to his will. A prime minister thought to be leading his party to electoral disaster is likely to find that his colleagues increasingly question his judgment and are reluctant to acknowledge his authority. By contrast, a prime minister believed to be an election winner will almost certainly find that outside prestige can be translated into inside influence.[29]

This can be applied to the Japanese prime minister. His high popularity may add votes crucial to a ruling party candidate who runs a close race.[30] When the level of public support for the prime minister and his cabinet is low, Diet members of the ruling party are uneasy in running an election campaign under his leadership. This causes internal pressure within the ruling party. Such pressure erodes the leadership of the prime minister and sometimes leads to his resignation.

The prime minister, whether effective or not, is the most visible political figure. At a macro level, popular support for his administration and for him personally can affect many members of the ruling party. At a micro level, the campaign support received by individual members through the personal involvement of a popular prime minister can help their reelection effort. Especially in the 1950s and early 1960s, the prime minister's campaign visit, a show of support for a candidate, was very important because people in the countryside did not usually see famous politicians and were impressed by his visits. Because it is understood that the prime minister's time is limited, his visit in an election campaign shows that the candidate is well connected to the most powerful political figure.

However, when public support of the existing administration is weak, the prime minister's personal involvement is not welcomed by individual candidates. In April 1974, high inflation after the oil shock was still hurting the pocket books of Japanese households. Prime Minister Tanaka Kakuei and his policy of restructuring the Japanese archipelago were seen as at least partially responsible for the hyper inflation rate. An anti-LDP mood was so strong that the LDP affiliated incumbent mayor of a major Japanese city, who was running for reelection, asked the LDP not to support him in a visible manner and uninvited the prime minister to participate in his campaign. But the mayor could not totally erase his pro-LDP image, and he lost the election.[31] This is a typical example of how an economic recession can negatively affect the popularity of the prime minister in both the public eye and among his party members.

Public support for the prime minister also helps in the policy area. When Prime Minister Tanaka was trying to normalize relations with China, for example, he faced strong opposition from conservative politicians within the party who were in a position to block his policy. However, the opposition parties, big business, partisan promotional groups, and public opinion all supported the basic direction in which Tanaka was publicly committed.[32] Tanaka took advantage of the public climate and successfully normalized relations despite the opposition of right-wingers within the party.

Popular and media support again worked against Tanaka in the Lockheed scandal in which Tanaka accepted a bribe to select Lockheed planes for a major Japanese airline. Public support strongly encouraged Tanaka's successor, Prime Minister Miki Takeo, a leader of the smallest LDP faction, to uncover the scandal, despite strong opposition from within the ruling party. After failing to get the information acquired by the U.S. Congress on the Lockheed scandal through diplomatic channels, on February 23, 1976, Miki announced at a Diet meeting that he would send a request directly to President Gerald Ford asking the United States for the investigative information without first consulting any other LDP leader.[33] This upset LDP leaders outside the Miki faction. Many LDP members saw Miki's action as purely self-promoting and began forming a coalition against him.

Miki was firmly determined to pursue the scandal despite the strong reaction of his opponents in the party. He told a political critic, "I have to get this through. I must do so even if it leads to my death."[34] Despite the pressure from within the ruling party against Miki, the public and the media continued to support his efforts.[35] Because of this strong public support, the anti-Miki coalition could not force Miki out of office. One member of the anti-Miki movement recalls: "The professional political community viewed Mr. Miki as an incompetent party leader [and could have forced him out of office]. But such action might have created strong public reaction."[36] Miki himself stated: "I did not think that I would receive this much support. It is the first time in my long political life [that I have experienced this]."[37] Although the anti-Miki sentiment within the LDP forced Miki to resign after the LDP suffered a defeat in the election in December 1976, public support made it possible for him to pursue the scandal right up to his resignation. His efforts eventually resulted in the arrest of the powerful former prime minister Tanaka Kakuei.

Public support gives a prime minister strong leverage in pursuing his policies. Nakasone Yasuhiro was a prime minister who was keen on the power of public support. Administrative reform under his administration was politically difficult to pursue. The prime minister met opposition from all directions within the political circles—from within the LDP, and from the bureaucracy as well as from the opposition parties. Along with the support of the business community came strong public support. Nakasone once compared his efforts to a glider, saying, "As long as the winds of public and mass-media support continue to blow, it can fly. If the wind of support diminishes, the glider will stall and crash." Nakasone was well aware of the importance of public support and successfully maintained public attention on his administration. He eventually achieved a significant administrative reform that cut wasteful governmental spending.

Without public support, a prime minister has difficulty acquiring enough internal support to be effective, and he thus pays particular attention to public relations. As Robert C. Tucker suggests, "Whatever the system of government, people do not normally give their active support to a policy unless they are persuaded."[38] Therefore, the prime minister must communicate with the public and the media. Several prime ministers have even employed journalists in the top personal assistant post to advise them on media relations—how to use the media to build a positive public image.[39] Different prime ministers have established their public image in this way.

Prime Minister Ikeda Hayato was very active in public relations because he learned from his predecessor Kishi Nobusuke's lack of effort in achieving public understanding, and thus public support, in handling the revision of the U.S.–Japan Security Treaty in spring 1960. When Ikeda became prime minister, there was still considerable resentment, with many people believing that the government was too arrogant in making a critical national decision without listening to the voice of the people.

In an attempt to change the gloomy mood created by the turmoil to a positive one by focusing national attention on an optimistic economic policy, Ikeda introduced the "income-doubling plan" to double the national income within ten years. In October 1960, Prime Minister Ikeda dissolved the lower house. He then traveled throughout the country on the campaign trail to explain his economic policy.

Ikeda's strategy was a populist approach. Journalist Watanabe Tsuneo recalls Ikeda's campaign: "Ikeda was illustrating prices of tofu as well as tomato, cabbage, mackerel and sardines in order to explain the income doubling policy. He avoided intellectual discussion on foreign and defense policies and tried to overlap the image of the prime minister and the housekeeping book. By doing so, he seemed to try to close the distance between the public and him, to grasp their hearts, and to win popularity."[40] Ikeda's strategy was successful. The LDP won 296 seats, the greatest number to date. The election victory was the go-ahead sign for the implementation of Ikeda's income-doubling plan. The plan doubled national income in five years, a more successful result than even the most optimistic forecast had predicted. Throughout his term, Prime Minister Ikeda enjoyed continued public support resulting from his personal public relations efforts that were enhanced by his successful economic policy.

Ikeda's successor, Satô Eisaku, did not enjoy dealing with the media nor personally promoting public support. Instead, Satô hired a journalist as his top personal assistant to handle media relations for him. The assistant remembers: "I had to devote most of my energy to keeping a fierce tiger named Satô Eisaku in his cage. Fortunately, with the support of friends from my journalism days, there was no major trouble with the media during much of his term."[41] However, during the course of Satô's long administration, criticism did arise in the media. Especially when the newspapers strongly attacked, Satô began openly expressing his dislike of the press. In his final act as prime minister, he held a press conference to announce his resignation and requested that all newspaper reporters leave the conference room. His ex-journalist assistant lamented: "The tiger regained its wild nature, broke the cage rather effortlessly, and roared on the free land."[42]

After seeing Satô's troubled relationship with the press, the new prime minister Tanaka Kakuei stated at his first press meeting that he would respect the media, since avoiding the media would lead to "closed door" politics. The media welcomed his statement and portrayed this youngest-ever prime minister who had no formal higher education as a success story. The public also felt close to him; the Tanaka cabinet received the highest approval record to date just two months into its term.[43]

Tanaka had considerable influence over the television stations and their affiliated newspaper companies. When Tanaka was minister of posts and communications, he issued broadcasting licenses for major newspaper companies, permitting them to open television stations. As prime minister, he took advan-

Figure 4.1
Support Rate for the Tanaka Cabinet (Jul 1972–Dec 1974)

Source: Asahi Shimbun, October 23, 1991

tage of these connections, by reportedly threatening journalists covering him not to write negative reports on him.[44] Although Tanaka was confident of his control over the media, his financial scandal was exposed by media coverage. The story first broke, not in a newspaper or in television coverage, but in a magazine article not affiliated with those under his influence.

Tanaka experienced a significant decline in public support. Upon assuming office, he enjoyed a high popularity rating. Backed by public support, he successfully normalized relations with China. Then the oil shock hit Japan. Tanaka's popularity declined with the public feeling that his economic policy was exacerbating hyper inflation. The financial scandal further lowered his popularity, which forced him out of office (see Figure 4.1).

Miki Takeo, with a weak support base from within the party, tried to maximize his political power by strategically using the mass media. Miki's media advisor notes how much attention Miki paid to television appearances: "Mr. Miki was very picky about his TV appearances. He strongly requested to appear on television stations at 8:30 P.M. [the time of the highest viewing rate among an adult audience]. Prime Minister Miki even requested interviewers whom he liked."[45] Miki's usage of the media proved effective, and public support jumped (see Figure 4.2). This helped the prime minister pursue the Lockheed scandal incident. Although the anti-Miki coalition was a huge majority, it could not force Miki out of office until the LDP's defeat six months later in the November 1976 election.

Nakasone Yasuhiro was also a prime minister who attempted to maximize the effect of public relations. He became famous for his "performances." Nakasone himself said at an LDP seminar: "I have made performances acceptable to the new generation, which is growing in size. Since today is a visual age,

Figure 4.2
Support Rate for the Miki Cabinet (Dec 1974–Dec 1976)

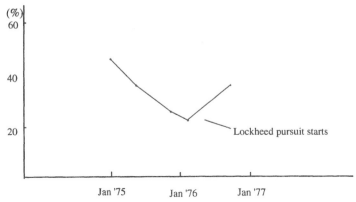

Source: *Asahi Shimbun*, October 23, 1991

the image of a party leader is important."[46] On April 9, 1985, Nakasone held a television conference to discuss his external economic policies. The conference was unique in that Nakasone used extensive graphs to explain exports and imports, and he appealed to the public to buy more imported goods. His performance was well received by the foreign community, especially the United States. Two weeks later, the prime minister visited a department store in downtown Tokyo and bought imported goods—an event carried by the mass media worldwide.

Nakasone relied on public relations to pursue his policies. One area Nakasone emphasized was the creation of an internationalist image. In his first visit to the United States in January 1983, Nakasone at a joint press conference with President Ronald Reagan made a brief statement in English. Although he made several obvious mistakes, his effort to communicate directly with Americans was well received. Four months later, at the Williamsburg summit in May 1983, Nakasone aggressively supported President Reagan's effort to unite the Western countries against the Soviet Union. At a photograph session with G-7 leaders, Nakasone stood next to Reagan, a move significant to the Japanese people because it indicated equality. This situation was a fresh surprise for the Japanese people, who were used to seeing their leader standing at the end of the lineup.[47] The photograph and the news report that described Nakasone's effort at the summit established a public image of Nakasone as a leader in the international community. In a survey by *Mainichi Shimbun*, the approval rate for the Nakasone cabinet increased to 40 percent. The prime reason for this support was his foreign policy stance.[48] His cabinet approval rate rose further as Nakasone established his international image. A survey by a public television network, *Nihon Hôsô Kyôkai* (NHK) in September 1985, for example, recorded 65.7 percent

Figure 4.3
Support Rate for the Hosokawa Cabinet (Aug 1993–April 1994)

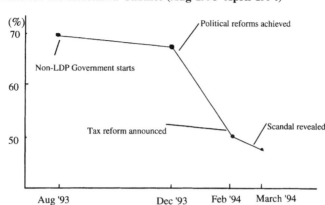

Source: Nihon Keizai Shimbun, March 29, 1994

approval rate for the Nakasone cabinet. This public support helped Nakasone to promote his efforts to internationalize the Japanese economy, namely, his action plan to lower tariffs on many different products.

Another prime minister who paid special attention to public relations is Hosokawa Morihiro, the first non-LDP politician to reach the premiership since 1955 when the LDP first took control. After unprecedented deliberations, Hosokawa emerged as the leader of a fragile coalition of eight different political groups. For Hosokawa, who represented only the fourth largest political group among the eight, it was essential to capture and maintain public support in order to pass a package of political reforms. Hosokawa emphasized the need for change and tried to create a different image by taking off his Diet member pin and handling, by himself, questions at press conferences. The Japanese public liked the new leadership style, and the public support rate for the Hosokawa cabinet soared to 70 percent at the beginning of his term, the highest level recorded by a single cabinet in postwar history.

Although Hosokawa's popularity significantly helped to achieve political reforms, the eventual decline in popularity over the course of eight months significantly weakened the prime minister's political power and eventually led to his resignation (see Figure 4.3). Hosokawa's public support significantly declined with the abrupt announcement of an unpopular proposal to raise the consumption tax. Later, in March 1994, the LDP persistently attacked Prime Minister Hosokawa in the Diet, citing his financial scandals. These attacks held up any deliberations on the government budget proposal. Hosokawa's popularity further declined as these scandals were revealed. Surprising many, on April 8 Prime Minister Hosokawa announced his resignation in order to take responsibility for the political disaster.

As noted, popularity can help, but it alone cannot achieve policies. Prime Minister Kaifu Toshiki, for example, maintained a high public support rate for his cabinet throughout his administration. In the aftermath of the Recruit scandal, in which an ambitious business owner gave many senior LDP leaders his company's unlisted stocks in order to acquire favorable treatment for his corporate group, the LDP appointed to the premiership a man with an "untainted, clean" image—Kaifu. The public, who were fed up with the scandal, welcomed the young, fresh national leader. He enjoyed a high level of popular support, with an approval rate that soared to 63 percent during 1990. But Kaifu did not take advantage of his personal popularity in pursuing his policies.

Prime Minister Kaifu managed to run the government until an emergency revealed his inexperience. When Saddam Hussein invaded Kuwait on August 2, 1990, Kaifu failed to identify the incident as a crisis. His failure to make a decision created delays in the Japanese government's response, and this drew both domestic and international criticism. To contribute to the multinational forces in the Gulf crisis, the Kaifu cabinet eventually introduced legislation that included the dispatch of the Self Defense Forces overseas. At the Diet debate in October 1990, however, the ideologically dovish prime minister denied the possibility that the Self Defense Force might be put in combat situations. When the opposition parties found that the wording of the bill would indeed allow the Self Defense Force to engage in combat, they accused the prime minister of misleading them and forced the LDP to withdraw the bill.

Kaifu, who had become prime minister because the leading candidates had been involved in scandals, had repeatedly stated that as the last effort for his administration, he would stake the life of his cabinet on reforming the electoral and campaign finance systems. This reform was highly encouraged by a public tired of corruption. When the opposition within the ruling party brought an end to the reform bills, Kaifu expressed the possibility of dissolution of the lower house. However, his supporters within the ruling party did not favor such an action. Kaifu had to give up on the dissolution. Three weeks later, despite his high popularity he announced his resignation.

To summarize, as a result of his mishandling of various political issues, an inexperienced national leader upset the leaders of the ruling party. Despite Kaifu's publicly popular image, his poor reputation in the political community was responsible for his ouster. Kaifu failed to utilize his popular support to develop support within the ruling party.

In general, public support has grown in importance to the political survival of prime ministers. As seen in the case of Tanaka Kakuei and the oil shock, bad economic conditions may negate the popularity of the national leader. In contrast, the high economic growth created by Ikeda Hayato's policy significantly helped him to maintain stability, allowing him to run the government. Further, scandals involving the prime minister or the ruling party often erode the popularity of the prime minister, whereas a clean image, in contrast, helps build public support, as in the cases of Miki Takeo and Kaifu Toshiki.

As public support became more important to their tenure and pursuit of their policies, prime ministers sought to establish better relations with the media. Media coverage creates momentum for many political activities. When the media is supportive of the prime minister's policies, it is more difficult for his political rivals in the ruling party and in the opposition parties to openly attack him. For prime ministers with weaker party control, such as Miki Takeo and Nakasone Yasuhiro, public support was one of their most powerful tools. An effective prime minister knows how to maximize the impact of public relations in his favor.

Brain Trust

Regardless of whether the prime minister is publicly popular, he is "a very isolated individual. Many officials in the government are afraid of taking responsibility for policy making, and hesitant to make recommendations to him," says a former advisor to Prime Minister Nakasone Yasuhiro.[49] The prime minister continuously faces a series of issues for which he must formulate a decision. Former prime minister Fukuda Takeo states: "I can say that [being prime minister] is to face continuous decisions. Among many different alternatives for the nation, he chooses what he thinks is best. To not make mistakes in such decisions is probably what all prime ministers desire the most strongly."[50] Prime ministers select a group of private advisors or a brain trust to ease such pressures.

Even Prime Minister Yoshida Shigeru, who is often portrayed as an autocratic leader, called on a long-time friend (a business leader) and a political critic for policy advice. Their role as advisors, however, was unofficial and limited to behind-the-scenes contact.[51]

Ikeda Hayato had a more organized brain trust that helped develop his income-doubling policy. His policy study group was formed two years before he became prime minister for this specific purpose. Most members of the study group were ex-bureaucrats from the Finance Ministry who worked under Ikeda when he was finance minister. They provided a theoretical base for the economic policy. Ikeda depended totally on this group for policy development.[52]

Whereas Ikeda's advisors were mostly bureaucrats, Ikeda's successor, Prime Minister Satô Eisaku, used many scholars as advisors. Prior to Satô's taking office, his assistant formed a private task force to formulate policies and invited journalists, scholars, and bureaucrats to this team.[53] When Satô became prime minister, he formed official advisory councils on the Okinawa and the China issues, which helped him to formulate his foreign policy.

Prime Minister Ôhira Masayoshi was the first prime minister to use advisory groups extensively. Ôhira created the posts of special assistants to the prime minister and recruited three bureaucrats to administer nine study groups comprising 219 advisors: 130 scholars and intellectuals and 89 senior bureaucrats. The nine groups covered the following topics: (1) culture; (2) city planning; (3) family; (4) the Pacific Basin; (5) comprehensive national security; (6) external

economic policy; (7) economic policy; (8) science and technology; and (9) life-
style.[54] One of the three assistants recalls, "Despite his busy schedule, he attended the study group meetings so often that people around him complained
to me. Mr. Ôhira really enjoyed talking with the members of these groups."[55]
Ôhira's study groups were charged with providing long-term goals for the nation
instead of advising on immediate policy. The goals were to be presented in a
series of reports culminating in one overall report. As Ôhira's assistant describes:
"Mr. Ôhira asked me to recruit younger leaders, mainly in the 35 to 45 age
range, who would be alive at the turn of the century. He did not think change
could happen during his term as premier. What he wanted to do was to maximize
the potential for the next generation."[56] However, Ôhira died before the final
report was published.

Nakasone Yasuhiro carefully read the Ôhira's study groups' final report. He
recognized the usefulness of such advisory groups, and many of Ôhira's advisors
were invited to join Nakasone's advisory councils. As a cabinet member in
charge of administrative reform under the Suzuki Zenkô administration, Nakasone formed the Second Ad Hoc Committee on Administrative Reform (Rinchô).
He appointed an elderly, charismatic business leader, former Keidanren chairman Dokô Toshio, to head the committee and staffed it with his private advisors
as expert members.[57] After succeeding Suzuki as prime minister, Nakasone gave
administrative reform the highest policy priority. With the recommendation of
Dokô's committee, he successfully privatized the three largest public corporations (see Chapter 5 for details). Several other advisory councils spanning a
variety of policy areas were formed; indeed, advisory councils became the center
of Nakasone's leadership style.[58]

Advisory councils were not new to the Japanese government, which had more
than 200 advisory councils. However, many of these were used by ministries to
justify their own policy initiatives, and selection of the members as well as the
agenda for meetings was often strongly controlled by the relevant ministry.[59]

Nakasone developed a new strategy for setting up advisory committees by
having them report directly to the prime minister to combat the power of the
entrenched bureaucracy and their patron zoku members.[60] Nakasone used the
committees to effectively identify existing problems and to raise public interest
in the issues. If the public strongly supported an advisory council's recommendations, it would be difficult for the sectional interests within the ruling party
and government to oppose them. Nakasone was fully aware of the importance
of public support. In a show of commitment to the Advisory Council on International Economic Cooperation, Nakasone attended 11 out of 13 of their break-
fast meetings. Media coverage increased because of the prime minister's
attendance, and so did public attention. This made government agencies recognize the importance of the council's recommendations. Nakasone effectively
used public support as leverage to implement policies opposed by the sectional
interests within the government.

More recently, Obuchi Keizô made his first policy priority economic recovery and set an advisory council in August 1998. This council, the Economic Strategy Council, was chaired by Higuchi Hirotarô, Chairman of Asahi Beer, and composed of four scholars and six business leaders. As the prime minister admitted himself, his own expertise in economic policy was limited. Thus, he needed an advisory body. The Economic Strategy Council produced a timely proposal to recover and restructure the Japanese economy.

Support from the Business Community

Business leaders have played an important role in the tenure of all postwar prime ministers as advisors and fund-raisers. In prewar Japanese politics, the so-called *zaibatsu* (business families) were official financial sponsors to political parties. Two of the largest business families, Mitsui and Mitsubishi, supported two major prewar political parties.[61] However, after the war, *zaibatsu* groups were broken up by order of the American Occupation authorities in an attempt to diffuse the money and power inherent in the *zaibatsu* and the political world. When official sponsorship by business leaders ended, business leaders and the political world developed relationships at the personal level.

Yoshida Shigeru enjoyed a long-time friendship with a business leader who not only helped with fund-raising for the Yoshida faction in the Liberal Party but also advised Yoshida on issues such as cabinet appointments.[62] For example, upon his recommendation Yoshida appointed Ikeda Hayato, a then-freshman politician, to the prestigious post of finance minister.[63]

The business connection of the Yoshida administration, however, led to the revelation of bribery in what is known as the Shipbuilding scandal—a bribery case in which shipbuilders attempted to influence government allocation of subsidies for ship construction plans. Shipping companies, which received government subsidies at that time, were not allowed by law to make political contributions, but the intimate relationship with Prime Minister Yoshida led companies to think they could influence the government through bribery. The largest-ever investigation was organized, involving 40 public prosecutors with 100 staffers to investigate more than 1,000 people. Public resentment came to a head when Yoshida directed the justice minister to block the investigation, thus blocking the arrest of his party's secretary general, Satô Eisaku. Business leaders repeatedly requested the resignation of Yoshida in order to regain public trust.[64]

Yoshida complied, and Hatoyama Ichirô became prime minister in December 1954. In the next month, *Keidanren* vice chairman Uemura Kôgorô and other business leaders, concerned that other financial contribution cases of corruption might arise, established the *Keizai Saiken Kondankai* (Economic Reconstruction Forum) as the official, unified channel for political contributions from the business community. Uemura persuaded other business leaders to support its formation: "The conservative party is a prodigal son, but the only son. We must support him for his survival."[65] In the words of a *Keidanren* official, such constant contributions were "an insurance fee to maintain a free economy," which the LDP was committed to sustaining.[66] By establishing such channels, business leaders attempted to avoid any direct financial connection between individual corporations and politicians that might lead to another scandal.

Prime Minister Hatoyama, however, did not receive support from mainstream business leaders for his policy of normalizing relations with the Soviet Union. The national leader, who was confined to a wheelchair, was pursuing this policy with the assistance of Kôno Ichitrô, whom many business leaders distrusted. In September 1955, representatives of the top four business organizations urged the LDP to change its leader, thereby indirectly calling for the resignation of Hatoyama.[67] Although Hatoyama was persistent in his efforts and successfully normalized relations with the Soviet Union, pressure from the business community significantly contributed to his resignation two months after normalization.

Good relations with the business community can, in contrast, contribute to a stronger premiership, as in the case of Ikeda Hayato. He served as finance and MITI minister for long periods, developing close ties with the financial circle and the heavy industry sector. As prime minister, he was able to call on powerful business leaders to serve as advisors.[68] These business leaders supported the formation in 1957 of a group within the ruling party called *Kôchikai*, the first institutionalized LDP faction. Ikeda's assistant explains: "*Kôchikai* was a group formed in order to make Ikeda the prime minister. Before the establishment of the group, fund-raising was a big hassle, with Ikeda raising funds alone. But after this group was formed, a group of business leaders regularly contributed political funds."[69] Even after Ikeda's death, this group maintained the close ties with big business developed by Ikeda.

Even though Prime Minister Ikeda had personal ties with the business community, he faced dissatisfaction concerning the Economic Reconstruction Forum from business leaders who felt that the forum misused money for factional purposes. Further, the organization was widely perceived as a symbol of an intimate relationship between the LDP and business.[70] The forum was abolished in March 1961. To fill the fund-raising void, the LDP established an affiliate organization, the *Kokumin Kyôkai*, to oversee fund-raising as well as public relations functions. The original plan was to raise contributions from individuals and corporations. But individual contributions were limited, and the *Keidanren* eventually absorbed most of the actual operations of collecting corporate funds for the *Kokumin Kyôkai*.

During his 1964 campaign, Prime Minister Satô Eisaku received support from the business community. Satô, nearly arrested over the shipbuilding scandal, was cautious to promote close relations with business leaders. One business leader describes Satô's relationship with the business community: "Mr. Satô looked down on us. He did not feel the necessity of cultivating ties with business leaders who sincerely consider and recommend national policies."[71]

At the end of the Satô administration, however, business leaders began to criticize the prime minister. Whereas the international community shifted its China policy in 1971—for example, the announcement of Nixon's Peking visit and the United Nations' invitation to Peking for membership—the Satô administration did not change its traditional pro-Taiwan stance. Japanese business leaders in favor of normalizing Japan-China relations formed a mission to visit Peking in November 1971 in an attempt to advance the normalization process.[72] When Nixon visited Peking in February 1972, pro-China business leaders openly expressed their hope for subsequent normalization of Japan-China relations and called for a new leader in Japan who would support this stance. Four months later, Satô resigned as prime minister, thus dismantling the pro-Taiwan administration.[73]

When Tanaka Kakuei succeeded Satô, business leaders were divided in his favor. Many mainstream leaders saw Tanaka, with his unusual background, as an unpredictable national leader. Other business leaders, such as Nakayama Sohei of the Industrial Bank of Japan, were impressed by Tanaka's political skill in handling issues when he was finance and MITI minister, and viewed his vitality as potentially useful in the rapidly changing world situation after the Nixon shock. Nakayama stated in an interview: "Ex-bureaucrat politicians tend to think within the conceptual framework of bureaucrats and often lack flexibility. At that time, in order to handle problems existing in the changing world, Mr. Tanaka's flexibility was needed."[74]

Tanaka's vigorous political style enabled the normalization of relations with China, a move supported by the business community, but his economic policy exacerbated an already rising inflation rate. The *Keidanren* contributed an unusually large sum of 26 billion yen to the LDP.[75] Tanaka used it for the upper house election campaign of 1974 in which the LDP barely maintained a majority. After this election, Tanaka's use of excessive monies in the campaign received heavy criticism. In August 1974, the *Keidanren* chairman told Tanaka that his organization would not help with further fund-raising efforts for the LDP unless Tanaka would work toward political reform. All the electric power companies and four major gas supply companies declared that they too would no longer make political contributions to the LDP.[76] In the fall, even business leaders who had supported Tanaka publicly urged him to resign. In the midst of mounting criticism against the prime minister, a magazine article illustrating his financial wrongdoing was published in October and precipitated Tanaka's resignation the next month.

Miki Takeo's clean image helped him to be chosen to succeed Tanaka. In December 1974, several weeks after his administration began, Miki announced his proposal for revising the Political Fund Control Law to include the abolishment of any corporate political contributions in three years' time. This clause met with strong objection from within the LDP and was removed from the bill submitted to the Diet. In July 1975, however, the final bill passed the Diet to limit the amount of political contributions and to require the registration of large-sized contributions.[77]

Miki did not have strong ties with the business community. One of his major policy goals was to revise the Anti-Trust Law, which would restrict the business activities of large corporations. Business leaders were upset, and *Keidanren's* chairman Dokô Toshio openly criticized the prime minister.[78] Although the bill passed the lower house in June 1975, it later died in the upper house. When Miki had difficulty raising funds for the election campaign of December 1976, business leaders gave him no assistance. Major banks refused to loan money to the LDP under Miki's leadership. Partly because of the lack of funds, the LDP lost the election, which forced Miki's resignation.[79]

Strong support and opposition by mainstream business leaders influence policy outcomes. In 1979, Prime Minister Ôhira Masayoshi announced his intention to introduce a general consumption tax. *Keidanren* chairman Dokô publicly criticized Ôhira's tax policy: "Increase taxes after achieving administrative reform. I will not accept any tax increase before then."[80] The public echoed Dokô. With such increased pressure, the prime minister had to withdraw his tax proposal.

Prime Minister Hosokawa Morihiro, though not working in a traditional LDP-led postwar government, appointed a prominent business leader, *Keidanren* chairman Hiraiwa Gaishi, to chair his advisory council on Japan's economic restructuring in 1993. Hosokawa recognized that assistance from the private sector, especially from business leaders, was essential in tackling government regulations and other red tape. Ironically, it was business leaders who ultimately pressured Hosokawa to resign the premier post. When the Diet session became chaotic with the accusation of Hosokawa's financial wrongdoing, Hiraiwa and Nakayama Sohei, one of the most senior business leaders, as well as Yotsumoto Yoshitaka, who claimed to be Hosokawa's close advisor, met with the prime minister. They advised Hosokawa "how to prepare for resignation."[81] Two days later, Hosokawa suddenly announced he would resign.

More recently, when Prime Minister Hashimoto Ryûtarô tried to promote administrative reform, the business community showed full support. As he faced strong opposition from within the LDP, the business leaders formed "The Committee of 100 Supporters" to publicly encourage the prime minister. This group eventually expanded to become "The Committee of 500 Supporters." However, when Hashimoto's economic policy failed to recover the economy, criticism against him rose within this same business community. Tsutsumi Seiji, chairman of the Political Affairs Committee of *Keizai Dôyûkai*, openly commented in April 1998 that the prime minister should resign in order to refresh the nation's economic policy. A few months later, voters expressed frustration with the government's handling of the economy in the upper house election, leading to Hashimoto's resignation.

The business community has long served as fund-raiser and advisor to postwar prime ministers. For example, its support was influential in major policy changes such as Tanaka's China policy. Its withdrawal of support often led to the demise of several prime ministers. Under the non-LDP Hosokawa administration, the

Political Fund Control Law was revised to provide political parties with public money of some 30 billion yen per annum, and the *Keidanren* announced that it would no longer collect corporate funds for any political party. As a result, the dependence on the business community for political funds significantly decreased. Okano Tadashi, a staff member of *Keizai Dôyûkai*, observes the recent changes in relations between politics and business: "Even as the financial dependence on the business community decreased, the business leaders can be helpful to the political community. As Japan's economy faces significant structural changes, the government needs advice from those who know the market."[82] It is likely that Japanese business leaders will remain vocal and visible in the public to support or criticize government policies.

Support from the United States

Another group prime ministers are often willing to listen to are Americans. Bilateral relations with the United States are Japan's most important foreign dealing. Japanese political leaders are quite sensitive about their American reception. Most prime ministers choose the United States as the destination of their first overseas visit. These visits are important in creating the image of the prime minister as well as for their symbolic political ceremony.

Some prime ministers have developed personal relationships with U.S. presidents, and these ties have become political assets at home. For a prime minister with close ties to world leaders, the ties can help to keep him in his post: As in the case of Kaifu Toshiki, the LDP was hesitant to replace him because he had developed good relations with American leaders at a time when important bilateral issues were on the table.

Under the American Occupation in the immediate postwar period, U.S. support was a must for the prime minister. Japan's prime ministers were chosen largely on the basis of their ability to negotiate with the Occupation authorities and to be accepted by the Americans. Prime Ministers Shidehara Kijûrô, Ashida Hitoshi, and Yoshida Shigeru were ex-diplomats with liberal ideas who had acted against the Japanese military in the prewar period or during the war.

Yoshida, who led the longest reign in the Occupation era, is often referred to in magazine articles as the most respected postwar prime minister primarily because of his relationship with the United States. Yoshida was disliked by some Occupation officials but he was liked by General Douglas MacArthur. He spoke with Americans in a straightforward manner and did not always obey the powerful Occupation authorities; yet he stayed in MacArthur's favor, allowing him to remain effective. For example, Yoshida strongly rejected the American request for Japan's rearmament, and he won MacArthur's support and understanding. His ability to resist the Americans was the primary source of his popularity and power within the party.[83]

Kishi Nobusuke was the first prime minister to visit the United States and was warmly welcomed by President Dwight D. Eisenhower. On that tour, Kishi successfully acquired U.S. support for Japan's membership in the United Nations Economic Council, for which Japan's Foreign Ministry had been hesitant to ask.[84] This was an especially important victory for Kishi, who had been the minister of commerce and industry in the wartime cabinet and had been labeled a war criminal after the war. His successful trip demonstrated, in a sense, approval by the U.S. government and helped enhance his image, softening his image as a war criminal.

For the United States, the growth of Japan's economy and subsequent social stability meant a more dependable ally in an unstable East Asia. When Ikeda Hayato visited the United States in June 1961, the first civilian American ambassador to Japan, Edwin O. Reischauer, saw the importance of Japan for his nation and was helpful to Ikeda. The ambassador suggested a concept of "equal partnership" instead of an alliance that might have disturbed Japanese sensitivity concerning military affairs. Both Prime Minister Ikeda and President John F. Kennedy picked up Reischauer's term and confirmed close relations between the two countries. During the same trip, Ikeda successfully persuaded the U.S. government to recognize Japan's potential sovereignty over Okinawa. Ikeda proved his ability in diplomacy and gained confidence as a national leader.[85]

Conversely, poor relations with the U.S. government can force a Japanese prime minister out of office. After the 1981 summit talk between Prime Minister Suzuki Zenkô and President Ronald Reagan, a joint statement was released. Prenegotiated by diplomatic officers, the statement included the word "alliance" for the first time in a joint statement between the two nations. In an attempt to deny that the use of the word implied Japan's newly increased military role, Suzuki at a press conference and again in a Diet committee meeting repeated that "alliance" did not connote a military component for Japan.[86] After Suzuki's statement, the foreign vice minister commented to reporters that an alliance without a military context would make no sense, especially with the security pact between the two countries. This was a rare occasion in which a high government official publicly criticized a prime minister. The foreign minister fully supported the top foreign service officer. The media widely reported this incident as a case of a disagreement within the cabinet. After Suzuki denounced the Foreign Ministry at the cabinet meeting, the minister and the vice minister of foreign affairs submitted their resignations to the prime minister as a form of protest.

Their resignations were not the end of the story. A new foreign minister commented to reporters in the Philippines that the U.S.–Japan joint statement lacked the legal binding of a treaty. Kishi Nobusuke, the former prime minister who had sacrificed his administration to revise the U.S.–Japan Security Treaty, was very disappointed in Suzuki. Under fear of worsening relations with the United States, Kishi and his faction followers began an anti-Suzuki movement. This led to the resignation of Suzuki.[87]

Suzuki's successor, Nakasone Yasuhiro, quickly moved to improve relations with the United States. However, his first overseas trip was to South Korea.

Japan had an unresolved problem with South Korea over Japan's economic assistance to the country. Nakasone, who saw bad relations between the two countries as a concern for the United States as well, decided to resolve that problem with a visit first to Korea.[88] When Nakasone visited the United States in January 1983, President Ronald Reagan welcomed Nakasone by recognizing that he had improved Japan-Korea relations, allowed military technology transfers to the United States, expanded the defense budget for the 1983 fiscal year, and opened the market for American chocolates and cigarettes. Nakasone successfully built a personal relationship with the U.S. president, which the media portrayed as the "Ron-Yasu relationship."

Four months later in May 1983 at the Williamsburg summit, Nakasone aggressively supported Reagan's policy of deploying intermediate nuclear forces in Europe as a counter to the Soviet Union's missile buildup in the region. This gave many Japanese the feeling that Nakasone was a world leader. After the summit meeting, the rate of support for the Nakasone cabinet rose from 34 percent to 40 percent, an even higher rate than Nakasone had boasted when entering office.[89]

A close personal relationship between Reagan and Nakasone brought a certain stability to bilateral relations. Although the mid-1980s saw many economic and trade problems between the two countries, the personal relationship at the top level minimized the damage from disputes that could have otherwise been devastating. Nakasone had 12 meetings with the U.S. president during his five year tenure, more meetings than held by any postwar prime minister.[90] This relationship was an effective tool for Nakasone in gaining support at home, particularly public support.

Prime Minister Kaifu Toshiki enjoyed friendly relations with President George Bush and had frequent phone conversations during the 1991 Gulf War, a conflict that required close cooperation between the two countries as well as among Western nations. Some LDP members viewed the early attempt to remove Kaifu from office as a move against the interest of the Bush administration, and therefore the attempt was abandoned.[91]

When the Socialist leader Murayama Tomiichi was elected as prime minister by a coalition of the LDP, the Socialist Party, and *Sakigake*, many Japanese as well as Americans were caught by surprise. American officials did not even know if Japan's new leader would be able to depart from the traditional Socialist stance against the will of many other Socialist members to support the U.S.–Japan alliance and Japan's Self Defense Forces.

Murayama was eager to remove such American anxiety. An opportunity to do so came within his first ten days in power when he attended the G-7 economic summit in Naples. In his memoir, Murayama confesses that he was very nervous about whether or not he could reach a basic understanding with President Clinton. At the summit meeting with the American leader, Murayama opened the conversation by asserting that he was committed to maintaining Japan's established foreign policy and firmly supported the bilateral security ties. Further, he was committed to promoting the democratic political process. Clinton expressed his satisfaction with Murayama's statements.[92] At a press conference Murayama and Clinton affirmed the need to proceed with the framework trade talks. Murayama thus successfully completed his first major international mission.

As described in Chapter 2, Murayama's commitment to support the U.S.–Japan Security Treaty and the Self Defense Forces was firm. In accordance with his promise to President Clinton, the Socialist prime minister officially declared in the Diet that the Self Defense Forces were constitutional. At the national convention of the Socialist Party in September 1994, Murayama successfully defended his decision. In the end, the party approved this "historical policy shift."

Support from the United States is a valuable asset for the prime minister. In the immediate postwar period, ties with American authority were essential for the prime minister. As Japan became an economic power and the Cold War ended, Japan became less dependent on the United States. At the same time, however, Japan's role in the international community increased, keeping the prime minister's ability to communicate with Japan's most important ally valuable.

SUMMARY

Because the prime minister's legal authority is limited, he relies on other sources of power for his leadership credentials. His effectiveness as a national leader depends largely on his support base within the ruling party or coalition. Under either an LDP-led government or a coalition government, the prime minister's control over the ruling party has been relatively weak as a result of its loose organization. Decentralization of power within the party in the 1970s further weakened party leadership under the LDP government. A prime minister with weak control needs a process of consensus building in order not to disturb harmony within the ruling party. In the process, numbers play a significant role. The prime minister needs to receive support from a majority of the ruling party to operate his policies smoothly. The larger his group, the easier it is to formulate a consensus to support his policy. He can use his fellow faction or party members to actively persuade other members.

The prime minister's effectiveness as a leader also depends on his experiences and accomplishments before assuming office. His administrative skill in controlling the bureaucracy is a crucial determinant of how successfully he can pursue his policies. By cooperating with the bureaucracy, the prime minister, even with a very small Cabinet Secretariat, can act on policy decisions. A policy made within the government then has to go through the legislative process. The prime minister's relationship with the opposition parties, which is usually established before his becoming prime minister, can become a decisive factor in his ability to enact policy smoothly.

Informal sources of power for the prime minister are not limited to the political circle. Popularity has become increasingly important for the effectiveness of his leadership. Members of both the ruling party and the opposition parties find it difficult to openly attack a popular prime minister's policies that the public strongly supports. At the same time, ruling party Diet members are reluctant to run their own elections under a publicly unpopular party leader, for the lack of public support may force him out of office.

To improve their public support base, prime ministers have put energy into public relations activities. Miki Takeo and Nakasone Yasuhiro are among the prime ministers who effectively used the mass media. In the television age, a major part of public image is formulated by his appearance and eloquence on the air. Even the spoken word is now analyzed in the written media and replayed on the networks. Slips of the tongue do not go unnoticed and may erode a prime minister's leadership. Yoshida Shigeru, for example, was forced to dissolve the lower house because of an improper remark made in the Diet. Nakasone ruined his own internationalist image by making a statement with racial connotations. Because the media and the public pay close attention to each word of the national leader, his ability to deliver his message without creating misunderstanding or leading to misconstrued meanings is essential to building and maintaining public support.

Support from the business community and the United States does not necessarily play an important role in the selection of a prime minister, but once the prime minister takes office, their support is important in maintaining the stability of his administration. In the same light, their disapproval can lead to his resignation. Yoshida Shigeru, Hatoyama Ichirô, Tanaka Kakuei, and Miki Takeo left office soon after the business community requested their resignation. Suzuki Zenkô's poor handling of relations with the United States led to the anti-Suzuki movement within the party, which resulted in his resignation.

In short, various factors affect the leadership of the prime minister. The prime minister can supplement his institutional power with personal power and his status as a leader of the ruling party. His ability to do so determines his effectiveness as a national leader. The following three chapters will analyze how very different prime ministers—Suzuki Zenkô, Nakasone Yasuhiro, Takeshita Noboru, and Hashimoto Ryûtarô—utilized or failed to utilize their sources of power in pursuing major economic policies.

NOTES

1. Haruhiro Fukui, *Party in Power* (Berkeley: University of California Press, 1970), pp 95–96.

2. The post of the LDP secretary general was considered a crucial step toward the premiership. All ten prime ministers from Kishi Nobusuke to Takeshita Noboru (1957–89) had held the secretary general post of the ruling party, with one exception—Suzuki Zenkô, who unexpectedly became LDP president after the sudden death of Ôhira Ma-

sayoshi. In other words, this was the best position for an LDP member to develop his political skill, experience, ties with other factions and parties, and political resources.

3. Nakamura Keiichirô, *Miki Seiken 747 nichi* [The Miki administration: 747 days] (Tokyo: Gyôsei Mondai Kenkyû-sho, 1981), p. 49.

4. Nakamura Keiichirô, interview by author, Tokyo, December 17, 1992.

5. Nakamura, *Miki Seiken*, pp. 63–70.

6. Asahi Shimbun Seiji-bu, *Takeshita-ha Shihai* [The control by the Takeshita faction] (Tokyo: Asahi Shimbun-sha, 1992), pp. 177–78.

7. Gotôda Masaharu, interview by author, Tokyo, December 15, 1992.

8. Miyawaki Raisuke, interview by author, Washington, D.C., December 9, 1992.

9. Konaga Keiichi, interview by author, Tokyo, December 14, 1992.

10. Kusuda Minoru, *Shuseki Hishokan: Satô Sôri tono Jûnenkan* [Chief secretary: Ten years with Prime Minister Satô] (Tokyo: Bungei Shunjû, 1975), p. 43.

11. Kent Calder views Fukuda Takeo as a typical ex-bureaucrat prime minister who took advantage of his experience at the Ministry of Finance to achieve financial policies. Kent E. Calder, "Kanryô vs. Shomin: Contrasting Dynamics of Conservative Leadership in Postwar Japan," in *Michigan Papers in Japanese Studies No. 1: Political Leadership in Contemporary Japan*, ed. Terry Edward MacDougall (Ann Arbor: Center for Japanese Studies, University of Michigan, 1982), pp. 9–10.

12. See Kôsaka Masataka, *Saishô Yoshida Shigeru* [Prime Minister Yoshida Shigeru] (Tokyo: Chûô Kôron-sha, 1968), pp. 46–47.

13. Ohira Masayoshi, *Watashi no Rirekisho* [My personal history] (Tokyo: Nihon Keizai Shimbun-sha, 1978), p. 104.

14. Katô Hiroshi, *Nihon Keizai Jiko Henkaku no Toki* [Time for Japan to change] (Tokyo: PHP Kenkyû-sho, 1991), p. 103.

15. About 6,000 are national government-related, and 14,000–15,000 are under the jurisdiction of prefectural governments. *Nihon Keizai Shimbun* (March 4, 1991).

16. Tanaka Zen'ichirô, "Daiichiji Tanaka Naikaku" [The first Tanaka cabinet], in *Nihon Naikaku Shiroku* [The history of the Japanese cabinet], ed. Hayashi Shigeru and Tsuji Kiyoaki (Tokyo: Dai-ichi Hôki, 1981), pp. 321–12.

17. Kent Calder, "Kanryô vs. Shomin," pp. 10–11.

18. Konaga Keiichi, interview by author, Tokyo, December 14, 1992.

19. Nakamura Keiichirô, interview by author, Tokyo, December 17, 1992.

20. Ide Ichitarô, chief cabinet secretary under the Miki cabinet, interview by Suzuki Kenji, in Suzuki Kenji, *Rekidai Sôri Sokkin no Kokuhaku* [Confessions by close associates of the prime ministers] (Tokyo: Mainichi Shimbun-sha, 1991), pp. 100–102.

21. Nakamura, *Miki Seiken*, p. 107.

22. Matoba Junzô, interview by author, Tokyo, December 16, 1992. I retold this story to Justice Minister Gotôda, who listened with a nod and smile.

23. The number of cabinet bill submitted to the Diet has decreased to 100 since the late 1970s. Until the mid-1950s, it counted more than 200. Iwai Tomoaki explains the decrease as a sign of a more mature legal system. Iwai Tomoaki, *Rippô Katei* [The legislative process] (Tokyo: Tokyo Daigaku Shuppan-kai, 1988), pp. 86–89.

24. Mike Masato Mochizuki, "Managing and Influencing the Japanese Legislative Process: The Role of Parties and the National Diet" (Ph.D. dissertation, Harvard University, 1981), p. 48.

25. Iwai, *Rippô Katei*, pp. 130–31.

26. Ibid., pp. 136–39.

27. See Fujimoto Kazumi, ed., *Kokkai Kinô Ron: Kokkai no Shikumi to Un'ei* [Arguments for the functional Diet: The mechanism and operation of the Diet] (Tokyo: Hôgaku Shoin, 1990), pp. 118–20.

28. Richard E. Neustadt, *Presidential Power and the Modern Presidents: The Politics of Leadership from Roosevelt to Reagan* (New York: Free Press, 1990), p. 78.

29. Anthony King, "Margaret Thatcher: The Style of a Prime Minister," in *The British Prime Minister*, ed. Anthony King (Durham, North Carolina: Duke University Press, 1985), p. 109.

30. A 1991 study suggests that the prime minister's popularity was one of the factors that made a difference in outcome between the 1989 upper house election and the 1990 election. Kobayashi Yoshiaki, *Gendai Nihon no Senkyo* [Contemporary Japanese elections] (Tokyo: Tokyo Daigaku Shuppan-kai, 1991), pp. 141–47.

31. Nakano Shirô, *Tanaka Seiken 886 nichi* [The Tanaka administration: 886 days] (Tokyo: Gyôsei Mondai Kenkyû-sho, 1982), p. 331.

32. Haruhiro Fukui, "Tanaka Goes to Peking," *Policymaking in Contemporary Japan*, ed. T. J. Pempel (Ithaca: Cornell University Press, 1977), p. 97.

33. Nakamura, *Miki Seiken*, p. 186. Also see an interview with former chief cabinet secretary Ide Yoichirô by Suzuki Kenji, in Suzuki, *Rekidai Sôri*, pp. 111–12.

According to Nakamura Keiichirô, U.S. secretary of state Henry Kissinger was hesitant to provide information to Japan, knowing that the political impact would be tremendous to America's ally. Nakamura, pp. 184–85.

34. Miki's conversation with Fujiwara Kôtatsu quoted in Miki Mutsuko, *Shin Nakuba Tatazu: Otto Miki Takeo to no Gojûnen* [No rising without his belief: Fifty years with my husband, Miki Takeo] (Tokyo: Kôdan-sha, 1989), p. 280.

35. Miki's wife looks back: "There were enormous numbers of letters and phone calls to Miki from around the nation every day. The three phones [at the prime minister's official residence] were always ringing, and [the phone calls] were to encourage Miki with sincerity. Every day, we were moved [by such encouragement]. . . . At that time the public interest was so significant. Politics went into the average household. Everybody was observing and emotionally involved with the proceedings of the incident. I think that such energy of the people supported Miki throughout this ordeal." Ibid., p. 284.

36. Kurihara Yûkô, *Ôhira Moto Sôri to Watashi* [Former prime minister Ôhira and me] (Tokyo: Kôsai-dô, 1990), p. 52.

37. Nakamura, *Miki Seiken*, p. 230.

38. Robert C. Tucker, *Political Leadership* (Columbia: University of Missouri Press, 1981), p. 62.

39. Journalists who served as personal secretary to the prime minister include: Itô Masaya (*Nishi Nihon Shimbun*) served for Ikeda Hayato; Kusuda Minoru (*Sankei Shimbun*) for Satô Eisaku; Fumoto Kuniaki (*Kyôdô News* Service) and Hayasaka Shigeo (*Tokyo Times*) for Tanaka Kakuei; Nakamura Keiichirô (*Yomiuri Shimbun*) for Miki Takeo. Abe Shintarô, son-in-law of Kishi Nobusuke who served as a personal secretary to Kishi, was also a journalist.

40. Watanabe Tsuneo, *Habatsu to Tatôka Jidai* [Factions and the multiparty era] (Tokyo: Sekka-sha, 1967), p. 103.

41. Kusuda Minoru, ed., *Satô Seiken: 2797 nichi* [The Satô administration: 2,797 days], vol. 2 (Tokyo: Gyôsei Mondai Kenkyû-sho, 1983), p. 391.

42. Ibid.

43. According to a survey conducted by *Asahi Shimbun* at the end of August 1972,

the approval rate for the Tanaka administration was 62 percent with 10 percent disapproving.

44. Niimura Masashi, *Desk Memo 3*, 1973, pp. 245–48, quoted in Tanaka Zen'ichirô, "Daiichiji Tanaka Naikaku," pp. 240–41.

45. Nakamura Keiichirô, interview by author, Tokyo, December 17, 1992.

46. The speech took place in Karuizawa on August 30, 1986. Quoted in Maki Tarô, *Nakasone Seiken 1806 nichi* [The Nakasone administration: 1,806 days], vol. 2 (Tokyo: Gyôsei Mondai Kenkyûsho, 1988), p. 229.

47. Nakasone states in his memoirs that he did not plan to stand by Reagan. Nakasone Yasuhiro, *Seiji to Jinsei* [Politics and life] (Tokyo: Kôdansha, 1992), p. 317.

48. *Mainichi* survey announced on June 9, 1983. The second reason was his effort for administrative reform, and the third was his leadership.

49. Miyawaki Raisuke, interview by author, Washington, D.C., March 10, 1993.

50. Fukuda Takeo, interview in "Waga Shushô Jidai" [My time as the prime minister], *Chûô Kôron* (October 1980): 291–95.

51. See Sakurada Takeshi and Shikanai Nobutaka, *Ima Akasu Sengo Hishi* [The secret postwar history revealed now] (Tokyo: Sankei Shuppan, 1983), pp. 7–60.

52. Yoshimura Katsumi, *Ikeda Seiken 1575 nichi* [The Ikeda administration: 1,575 days] (Tokyo: Gyôsei Mondai Kenkyû-sho, 1985), pp. 50–51. See also Miyazawa Kiichi, *Sengo Seiji no Shôgen* [Testimony on postwar politics] (Tokyo: Yomiuri Shimbun-sha, 1991), pp. 105–10; Itô Masaya, *Ikeda Hayato Sono Sei to Shi* [Ikeda Hayato: His life and death] (Tokyo: Shiseidô, 1966), pp. 84–93.

53. Kusuda, *Shuseki Hishokan*, pp. 26–31.

54. See Nagatomi Yûichirô, *Kindai wo Koete: Ko Ôhira Sôri no Nokosareta mono* [Beyond the contemporary era: What late prime minister Ôhira left for us] (Tokyo: Ôkura Zaimu Kyôkai, 1983).

55. Nagatomi Yûichirô, interview by author, Tokyo, December 17, 1992.

56. Ibid.

57. Dokô Toshio, *Watashi no Rirekisho* [My personal history] (Tokyo: Nihon Keizai Shimbun, 1983), pp. 20–22.

58. First, Nakasone gathered his own private advisory council on culture and education in June 1983. Two months later, he formed another private advisory council, the Research Council on Peace Issues. Besides these, Nakasone brought together advisory councils on the Yasukuni shrine issue, on economic policy, on education, and on international harmonization.

59. *Keidanren* chairman Hiraiwa Gaishi complains about the existing advisory councils by saying: "Some of them are created for the ministries to protect themselves or to gain time. Since the bureaucracy is in charge of their secretariat, they manipulate advisory councils to serve for the bureaucracy." *Nihon Keizai Shimbun* (March 4, 1991).

60. Nakasone's senior assistant, Matoba Junzô states: "Mr. Nakasone used advisory councils as a way of removing the problem of sectionalism in the bureaucracy. The prime minister challenged the limitations allowed under the National Administrative Organization Law." Matoba Junzô, interview by author, Tokyo, December 16, 1992.

61. While the Mitsui House supported *Rikken Seiyûkai*, founded by Japan's first prime minister, Itô Hirobumi, the Mitsubishi House backed the *Kenseikai*. In addition to *Kenseikai*'s first president, Katô Takaaki, Mitsubishi sent their prominent members to the political world. See Haruhiro Fukui, *Party in Power*, pp. 9–31.

62. The business leader was Miyajima Seijirô, president of *Nisshinbô*.

63. Sakurada Takeshi originally introduced Ikeda to Miyajima. Itô Masaya, *Ikeda Hayato*, p. 8. See also Sakurada and Shikanai, *Ima Akasu*, pp. 33–42.

64. Uchida Kenzô, *Sengo Nihon no Hoshu Seiji* [Conservative politics in postwar Japan] (Tokyo: Iwanami Shoten, 1969), pp. 85–88. See also Masumi Junnosuke, *Sengo Seiji 1945–55 nen* [Postwar politics, 1945–55] (Tokyo: Tokyo Daigaku Shuppan, 1983), p. 431.

65. Masumi, *Sengo Seiji*, p. 437. For the discussion of the establishment of the Economic Reconstruction Forum, see Hanamura Nihachirô, *Seizaikai Paipu Yaku Hanseiki* [My life as a channel between the political and business worlds] (Tokyo: Tokyo Shimbun, 1990), pp. 83–85.

66. Hanamura, *Seizaikai Paipu Yaku Hanseiki*, p. 85.

67. Sakurada and Shikanai, *Ima Akasu*, pp. 224–41. According to Hanamura Nihachirô, *Keidanren* chairman Ishizaka Taizô visited Hatoyama's private residence and personally told Hatoyama that he should resign. Hanamura, *Seizaikai Paipu Yaku Hanseiki*, p. 97.

68. The business leaders included Kobayashi Ataru (president of the Japan Development Bank), Mizuno Shigeo (president of Sankei Shimbun), Sakurada Takeshi (president of Nisshinbô), and Nagano Shigeo (president of Fuji Steel).

69. Itô, *Ikeda Hayato*, p. 37. See also Miyazawa, *Sengo Seiji no Shôgen*, pp. 100–101.

70. Masumi Junnosuke, *Gendai Seiji 1955 nen igo* [Contemporary politics after 1955] (Tokyo: Tokyo Daigaku Shuppan, 1985), pp. 355–57. See also Fukui, *Party in Power*, pp. 146–48.

71. Sakurada and Shikanai, *Ima Akasu*, p. 198.

72. The mission included Nagano Shigeo (chairman of the Japan Chamber of Commerce) and Kikawada Kazutaka (chairman of the *Keizai Dôyûkai*).

73. Tsuda Tatsuo, *Zaikai-Nihon no Shihaisha Tachi* [The business community: The people who rule Japan] (Tokyo: Gakushû no Tomo-sha, 1990), pp. 173–82.

74. Nakayama Sohei, interview by author, Tokyo, December 15, 1992. See also interview with Nakayama Sohei, *Shûkan Asahi* (May 4, 1973), pp. 142–46.

75. Hanamura, pp. 112–14.

76. Nakano, *Tanaka Seiken*, pp. 360–61. See also Hanamura, *Seizaikai Paipu Yaku Hanseiki*, pp. 122 and 183–86.

77. See Nakamura, *Miki Seiken*, pp. 44–48 and 71–79.

78. Miki, *Shin Nakuba Tatazu*, p. 262.

79. Nakamura, *Miki Seiken*, pp. 301–9.

80. Dokô, *Watashi no Rirekisho*, pp. 18–19.

81. Nakayama Sohei, interview by author, October 24, 1996.

82. Okano Tadashi, interview by author, December 15, 1998.

83. For the discussion of Yoshida's relation with the American occupation authority, see Kôsaka, *Saishô Yoshida Shigeru*, pp. 25–33 and 234–47.

84. For Kishi's description of the visit, see Kishi Nobusuke, *Kishi Nobusuke Kaisôroku* [Memoirs of Kishi Nobusuke] (Tokyo: Kôsaido, 1983), pp. 331–37.

85. About Reischauer's account of the trip, see Edwin O. Reischauer, *My Life between Japan and America* (New York: Harper and Row, 1986), pp. 202–3. See also Miyazawa, *Sengo Seiji no Shôgen*, pp. 117–22; Yoshimura, *Ikeda Seiken*, pp. 119–30; and Itô, *Ikeda Hayato*, pp. 126–29.

86. Even Suzuki himself admits that this word usage was not well explained. Suzuki Zenkô, interview by Suzuki Kenji, in Suzuki, *Rekidai Sôri*, p. 160.

87. Uji Toshihiko, *Suzuki Seiken 863 nichi* [The Suzuki administration: 863 days] (Tokyo: Gyôsei Mondai Kenkyû-sho, 1983), pp. 170–222.

88. Nakasone admits that he planned to improve the relations with Korea for the betterment of the U.S.–Japan relations. Nakasone, *Seiji to Jinsei*, pp. 312–13. See also Gotôda Masaharu, *Naikaku Kanbô Chôkan* [Chief cabinet secretary] (Tokyo: Kôdan-sha, 1989), pp. 28–30.

89. *Mainichi Shimbun* poll on June 9, 1983. Maki, *Nakasone Seiken*, vol. 1, pp. 130–31.

90. The second are five times by Satô Eisaku, Tanaka Kakuei, and Kaifu Toshiki. Suzuki, *Rekidai Sôri*, pp. 274–90.

91. At one point, the media jokingly reported that Kaifu from the smallest LDP faction belonged to the strongest faction in the ruling party, "the Bush faction."

92. Murayama Tomiichi, "Watashi no Rirekisho" [My personal history], *Nihon Keizai Shimbun*, June 27, 1996.

Part III

Major Reform and the Prime Minister

Chapter 5

Administrative Reform by Suzuki and Nakasone

In the 1980s, fiscal reconstruction was the primary policy goal of Japanese politics. The Suzuki Zenkô (1980–82) and Nakasone Yasuhiro (1982–87) administrations tried to cut government spending through administrative reform, and the Nakasone and Takeshita Noboru (1987–89) administrations pursued tax reform to introduce a new indirect tax.

Throughout the 1970s, the national budget grew continuously. Total government expenditures in FY 1980 amounted to 42 percent of the national income, compared to 25 percent in FY 1970. In the early 1970s, the Satô Eisaku and Tanaka Kakuei administrations extended the expenditures on social welfare and education. The continuous expansion of entitlement payments was institutionally built into the budget structure. Between 1973 and 1981, for example, overall social security expenses increased four times and welfare pension payments five times. Because LDP *zoku* members and the related government ministries tried to protect other existing programs for their industries, total expenditures continued to expand. For the decade of the 1970s, the general account budget averaged a 19.2 percent annual increase.

Whereas spending grew, government tax revenues fell far behind. Japan had experienced remarkable growth for more than two decades, and the country progressed from a war-devastated nation to an economic power. In the 1960s, Japan's real (inflation-adjusted) rate of economic growth averaged as high as 12.1 percent. As the Japanese economy matured, though, it could no longer maintain such rapid growth and entered a stable growth period. Between 1970 and 1973, Japan's growth rate slowed to an average of 7.5 percent. After the oil shock (1974–85), it dropped to an average of 3.7 percent. The result was lagging tax revenues. During the rapid growth from 1961 to 1973, tax revenues grew at an average annual rate of 15.7 percent, keeping pace with government spending. However, from 1974 to 1979, annual revenue growth slowed sharply to 11.7 percent, widening the discrepancy with expenditures.

The gap between revenues and expenditures was filled with public debt. The average ratio of deficit to total expenditures increased from 9.2 percent during 1970–74 to 32.9 percent during the period 1976–80. Bond revenues in the initial budget of FY 1979 were almost 40 percent of government revenue. The amount of outstanding national bonds accumulated to more than one-third of the national income. This created a nightmare situation for the austerity-minded Ministry of Finance, which had long maintained a tradition of balancing the budget. One MOF official lamented: "This is not a fiscal crisis or failure. It is the bankruptcy of the nation."[1]

Prime Minister Ôhira Masayoshi, a former MOF official who served as finance minister when the government issued deficit-financing bonds in 1975, shared the MOF concerns about the deficit.[2] There are two ways to deal with a budget deficit: cutting expenditures or increasing revenues by raising taxes. Ôhira was pessimistic about saving a sizable amount through administrative reform because he would have to deal with the resistance of the bureaucracy.[3] Direct taxes, such as income and corporate taxes, already accounted for a growing proportion of total tax revenues. For Ôhira, the introduction of a large scale indirect tax was the only plausible solution to Japan's debt crisis.

The introduction of the new indirect tax did not originate with Prime Minister Ôhira. The Tax Commission, an advisory group to the Ministry of Finance, had recommended the introduction in October 1977 and in September 1978 both times to the Fukuda Takeo administration. At that time, Fukuda was contemplating calling a general election and was unwilling to take action because such a tax proposal would negatively affect the LDP in an election.[4]

Ôhira took a different approach. When briefed by top Finance Ministry officials in December 1978, the newly elected prime minister asked them to prepare for the new tax: "Bring the horse to the water. Then I will feed it water."[5] In his policy speech on September 3, 1979, Ôhira announced that financial reconstruction was his top policy priority, and he dissolved the lower house in order to call for public support four days later. But public reaction was different from what Ôhira had anticipated. Voters opposed the new indirect tax. Business leaders, such as *Keidanren* chairman Dokô Toshio, strongly criticized Ôhira for introducing a tax increase instead of cutting government spending. LDP Diet members formed a coalition against the introduction of the new tax, and 214 out of 383 members joined the coalition. Even Finance Minister Kaneko Ippei publicly questioned the timing of the new tax. This election pressure forced Ôhira to withdraw his proposal. Despite this withdrawal, the LDP lost in the October 1979 general election.

The LDP's defeat was a severe setback for the government in terms of introducing a new tax. Two months later, the Diet adopted a resolution to reconstruct the financial situation without a new indirect tax. Thus only one option remained for financial reconstruction—administrative reform. After Ôhira's sudden death on the campaign trail of the 1980 general election, administrative reform, combined with fiscal reconstruction without a tax increase, became the top priority of the two successive administrations of Suzuki Zenkô and Nakasone Yasuhiro.

This chapter analyzes both the failed and the successful attempts to reform the administrative system. To reduce the fiscal deficit, the government had to tackle the so-called three K's—*Kokutetsu* or the Japan National Railways, *Kenkô Hoken* or health insurance, and *Kome* or rice price subsidies. These three main budget deficit items were politically difficult. The national railways, with 400,000 employees and an annual deficit of 2 trillion yen, needed major reform. But the opposition parties, backed by strong labor union support, were expected to resist drastic reform measures such as large-scale layoffs. Health care issues were controlled by LDP welfare *zoku* members who represented powerful interest groups such as the pharmaceutical industries and the Japan Doctors' Association. Rice price was one of the most politically sensitive issues for the LDP Diet members who represented agricultural districts (60 percent of electoral districts were considered agricultural). All three areas presented potential barriers to reform.

Success was contingent on the ability of each prime minister to actually utilize his formal and informal sources of power. Prime Minister Suzuki was unsuccessful because he could not show leadership in key areas, nor could he balance domestic and international challenges. Prime Minister Nakasone, to the contrary, took appropriate and calculated risks to maximize his leadership and was successful in substantially reducing the fiscal deficit.

SUZUKI UNDERTAKES ADMINISTRATIVE REFORM

After Ôhira Masayoshi's sudden death, the Liberal Democratic Party took about one month to decide Ôhira's successor. Following lengthy discussions among LDP factions, Suzuki Zenkô was chosen for the premiership. After the fierce interfactional conflicts in the 1970s, especially between the factions of Tanaka Kakuei and Fukuda Takeo, the LDP wanted a party president with a wider support base within the party to avoid serious conflicts. Suzuki had served for seven terms as chairman of the LDP's Executive Council, the party's highest decision-making institution. Because decisions made by the council required unanimous consent, its chairman needed skills to coordinate among conflicting interests to build party consensus. Suzuki's ability in this area was highly respected and was seen as a necessary attribute for a prime minister. Suzuki knew exactly why he was chosen for the post and repeatedly emphasized his role in keeping party harmony.[6]

When Suzuki entered office in July 1980, more than one-third of the national budget for FY 1980 depended on national bonds. The failure of Ôhira Masayoshi to introduce a new indirect tax left Suzuki with no option but to introduce spending cuts for fiscal reconstruction. Suzuki, who succeeded the premiership and the leadership of Ôhira's faction, committed himself to Ôhira's political goal of reducing the deficit. "Financial reconstruction without tax increase" became a political slogan of his administration.

Suzuki began work on administrative reform by appointing Nakasone Yasuhiro, a potential candidate to succeed the prime minister, to the post of director general of the government body responsible for administrative reform, the Administrative Management Agency (AMA). Prime Minister Suzuki used his cabinet appointment authority to make his potential challenger loyal to his administration's top policy priority. The ball was thus lobbed to Nakasone to determine how the government should deal with the reform, and Suzuki sat back to observe. An LDP Diet member of the Suzuki faction looks back: "Administrative reform is . . . one of the most difficult themes in our political tradition, one generally considered unlikely to succeed. We waited, with breathless interest, for a plan to handle the difficult problem from Director General Nakasone who was seeking to succeed the premiership after Suzuki."[7]

Many saw the appointment to the AMA directorship as an insult to Nakasone. Nakasone himself was at first dissatisfied with the new post, which was generally considered a junior cabinet position with authority limited to minor administrative operations. His own faction member, Watanabe Michio, was appointed to the prestigious post of finance minister, the post Nakasone had wanted. Moreover, Nakasone's predecessor was another member of his faction. It was quite unusual for a faction leader to succeed the post previously held by a member of his own faction.[8]

The AMA's administrative deputy director suggested to Nakasone that a Second Ad Hoc Commission for Administrative Reform, or *Rinchô* (abbreviation of *Dainiji Rinji Gyôsei Chôsa Kai*) be established. Nakasone, who wanted a major political role in the Suzuki cabinet as a stepping stone to becoming prime minister, took the suggestion seriously.[9]

In August 1980, Nakasone and other agency officials began work to establish the *Rinchô*. The deputy director met with the chief of the Ministry of Finance's Budget Bureau and asked for the ministry's cooperation. Initial reaction, however, was negative; ministry officials were cautious about administrative reform because the first *Rinchô* had proposed to shift the budget-making power to the cabinet. Later, MOF officials found out that Nakasone had no such intention, and subsequently the MOF Budget Bureau chief promised his ministry's cooperation on administrative reform. The reform to reduce wasteful government spending would be in the ministry's best interest, since it wanted to reduce the fiscal deficit.[10] In September 1980 after consulting other government agencies, AMA director general Nakasone proposed at a cabinet meeting the establishment of the second *Rinchô*, an outside advisory council that would recommend administrative reforms difficult to propose internally.

Because the first *Rinchô*, which had existed from 1962 to 1964, had not worked well, the policy community was skeptical about the success of the second commission. Without any immediate crisis, the Ikeda Hayato and Satô Eisaku administrations felt reluctant to implement the recommendation from the first *Rinchô* for the reorganization of government agencies. With high economic growth and increasing government revenues, these two administrations were more interested in establishing offices, such as the Environmental Agency and the Land Agency, to meet the new needs of the nation than in rationalizing and restructuring the government. Critics thought that the second commission would again produce ideas but no action. But this time a crisis did exist—the budget deficit.

Setting up the Rinchô

The *Rinchô* drew more serious attention in January 1981 when Nakasone named Dokô Toshio as head of the commission. Dokô was a prominent business leader who had just retired as president of *Keidanren*, or the Federation of Economic Organizations. Nakasone explained the reason for this appointment: "Mr. Dokô was a big figure in the business community. If he shows initiative, all business leaders will have to cooperate. Therefore, we need to bring Mr. Dokô in so that we can pursue administrative reform."[11] Nakasone was right. As soon as Dokô was named, the leaders of the five major business groups formed the "Five-Man Committee to Promote Administrative Reform" to support Dokô.[12] This meant that the *Rinchô* would be much more powerful than were 200 other government advisory councils, which usually were under the strong control of the bureaucracy.

The appointment of Dokô not only added weight to the new commission but also assured the commitment of the prime minister. On March 11, five days before the official appointment, Dokô visited the prime minister's office and presented four conditions for accepting his appointment in a written memorandum. Among them, Dokô demanded a promise from Suzuki that the prime minister would fulfill the recommendations the committee would present and that financial reconstruction would be pursued without a tax increase. Dokô also demanded that the government deal with the reform of the so-called three K's—government subsidies for rice, health insurance, and the national railways—which made up a large portion of the government deficit. The ball of administrative reform, which had been lobbed by Suzuki to Nakasone, was thrown back to the prime minister by Dokô. Suzuki caught the ball and verbally promised Dokô that he would carry out the recommendations submitted by the *Rinchô*.

On March 16, 1981, the *Rinchô* was officially instituted with 9 regular members to handle overall reform efforts, and 21 expert members to handle specific plans. The regular members were composed of three business leaders, including Dokô, two labor leaders, one ex-bureaucrat, one scholar, and one representative each from the local community and from the media.[13] Nakasone, without Suzuki's involvement, had considerable control over the appointment of the expert members. The majority of them were "Nakasone's inner circle of friends and former colleagues."[14] Two days later, before a group of LDP Diet members, Prime Minister Suzuki promised no tax increase for the fiscal 1982 budget, as the *Rinchô* chairman had suggested. On that same day, Suzuki publicly stated that he would stake his political life on administrative reform. Through this statement, Suzuki clearly identified reform as his top priority issue in his political agenda, seeming to suggest his preparedness to act.

The prime minister's pledge became an effective weapon for the commission. The Ministry of Finance could no longer raise taxes to reduce the fiscal deficit. Five days later, Finance Minister Watanabe Michio complained to Dokô about the commission's policy: "[The pledge for] financial reconstruction without a tax increase is to us like being hit by a mega-ton class bomb. . . . It is difficult to do without a tax increase." Dokô replied simply, "The prime minister has already decided."[15] In Dokô's view, without strong restrictions, the bureaucracy constantly strove to expand its programs. Such expansions would lead to a rise in government spending and thus to tax increases that Dokô did not want to see.[16] The prime minister's "no tax increase" promise eliminated the option of increasing taxes and forced the Ministry of Finance to prepare for a freeze in government spending.

When "financial reconstruction without tax increase" was announced, three groups with slightly different priorities—the prime minister and the Ministry of Finance, the AMA, and the *Rinchô*—began acting together. Prime Minister Suzuki and the Ministry of Finance wanted to cut the fiscal deficit.[17] The prime minister had included this goal in his first policy speech on October 3, publicly promising to decrease the issuance of national bonds by 2 trillion yen before announcing his decision on administrative reform. On the other hand, Nakasone and the Administrative Management Agency's goal was to reorganize the government agencies—to update their structure and improve efficiency.[18] Meanwhile, Dokô and other business leaders were strongly against increasing the tax burden. Dokô had repeatedly made public statements that the government needed to reorganize and rationalize its structure to cut wasteful spending. The three different groups formed a coalition to pursue administrative reform.

The Introduction of the Zero Ceiling

As the first job for the *Rinchô*, Prime Minister Suzuki asked the commission to form guidelines for the budget formation for FY 1982 and to submit them by July 1981. Upon the suggestion of *Rinchô* member Sejima Ryûzô, Suzuki and AMA Director General Nakasone asked the commission to make their proposal both feasible and practical.[19] The *Rinchô* established two special subcommittees to form their first recommendation, one of which was in charge of budget issues. The Ministry of Finance, which strongly desired deficit reduction, asked the *Rinchô* to include their representatives in the commission. This triggered active participation from other ministries.[20] As a result, 50 councilors who represented various government agencies as well as related interest groups were added to the already existing membership of the *Rinchô*. Virtually all ministries of the government became involved in this commission. Their participation was important because they helped generate feasible solutions to spending cuts.

Meanwhile, the Ministry of Finance was preparing a proposal to freeze the spending of each ministry—the so-called zero ceiling—in order to cooperate with *Rinchô*'s principle of fiscal reconstruction. On May 27, after consulting with the *Rinchô* and the AMA, the Ministry of Finance announced the zero ceiling for each ministry's initial budget proposal (except defense and overseas economic cooperation programs, which were exempted for foreign policy reasons).[21] All ministries and government agencies would thus share equally in the burden, and the government could avoid unnecessary conflicts among the agencies. With all bearing the same burden, unity in achieving reform was facilitated. Prime Minister Suzuki successfully persuaded his cabinet members to follow this policy, and the cabinet approved the zero-ceiling approach at a cabinet meeting within ten days of its announcement.[22] However, Suzuki's conviction to this milestone would not hold true when later challenged with respect to the rice pricing one year later.

The first *Rinchô* proposal was presented to the prime minister on July 10, 1981. The proposal reconfirmed the zero ceiling and contained recommendations such as a reduction of subsidies and personnel as well as a significant decrease in spending on welfare and public work programs. The Suzuki cabinet accepted this proposal and approved a cabinet decision to cut 10 percent from subsidies across the board in the FY 1982 budget outline.

This across-the-board freeze (and later reduction) approach for all administrative agencies was called the "starve-out" strategy by an opposition party leader. This strategy was effective, particularly when combined with the *Rinchô* principle of making "feasible and practical" proposals and involving the bureaucracy in policy making. The *Rinchô* and its Secretariat kept contact with the individual ministries and their patron LDP *zoku* members in order to make their proposals feasible and practical before they were made public. With a ceiling on total spending for the individual ministries, LDP members and the ministries had to reveal the subsidies and administrative operations that were the most wasteful. By the time the actual proposal was announced, a basic agreement had been reached between the *Rinchô* and the ministry, creating a situation in which the individual ministry and the LDP could not refuse the agreement.[23]

Prime Minister Suzuki showed his leadership by successfully fulfilling the *Rinchô* recommendation. On September 11, the Suzuki cabinet approved a cabinet decision to reduce government personnel by 5 percent within five years. In the November 30 cabinet reshuffling, three days after the passage of the administrative reform bill, Prime Minister Suzuki reappointed Director General of the Administrative Management Agency Nakasone and Finance Minister Watanabe to their posts, thereby showing his determination to continue his support of their efforts in administrative reform. One month later, the new Suzuki cabinet approved a budget proposal that reflected the *Rinchô* proposal. The increase in the total budget was kept to 1.8 percent, the lowest level since the 1960s. The deficit-financing bond was reduced by 1.83 trillion yen, just below the goal of 2.0 trillion yen the prime minister had publicly announced.

Suzuki Makes a Pledge

Prime Minister Suzuki repeatedly reaffirmed his determination to achieve administrative reform and financial reconstruction. In the slow-growth economy, some LDP leaders called for fiscal expansion. Suzuki did not allow fiscal expansion, however, and he never withdrew his pledge of terminating the issuance of deficit-financing bonds by FY 1984. On February 3, at a lower house committee meeting, he officially announced that he would stake his political life on achieving the bond reduction goal. This meant that he would take full responsibility and leave the premiership should the goal not be met. In July the prime minister introduced the so-called minus ceiling to cut government spending by further lowering the ceiling for the FY 1983 budget request for each government agency by 5 percent from the previous year.

Meanwhile, since fall 1981, the *Rinchô* had organized four expert committees, one of which was in charge of restructuring public corporations. Prime Minister Suzuki privately and publicly expressed his determination to privatize three public corporations, the Nippon Telegraph and Telephone Public Corporation, the Japan Tobacco and Salt Public Corporation, and the Japan National Railways (JNR). The privatization of the national railways, with 400,000 employees and an accumulated debt of 13 trillion yen, was considered politically the most difficult task the *Rinchô* would undertake because of its strong union. JNR union members were a large part of the General Council of Trade Unions of Japan, or *Sôhyô*, on which the Japan Socialist Party relied for its electoral base.

Japan National Railways reform would involve great political risk and require commitment of the prime minister. At a private meeting with the expert committee chairman Katô Hiroshi, Suzuki affirmed that he would definitely support the reform of all three public corporations.[24] As AMA director general, Nakasone spent considerable energy on privatizing the Japan National Railways. He formed the so-called Shadow *Rinchô* to discuss the JNR issue and other reform issues.[25] *Rinchô* chairman Dokô also devoted special attention to the reform of the JNR because this was the most visible issue and likely to become a symbol of the entire administrative reform effort.[26]

On February 10, 1982, the *Rinchô* announced its second proposal, which focused on the reduction and rationalization of government regulations and authorizations that complicated licensing and approval procedures for businesses and created inefficiencies and large administrative costs for the government. By the time the *Rinchô* was preparing for their third report in spring 1982, administrative reform had become a national movement. *Rinchô* chairman Dokô Toshio had asked well-respected business leaders Honda Sôichirô, a founder of

Honda Motors, and Ibuka Masaru, a cofounder of Sony, to cooperate with him to gain public support. Honda and Ibuka organized the National Forum to Promote Administrative Reforms. The Forum held many meetings throughout the country, and by June 1982 more than 20,000 of its members were helping to develop public support for administrative reform. Dokô also asked a group of young business leaders, the *Nihon Seinen Kaigisho*, with 700 branches and 60,000 members, to cooperate. In July 1982, nearly 3,000 young business leaders from all over the nation participated in a conference in which Dokô passionately spoke on administrative reform.[27] An expert member of the *Rinchô* and former chairman of the *Seinen Kaigisho* noted: "The *Rinchô* was at the beginning merely one of many advisory councils. With the leadership of a national hero, Dokô Toshio, the commission has grown to develop a large-scale national movement to reform the society.[28]

Public support particularly for reform of the Japan National Railways grew as the *Rinchô* movement progressed. One of the *Rinchô*'s expert members and journalist wrote an article in an influential opinion magazine on the inefficiencies of the railways.[29] The public, already dissatisfied with continuous fare increases and the low quality of service, showed strong reaction to this article. This public attention forced the Japan National Railway to conduct an internal survey of its own operations. The results of the survey announced in an April 1982 report surprised even the JNR president at how bad JNR operations were. This created additional leverage for the *Rinchô*'s efforts.

Whereas administrative reform attracted public support, the prime minister suffered a setback in his efforts to reduce the deficit. Despite his determination, Prime Minister Suzuki could not break from traditional-style of Japanese politics. Suzuki, who emphasized the importance of party harmony, did not intervene in the process of setting the rice price within the LDP. Such intervention in a politically sensitive issue might create disharmony within the party. Suzuki chose not to intervene in the process rather than to risk party disharmony. As a result, on July 21, the government decided to increase the rice price by 1.1 percent, against the *Rinchô*'s recommendation to freeze the price to which Suzuki had earlier committed. Seeing that Suzuki broke his own pledge to follow the *Rinchô*, Chairman Dokô was sufficiently disappointed to express his desire to resign from the chairmanship. Although the price increase was small, it violated the *Rinchô*'s principle of an across-the-board budget ceiling that gave equal burden to various ministries. Many thought that this exceptional step would trigger other interest groups' demands and lead to the collapse of the entire administrative reform effort, catalyzed by Suzuki's unwillingness to stand up for the hard-line measures to tackle one of the three symbolic major deficit items. AMA director general Nakasone, scrambling to recover from Suzuki's blunder, apologized to Dokô for the increased rice price and asked him to continue as chairman. Dokô told him he would stay. As a result of this incident, the *Rinchô*'s influence increased further. The government would now have to follow the *Rinchô*'s proposals more closely.

At the end of July 1982, the *Rinchô* announced its third proposal, called the "basic" proposal, which was an extensive and systematic report of the basic philosophy and ideals of administrative reform. It also included a controversial recommendation that called for the privatization and breakup of the Japan National Railway, which would change the structure of Japan's labor movement, weakening the influence of *Sôhyô*, an umbrella organization of public-sector labor unions. On August 10, the Suzuki cabinet approved a cabinet decision that agreed to pay "full respect" to the recommendations. Two weeks later, the cabinet approved the *Rinchô*'s policy to establish the National Railways Reconstruction Management Committee to prepare for the privatization and partitioning of the Japan National Railways.[30]

Suzuki Takes Responsibility

Timing was not with Suzuki, for the recession presented additional difficulty for fiscal reconstruction. Decreased tax revenues further enlarged the government deficit. When it became obvious in summer 1982 that the government would fall 6 trillion yen short for FY 1982, Prime Minister Suzuki's pledge of "no deficit-financing bonds in FY 1984" seemed impossible to fulfill. When Finance Minister Watanabe Michio told Suzuki that he would resign, taking responsibility for the shortage, the prime minister persuaded him to stay. On September 16, Suzuki publicly declared a budget state of emergency. He froze the salaries of workers in the public sector for a year,[31] a politically controversial step that affected millions of public-sector employees. Some LDP members, including former prime minister Fukuda Takeo, criticized Suzuki's decision. Unrest within the LDP began to surface.

Prime Minister Suzuki, who emphasized party harmony, now faced disharmony. The situation was further exacerbated by Suzuki's mishandling of relations with the United States involving his statement on the U.S.–Japan "alliance." Former prime minister Kishi Nobusuke, who had staked his political life on the revision of the U.S.–Japan Security Treaty in 1960, began an anti-Suzuki movement (see Chapter 4), a movement Suzuki was unable to quiet. When the prime minister's pledge of "no deficit-financing bonds in FY 1984" became obviously impossible to fulfill, political pressure against the prime minister within the LDP mounted. The public showed disappointment in the Suzuki administration. Public support for the Suzuki cabinet, which had been over 50 percent at the beginning of his term, was now down to less than 30 percent. Surprising many both within and outside the political circles, Suzuki announced that he would not run for the LDP presidency on October 12. His reason was that he could no longer maintain the party harmony necessary to tackle the difficult problems Japan was facing domestically and internationally.[32] His inconsistency in policy statements versus actions taken, his lack of foresight to nurture party support, and his unwillingness to play an active part in the reform efforts led to the exact situation Suzuki had wanted to avoid—party disharmony.

The only powers used by Suzuki were to appoint Nakasone to a key post, make public statements (though unrealistic) in the Diet, and see that a few key decisions received approval in the cabinet. Upon his resignation, Suzuki said to Nakasone: "I have no intention to remain prime minister. I am not so foolish as to continue with so many difficult problems and with the public opinion against me."[33] His passive approach, ending with his bailout, dramatically contrasts with Nakasone's assertive and often courageous approach.

NAKASONE TAKES OVER REFORM

On November 24, 1982, Nakasone Yasuhiro, who had been the cabinet minister in charge of administrative reform, was elected LDP president.[34] Two days later when the Diet officially appointed Nakasone to the prime ministership, Nakasone met with *Rinchô* chairman Dokô Toshio to affirm the new prime minister's pledge to continue to pursue administrative reforms.

A cabinet appointment that would prove critical for administrative reform was the recommendation of Gotôda Masaharu, former director of the Police Agency and member of the Tanaka faction, as chief cabinet secretary, a post usually reserved for a member of the prime minister's own faction.[35] To pursue reform, Nakasone needed Gotôda's skill and experience in controlling the bureaucracy. In addition, by having Gotôda in the Cabinet Secretariat, Nakasone could take advantage of the support of the Tanaka faction.[36]

On his fourth day as prime minister, Nakasone spoke at a *Rinchô* meeting and confirmed that his policy priority would be administrative reform.[37] Four months later, the *Rinchô* submitted its last proposal to the prime minister, urging the government not only to fulfill the commission's proposal but also to further pursue administrative reform. Nakasone promised Dokô that he would try to carry out the recommendations.

Two months later in his policy speech of January 24, 1983, Nakasone emphasized the need for administrative reform and introduced his political slogan, "Clearing the Postwar Political Legacy." According to the prime minister, Japan was at a turning point in its postwar history. Many administrative operations that had supported Japan's postwar economic development had become dated. Nakasone stated that updating the postwar administrative system was crucial for future government operations and the economy. His slogan provided the public and the media an historical perspective of the situation requiring Japan to reform its administrative systems and helped increase public support for reform efforts—cultivated support that would prove imperative.

Continuing Reform Efforts

Prime Minister Nakasone kept his word. On May 13, 1983, he managed to pass the bill that established a committee to proceed with the reform of Japan National Railways despite opposition from the organization itself and the Transportation Ministry. As requested in the *Rinchô*'s fourth proposal, a bill to establish the Advisory Council on Enforcement of Administrative Reform (*Rinji Gyôsei Kaikaku Suishin Shingikai*, or *Gyôkakushin*) was enacted on May 20. Nakasone asked *Rinchô* chairman Dokô Toshio again to chair the *Gyôkakushin*. Dokô at first refused Nakasone's request citing his age (then 86 years old), but he was persuaded to chair the council for another three years. On June 7 in a meeting with members of *Keidanren*'s Special Committee on Administrative Reform, the new AMA director general, Saitô Kunikichi, told business leaders that the *Gyôkakushin* would serve as a general planning group for reform. The council was thus confirmed as a leading actor in administrative reform rather than a mere overseeing body.[38]

The first meeting of the *Gyôkakushin* was held on July 8. The council was comprised of seven regular members, including Chairman Dokô and many ex-bureaucrats as councilors. As seen in the *Rinchô*, their involvement was important in making realistic proposals. Although ex-bureaucrats served as representatives of their former home ministries by resisting proposals that could harm the agencies, they would be responsible for implementation of the proposals once adopted by the council. On August 4, the *Gyôkakushin* submitted a proposal to schedule legislation on administrative reforms. Prime Minister Nakasone then asked the Cabinet Secretariat and individual ministries to make a schedule for its implementation. Chief Cabinet Secretary Gotôda looks back: "In the schedule, everything was written: what operation would be completed by when. This needed to be legislated, and that would be announced as a government order. [Mr. Nakasone] had the LDP authorize [such schedules], and created a situation in which the government and the party together had to act quickly. He was very tactful."[39] By having the schedule authorized, Nakasone successfully made its implementation a matter of fact in his political agenda.

In his policy speech on September 10, 1983, Prime Minister Nakasone continued his determination to achieve financial reconstruction by announcing a new goal of "no deficit-financing bonds by FY1990." This was a more realistic goal than Prime Minister Suzuki's pledge to achieve the same outcome within three years. Nakasone intentionally presented no specific figure for the short term, which was opposite of Suzuki's attempt at a 2 trillion-yen reduction of deficit-financing bonds per annum. By doing so, the prime minister avoided a situation in which he would have to resign because he failed to meet his own goal.

Getting over the "Tanaka Problem"

The Nakasone administration and the LDP had to face another political issue. On October 12, the Tokyo District Court found former prime minister Tanaka Kakuei guilty of the charges stemming from the Lockheed scandal and sentenced him to four years in prison for receiving bribes from the American aircraft maker to influence a Japanese airline's procurement decision. Tanaka criticized the sentence and expressed his strong intent to appeal the decision in a higher court. The opposition parties submitted a resolution to urge Tanaka's resignation from the lower house, and the normal legislative process virtually came to a standstill. Within the LDP, Tanaka's political rivals, former prime ministers Fukuda Takeo and Miki Takeo, urged Tanaka to resign and asked Nakasone to help.

Chief Cabinet Secretary Gotôda Masaharu and LDP secretary general Nikaidô Susumu, both senior members of the Tanaka faction, arranged a meeting for November 28 between Nakasone and Tanaka under the condition that the prime minister would not ask for Tanaka's resignation. Nakasone reported on his meeting with Tanaka at an LDP meeting. However, many LDP members were not satisfied with his report and forced him to make another statement at an LDP meeting. This time the prime minister told LDP members with tears in his eyes that he had asked Tanaka to revise his public statement, and that the former prime minister had agreed to do so. Although not all the LDP members were fully satisfied by the second explanation, they agreed to stop calling for Tanaka's resignation. Many LDP Diet members did not want to escalate the intraparty conflict that might have lead to the dissolution of the lower house.[40]

However, the opposition parties accelerated their attack on the LDP and stopped Diet operations, demanding dissolution of the lower house. In the shadow of the Lockheed scandal, it was obvious that the LDP would lose in the general election. Despite the probable loss, Nakasone decided to call an election. But before Nakasone did so, he successfully negotiated with the opposition parties that if the prime minister promised to dissolve the lower house, they would immediately normalize Diet operations.[41] Nakasone was able to get the reform bills passed in the Diet, and he dissolved the lower house on November 28. In his diary Nakasone wrote, "There was something unusual during this 100th Diet session. The government passed all the bills by threatening the opposition parties not to dissolve the lower house. This was opposite to the usual pattern in which the government uses the threat of dissolution."[42] The LDP, as expected, lost in the December 1983 general election; but despite setbacks, Nakasone controlled the situation enough to get the reforms through.

The LDP's loss of 38 lower house seats was even greater than Nakasone had expected; the LDP could claim only 250 of 511 seats, which meant that the LDP no longer maintained a majority in the lower house.[43] Prime Minister Nakasone successfully persuaded the New Liberty Club to join the LDP in a coalition government. He also succeeded in recruiting conservative candidates who ran independent campaigns to join the LDP. This returned to the LDP secure control in all the lower house committees—a desirable condition to complete reform efforts. In his memoirs, Nakasone claims that his dissolution of the lower house and the formation of the coalition afterward were turning points in the successful completion of administrative reform.[44] The LDP and the New Liberty Club announced their coalition policy platform, which included their commitment to administrative reform. The coalition secured a stable majority, assuring the LDP that its party members would hold the chairmanships of all the lower house committees.

LDP leaders, especially former Prime Minister Miki Takeo, were critical of Nakasone and Tanaka for the LDP election losses. Prime Minister Nakasone and LDP secretary general Nikaidô Susumu, a senior leader of the Tanaka faction, in an attempt to calm any anti-Nakasone sentiment, visited all LDP supreme advisors—former prime ministers and former speakers of the legislative houses. Former prime minister Kishi Nobusuke, who led the anti-Suzuki campaign after Suzuki had mishandled relations with the United States, gave his support to Nakasone to remain premier because he was satisfied with Nakasone's relationship with U.S. President Ronald Reagan. However, to satisfy other leaders, Nakasone agreed that the administration would eliminate Tanaka's influence. This statement not only kept Nakasone in power but also enabled the prime minister to be more independent from the Tanaka faction, still the largest LDP faction.[45]

Implementing Reform Plans

On December 30, *Gyôkakushin* chairman Dokô Toshio and his vice chairman submitted the commission's recommendation of the need for continued financial reconstruction without a tax increase in the budget for FY 1984. Among specific recommendations, the commission fully supported the Ministry of Health and Welfare's proposal to reform the health insurance program—one of the three major deficit items—by requiring 20 percent of medical costs to be borne by patients. On February 24, 1984, the Nakasone cabinet approved the health insurance reform.

This issue was politically sensitive. The media predicted that the elderly and the poor would be hard hit by the reform. Powerful interest groups, such as the Japan Doctors' Association and pharmaceutical companies, were strongly opposed to the change. It was the Ministry of Health and Welfare who had decided to support the health insurance reform. For a ministry that usually protected client interest groups, with the given "minus ceiling" for its budget, the reform was the only way to reduce its spending.[46] The "starve-out" strategy of the *Rinchô* and the *Gyôkakushin* was effective in this instance.

In his policy speech on February 6, Nakasone publicly announced that in this Diet session his administration would submit legislation on health insurance reform as well as on privatization of two state-owned corporations, the Nippon Telegraph and Telephone (NTT) and the Japan Tobacco and Salt Public Corporation. Achieving the privatization of the two state-owned corporations was an important step toward the privatization of the Japan National Railways, another politically sensitive issue with which the prime minister was planning to deal the next Diet session.

Nakasone's handling of foreign affairs and administrative reform brought him an increase in public support in spring 1984. According to a *Yomiuri Shimbun* survey, 49.2 percent of the people polled supported the Nakasone cabinet, up by 12 percent from fall 1982. Riding the tide of growing public support, Prime Minister Nakasone extended the ordinary Diet session on May 23 for 77 days in an attempt to pass legislation to reform the health insurance program and to privatize the public corporations.

Nakasone drew upon his experience as a bureaucrat. He had the support of his former colleagues at the prewar Home Ministry who were now senior LDP politicians. Nakasone writes: "As administrative reform drew near to the final stage, Mr. Kataoka Seiichi and others formed *Naiyûkai* with 47 Diet members [a group of former colleagues from the ministry to support Nakasone]. . . . This group became a powerful engine in the promotion of administrative reform."[47]

Although the LDP barely maintained a majority in the lower house, controlling the Diet operation did not prove to be overly difficult for Nakasone, given strong public support. Gotôda Masaharu looks back: "With less Diet seats, it usually is more difficult for the ruling party to legislate bills. But administrative reform, creating a lean government and lean administrative operations, and improving administrative efficiency, was a theme that attracted public support. Diet operations were not so severe."[48] On July 25, the *Gyôkakushin* submitted another report to reinforce the administration's effort on administrative reform. Six days later, the Nakasone administration decided to maintain the "minus ceiling" in the budget. On August 3, bills to privatize the Japan Tobacco and Salt Public Corporation were passed; and on August 7, the bill to reform the health insurance program was enacted. Although another major administrative reform bill on the privatization of the Nippon Telegraph and Telephone Public Corporation was awaiting passage, it had already gained support from its labor union. The labor union was dissatisfied with the public corporation status that had kept their wages at the same low level as those of the workers of Japan National Railways—a state-owned corporation that had run a huge deficit. (This bill did pass by the end of 1984.) On August 10, the National Railways Reconstruction Management Committee announced its policy to privatize and break up Japan National Railways, as the *Rinchô* had recommended.

Privatizing the National Railways

The JNR reform became a central issue in the political scene of 1985–86. When the 102nd ordinary Diet session opened on January 24, 1985, Prime Minister Nakasone noted in his policy speech that among the so-called three K's, the sectors that were contributing a large part of the fiscal deficit, two of them— rice and health insurance—were successfully handled within the framework of administrative reform. The prime minister then declared that the government would deal with the last major issue—the reform of the Japan National Railways.[49] Nakasone repeatedly stated the need for an immediate reform to deal with this crisis situation.

The reform movement, which would lead to large-scale layoffs of employees, met strong objection from within the Japan National Railways. Although JNR president Nisugi Iwao had been appointed to the office by Nakasone on the condition that he would cooperate with the company's privatization and partition, his attitude changed because of pressures put on him by the JNR leadership.[50] In June 1985, Nakasone asked the JNR president and his vice president for their resignations. In addition, five other board members, who were opposed to the breakup of the JNR, were replaced. Nakasone says in his memoirs: "I received the resignation of the JNR president. This added critical momentum to promoting the reform."[51] Nakasone utilized his authority as prime minister to appoint and dismiss executive officials at public corporations.

One month after the resignation of the top executives, the National Railways Reconstruction Management Committee submitted its final proposal, a concrete plan to privatize and partition the Japan National Railways. The next day, Prime Minister Nakasone publicly expressed his determination to conclude the JNR reform: "The administration is finally determined to fulfill the proposal at any cost. Even in the face of any trouble or chaos, we must achieve the JNR reform by acquiring the understanding of the public and the cooperation from the opposition parties."[52] Prime Minister Nakasone put this promise into action by adapting, through a cabinet decision, the committee's plan to privatize the company and regionally divide it into six different corporations by April 1987. In his policy speech at the 103rd extraordinary Diet session, Nakasone stated that Japan National Railways was in a crisis situation and called its reform "the most important national issue requiring an immediate solution." Nakasone again affirmed that his administration would zealously pursue JNR reform with full respect given to the proposal of the National Railways Reconstruction Management Committee.[53] With this constant affirmation of the prime minister's determination, Nakasone's administrative reform effort went into its final stage.

In December the prime minister ordered staffers of the Cabinet Legal Bureau to spend the New Year's break reviewing 200 laws related to the JNR reform and to prepare a draft bill. On February 28, the Nakasone cabinet approved five JNR reform bills as a cabinet decision. The biggest project in Nakasone's administration now awaited only Diet passage.

The opposition parties could not strongly attack the JNR reform bills because they had strong public support. The opposition feared the possible dissolution of the lower house, which would be followed by an LDP victory in a general election. They were thus unwilling to voice strong negative opinions in the Diet that would give Prime Minister Nakasone a good excuse to call for an election.

The opposition parties were most afraid of a double election involving both the upper and lower houses, a situation likely to benefit the LDP because of expected high turnout in the voting. However, the election call found another legitimate reason. According to the Supreme Court, the current lower house with unequal representation was in an unconstitutional situation: The Diet needed to reapportion some electoral districts. The opposition parties' strategy to avoid strong confrontation in the Diet helped pass the reapportionment bill. Ironically, this gave Nakasone a legitimate reason to dissolve the lower house "to correct its unconstitutional status." Nakasone's cabinet tricked the opposition parties by making a decision to open an extraordinary session where the LDP could legislate to postpone the upper house election so that a double election could take place. (For a detailed explanation, see Chapter 3.) The double election left the LDP with its largest majority ever, 304 out of 512 seats in the lower house. Nakasone won an exceptional one-year extension of the LDP presidency as a result of this victory as well as the achievement of a more stable power base within the party.

After the election, Prime Minister Nakasone formed his fifth cabinet. Takeshita Noboru was appointed LDP secretary general; and Kanemaru Shin, who had been at this post, was appointed deputy prime minister. Gotôda Masaharu was reappointed chief cabinet secretary. Hashimoto Ryûtarô, who had been instrumental as chairman of the LDP's research committee on administrative and financial policy in building a party consensus on administrative reform, was awarded with an appointment to minister of transportation under which the JNR reform fell.[54] The Tanaka faction, to which these cabinet members belonged, was not happy about this reshuffling, especially the reappointment of Gotôda and Takeshita. The faction requested Nakasone to appoint them outside of the quota allowed to their faction, but the request was denied.

This event highlighted the already weakening political influence of Tanaka Kakuei. In February 1985, Takeshita and Kanemaru formed a faction within the Tanaka faction. After Tanaka suffered a stroke in the same month, they further expanded their control over the faction. In this intrafactional conflict, Nakasone sided with Takeshita and Kanemaru.[55] Their appointment to the new cabinet was Nakasone's pledge of support to them.

Nakasone, at a press conference after the cabinet reshuffling, told reporters: "[The JNR reform] is the biggest challenge I have faced. The passage of the eight JNR reform–related bills is the largest issue of this cabinet."[56] The stage and cast were set to finalize the JNR bill.

On September 10, the extraordinary Diet session was called into session. Backed by the LDP's overwhelming majority in the lower house, the eight JNR reform bills passed the lower house special committee on October 24 and passed in the lower house floor four days later. Two opposition parties, *Kômeitô* and the Democratic Socialist Party, decided to support the bills under the condition that the status of the reform would be reported to the Diet each year for five years. The Nakasone administration had hurdled the biggest obstacle in the JNR reform.

On November 28, after one month of consideration, the JNR reform bills passed the upper house and were enacted. On that day, Chief Cabinet Secretary Gotôda wrote in his schedule book: "The JNR bills passed. We have overcome the biggest challenge in administrative reform."[57]

Nakasone's administrative reform was successful. Nakasone later called the reform the greatest achievement of his administration. All three of the so-called

three K's—Japan National Railways, rice price subsidies, and health insurance—
were successfully reformed under the umbrella of administrative reform. Because of Nakasone's skill and handling the most controversial reform, that of
Japan National Railways, was achieved without creating political turmoil. Furthermore, partly helped by the economic recovery that had began in spring 1983,
Nakasone's goal for financial reconstruction, "no deficit-financing bonds in FY
1990," was achieved after he left office, just as he had planned.

The privatization of Japan National Railways led to the reorganization of
Japan's labor unions and thus to a major change in the support base of the
opposition parties. The JNR labor group had been the most influential labor
group within the General Council of Trade Unions of Japan, or *Sôhyô*, the
traditional support base of the Japan Socialist Party. However, the JNR labor
union lost its influence over and membership in *Sôhyô*. In 1987, *Dômei*, or the
Japanese Confederation of Labor, which had comprised the support base of the
Democratic Socialist Party, was dissolved to form the Japan Federation of
Private-Sector Labor Unions, or *Rengô*, combining with other private-sector unions in *Sôhyô*. The new umbrella organization, which united virtually all the
major private-sector labor unions, was more cooperative with the LDP than the
traditional anti-LDP labor group. Administrative reform eventually weakened
the power of the anti-LDP groups.

Nakasone took advantage of his commission, the *Rinchô*. Compared with
other advisory groups that served legitimizing government policies, members of
the commission took a "really substantive role in the preparation of the proposals."[58] During the five years and three months of the *Rinchô* and the *Gyôkakushin* period, 46 reports were written, 16,000 different subjects were discussed,
and 13 official recommendations were submitted to the government. Chairman
Dokô Toshio attended 313 formal meetings. In addition, 914 subcommittee
meetings were held. In short, the administrative reform was a very large-scale
project involving many people.[59]

Gotôda Masaharu, who closely assisted Prime Minister Nakasone on administrative reform, described the reasons for the success:

First of all, it was good timing. Prime Minister Nakasone's administrative reform
matched the worldwide trend. Many Western nations were going for deregulation. In the
United States the Reagan administration called for a small government with more efficiency. It was also when many people talked about the Great Britain disease. Ideology
for a controlled economy and society declined and the world leaned further toward the
free economic system. Prime Minister Nakasone then came up with his administrative
reforms with the slogan of "Clearing the Postwar Political Legacy." It was just good
timing. Second, we had a charismatic business leader as a head of the Council. Mr. Dokô
Toshio became a symbol for the reform. This helped significantly. Third, Mr. Nakasone
had a determined political attitude toward the reform. His way of handling the issue
sometimes created friction within the party. The good timing, however, helped the prime
minister.[60]

Gotôda then concluded by saying, "The Japanese people wanted to see political leadership in this issue."

SUMMARY

Administrative reform was, in a way, a typical prime-ministerial issue, an issue so vast that it involved almost all administrative agencies. The prime minister's involvement was required for policy coordination and advancement for successful reform.

Ôhira Masayoshi had been devoted to financial reconstruction by introducing a general consumption tax. Prime Minister Suzuki Zenkô, who succeeded the office, shared Ôhira's view on the need to cut the budget deficit, publicly stating that he would stake his political life as prime minister. However, Suzuki was not interested in how spending was cut; choosing to remain closer to the sidelines, he delegated much of the decision making to Nakasone Yasuhiro, whom he had appointed as director general of the Administrative Management Agency. Suzuki had no way of knowing how seriously Nakasone would take the reform challenge and found himself surrounded by aggressive movements.

Suzuki, who emphasized party harmony, was inconsistent in his efforts to see through administrative reform. He disappointed *Rinchô* officials by giving up on freezing the price of rice; he was unwilling to cause disharmony by standing up to agricultural interests and their patron LDP *zoku* members (see Figure 5.1).

Economic conditions provided additional difficulty for Suzuki. The economic recession lasted longer than had been expected and handed the Japanese government a 6-trillion-yen revenue shortage in FY 1982. This dismantled Suzuki's already fairly unrealistic pledge of "no deficit-financing bonds in FY 1985." Meanwhile, Suzuki's mishandling of relations with the United States triggered an anti-Suzuki movement within the LDP, led by a former prime minister and other members of the Fukuda Takeo faction. Suzuki was passive in striving to maintain intraparty support for his administration, leaving him powerless to outlive the criticism. Unable to maintain party harmony, Suzuki resigned as prime minister in the midst of administrative reform efforts. Throughout his term, Suzuki, though verbally expressing commitment to reform efforts, did not actively participate in the progress. In the end, beaten by the challenge, he withdrew. Had Suzuki been willing to take bold steps, such as intervening in the rice price setting and combating the anti-Suzuki movement, the manner in which he left office could have been remarkably different.

Nakasone Yasuhiro, who succeeded Suzuki, had already been personally involved in the efforts of administrative reform. Nakasone knew the details of the issue before he became prime minister and kept himself deeply involved. Nakasone enthusiastically sought public support for his policy. Advisory councils for Nakasone were tools to identify problems and to gain public support to deal with issues.

Figure 5.1
Suzuki and Administrative Reform

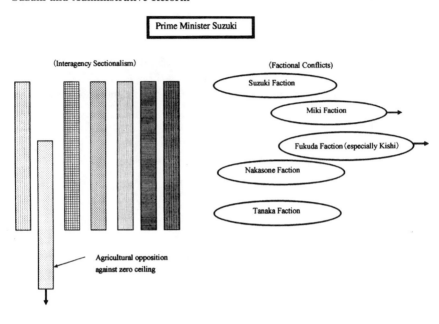

After the *Rinchô* was closed, Nakasone quickly moved to persuade Dokô to chair the commission that would oversee the implementation of administrative efforts. Nakasone was fully aware of the importance of this business leader as a symbol of reform. Under the leadership of Dokô, administrative reform had become a national movement supported by the people, thus muting any criticisms from the opposition parties.

Nakasone successfully contained sectionalism by maintaining the minus-ceiling policy. The so-called starve-out strategy forced government agencies to come up with their own feasible solution. Because every agency was "starved out," no single agency could complain of hunger. The politically difficult privatization of the Japan National Railways, which was under the jurisdiction of the Transportation Ministry, was conducted after the privatization of the two other public corporations, Japan Tobacco and Salt Public Corporation, under the Finance Ministry and the Nippon Telegraph and Telephone Public Corporation. The railways thus could not maintain an antiprivatization position. Further, to assist the government agencies in finding feasible solutions, Prime Minister Nakasone appointed, and had the help of Chief Cabinet Secretary Gotôda Masaharu, a former bureaucrat who knew the limitations of the bureaucracy well.

Because the government deficit was recognized as a serious problem, LDP members could not oppose the general direction of the administrative reform effort. Because all the agencies suffered, their patron LDP members could not

Figure 5.2
Nakasone and Administrative Reform

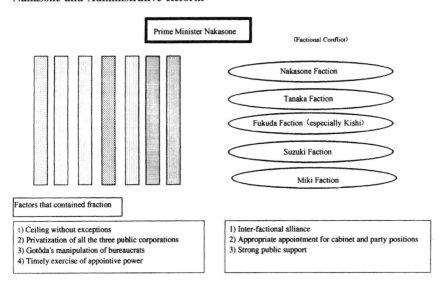

complain, and thus there was no serious disagreement among various *zoku* groups. Nakasone assertively recruited the support of an interfaction group of senior LDP members who used to work for the prewar Home Ministry. They shared Nakasone's view on administrative reform and organized to support the effort. This helped bind different factions within the LDP and thus maintain party unity (see Figure 5.2).

Prime Minister Nakasone took political risks in the process of the reform efforts. After Tanaka Kakuei received a guilty sentence in the Lockheed trial, Nakasone dissolved the lower house, choosing to suffer defeat in the election in a calculated exchange for passing six administrative reform bills. The prime minister used his authority to oust JNR officials who did not support the reform efforts. Nakasone asked for a concrete time schedule to legislate the reform-related bills and then approved the plan at meetings of his cabinet. All these steps required the involvement of the national leader, and Nakasone was fully committed to seeing the issues through, acting in a timely and bold manner. Nakasone later recalls these events by saying, "The ultimate factor in politics is the determination of the top leader."[61]

Nakasone was helped by timing. Western industrialized nations were suffering from large governments that discouraged the vitality of the private sector. The Reagan administration cut taxes in an attempt to reduce government. The Japanese people were fully aware of the need to cut the budget deficit, and administrative reforms to cut the wasteful spending in the public sector were a popular solution. Nakasone took necessary actions to ensure their knowledge of the issues to secure their support.

In short, Prime Minister Suzuki Zenkô could not succeed in his administrative reform attempt because his involvement was indirect and passive and because he avoided political confrontation within the ruling party. Prime Minister Nakasone Yasuhiro, in contrast, achieved administrative reform by effectively using different sources of power without causing a serious division with public opinion, disharmony among LDP factions, or conflicts of interest among various government agencies and their patron LDP *zoku* members.

NOTES

1. Quoted in Shindô Muneyuki, *Zaisei Hatan to Zeisei Kaikaku* [Financial breakdown and tax reform] (Tokyo: Iwanami Shoten, 1989), p. 34.

2. According to Ôhira's assistant, Nagatomi Yûichirô: "Prime Minister Ôhira strongly felt responsible for the financial reconstruction. He thought that the government must get out of the situation of issuing a huge number of national bonds, especially deficit-financing bonds." Nagatomi Yûichirô, *Kindai wo Koete: Ko Ôhira Sôri no Nokosareta mono* [Beyond the contemporary era: What late prime minister Ôhira left for us] (Tokyo: Ôkura Zaimu Kyôkai, 1983), p 457.

3. Ohira Masayoshi, *Watashi no Rirekisho* [My personal history] (Tokyo: Nihon Keizai Shimbun-sha, 1978), pp. 147–50. See also an interview with a former finance vice minister Ôkura Masataka. Ôkura Masataka, interview by Andô Hiroshi, *Sekinin to Genkai: Akaji Zaisei no Kiseki* [Responsibility and limitation: Tracing fiscal deficit], vol. 2 (Tokyo: Kin'yû Zaisei Kenkyû-sho, 1987), pp. 113–14. For further reference, see Yanagisawa Hakuo, *Akaji Zaisei no Jûnen to Yonin no Sôri tachi* [Ten years of fiscal deficit and four prime ministers] (Tokyo: Nihon Seisansei Honbu, 1985), pp. 39–44; and Michio Muramatsu and Masaru Mabuchi, "Introducing a New Tax in Japan," in *Parallel Politics: Economic Policymaking in Japan and the United States*, ed. Samuel Kernell (Washington, D.C.: Brookings Institution, 1991), p. 188.

4. According to a former finance ministry officer, Yanagisawa Hakuo, Prime Minister Fukuda when receiving the briefings said, "I understand that the report argues the necessity of a general consumption tax for financial reconstruction. However, avoid any possibility of creating discussion on a sales tax or consumption tax at the time of an election." Yanagisawa, *Akaji Zaisei no Jûnen*, p. 27.

5. Yanagisawa Hakuo, who sat in the briefing as an assistant to the chief cabinet secretary, recalls, "It was a heavy statement. We, who heard [the prime minister's statement], became more tense [than the prime minister]." Ibid., p. 38.

Ôhira's close associate, then deputy chief cabinet secretary Katô Kôichi recalls: "Mr. Ôhira thought he would be the prime minister for four or five years. He, therefore, recognized that he would not be able to escape from the issue of financial reconstruction. He strongly believed that he should bring the issue on the table and that the Japanese people would understand [the need for general consumption tax] if he told the truth." Quoted in Kawauchi Issei, *Ôhira Seiken 554 nichi* [The Ôhira administration: 554 Days] (Tokyo: Gyôsei Mondai Kenkyû-sho, 1982), pp. 159–60.

6. Suzuki stated in an interview: "The reason why I became the prime minister/LDP president without a presidential election was that the LDP was tired of factional conflicts such as 'the 40-days conflict' [under the Ôhira administration] which was heavily criticized by the public. I, who proposed 'politics of harmony,' was seen as appropriate in

such circumstances." Suzuki Zenkô, interview by Suzuki Kenji, in Suzuki Kenji, *Rekidai Sôri Sokkin no Kokuhaku* [Confessions by close associates of prime ministers] (Tokyo: Mainichi Shimbun-sha, 1991), pp. 171–72.

7. Yanagisawa, *Akaji Zaisei no Jûnen*, p. 56.

8. Nakasone himself admits his disappointment: "In fact I was at a loss for what I should do at the time I was appointed to the director general of the Administrative Management Agency. I found myself in a very complicated and delicate political environment." Nakasone's speech at Japan Press Club on August 18, 1980, quoted in Uji Toshihiko, *Suzuki Seiken 863 nichi* [The Suzuki administration: 863 days] (Tokyo: Gyôsei Mondai Kenkyû-sho, 1983), pp. 96–97.

9. See Gotôda Masaharu, *Naikaku Kanbô Chôkan* [Chief cabinet secretary] (Tokyo: Kôdan-sha, 1989), pp. 67–68.

10. Nakasone Yasuhiro, *Tenchi Ujô* [Affection in heaven and on earth] (Tokyo: Bungei Shunjû, 1996), pp. 338 and 525. Matsushita Yasuo, interview, in Andô, *Sekinin to Genkai*, vol. 2, pp. 209–10.

11. A statement by Katô Hiroshi, in Katô Hiroshi and Sandô Yôichi, *Dokô san to tomo ni 730 nichi* [Seven hundred thirty days with Mr. Dokô] (Tokyo: Keizai Ôraisha, 1983), p. 21.

Nakasone asked Dokô through his friends, Hanamura Nihachirô and Sejima Ryûzô, to chair the committee. On January 1, 1981, Nakasone told Prime Minister Suzuki that he would appoint Dokô Toshio, former chairman of Toshiba, and Ishikawajima Harima, who also served as chairman of *Keidanren*. Suzuki agreed with this appointment by saying, "He will fit in the post." See Nakasone Yasuhiro, *Seiji to Jinsei* [Politics and life] (Tokyo: Kôdansha, 1992), p. 300. See also Hanamura Nihachirô, *Seizaikai Paipu Yaku Hanseiki* [My life as a channel between the political and business worlds] (Tokyo: Tokyo Shimbun, 1990), pp. 187–89; and Dokô Toshio, *Watashi no Rirekisho* [My personal history] (Tokyo: Nihon Keizai Shimbun, 1983), pp. 19–20.

12. The establishment of the committee was announced on February 13, 1981. Members were Inayama Yoshihiro of *Keidanren*, Nagano Shigeo of the Japan Chamber of Commerce, Ôtsuki Bunpei of the Japan Employer's Federation, Sasaki Sunao of *Keizai Dôyûkai*, and Hiyûga Hôsai of the Kansai Economic Federation. See Tsuda Tatsuo, *Zaikai-Nihon no Shihaisha Tachi* [The business community: The people who rule Japan] (Tokyo: Gakushû no Tomo-sha, 1990), p. 303.

13. The two other business leaders were Sejima Ryûzô of Itochû Company and Miyazaki Kagayaki of Asahi Kasei Kogyo Company, and the two labor leaders were Maruyama Yasuo of *Sôhyô* and Kanasugi Hidenobu of *Dômei*. The other representatives were Tanimura Yutaka of Tokyo Security Exchange (ex-bureaucrat), Tsuji Kiyoaki of Tokyo University (scholar), Hayashi Keizô of the Local Institutional Research Council (the local community), and Enjôji Jirô of *Nihon Keizai Shimbun* (the media). Nakasone's original plan was to have only two business representatives, including Dokô. Dokô, however, insisted on two more business leaders. Liberals criticized that big business was overrepresented.

14. Shumpei Kumon, "Japan Faces Its Future: The Political-Economics and Administrative Reform," *Journal of Japanese Studies* 10, no. 1 (winter 1984): 143.

15. Finance Minister Watanabe Michio's conversation with Dokô Toshio, printed in Andô, *Sekinin to Genkai*, vol. 2, p. 221.

16. Nakasone also sensed Dokô's distrust, Nakasone writes in his memoirs: "At the beginning of *Rinchô*, Mr. Dokô seemed to see bureaucrats as untrustworthy and politi-

cians as suspicious men who often go around their promises." Nakasone, *Seiji to Jinsei*, p. 301.

17. As early as September 7, 1980, at an LDP meeting in Hakone, Prime Minister Suzuki had stated his intention to decrease the issuance of deficit bonds by 2 trillion yen per year so that the government would terminate the issuance of deficit-financing bonds at the end of three years' time. Finance Minister Watanabe Michio was surprised to hear this announcement, and he phoned the prime minister. Suzuki told the finance minister that only the prime minister's words could make the administration and the ruling party take the goal seriously. Watanabe Michio, interview by Fukuda Yukihiro, in Fukuda Yukihiro, *Zeisei Kaikaku e no Ayumi* [Steps toward tax reform] (Tokyo: Zeimu Keiri Kyôkai, 1987), p. 620.

18. Nakasone's view is expressed in his essay in an LDP public relations magazine: "We need to review all the administrative policies and operations and establish an administrative and financial base that would meet our future needs. By establishing such a base, it is important to come up with a mid- to long-term philosophy and system for the government that can last ten to twenty years after the 1980s." Nakasone Yasuhiro, "Kokumin Rinchô to Jiritsu Jijo no Gyôkaku" [*Rinchô* for the people and administrative reform for self-reliance] *Jiyû Minshu* (June 1981): p. 16.

19. Whereas an expert member of the *Rinchô*, Kumon Shumpei, suggests that this was a request of Prime Minister Suzuki, Gotôda Masaharu says that it was Nakasone's idea. Nakasone reveals in his memoirs that it was originally Sejima's idea. Nakasone Yasuhiro, *Seiji to Jinsei*, p. 303. See also Kumon, "Japan Faces Its Future," p. 145; and Gotôda, *Naikaku Kanbô Chôkan*, p. 74.

20. Katô and Sandô *Dakô san to tomo ni*, pp. 29–30, Katô and Sandô were *Rinchô*'s expert members.

21. There was a debate about who should announce the zero ceiling. The Finance Ministry's Budget Bureau director general Matsushita Yasuo successfully took this initiative by arguing that the zero-ceiling principle should be announced before July so that the other ministries could prepare their budget proposals. See Matsushita Yasuo, interview by Andô, *Sekinin to Genkai*, vol. 2, pp. 217–19.

22. The director general of the MOF Budget Bureau gives credit to Prime Minister Suzuki: "The setting of the zero-ceiling principle went surprisingly smooth. By then, the notion that the zero ceiling was the only option had penetrated not only to the party leadership but also the subcommittee level of the LDP's Policy Affairs Research Committees. One of the reasons for this was that Prime Minister Suzuki with strong enthusiasm took the initiative and gave instructions to each minister himself." Matsushita Yasuo, interview by Andô Hiroshi, in Andô, *Sekinin to to Genkai*, vol. 2, p. 228.

23. See Gotôda, *Naikaku Kanbô Chôkan*, p. 74; and Kumon, "Japan Faces Its Future," pp. 161–62.

24. Katô Hiroshi recalls Suzuki's comment: "[Prime Minister Suzuki told me,] 'Reform all three, not just one of them.' I asked him if this was really okay. Mr. Suzuki always told me, 'It is okay. I will certainly follow through.' His determination [on this issue] never changed." Katô and Sandô, *Dakô san to tomo ni*, p. 124.

25. Nakasone describes this informal gathering, which included Katô Hiroshi, who headed a subcommittee in charge of JNR reform. According to Nakasone, participants included Nakasone himself, parliamental vice ministers Horiuchi Mitsuo and Nakamura Yasushi, administrative vice minister Kaji Natsuo, LDP's Research Committee on Administrative and Financial Operations chairman Hashimoto Ryûtarô, *Rinchô* member Se-

jima Ryûzô, close advisor to Nakasone and former MITI vice minister Akazawa Shôichi, *Rinchô*'s forth committee chairman Katô Hiroshi, and its first committee chairman Umemoto Sumimasa. Nakasone, *Seiji to Jinsei*, p. 304.

26. See Katô and Sandô, *Dakô san to tomo ni*, pp. 84–86.

27. See Kaminogô Toshiaki, *Sôri wo Shikaru Otoko: Dokô Toshio no Tatakai* [The man who scolded the prime minister: The fight of Dokô Toshio] (Tokyo: Kôdansha, 1983), pp. 9–33.

28. A comment by Ushio Jirô. Ibid., pp. 32–33.

29. Yayama Tarô, "Kokutetsu Rôshi Kokuzoku-ron" [Argument that JNR employers and employees are both traitors to the nation] *Bungei Shunjû* (April 1982): 92–112.

30. The legal status of the National Railways Reconstruction Management Committee was a controversial issue. Representatives of the private sector supported an administrative committee based on Article 3 of the National Administrative Organization Law, which would give strong legal authority to the committee equivalent to ministries, whereas the representatives of the Transportation Ministry and the Japan National Railways stood for an advisory committee status based on Article 8 of the same law, but the recommendations of that committee would have little legal binding. Media observations on the outcome were that the administrative committee status would mean progress, whereas the advisory committee status would signal a retreat. Nakasone asked a *Rinchô* member, Sejima Ryûzô, to mediate. A compromise was reached. The committee would have an advisory committee status, but the prime minister would be responsible for fulfilling its recommendations. According to a *Rinchô* expert member, Katô Hiroshi, the status was actually what the *Rinchô* wanted because both committees based on Articles 3 and 8 had demerit. Katô and Sandô, *Dakô san to tomo ni*, pp. 132–39.

31. This announcement was made despite the recommendation of the National Personnel Authority to increase wages by a 4.58 percent for annual adjustment.

32. Suzuki notes: "Over two years into the term, factionalism arose. . . . If I tried to keep my post, there might have been some movement against me. Such a movement would have forced me to counterattack. This would have created another fierce conflict within the party, and would have spoiled everything. So I decided [to resign]." Suzuki Zenkô, interview by Suzuki Kenji, Suzuki, *Rekidai Sôri*, p. 172.

33. Suzuki's statement was recorded in Nakasone's diary. See Sekai Heiwa Kenkyûsho, ed., *Nakasone Naikakûshi* [The history of the Nakasone cabinet], vol. 3 (Tokyo: Sekai Heiwa Kenkyûsho, 1995), p. 617.

34. The selection process of the LDP leader was complicated. In the race for the LDP presidency, Nakasone along with three other LDP leaders declared his candidacy. With support from the largest Tanaka faction and the Suzuki faction, Nakasone gained nearly 60 percent of the votes in a nationwide primary election. Nakasone's overwhelming victory in the primary race prompted the other three candidates to withdraw from the final race.

35. Gotôda, *Naikaku Kanbô Chôkan*, p. 21.

36. Gotôda Masaharu evaluated his relations with Nakasone: "Mr. Nakasone's ideas for the administrative reform matched mine. I had worked on the same topic as a vice chairman of LDP's committee on administrative and finance reform. Getting down to the reality of how well the prime minister and his chief cabinet secretary work together really depends on their personal relationship. Since our political goals and objectives were the same, we worked well together." Gotôda Masaharu, interview by author, December 18, 1992.

37. Kaminogô, *Sôri wo Shikaru Otoko*, pp. 68–70.

38. Maki, *Nakasone Seiken*, vol. 1, p. 134.

39. Gotôda, *Naikaku Kanbô Chôkan*, p. 74. Gotôda also told a similar story to author, "Mr. Nakasone was very good at having recommendations on administrative reform approved as cabinet decisions and authorized by the LDP. He did it so splendidly." Gotôda Masaharu, interview by author, December 18, 1992.

40. This was Gotôda's observation. Gotôda Masaharu, *Jô to Ri* [Emotion and logics], vol. 2 (Tokyo: Kôdansha, 1998), p. 80. See also Gotôda, *Naikaku Kanbô Chôkan*, pp. 43–48, and Nakasone, *Tenchi Ujô*, p. 474.

41. Gotôda said to Nakasone: "Even if we do not dissolve the lower house, the Diet operation will not be normalized until early next year. It would stop the legislative schedule for the budget committee, and possibly delay the budget enactment for a long time. Under such circumstance, the Nakasone Cabinet would die in the gutter. Dissolution is the only choice." Gotôda, *Naikaku Kanbô Chôkan*, p. 49.

42. Nakasone, *Tenchi Ujô*, p. 478.

43. When Nakasone asked Gotôda for his prediction, he answered that the LDP would lose about 20 seats. Gotôda Masaharu, *Jô to Ri*, vol. 2, p. 84.

44. Nakasone, *Seiji to Jinsei*, p. 305. See also Nakasone, *Tenchi Ujô*, pp. 477–82, and Gotôda Masaharu, *Jô to Ri*, vol. 2, p. 80.

45. See Nakasone, *Tenchi Ujô*, pp. 483–85.

46. Yamaguchi Mitsuhide, interview by Andô Hiroshi, Andô, *Sekinin to Genkai*, vol. 2, p. 241.

47. Nakasone, *Seiji to Jinsei*, p. 304. See also Nakasone, *Tenchi Ujô*, pp. 509–14.

48. Gotôda, *Naikaku Kanbô Chôkan*, p. 76.

49. Prime Minister Nakasone's policy speech, *Yomiuri Shimbum*, evening edition (January 25, 1985).

50. Gotôda Masaharu states: "I had the responsibility of his appointment. On several occasions I called [Nisugi] to the office of the Director General of the Management and Coordination Agency. He was a cheerful person, and said, 'I know [the government's position]. I will cooperate,' in our discussion. But when he returned to the JNR, he was strongly pressured by the vice president and others and was unable to act on his own accord. Vice president Nawata and others were supportive of privatization but opposed to the breakup of the JNR. . . . I asked the opinion of a JNR board member. He said, 'Reform cannot be done under the current top executives.' This was the conclusion." Gotôda, *Naikaku Kanbô Chôkan*, p. 80.

51. Nakasone, *Seiji to Jinsei*, p. 305.

52. Prime Minister Nakasone's speech in Karuizawa on July 27, 1985. Quoted in Maki, *Nakasone Seiken*, vol. 2, p. 20.

53. Prime Minister Nakasone's policy speech on October 14, printed in *Mainichi Shimbun*, October 15, 1985).

54. For Nakasone's reason of Hashimoto appointment, see Nakasone, *Tenchi Ujô*, p. 512.

55. In his diary on February 15, 1985, Nakasone wrote, "Nakasone and Kanemaru relationship has acquired the entire initiative." Sekai Heiwa Kenkyusho, ed., *Nakasone Naikakushi*, vol. 3, p. 641.

56. Quoted in Maki, *Nakasone Seiken*, vol. 2, p. 204.

57. Gotôda, *Naikaku Kanbô Chôkan*, p. 81.

58. One expert member recalls: "On average, expert members and councilors not only

spent about one thousand hours in formal hearings and discussions, but also spent even more time in informal activities such as listening to the appeals of related ministries and organizations, giving public lectures concerning the administrative reforms, and directly negotiating with individual ministries with respect to the details of the reform items. Some members even wrote parts of the proposal drafts." Kumon, "Japan Faces Its Future," p. 145.

59. Nakasone, *Seiji to Jinsei*, p. 306.
60. Gotôda Masaharu, interview by author, December 18, 1992.
61. Nakasone, *Tenchi Ujô*, p. 514.

Chapter 6

Tax Reform by Nakasone and Takeshita

NAKASONE TAKES THE INITIATIVE

When Nakasone was reelected LDP president in October 1984, he wanted to introduce another major issue after administrative reform to tackle in his second two-year term. The need for a tax reform had been pointed out by a group of tax experts in the Government Tax Commission. Chief Cabinet Secretary Gotôda Masaharu, who was a tax expert as former director general of the Ministry of Home Affairs Tax Bureau, suggested to Nakasone that it was time to bring up tax reform.[1]

Tax reform was a fitting policy goal for the reelected prime minister. It matched his political slogan, "Clearing the postwar political legacy." Japan's tax system was created during the postwar U.S. Occupation and was based on the recommendation of Columbia University professor Carl S. Shoup. Because the immediate postwar era consumption level in Japan was low, Shoup suggested the adoption of a highly progressive income tax rate in an attempt to redistribute individual income more equally.

As the economy expanded, however, it became obvious by the late 1970s that the out-of-date tax system was creating many distortions. First, salaried workers in Japan complained that they suffered a disproportional tax burden. Their complaints were symbolized in the so-called 9-6-4 problem, in which the government could ascertain and tax 90 percent of salaried employees' income, compared to 60 percent of self-employed workers' income and only 40 percent of that of farmers. Under the Japanese tax system, the income tax of salaried employees is levied through their employers; thus, virtually all income earned by salaried workers is identified and reported to the tax authority. Yet, the income of self-employed workers is not always correctly identified or reported.

Because Japan does not have an individual tax identification numbering system, it is impossible for the tax authorities to identify all the earnings of individual taxpayers. Further, self-employed workers can relatively easily manipulate their declared income by claiming their spending as business costs. In 1983, almost 90 percent of salaried employees paid taxes, whereas only 40 percent of self-employed workers (non-farmers) and 20 percent of farmers did so.[2]

The second distortion in the tax system was that commodity and consumption taxes violated the principle of fairness and equality. The postwar tax system had imposed an indirect tax on luxury items. The concept of luxury, however, was ambiguous and relative. It was difficult to judge whether a newly introduced commodity was luxurious or not. Televisions and refrigerators were once luxury items but are now considered necessities for a household. An industry that was protected by powerful politicians could be exempt from commodity taxes for no apparent reason. As a result, there were numerous distortions and inequalities in taxes on commodities. For example, a commodity tax was imposed on coffee and cocoa, but not on tea or green tea. Consumers paid a tax on water skis, but not on snow skis.

Yet another distortion in the tax system was that the tax base for the commodity tax was limited to 85 items because of aggressive lobbying for tax exemption status by the relevant industries. This led to the government's heavy reliance on direct taxes, namely, individual and corporate income taxes. In 1985, 73.4 percent of tax revenue came from direct taxes, compared with 55 percent in 1950. However, direct taxes are relatively unstable revenue sources because individual and corporate incomes fluctuate more than does consumption. In addition, because the forthcoming aging society would have a considerably smaller ratio of income earners to support them, the government's tax revenue would also decrease. Because Japan's consumption level had grown to provide a large tax base, from the government's point of view, it was more effective to balance the sources of tax revenue among incomes, assets, and consumption. The Ministry of Finance wanted a consumption tax that would be a stable source of revenue.

Furthermore, tax reform was expected to contribute to the internationalization of the tax system. With business transactions becoming increasingly international, continued heavy reliance on individual and corporate income taxes was an ineffective policy. In Gotôda Masaharu's words, "Too heavy an individual income tax drives [high income earners] overseas, and too heavy a corporate income tax drives companies to off-shore activities."[3] In the eyes of tax experts, Japan needed to change the ratio of direct and indirect taxes by introducing a new indirect tax, as many Western countries had done.

In December 1984, the prime minister expressed to journalists his willingness to deal with the issue: "[Tax reform] would not change taxpayers' burden, but would focus on changing the direct-indirect tax ratio."[4] His emphasis on tax reform was a revenue-neutral and tax-cut-first approach.[5] By first providing the same amount of tax *cuts* in individual and corporate income taxes as the tax *increase* in indirect taxes, the prime minister thought he would be able to gain support from middle-class salaried employees and the business community, both suffering from a heavy tax burden.

In July 1985, Nakasone instructed the Ministry of Finance on his tax reform plan. In this plan, he suggested his approach. MOF officials, who wanted a stable revenue source, were generally pleased that the prime minister was willing to pursue the politically difficult reform, but they were concerned about the tax-cut-first approach. In a political compromise, the government might end up giving tax cuts without the introduction of a new tax. When MOF officials first met the prime minister on tax reform, they tried to persuade him that the introduction of a new tax and tax cuts must be introduced simultaneously. Not totally convinced, Nakasone emphasized the significance of his political approach to the situation.[6]

Nakasone had some distrust of the Ministry of Finance's motives because of its reccurring desire to implement a tax increase to reduce the fiscal deficit. Nakasone had doubtlessly learned a lesson from Prime Minister Ôhira Masa-yoshi's efforts to introduce a general consumption tax to reduce the fiscal deficit. Ôhira's efforts had met with strong opposition from the public and had created inner-party conflicts. These conflicts greatly fatigued the prime minister and contributed to his sudden death during the 1980 election campaign. Later, Nakasone expressed his distrust of bureaucrats: "So far [tax reform] has been led by the Ministry of Finance. As a result, one politician [Ôhira] was killed. I will not be killed. We have to do it in such a way that politicians lead the move."[7]

The Tax Policy Process

The question the prime minister faced was how to exercise his leadership. Prime Minister Nakasone was not a tax expert, and the tax policy-making process was complicated, involving the Government Tax Commission, the Liberal Democratic Party's Tax Commission, and the Ministry of Finance.

The MOF Tax Bureau is the office in charge of drafting tax legislation. Until 1959 when the Government Tax Commission was promoted to the level of advisory group to the prime minister, the MOF Tax Bureau had presented their own legislation to the Diet.[8] The commission was composed of fiscal policy scholars and some representatives of the private sector. The bureau formally delegated the responsibility of considering the general direction of tax policy to the commission. Because its Secretariat, which provided information and organized commission meetings, was located in the Ministry of Finance, the Tax Bureau could maintain considerable control over the course of discussions in the Tax Commission. This commission often merely approved the policy that the Ministry of Finance wanted to pursue.

Under the Suzuki and Nakasone administrations, a major power shift took place in the tax policy-making process: The LDP Tax Commission grew in influence vis-à-vis the Government Tax Commission. During the period of economic growth when the Government Commission usually proposed tax cuts, the LDP Tax Commission had played a relatively minor role. LDP politicians had no strong reason to oppose tax cuts, a politically popular policy. Once the economy entered its slow-growth period after the two oil shocks in the 1970s, the government began to propose tax increases instead of cuts. The LDP Commission could no longer play only a minor role.

According to one member of the Government Tax Commission, a drastic change occurred after the failure of Prime Minister Ôhira Masayoshi's attempt to introduce a general consumption tax.[9] As part of administrative reform, government spending for each ministry was frozen for five years. It became much more difficult for LDP Diet members to use their political influence and maneuvering on behalf of their constituency in the budget-making process. The arena in which the LDP members sought to wield their political power shifted to tax policy. Because they could no longer influence the spending side, they became more involved in the revenue side. An official at the MOF Tax Bureau described the shift: "In the budget-making process, lobbying by an LDP politician seldom causes a budget subexaminer [*Shusa*, a middle-level bureaucrat in charge of making decisions for detailed programs in government spending] to increase the budget even by a small amount on the spending side. In the tax policy-making process, on the other hand, LDP members often get tax savings of billions of yen for their clients."[10] More LDP members became interested in tax policy making, and in the late 1980s more than a majority of the LDP Diet members participated in the LDP Tax Commission.

When the LDP Tax Commission held a general meeting, more than 200 members attended to show that their client industries and constituencies were well represented. The top executives of the commission, respected as tax experts by other LDP members, coordinated the interests of the members and created a set of final tax proposals with the cooperation of the MOF Tax Bureau.[11] The political power of the commission's chairman was so strong that he was often referred to as "the finance minister in charge of tax policy," and he enjoyed considerable freedom in the decision-making process. One former chairman, Yamanaka Sadanori, for example, said in an interview: "As long as I was the chairman of the LDP Tax Commission, I did not allow even the prime minister to intervene in my decisions."[12]

Prime Minister Nakasone, with his limited knowledge of tax issues, had to pursue tax reform with the two commissions. Because the Government Tax Commission existed as an advisory council to the prime minister, Nakasone could not use the strategy of forming his own private advisory council, like the *Rinchô*, which was independent from the bureaucracy, an effective source of power described in the previous chapter. Instead, he used his appointment authority and appointed ten of his private advisors to the Government Tax Commission in an attempt to control the discussion on tax reform.[13] He justified his appointments at a press conference: "I would like to appoint some people outside of the bureaucratic circle so that the commission can reflect the voice of the private sector. So far the Government Tax Commission has been too respectful of the opinions of the Finance Ministry. It is better to have some 'Wild Stallions' [who can add new perspectives] in the commission."[14]

Forming a New Tax

In September 1985, Prime Minister Nakasone officially requested the Government Tax Commission to design a tax reform proposal. In his request, Nakasone asked the commission to first outline a policy for tax reduction and the rationalization of the tax system. He then asked for a new tax policy to supplement the reduced tax revenue. In his request, Nakasone reinforced his revenue neutral policy and emphasized a tax-cut-first policy to make the new indirect tax more politically acceptable.

MOF officials specifically asked the prime minister to make a speech at the meeting. Mizuno Masaru, then director general of the Tax Bureau, states why: "Looking back on the history of tax reform, most major reforms took place under extraordinary circumstances such as war. During normal times, government officials need to have not only strong determination but also the strong leadership of the prime minister in order to pursue major reforms. We needed the prime minister to express his determination."[15] The MOF officials wanted the visible involvement of the prime minister to give them leverage in their negotiations with other government agencies and LDP Diet members.

In his policy speech in January 1986, Nakasone labeled tax reform "a national issue requiring immediate treatment."[16] In April, the Government Tax Commission presented its proposal for a tax cut for individual and corporate income taxes, as Nakasone had requested. In the following month, the LDP Tax Commission presented its tax cut plan, basically confirming the Government Commission's proposal. These tax cuts were proposed at a time when they could benefit the LDP in the upcoming general election in July. As Nakasone later told junior LDP members: "First, we offer a tax cut to make people happy. Then, when we face the need to finance the tax cut, we introduce a tax hike because we have no alternative revenue. It is a two-step procedure."[17] This was Nakasone's election tactic.

Confident about gaining an increase in the number of LDP-held seats from an election, Prime Minister Nakasone dissolved the lower house on June 2. Four days later, however, LDP Policy Research Council chairman Fujio Masayuki said in a television debate, "The government would introduce a large-scale indirect tax to supplement government revenues lost by a cut in income taxes."[18] It prompted strong reaction all over the nation. Opposition parties attacked the government for considering such a large-scale tax increase. In a counterargument, Nakasone promised that he would not introduce a "large-scale indirect tax with which the Japanese people and LDP party members would disagree."[19] Early the next morning, two top Finance Ministry officials visited the prime minister and asked him to revise his statement. Nakasone did not take the situation so seriously and told them that they need not worry about his statement.[20] The public, however, took the prime minister's statement as an LDP campaign promise. In the July 6 double election, the LDP won an overwhelming victory, achieving a record-high 304 seats and earning Nakasone an exceptional one-year extension of his LDP presidency.

With this victory, Prime Minister Nakasone formed his fifth cabinet to pursue the tax reform issue as well as to finalize his administrative reform. Nakasone appointed two senior members, who had tight control over most of the members of the Tanaka faction, to top posts: LDP secretary general Kanemaru Shin became deputy prime minister and Takeshita Noboru took over as LDP secretary general. Kanemaru and Takeshita were also known as experts in Diet relations and were expected to play a crucial role in handling negotiations with the opposition parties. Abe Shintarô, who succeeded the leadership of the Fukuda faction, became chairman of the LDP Executive Council to build consensus within the party. Miyazawa Kiichi, who would soon take over as head of the Suzuki faction, was appointed finance minister and would be in charge of the policy side of tax reform. All the new leaders and potential prime ministerial candidates were now required to do their part to cooperate with the prime minister in the tax reform effort. It was also to their benefit to complete the politically difficult tax reform procedure under the Nakasone administration rather than having to deal with the issue if and when they became prime minister.

Nakasone appointed Yamanaka Sadanori to a crucial post in the tax reform scheme, chairman of the LDP Tax Commission. Although Yamanaka was a member of the Nakasone faction, he had a strong sense of rivalry toward Nakasone that originated in an early stage in their political careers. Yamanaka, proud of his independent power in tax policy making, would be difficult for Nakasone to control. However, the prime minister needed Yamanaka's expertise in the tax area, his political skill within the LDP, and his control over the Ministry of Finance to effectively pursue a reform of the tax structure. New tax committee chairman Yamanaka asked Nakasone about his commitment to tax reform. Nakasone stressed that tax reform was the final major policy objective of his cabinet. Yamanaka, recognizing Nakasone's firm determination, promised to do his best to help.[21]

The personal appointments for tax reform were set, but Nakasone's campaign promise not to introduce a large-scale indirect tax presented an obstacle. Two weeks after the election, the Government Tax Commission's subcommittee presented an interim report that suggested three different types of indirect taxes—a manufacturers' sales tax, a retailers' sales tax, and a Japanese-style value-added tax (VAT). Among the three, Nakasone preferred a manufacturers' sales tax, which would be imposed only on manufacturers and thus would not violate his campaign pledge.[22] LDP tax experts and the Ministry of Finance were against the prime minister's choice. One LDP tax expert told Nakasone that a manufacturer's sales tax would not be a large source of revenue unless the rate were set as high as 15 percent, which would clearly create unequal taxation on manufacturing and service industries.[23] Because of his lack of knowledge of tax issues, Nakasone had inadvertently chosen a system that would not be supported by LDP tax experts or by MOF officials who played important roles in tax policy making.

Originally the Ministry of Finance had planned to pursue a VAT, which would have provided a broad base for taxation. A majority of the Government Tax Commission agreed with ministry officials and expressed their preference for a VAT. Nakasone began to lose control. Even though Nakasone had appointed his private advisors to the commission, he was unable to influence their discussion. One of Nakasone's advisors on the commission commented: "Since we were newcomers and nonexperts on tax issues, we could not be influential in the commission's deliberations."[24]

In addition to the opposition stemming from both the party and the government, another group, the *Keidanren*, applied pressure on the prime minister. The *Keidanren* is an influential group of big businesses whose members are mostly manufacturers. Its chairman visited the prime minister's official residence after 9 P.M. on October 21, 1986—an unusual time for any official visit to the prime minister—and successfully persuaded Nakasone to drop the manufacturers' sales tax.[25] Nakasone could not deny this request from the influential business group. Nakasone was not, however, totally sold on a VAT. According to Nakasone's private advisor, the prime minister continued to seek an alternative between the manufacturing sales tax and the large-scale VAT.[26] There was none.

On October 28, the Government Tax Commission submitted its final proposal for tax reform, giving three alternative plans and its preference for a VAT. At that time, having been persuaded, Nakasone publicly expressed his endorsement of the VAT. At the lower house budget committee meeting on November 7, the prime minister stated that "the Japanese-style value-added tax, with tax-exempt items, would be possible" without violating his campaign pledge. According to Nakasone's argument, a VAT would not be a comprehensive, across-the-board indirect tax, with exceptions.

Meanwhile, the LDP Tax Commission began its deliberations on tax reform. Chairman Yamanaka Sadanori tried to proceed with deliberations in a relatively closed meeting of 38 members.[27] However, because the tax issue was closely related to many LDP members' constituencies and client industries, LDP leaders demanded a forum to express their views. On October 30 when the commission held a general meeting, 150 Diet members attended.

In the open meeting, the three top leaders of the commission—Chairman Yamanaka, Deputy Chairman Murayama Tatsuo, and Subcommittee Chairman Yamashita Ganri—all supported a value-added tax because a VAT would provide the broadest tax base. During deliberations, tax exemptions were introduced—for small business with annual sales of less than 100 million yen and for seven categories of goods and services such as food, medical service, education, housing and real estate rent, and transportation—that made the new tax neither "across-the-board" nor "large-scale."

Even after the announcement of these exemptions, a fierce battle took place in the LDP Tax Commission among interest groups and their patron *zoku* LDP members who were trying to win tax exempt status. As LDP Tax Commission chairman Yamanaka Sadanori recalls: "We first decided that warehouses could be exempted because storing goods does not add value to the goods. Then representatives of the refrigerated warehouse industry came to us and asked for exemption, arguing that they are no different from ordinary warehouses except in room temperature. It sounded reasonable. Then the refrigerated freight industry asked for an exemption. It became difficult to draw the line and many controversies arose."[28] Subsequently, on December 20, 26 categories were added to the original 7. In the final proposal, 41 categories received tax exemptions.

These tax exemptions helped legitimize Nakasone's claim that his sales tax proposal was not large-scale, but they created new distortions and inequalities— the very characteristics that the government had intended to eliminate with the introduction of the new tax. Deputy Chairman Murayama Tatsuo stated: "It was not a good idea to open the tax discussion to LDP members before the basic framework was completed. LDP members, who represented certain industries, asked for exemptions for their client industries. This distorted the tax proposal."[29] The indirect tax created dissatisfaction among tax experts, who had wanted a fairer, more equal tax system, as well as industries that did not receive tax exemption status for their products and services. Among the most vocal industries was the textile industry. According to an MOF official, its representatives argued that among the three basics in life—clothing, food, and housing— clothing was the only one that would be taxed. This discrepancy led them to vigorously oppose the sales tax.[30] The Ministry of Finance's Tax Bureau chief looks back: "The new tax framework was introduced in December, and by the end of the month everything was decided. I felt the frustration of various industries: they had not had enough time to receive an explanation of the reform measures and to submit requests."[31] This further weakened support for the VAT.

Meeting the Oppositions

December 29 saw the opening of the 108th ordinary Diet session, which came to be known as the "Sales Tax Session." Prior to the opening, the opposition parties had formed a coalition against the sales tax. In the private sector, retailers, including those from supermarkets and department stores, and wholesalers had formed organizations to oppose the new tax and had teamed up with the opposition parties on this issue. The tax reform was supposed to reduce the tax burden on salaried employees, but a report by an independent group of scholars announced that the tax reform would actually increase the burden for those with an income of less than 6 million yen. This created strong public resentment against the new tax. Prime Minister Nakasone lost the support of urban salaried workers, on which he had counted.

The Diet session reopened after a recess on January 26, 1987, and Nakasone gave his policy speech. Although he restressed the need for tax reform, he neglected to mention the name of the new tax system his administration planned to introduce. This gave the opposition parties an opportunity to attack the ruling party and thus delayed the Diet deliberations for a full month.[32] The sales tax Diet session showed signs of trouble from the beginning.

Despite the opposition from the private sector and the opposition parties, the Ministry of Finance proceeded drafting tax reform. MOF officials originally wanted to draft one legislation with both the introduction of sales tax and tax cuts so that Prime Minister Nakasone could no longer seek a tax-cut-first approach. The Cabinet Legal Bureau opposed the idea of combining the revision of the existing law and the introduction of a new tax in the same legislation. Changing their tactics, MOF officials then drafted three bills—one on tax cuts, another on sales tax, and the third on details for the two new laws such as the date of effect, functionally combining the first two bills. Nakasone and his cabinet approved these MOF bills, officially abandoning his tax-cut-first approach.[33]

After introducing the tax reform bills on February 4, Nakasone asked 500 representatives from local LDP offices to support the new tax. "I do not care what would happen to me. I am tackling tax reform with the belief that the nation and its people are much more important than myself. Let me achieve this. I want to stake my political life on discharging my responsibilities as a statesman."[34] Nakasone explained that his sales tax proposal did not violate the campaign promise in which he had refused to introduce a large-scale indirect tax because of the many exemptions granted to different interest groups. However, Nakasone was not convincing and failed to gain support. In a closed question-and-answer session, local representatives criticized the way the LDP had handled tax reform.[35]

Some LDP Diet members were also critical. Younger LDP members from urban districts, whose electoral support base was primarily retailers, could not afford to support a sales tax. LDP members Fukaya Ryûji and Hatoyama Kunio, both from districts in downtown Tokyo, attended an anti–sales tax meeting organized by local retailers and pledged that they would oppose the new tax. Other LDP members voiced strong criticism against them, and LDP secretary general Takeshita Noboru warned them about going against the party's decision. The two apologized for attending the meeting that included Communist Party members, but they told Takeshita that they would not change their stance against the sales tax. For them, reelection was much more important than party discipline.

Diet deliberations were effectively stopped by the opposition parties; at the same time, opposition grew within the ruling party itself. A turning point in the political climate came in a by-election for an upper house seat in Iwate Prefecture. On March 8, an LDP candidate lost by a large margin—more than two to one (421,000 to 198,000 votes)—in the election for the seat previously occupied by her late husband. Because she was expected to win in the conservative prefecture, her loss shocked the LDP. The winner from the Japan Socialist Party told reporters that his victory was thanks to Prime Minister Nakasone, who had introduced an unpopular sales tax. JSP leader Doi Takako later wrote in her memoirs that the "Iwate shock" changed the direction of tax reform and eventually led to the death of the sales tax proposal.[36]

The election loss exacerbated the fear of LDP members who were facing local elections. On March 16, Deputy Prime Minister Kanemaru Shin noted the possible need for revising the proposal. LDP Policy Research Council chairman Itô Masayoshi complained: "It was like being shot in the back. When younger Diet members are holding back, an influential cabinet member must not make such a statement."[37] Just as Itô had expected, Kanemaru's statement triggered more open criticism against the sales tax among LDP members whose support base opposed tax reform.

Opposition at the local level was so strong that LDP affiliated candidates running for prefectural governors were worried about their election campaigns scheduled to begin on March 23. Tokyo governor Suzuki Shun'ichi of the LDP openly stated his opposition to the sales tax. No gubernatorial candidate asked Nakasone for his endorsement in the form of a speech in his or her district during the campaign. This was quite an unusual occurrence; prime ministers were usually popular in helping candidates during major election campaigns.

The anti–sales tax sentiment was so strong that the LDP lost in the gubernatorial elections in Hokkaido and Fukuoka Prefectures, two close races to which the party had paid the most attention. The LDP lost many seats in the local parliament as well—from 1,486 down to 1,382 in the prefectural assemblies and from 232 to 204 seats in city assemblies. Even LDP secretary general Takeshita Noboru admitted that the loss was largely attributable to the proposed sales tax.

"The public support rate of my cabinet before starting tax reform was over 60 percent. I am willing to sacrifice my popularity." Despite the loss in the election, Nakasone expressed his determination in front of his supporters from his electoral district.[38] At the lower house Budget Committee meeting on April 14, the prime minister stated that he had no intention of withdrawing the sales tax bills. On the same day at the party's executive council meeting, many LDP members expressed their opposition to the tax. Three days later, a private group of more than three hundred LDP Diet members adopted a resolution that urged the withdrawal of the sales tax bills, and handed it to Secretary General Takeshita and Chief Cabinet Secretary Gotôda. A majority of the LDP was now against forcing the sales tax bills through the Diet.

Backed by public support, the opposition parties accelerated their attack on the LDP. The budget proposal for FY1987, suspended in the Diet, was now held hostage by the opposition parties. Because deliberations on the budget were delayed, the government had to form a temporary budget to pay the salaries of government employees. LDP leaders, including Secretary General Takeshita Noboru, saw that passing the budget was more important than passing the tax reform bills in that session. On April 15, the LDP forced the budget proposal through the lower house Budget Committee with no prior consent from the opposition parties. Budget Committee chairman Sunada Shigetami stated: "We could not delay the passage of the budget any longer. The destiny of the Japanese economy was much more important than the destiny of Mr. Nakasone. I am proud of my committee for passing the budget bill."[39] The consequence was obvious: The opposition parties further hardened their position against the sales tax.

The Sales Tax Dies

Deliberations over the sales tax bills on the lower house were even tougher for the LDP. As Chief Cabinet Secretary Gotôda describes: "The unity of the opposition parties was firm, and their position was that they were determined to refuse talks unless [the LDP] withdrew the sales tax bills."[40] The opposition parties used a traditional filibuster in the Japanese Diet for the first time in 12 years, "cow-walking" (walking extremely slowly during their voting) to use up the already limited deliberation time allocated to the lower house for voting on the budget proposal. LDP secretary general Takeshita told Nakasone that the LDP would not be able to force the budget through the lower house because of the strong unity of the opposition parties and the disunity within the LDP. He asked the prime minister to decide how to deal with the tax reform proposal. Nakasone instructed Takeshita to have the speaker of the lower house mediate between the LDP and the opposition parties without killing the tax proposal.[41] Behind the scenes, Takeshita instructed Ozawa Ichirô, a younger leader of his own faction, to work on a political compromise with the opposition parties.[42]

As a result, the mediation of the speaker produced the following results: (1) the LDP and the opposition parties would continue to discuss the tax reform issue after the budget passed the Diet; (2) the sales tax bills would be dropped if they could not reach agreement; and (3) the lower house would establish a joint council to continue discussing tax reform. As Takeshita points out: "The mediation by the speaker was to set a new starting point to put tax reform back on track in return for dropping the sales tax bills."[43] The opposition parties agreed to these terms. This enabled the LDP to pass the FY 1987 budget in the lower house on April 23. One month later, the upper house passed the budget, and the "sales tax session" closed. The sales tax, on which Nakasone had placed top priority in his last year as prime minister, was officially dropped with the closing of the session.

Partial Reform Enacted

Prime Minister Nakasone's ambition to pursue tax reform, however, did not end. On May 25, the LDP and the opposition parties opened the first meeting of the Conference on Tax Reform, with 13 multipartisan members, to continue discussions. One of the issues discussed was a tax cut to stimulate the economy. Facing the G-7 Venice summit in the following month, the Japanese government was expected by other countries to expand domestic demand and increase imports. The Nakasone administration held a cabinet-level economic conference and decided on an emergency economic package, including a tax cut of no less than 1 trillion yen, which the prime minister would be able to present at the summit. Nakasone planned to link the tax cut in the stimulus package to tax reform so as to eliminate *maruyû*, or tax exemption for small-scale savings, previously included in tax reform bills. The tax-exempt small-scale savings system was considered an obstacle to increasing domestic consumption and was under international criticism.

"The Nakasone cabinet shall pass this through. It will create a path for tax reform"—the prime minister expressed his intent to abolish the tax exemption.[44] Tax Bureau chief Mizuno Masaru analyzes Nakasone's political intentions in relation to a new political development with the expiration of his term as LDP president in October 1987. "We needed some result in tax reform by September [before selection of the new prime minister in October]. Otherwise, Prime Minister Nakasone who initiated tax reform would resign without any achievement."[45] The abolition of the tax exemption was a must for Nakasone in order to maintain his political influence after leaving office.

After 12 meetings, the multipartisan tax conference submitted an interim report to the lower house. Although the LDP and the opposition parties agreed on the need for a sizable tax cut, they disagreed on the size of the cut and how to finance the decrease in revenues. The LDP proposed a 1-trillion-yen tax cut and the abolition of the *maruyû* to finance the cut. The opposition parties, in contrast, wanted 2 trillion yen in tax cuts and the continuation of the tax exemption system. Although disagreement was significant, agreement on the need for a tax cut was greater. On July 31 the Nakasone cabinet approved tax bills that would reduce individual income taxes by 1.3 trillion yen and abolish the tax exempt savings system, with an exception for single-mother families, the elderly, and the handicapped. The cabinet then presented the bill in the Diet. The stage for negotiations was forced outside parliament.

LDP secretary general Takeshita Noboru and Diet Policy Committee chairman Fujinami Takao contacted the opposition parties. Again, Takeshita asked Ozawa to negotiate with the opposition parties.[46] Partly because they no longer held the budget proposal hostage and partly because they too wanted the tax cut, the attitude of the opposition parties was more flexible than during the sales tax debates. The Democratic Socialist Party and *Kômeitô* showed interest in an LDP proposal to increase the amount that taxes would be reduced.

Takeshita presented a proposal that included a 1.5-trillion-yen income tax reduction. At first, the opposition parties refused this because the reduction level was still too small. Prime Minister Nakasone was upset by this response, and he refused to increase the tax reduction any further. Takeshita met with representatives from the opposition parties and presented a revised final proposal that included an additional 40-billion-yen tax reduction. Although the proposal was not fully satisfactory to the opposition parties, they agreed to participate in deliberations on the tax proposal in the Diet. This was in actuality a final political compromise needed for the passage of the tax bill. The tax reform to abolish the *maruyû* system passed the Diet on September 19, a month before the end of Prime Minister Nakasone's term. Nakasone saved face by passing a partial tax reform bill. The passage would help Nakasone maintain his influence in the LDP.

TAKESHITA'S CONSUMPTION TAX

The task of finishing the tax reform was handed down to the post-Nakasone administration. Three LDP leaders declared their candidacy for the LDP presidency and agreed to pursue the tax reform issue. At a joint press conference, however, Takeshita Noboru was the only one to cite completion of tax reform as his top policy priority.[47]

The three candidates preferred that the next prime minister be selected through negotiations in order to avoid any unnecessary hostility that might come with the election. They agreed to cooperate with the new administration to pursue policy goals regardless of who was the national leader, but their negotiations failed to produce agreement on who would succeed Nakasone. The three delegated the authority to decide who would be the successor.

Nakasone's pick was Takeshita, who had played an instrumental role as LDP secretary general in the attempt to introduce the sales tax.[48] Takeshita had been the finance minister not only under the Nakasone administration for four consecutive terms but also under the Ôhira administration when Ôhira tried to introduce his general consumption tax. In his policy platform in the LDP presidential race, Takeshita stated that Japan needed to establish a fair and simple tax system through open discussion in order to secure a revenue source to improve national welfare.[49]

Takeshita's knowledge of the tax system was widely known. Many in the government believed that the introduction of a new indirect tax would be possible only under Takeshita's leadership. "Consumption tax is not understood in this country. If someone introduces it, he would receive much criticism and be seen as a bad guy. For the future of Japan, somebody must do this despite the criticism. I am ready and determined to take the risk," Takeshita explained to his assistant.[50]

Making a New Proposal

Takeshita, with tax reform as his top policy priority, initiated his first move just one week after he took office by appointing 30 members to the Government Tax Commission and asking them to prepare a tax reform plan. In his first policy speech on November 27, 1987, the prime minister stressed that he would try not to overly influence the deliberations of the Government Tax Commission in order to encourage open discussion. Early in 1988, Takeshita's policy of open discussion was further emphasized by the commission. The commission held 20 public hearings throughout the country between February 8 and March 3, which served as an important information source for the Takeshita administration. An MOF official, who helped organize the hearings, said in an interview: "We have learned that the sales tax introduced under the Nakasone administration created fear among taxpayers, fear that the tax authority would tighten tax collection by requiring the presentation of invoices for every single business transaction. By getting rid of these concerns, we thought that we could successfully introduce a new tax."[51]

Reflecting the results of the public hearings, Prime Minister Takeshita suggested to his assistant from the Finance Ministry, "We should turn the table around by pointing out the problems that we need to overcome."[52] Takeshita indicated in the Diet on March 10 that taxpayers had several concerns about the introduction of a new indirect tax. These concerns were that such a tax might (1) weaken the redistribution effect of taxes; (2) increase the inequality borne by middle-class tax payers; (3) excessively increase the tax burden for nonincome earners; (4) make it easy for the government to increase taxes because a broadly based tax would be less of a burden to each tax payer; (5) increase administrative costs for small business; and (6) increase prices, thus inviting inflation. The prime minister expressed his willingness to deal with these problems, a statement that enabled further discussion with the opposition parties and allowed the introduction of a new tax.[53]

Takeshita provided the opposition parties with another reason to be involved in the deliberations of a new indirect tax. The Japan Socialist Party, Kômeitô, and the Democratic Socialist Party had requested a revision of the budget, including a 3-trillion-yen tax cut. Such a large-scale tax cut could not be achieved without drastic tax reform. The Liberal Democratic Party agreed with the request, and the LDP and the opposition parties agreed to further discuss how to finance it. The tax cut agreement served as Takeshita's invitation to deliberate a tax reform.

On April 28, the Government Tax Commission introduced its interim report. It presented three types of multilevel indirect taxes: a VAT with an invoice system, which was similar to Nakasone's sales tax; a VAT with an account-bookkeeping system; and an indirect tax on overall sales. The new tax had to be multilevel, or its administrative costs would be imposed only on retailers, the electoral base for many LDP members. An indirect tax on overall sales, which would impose more taxes on products that go through many distribution channels, was against the principle of equality.[54] The actual choices of a VAT were, therefore, limited to an invoice system or an account-bookkeeping system.

Having learned lessons from the Nakasone administration's experience and public hearings, Takeshita's pick was a new consumption tax with an account-bookkeeping system. An account-bookkeeping system would ease taxpayers' concerns in several ways. It would lessen the administrative costs and would not force small businesses to present the details of every business transaction.

In an account-bookkeeping system, taxes are levied, in principle, on all items. Without invoices, it is very difficult to decide which items are tax exempt. The no-exemption principle would avoid the political infighting and turmoil over tax exemption status that had led to rejection in the Diet of Nakasone's sales tax. Once Takeshita decided on the account-bookkeeping system and the no-exemption principle, it was not difficult for the LDP Tax Commission to reach its final decision. The commission's deputy chairman Murayama Tatsuo recalls: "The fact that the members of the largest faction, [Takeshita's] *Keiseikai*, made the decisions was one of the main factors for its successful introduction. When they decided on the account-bookkeeping system and the no-exemption principle, it was difficult for other LDP factions to oppose it."[55]

Takeshita's faction members competed to help their leader build a consensus within the ruling party. Successful passage would increase the political influence of the Takeshita faction over the party and the bureaucracy. Katô Hiroshi, chairman of the Government Tax Commission's Subcommittee on Indirect Tax, stated that the agreement among seven younger leaders of the Takeshita faction on the introduction of the consumption tax was important for its success. "The seven, especially those very closely associated with Takeshita such as then chief cabinet secretary Obuchi Keizô, worked hard to convince the entire faction and then actively persuaded other faction members," said Katô.[56] Many LDP members realized that another failed tax reform attempt would devastate the political influence of the LDP and increase that of the opposition parties.

On June 14, the LDP Tax Commission announced its final report. As expected, the report recommended a VAT with the account-bookkeeping system and limited categories for tax exempt items. It also lowered the tax rate of a VAT from 5 percent to 3 percent. This made overall tax reform a net tax cut of as much as 2.4 trillion yen. The Ministry of Finance, which had been preparing a revenue-neutral tax reform, was strongly opposed to the lowered rate, and Finance Minister Miyazawa Kiichi tried to persuade LDP Tax Commission chairman Yamanaka Sadanori to change the rate. Yamanaka flatly refused, explaining:

We failed in an attempt to introduce [Nakasone's] sales tax. We could not present a new proposal with the same 5 percent rate. We had to lower the rate so that the new tax would be more acceptable to tax payers. Finance Minister Miyazawa tried to persuade me to increase the rate to 5 percent. But I would not have allowed anybody, not even the prime minister, to intervene in my decision as the chairman of LDP's tax committee.[57]

MOF officials finally accepted Yamanaka's decision by saying, "The most important thing is to introduce a consumption tax."[58]

Prime Minister Takeshita allowed Yamanaka to make this significant decision. Takeshita had made the decision on the account-bookkeeping system and the no-exemption status, having Yamanaka make the 3 percent decision was, in a sense, a face-saving measure for the independent-minded Government Tax Commission chairman. Katô Hiroshi said in an interview: "The MOF was very upset by Yamanaka's decision, which was supported by Takeshita."[59] Yamanaka boasted in an interview, "Without me, the tax reform could have taken over ten years."[60] According to Yamanaka, his political career as a tax expert and reputation as a political fighter enabled him to stand up to MOF pressure. Takeshita's decision to reappoint Yamanaka to the chair contributed to the success of the tax reform.

The opposition parties announced their dissent of the LDP proposal. However, their unity was not as solid as it had been in their rejection of Nakasone's sales tax. Whereas the conservative Democratic Socialist Party agreed to further discuss the tax reform, the Japan Socialist Party, the Japan Communist Party, and *Kômeitô* demanded the dissolution of the lower house before the reform could be introduced. Some labor unions that could benefit from a reduction in income taxes pressured the party to start discussions on the tax reform measures.[61] The flexible attitude of the DSP enabled the LDP to deliberate the tax bills in the Diet.

Easing the Opposition

Prime Minister Takeshita ordered the various ministries to find ways to ease taxpayers' fear in each industry and to compensate them for their damage without making exceptions to the no-exemption principle regarding the 3 percent consumption tax rate. Takeshita was able to take advantage of his extensive personal network with individual bureaucrats. The general director of the MOF Tax Bureau said: "The Tax Bureau was the center of activities when promoting the Nakasone tax reform. But this time, the entire ministry concentrated its efforts to one end: asking all its bureaus to cooperate. We even asked the Ministry of International Trade and Industry to contact concerned industries."[62]

As the official pointed out, MITI was probably the ministry that worked most closely with the Ministry of Finance. The strongest opponents of sales tax, retailers and the textile industry among others, were under MITI jurisdiction. Despite the opposition of some industries, MITI decided to support the sales tax and the consumption tax. Tax reform would come with a reduction in corporate taxes, rates considered extremely high by international standards. Lower corporate taxes would allow the industries to invest more for future developments.

Following Takeshita's "open discussion" policy, MITI conducted public and private hearings with representatives of many industries to find out their complaints and their suggestions on how the government could improve the system. Each MITI division collected information for its client industries. MITI's Corporate Behavior Division in the Industrial Planning Bureau served as planning headquarters for the introduction of the tax reforms. The division's director recalls:

The Nakasone administration's sales tax was theoretically a well-structured tax system. It would not have created inequality on the side of tax collectors. But it ignored the taxpayers' side. In the Takeshita tax reform, we decided to listen to the taxpayers and learn reality from their point of view. The retailers of used automobiles, for example, complained that any form of consumption tax would encourage private sales of used cars, which would decrease their business. It was a good learning process for us.[63]

After listening to the complaints from each industry, MITI and the Ministry of Finance provided appropriate budgetary and tax compensations to rid or ease the industries' fears without violating the no-exemption principle.[64]

One group to which MITI and the LDP paid special attention was retailers. Traditionally pro-LDP, these small-size retailers were the core of the organized actions that had grown into a national movement against the Nakasone sales tax. Their opposition scared the LDP Diet members who represented urban commercial districts, and that fear led to the split within the party in the last tax reform attempt. An official of MITI's Retail Commerce Division said in an interview, "When the industry's representatives learned the government was even more serious, they changed their position to one of fighting for better conditions for compensation."[65] MITI offered low-interest loans and subsidies for shopping arcades under the guise of "consolidation of the community facility," simplified the tax-filing system for retailers, and lowered the corporate tax.

The LDP also decided that small business owners with annual sales of less than 30 million yen would be tax exempt. This would effectively exempt most farmers and many small retailers. The exemption gained the support of LDP members, most of whom were supported by these interest groups. (Tax exemption by business size did not create the same split in intraparty politics as did the tax exemption by item.) LDP Tax Commission chairman Yamanaka Sadanori looks back:

We held several public hearings and learned that many small commerce groups in the local communities, including groups of small retailers, were most strongly opposed. We, members of the LDP Tax Commission, decided to formulate a new tax that would be acceptable to those commerce associations even if local chambers of commerce [groups of larger business] would oppose it. This was the main reason that we decided the maximum tax exemption level of annual sales would be 30 million yen.[66]

With the government providing compensation and dealing with the specific concerns of each industry, LDP *zoku* members who had played their role as protectors of the industry no longer had a strong reason to oppose Takeshita's tax reform.

Takeshita punished those LDP members who had actively opposed Nakasone's sales tax through his appointment authority. For example, Hatoyama Kunio was one of the most vocal young members of the LDP who had participated in the anti–sales tax meetings and had appeared in the media publicly criticizing the tax reform initiative. The LDP punished Hatoyama by not appointing him chairman of LDP's Policy Subcommittee on Education. As an education *zoku* member, Hatoyama greatly wanted this post.[67] Instead, he was appointed director of the Public Speeches Bureau of the LDP and therefore was forced to take on the preparations for Prime Minister Takeshita's campaign to persuade taxpayers to support tax reform.

Another example was Sakurai Shin, one of the two strong candidates for the popular post of the construction vice minister. The post was not given to Sakurai, who had openly opposed the new tax system, but to another candidate who had worked hard on the Nakasone tax reform. All the faction leaders supported these punishments. The strong unity among faction leaders quieted the voices of those with an anticonsumption tax stance.

The Consumption Tax Session

As the consensus-building within the LDP neared completion, the stage moved to the Diet for the last tax reform battle. On June 23, Prime Minister Takeshita Noboru, at a press briefing in Hawaii, expressed his determination to see tax reform through by staking the destiny of his cabinet on the passage of the consumption tax bills.[68] Five days later, the Takeshita cabinet approved the Outline for Tax Reform submitted by the LDP Tax Commission, which included the introduction of the consumption tax.

As the LDP negotiated with the opposition parties in early July, the political environment dramatically changed. The Recruit scandal—a scandal exposed by an *Asahi Shimbun* scoop on June 18 in which an ambitious business leader attempted to build intimate ties with many politicians—drew wide public attention.[69] On July 6, the *Asahi Shimbun* reported that the assistants of former prime minister Nakasone Yasuhiro, LDP secretary general Abe Shintarô and Finance Minister Miyazawa Kiichi, received unlisted stocks of the Recruit Cosmos Company, the prices of which were destined to inflate when listed. This was seen as a new style of political contribution that could be labeled as bribery. On the following day, it was reported that an assistant to Prime Minister Takeshita and DSP chairman Tsukamoto Saburô had also received stocks.

This scandal changed the attitude of the opposition parties. The Japan Socialist Party and *Kômeitô* became interested in opening an extraordinary Diet session to discuss the scandal further. The LDP saw this as an opportunity to deliberate on the tax reform bills. When the LDP suggested the establishment of a special committee to discuss tax reform and the scandal, the opposition parties generally agreed. In return for participating in the deliberation, however, the opposition parties demanded that the government first introduce tax cuts, separately from the introduction of a consumption tax. The LDP accepted the condition.[70] This, of course, met strong opposition from MOF officials who had successfully stopped Nakasone's tax-cut-first approach earlier.

Takeshita instructed Deputy Chief Cabinet Secretary Ozawa Ichirô to persuade MOF officials. Ozawa, who had dealt with tax negotiation under the Nakasone administration, was already actively negotiating with the opposition parties and the government officials behind the scene.[71] Ozawa met Mizuno Masaru, MOF Tax Bureau chief, with his close associate Hirano Sadao. After Mizuno refused the tax-cut-first approach several times, Ozawa finally said, "It is a matter of trust. I am confident that *Kômeitô* and the DSP will cooperate in the end." Hirano added, "Mr. Ozawa, who in fact represents the Takeshita administration, said he is confident, considering the situation of *Kômeitô* and the DSP. If you don't trust him, that means you have no trust in the Takeshita administration." This threatened Mizuno, who responded, "I trust Mr. Ozawa, *Kômeitô*, and the DSP."[72] As the Ministry of Finance reluctantly accepted the tax-cut-first approach, the LDP and the opposition parties finally agreed on opening an extraordinary Diet session on July 19. The first hurdle for the passage of the consumption tax bills—setting a forum to deliberate the bills—was overcome.

The LDP kept its promise by introducing a bill on income tax cut as a separate legislation. After seeing its passage, deliberations over the tax reform bills began in the lower house on September 22. While the JSP and the Japan Communist Party refused to participate, the DSP and *Kômeitô* held to their commitment by joining the LDP in floor discussions. By this time, it was obvious that the chairmen of the two parties were involved in the scandals—the DSP chairman in the Recruit scandal and *Kômeitô* chairman in yet another political scandal. If the tax reform bills died and Prime Minister Takeshita dissolved the lower house, these two opposition parties would be at least as severely damaged as the LDP, if not more so. The threat of dissolution, often referred to as the prime minister's trump card, forced the two opposition parties to agree to participate in the Diet deliberations on the tax reform bills. With the attendance of these two parties, the LDP successfully extended the extraordinary session for another 59 days.

On November 10, after conducting the promised public hearing on the new consumption tax in three different cities, the chairman of the Special Committee of Tax Reform and the Recruit scandal opened a committee meeting. When the opposition parties refused to take part in further negotiations, the LDP forced the tax reform bills through the special committee without the presence of any opposition party member.[73] Now the reform bills awaited passage in the lower house floor.

All the opposition parties criticized the forced passage of the tax reform bills, but were not united on their next demand. The Japan Socialist Party and the Japan Communist Party demanded the dissolution of the lower house unless the LDP withdrew the bills. The JSP forced its Diet member involved in the scandal to resign, thus allowing the party to continue attacking the LDP. In contrast, *Kômeitô* did not force their Recruit scandal–tainted member to resign. It thus shared the weak position of the Democratic Socialist Party, whose chairman was involved in the scandal; neither could ask for the dissolution of the lower house because the subsequent election would lead to the defeat of their own party members. On November 15, the LDP reached an agreement with the DSP and

Kômeitô ensured that the government would disclose all the names involved in the Recruit scandal. *Kômeitô*, whose chairman was rumored to be involved in the scandal, badly wanted the disclosure of that list to prove its leader's innocence.[74] As instructed by Takeshita, Ozawa Ichirô met with *Kômeitô* chairman Yano Junya. Ozawa accepted the disclosure after securing agreement from *Kômeitô* leader that his party would continue discussions on tax reform.[75] This deal allowed the LDP to proceed with further negotiations on the tax reform bills with the opposition parties.

The Tax Reform Bills Enacted

The resulting negotiation session lasted until the morning of November 16. In the negotiations with the DSP, the LDP agreed to the DSP's conditions, including flexible implementation of the consumption tax. The LDP then began negotiating with *Kômeitô*. *Kômeitô* requested the implementation of several welfare programs, and the LDP agreed. These agreements assured the presence of the two opposition parties in the Diet for the vote on the tax reform bills. In the afternoon, the lower house meeting was held, and the tax reform bills with the modifications requested by the opposition parties were presented. The DSP and *Kômeitô* voted against the original bills but voted for the modified portions. In the end, the tax reform bills passed the lower house with the LDP's majority votes.

On November 24, the lower house voted for a further extension of the extraordinary session for another 34 days to deliberate the tax reform bills in the upper house. With this extension, the extraordinary session lasted 163 days. The Diet session of 313 days in 1988, combined with 150 days of the ordinary session, set a record. Takeshita took full advantage of the extraordinary session with two extensions as well as the fact that the government did not need to introduce a budget—in an ordinary session the budget is often held hostage by the opposition parties, as in the case of the sales tax.

During the extended session, Finance Minister Miyazawa Kiichi was accused of being dishonest about his assistant's involvement in the Recruit scandal. On December 1 in the upper house, Miyazawa admitted that his previous statements had been incorrect. He told Prime Minister Takeshita that he was prepared to resign at any time.[76] The possibility of Miyazawa's resignation became a trump card for the Takeshita administration and helped ease the attitude of *Kômeitô* and the DSP toward further deliberation in the upper house.[77]

After Miyazawa resigned, Takeshita assumed the post of the finance minister in addition to his responsibilities as prime minister. As Takeshita's assistant suggested, this was proof of how deeply the prime minister was involved in the tax reform. The assistant stated in an interview: "Mr. Takeshita was confident that he knew more about the reform than anybody and that he would not need another finance minister. It showed that Mr. Takeshita was the pivotal figure who orchestrated the tax reform, not Finance Minister Miyazawa."[78]

After holding a public hearing on December 16, 1988, the LDP informally told representatives of the opposition parties of its intent to count the votes on the reform at the special committee within a week's time. Although the opposition parties did not approve of this step, some members of *Kômeitô* and the DSP admitted that the minimum necessary time for deliberation in the committee had passed.[79] On December 21, the LDP suddenly cut off deliberations and forced the tax reform bills through the committee. After the bills' passage there, the LDP quickly approached *Kômeitô* and the DSP to secure their support in upper house deliberations. The two opposition parties, both wanting to avoid the dissolution of the lower house by any means possible, began renegotiations with the LDP. When the LDP accepted their conditions, the opposition parties agreed to participate in the upper house meeting.[80]

On December 23, the upper house met, including the members of the Japan Socialist Party and the Japan Communist Party. However, they joined the meeting only to engage in "cow-walking" by submitting nonapproval resolutions of several cabinet members—the same filibuster technique that had killed Nakasone's sales tax bills. But the impact this time was much weaker because *Kômeitô* and the DSP did not join in the filibuster. Twenty-six hours after the opening of the session, the tax reform bills passed the upper house and were finally enacted. On the same day, Prime Minister Takeshita Noboru said, "I believe that once the consumption tax is implemented and becomes familiar to the people . . . combined with a large direct tax cut, the people will understand that they are better off with this tax reform."[81]

Four months later, in the midst of the political turmoil surrounding the Recruit scandal, Prime Minister Takeshita resigned. The support rate for the Takeshita cabinet dropped to a record low 3 percent. The low popularity of the Takeshita administration, which partly reflected the introduction of the unpopular tax reform, strongly affected the July 1989 upper house election, in which the LDP lost a majority for the first time since its inception of 1955. As Takeshita predicted, however, a few years after the introduction of the consumption, criticism against it was rarely heard. Today tax reform is portrayed as the most significant political contribution of the Takeshita administration.

SUMMARY

Tax reform, initiated by the Nakasone administration and followed through in the Takeshita administrations, would affect various economic activities in the nation. Although the introduction of a new tax itself is under the jurisdiction of the Ministry of Finance, the overall tax reform efforts involved most of the government agencies and various groups of LDP *zoku* members. The process required the deep commitment of two prime ministers.

Prime Minister Nakasone Yasuhiro, who had successfully orchestrated administrative reform, was not able to handle the technical matters surrounding the tax reform issue. By appointing ten of his close advisors to the Government

Tax Commission, Nakasone tried to influence the policy process of reforming the tax system. However, these ten advisors did not have the necessary expertise on tax issues, so their influence remained limited. The tax experts on the commission dominated the deliberations.

Nakasone had limited bureaucratic experience and never assumed the post of finance minister. He failed to convince the Ministry of Finance to allow the tax-cut-first approach. This limited his room for political maneuvering. Also, Nakasone's lack of expertise in tax issues was evident in his preference for a manufacturers' sales tax over a value-added tax. His choice was opposed by tax experts in the government, by the LDP, and by the business community—camps he needed in alliance to achieve his goals. Support was thus lacking.

Nakasone stated that his administration would not introduce a large-scale indirect tax, reflecting his preference for the manufacturers' sales tax. This statement was taken as a campaign pledge for the 1986 double election, and many LDP candidates echoed the prime minister in their own campaigns to win their seat. This became a major constraint on Nakasone's efforts to reform the tax system, since he could not smoothly retract the statement after so much had been made of it.

Nakasone, knowing he was in his final year as prime minister, felt that he did not need to maintain public support. He was willing to sacrifice his popularity to see through a difficult policy agenda. When he veered from the position, the public and the media, as well as interest groups, felt that the prime minister had lied to them, and they strongly expressed their objections to any tax reform under Nakasone—trust was gone. Nakasone underestimated the public response. This was ironic because he had relied on public support for the successful conclusion of administrative reform.

The public and the media felt that the government was attempting to introduce a drastic change in the tax system without discussing the issue thoroughly. For many, tax reform became a hot debate only in December 1986, and it took just two months after this to introduce the tax reform bills in the Diet. Senior LDP members admitted that the proceedings on tax reform were hasty and that this haste and an inadequate explanation of the issue to the public were among the causes of its failure.[82] The lack of effort to persuade the public and industries accelerated the anti–sales tax movement. The opposition of interest groups such as retailers and textile industries mobilized both LDP and opposition party members to oppose the tax reform.

Ironically, the election victory in 1986, which introduced many new LDP members, hurt Nakasone's tax reform effort by weakening party unity. Junior LDP members, elected for the first time in the 1986 election pledging that no large-scale indirect tax would come out of an LDP administration, found themselves needing to campaign against the indirect tax in order to sustain the support base of these interest groups for their reelection.

In an attempt to ease criticism, Nakasone introduced many tax exemptions. In his view, an indirect tax with numerous exemptions would not be a "large-

Figure 6.1
Nakasone and Tax Reform

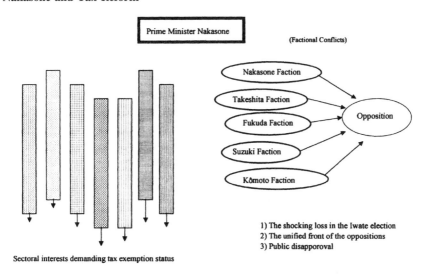

Sectoral interests demanding tax exemption status

scale" indirect tax. The introduction of exemptions, however, further weakened party disharmony. LDP *zoku* members who represented industries that did not receive a tax exempt status stood against the reform bills.

Now junior members and LDP *zoku* members were against Nakasone's tax reform. The LDP's defeat in local elections in spring 1987 further accelerated the anti–sales tax sentiment in the LDP. Even so, the sales tax bills were introduced in the Diet. There Nakasone found that the opposition parties had teamed up against the LDP and were backed by strong public and media support. This and the opposition from within its own party made it impossible for the LDP to force the bills through the Diet (see Figure 6.1).

Prime Minister Takeshita, who had played an important role in Nakasone's tax reform attempt as LDP secretary general, learned many lessons from the failure of the sales tax. In his consumption tax, Takeshita introduced the no-exemption principles so that there would be no winners or losers resulting from tax reform. This avoided a possible split among industry representatives within the LDP.

Takeshita enjoyed the benefits of being the leader of the largest LDP faction. Once Takeshita decided on the no-exemption principle, senior members of his faction actively sought party consensus by persuading members of the other LDP factions. The Takeshita faction boasted the largest number of various *zoku* members within the party. They played an important role in pushing for tax reform by persuading other *zoku* members, client industries, and related ministries to support the reform efforts. This worked to suppress the opposition.

Takeshita's long-time experience as finance minister gave him strong control over the Ministry of Finance. He frequently communicated with its officials to exchange views and to ensure smooth proceedings. At critical moments he successfully persuaded them. For example, Takeshita forced the ministry to accept the tax-cut-first approach by sending Ozawa Ichirô as a messenger. This was a source of power and leadership that Nakasone did not have.

Knowing that the lack of an explanation was one of the major causes of Nakasone's sales tax failure, Takeshita tried to develop the issue through "open discussions." His administration organized public hearings nationwide, and the prime minister undertook a speaking tour to explain the need for tax reform. These efforts had positive results in that administration officials were informed of the problems and complaints of taxpayers in different industries.

Reflecting these opinions, Takeshita's consumption tax was formulated to include a tax exemption for small business with annual sales of less than 30 million yen. This effectively exempted 90 percent of farmers and many retailers who constituted an important LDP voter base. The Ministry of Finance and the Ministry of International Trade and Industry provided subsidies and some compensation to each industrial sector without breaking the no-exemption principle. Interest groups and their patron LDP *zoku* members no longer had a strong reason to oppose the tax reform.

Prime Minister Takeshita also effectively used LDP Tax Commission chairman Yamanaka Sadanori. Yamanaka, who boasted of his power and autocracy, took most of the responsibility and blame for the political decisions made in the policy formation of the tax reform bills. Yamanaka, for example, decided that the consumption tax rate should be 3 percent instead of the proposed 5 percent rate in Nakasone's sales tax. With this rate, tax reform became a net tax cut. Economic conditions allowed Yamanaka to refuse the MOF request to raise the rate. The bubble economy created more tax revenue than had been expected. This allowed the consumption tax rate to be set at 3 percent without causing a serious revenue shortage. Yamanaka, who was seen as the main actor in the tax reform efforts, lost the 1990 election largely because of his involvement in the unpopular tax reform.[83]

After the tax reform bills were introduced in the Diet, Takeshita's policy strategy was tactful (see Figure 6.2). He chose an extraordinary Diet session as the forum for the tax deliberations, a session in which the LDP had two opportunities to extend the duration of the Diet, and in which the opposition parties could not use the tactic of taking the budget hostage because a budget bill was not introduced.

Prime Minister Takeshita used his authority to dissolve the lower house as a negotiating tool. The opposition parties, *Kômeitô* and the DSP, whose members were involved in scandals, could not risk a general election in which they would suffer a loss. Although they did not vote for the tax reform bills, they agreed to participate in the Diet floor sessions on the condition that they could amend the bills. This allowed the LDP to legitimately pass the bills in the Diet.

Takeshita took advantage of the Recruit scandal, which hit many LDP mem-

Figure 6.2
Takeshita and Tax Reform

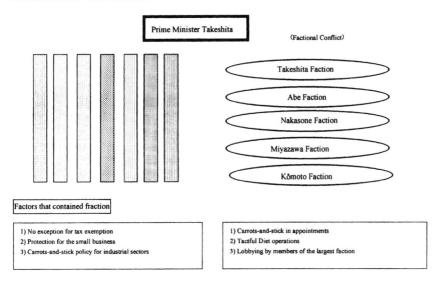

bers, eventually even Takeshita himself. By setting up a special committee to deal with both tax reform and scandal, the Takeshita administration drew the opposition parties into deliberations on the tax reform bills. Even the Japan Socialist Party and the Japan Communist Party joined the deliberation to seek avenues by which they could attack the LDP for its involvement in the scandal.

In short, Prime Minister Takeshita Noboru successfully introduced a controversial tax reform by persuading his faction, his party, various industries and their client LDP *zoku* members, the public, and, to some degree, the opposition parties to support his bills. Takeshita's skill in building a consensus within the party and orchestrating reform efforts was crucial to the successful introduction of the consumption tax.

NOTES

1. Gotôda Masaharu, *Naikaku Kanbô Chôkan* [Chief cabinet secretary] (Tokyo: Kôdan-sha, 1989), p. 216.

2. Murayama Chôsa-kai, *Zeisei Kaikaku ni Mukete* [Toward tax reform] (Interim Report, October 8, 1985), p. 16.

3. Gotôda, *Naikaku Kanbô Chôkan*, p. 217.

4. Quoted in ibid., pp. 215–16.

5. Nakasone once told an LDP member who was a tax expert, "From my experience in sales tax (*torihikidaka zei*), the introduction of a large-scale indirect tax, aimed at raising government revenue, will meet strong oppositions." Fukuda Yasuhiro, *Zeisei Kaikaku e no Ayumi* [Steps toward tax reform] (Tokyo: Zeimu Keiri Kyôkai, 1987), p. 626.

6. Mizuno Masaru, *Shuzei Kyokuchô no Sensanbyaku-nichi: Zeisei Bappon Kaikaku eno Ayumi* [Thirteen hundred days as the director general of the Tax Bureau: Steps toward drastic tax reform] (Tokyo: Ôkura Zaimu Kyôkai, 1993), pp. 44–49.

7. Ibid., pp. 91–92. See also Nakasone Yasuhiro, *Tenchi Ujô* [Affection in heaven and on earth] (Tokyo: Bungei Shunjû, 1996), p. 534.

8. There were tax commissions before 1959. The first commission, for example, was established in 1946 and headed by Tomabechi Yoshizô. However, it was not until 1959 that the commission became a direct advisor to the prime minister and responsible for tax policy making. See Kinoshita Kazuo, *Zeisei Chôsa-kai: Sengo Zeisei Kaikaku no Kiseki* [The Tax System Research Council: Trace of postwar tax reforms] (Tokyo: Zeimu Keiri Kyôkai, 1992), pp. 516–18, 562–66; and Fukuda, *Zeisei Kaikaku e no Ayumi*, pp. 49–50.

9. Mizuno Masaichi, *Zaisei Saiken to Zeisei Kaikaku* [Financial reconstruction and tax reform] (Nagoya: Nagoya Daigaku Shuppan-kai, 1988), pp. 157–58.

10. Watanabe Hiroshi, director of the Third Tax System Division, Tax Bureau of the Finance Ministry, interview by author, Tokyo, August 5, 1992.

11. See Kishiro Yasuyuki, *Jimintô Zeisei Chôsa-kai* [LDP Tax System Research Council] (Tokyo: Tôyô Keizai-Shinpô-sha, 1985).

Former director of the National Tax Agency Fukuda Yukihiro criticized the current situation in which the LDP Tax Commission, which did not have any legal authority or responsibility, had actual decision-making power in specific tax policies. Fukuda, *Zeisei Kaikaku e no Ayumi*, pp. 49–56.

12. Yamanaka Sadanori, interview by author, Tokyo, December 16, 1992.

13. The ten appointees were Iijima Kiyoshi (political critic), Ushio Jirô (chairman of Ushio Electric), Ezoe Hiromasa (CEO of Recruit Co.), Kumon Shumpei (professor at University of Tokyo), Sakaiya Taichi (writer), Tsuchiya Kiyoshi (chairman of the Sôgô Seisaku Kenkyûsho), Nakagawa Kôji (president of Nomura Research), Nagata Takao (Hitachi Shipbuilding), Hosomi Takashi (president of the Overseas Economic Coopera-tion Fund), and Miyake Hisayuki (political critic).

14. Quoted in Kishiro, *Jimintô Zeisei Chôsa-kai*, p. 138.

15. Mizuno Masaru, *Shuzei Kyokuchô*, pp. 52–53.

16. Prime Minister Nakasone's policy speech on January 27, 1986. *Yomiuri Shimbun*, evening edition (January 27, 1986).

17. *Nihon Keizai Shimbun* (October 29, 1986). See also Mizuno Masaru, *Shuzei Kyok-uchô*, p. 92.

18. Mizuno Masaru, *Shuzei Kyokuchô*, p. 76.

19. Prime Minister Nakasone's statement at a meeting of pro-LDP organizations in Tokyo on June 14, 1986.

20. The officials were Vice Minister Yoshino Yoshihiko and Tax Bureau director general Mizuno Masaru. Mizuno, *Shuzei Kyokuchô*, p. 77. Watanabe Michio, former finance minister who later succeeded the Nakasone faction leadership, explained Naka-sone's standpoint: "There is no way to measure people's opposition. The opposition of LDP party members could not be measured because we could not take a poll. In short, [Nakasone] meant that he would not introduce a large-scale indirect tax with which LDP Diet members, representing the Japanese people, would disagree." Watanabe Michio, interview by Fukuda Yukihiro, Fukuda, *Zeisei Kaikaku e no Ayumi*, p. 626.

21. Mizuno, *Shuzei Kyokuchô*, pp. 84–85.

22. Nakasone in his memoirs reveals that he recommended the manufacturers' sales tax. Nakasone, *Tenchi Ujô*, p. 534.

23. Watanabe Michio, interview by Fukuda Yukihiro, Fukuda, *Zeisei Kaikaku e no Ayumi*, p. 631.

24. Kumon Shumpei, interview by author, Tokyo, December 15, 1992.

Kumon was portrayed by the media as a strong supporter of the manufacturers' sales tax, which Nakasone preferred. Kumon, however, denies such portrayal: "As a deputy chairman of the subcommittee, I told reporters that there was a discussion over the manufacturers' sales tax. I believe, it was Professor Tachi who started the discussion without any relevance to the context of the meeting's proceeding. That was all I told at a press conference and the media began describing me as a strong supporter of the manufacturing sales tax."

25. Gotôda Masaharu looks back: "I think that [the chairman's visit] changed his mind from a manufacturers' sales tax to a Japanese-style VAT, *Uriagezei*." Gotôda, *Naikaku Kanbô Chôkan*, pp. 220–21. See also Nakasone Yasuhiro, *Tenchi Ujô*, p. 534.

26. Kumon Shumpei, interview by author, Tokyo, December 15, 1992.

27. The members included 19 executive commission members, 17 subcommittee chairmen of the LDP policy committee to represent each *zoku* group, and 2 chairmen of the Diet committee on the issue of Okinawa and Hokkaido.

28. Yamanaka Sadanori, interview by author, December 16, 1992.

29. Murayama Tatsuo, interview by author, August 10, 1992.

30. Watanabe Hiroshi, director, Third Tax System Division, Tax Bureau, Ministry of Finance, interview by author, Tokyo, August 5, 1992.

31. Mizuno, *Shuzei Kyokuchô*, pp. 117–18.

32. Chief Cabinet Secretary Gotôda Masaharu claims that it was by mistake that the words "sales tax" were not included in the speech. Gotôda, *Naikaku Kanbô Chôkan*, pp. 221–22.

33. Takeshita Noboru and Hirano Sadao, *Shôhizei Seido Seiritsu no Enkaku* [Development toward the introduction of the consumption tax system] (Tokyo: Gyôsei, 1993), pp. 100–101. See also Mizuno, *Shuzei Kyokuchô*, pp. 111–13.

34. Nakasone's statement at the National Conference for Promotion of Tax Reform on February 10, 1987. Maki Tarô, *Nakasone Seiken 1806 nichi* [The Nakasone administration: 1,806 days], vol. 2 (Tokyo: Gyôsei Mondai Kenkyûsho, 1988), p. 316.

35. Takeshita and Hirano, *Shôhizei Seido Seiritsu no Enkaku*, p. 106.

36. Doi Takako, "Watashi no Rirekisho," *Nihon Keizai Shimbun*, September 29, 1992. Mizuno Masaru also mentions this election's impact on sales tax. Mizuno, *Shuzei Kyokuchô*, p. 118.

37. See Gotôda, *Naikaku Kanbô Chôkan*, pp. 223–27; and Takeshita and Hirano, *Shôhizei Seido Seiritsu*, pp. 113–15.

38. Gotôda, *Naikaku Kanbô Chôkan*, p. 230.

39. Takeshita and Hirano, *Shôhizei Seido Seiritsu*, p. 122.

40. Gotôda, *Naikaku Kanbô Chôkan*, p. 236.

41. Nakasone himself believes that the government could have passed the tax reform bills. He states in his memoirs: "We could have overcome with one more day. There may have been an intention among some LDP members who concerned that the successful passage of sales tax would extend the term of the Nakasone Cabinet. I do not know." Nakasone, *Tenchi Ujô*, p. 536.

42. Takeshita Noboru, *Shôgen Hoshu Seiken* [Testimony on conservative administrations] (Tokyo: Yomiuri Shimbun-sha, 1991), p. 191.

43. Ibid.

44. Gotôda, *Naikaku Kanbô Chôkan*, p. 241.

45. Mizuno, *Shuzei Kyokuchô*, p. 138.

46. Takeshita, *Shôgen Hoshu Seiken*, p. 194.

47. Abe Shintarô mentioned the need for more contribution to the international community, and Miyazawa Kiichi raised the land problem.

48. "After considering many factors, including the introduction of an indirect tax and the stability within the party, I thought Mr. Takeshita would be a good pick. Mr. Miyazawa would not be effective at passing legislation. Mr. Abe would not be able to pay attention to details, and was not knowledgeable about the tax system. On the other hand, Mr. Takeshita was good at dealing with the opposition parties and had long-time experience as finance minister. He would be the best person for introducing an indirect tax." Nakasone, *Tenchi Ujô*, p. 586.

49. Takeshita writes in his memoirs: "Looking back, I had always been involved in the issue as the finance minister or LDP secretary general for eight years since the general consumption tax began being discussed. I thought that I needed to express my determination on tax reform in my policy plan. Reflecting the past experience, there were two points that I wanted to emphasize, 'open discussion' and 'improved national welfare.' " Takeshita, *Shôgen Hoshu Seiken*, p. 194.

50. Ishihara Nobuo, *Kantei 2668 nichi: Seisaku Kettei no Butaiura* [Twenty-six hundred sixty-eight days at the prime minister's office: Behind the scene of decision making] (Tokyo: NHK Shuppan, 1995), p. 86.

51. Saka Atsuo, budget examiner for the Prime Minister's Office, Budget Bureau, the Ministry of Finance, interview by author, Tokyo, August 6, 1992.

52. Ishihara, *Kantei 2668 nichi*, p. 87. After frequent discussions with MOF officials, the prime minister came up with these points. According to Deputy Chief Cabinet Secretary Ishihara Nobuo, this was a typical example of Takeshita's bottom-up leadership style. Ishihara Nobuo, *Kan Kaku Arubeshi* [How the bureaucrats should be] (Tokyo: Shôgakukan Bunko, 1998), p. 19.

53. Takeshita and Hirano, *Shôhizei Seido Seiritsu*, p. 250.

54. Katô Hiroshi, interview by Fukuda Yukihiro, in Fukuda Yukihiro, *Zoku Zeisei Kaikaku e no Ayumi* [Steps toward tax reform Part II] (Tokyo: Zeimu Keiri Kyôkai, 1988), p. 314.

55. Murayama Tatsuo, member of House of Representative and former finance minister, interview by author, Tokyo, August 10, 1992.

56. Katô Hiroshi, professor at Keiô University and the chairman of the Government Tax Commission, interview by author, Tokyo, August 6, 1992. The other six members were Hashimoto Ryûtarô, Hata Tsutomu, Kajiyama Seiroku, Okuda Keiwa, Ozawa Ichirô, and Watanabe Kôzô.

57. Yamanaka Sadanori, former chairman of the LDP's Tax System Research Commission and former minister of the Ministry of International Trade and Industry, interview by author, Tokyo, December 16, 1992. For a discussion of the argument over the tax rate, see Mizuno, *Shuzei Kyokuchô*, pp. 239–41.

58. Ishihara, *Kantei 2668 nichi*, p. 90.

59. Katô Hiroshi, professor at Keiô University and chairman of the Government Tax Commission, interview by author, Tokyo, August 6, 1992.

60. Yamanaka Sadanori, interview by author, Tokyo, December 16, 1992.

61. Takeshita and Hirano, *Shôhizei Seido Seiritsu*, p. 276.

62. Mizuno Masaru, *Aera* (May 24, 1988), p. 22. Translation by Michio Muramatsu and Masaru Mabuchi, "Introducing a New Tax in Japan," in *Parallel Politics: Economic Policymaking in Japan and the United States*, ed. Samuel Kernell (Washington, D.C.: Brookings Institution, 1991), p. 200.

63. Hirose Katsusada, secretary to Prime Minister Miyazawa Kiichi and former director of the Corporate Behavior Division of the Ministry of International Trade and Industry, interview by author, Tokyo, December 15, 1992.

64. Ibid.

65. A MITI official who requested not to be identified, interview by author.

66. Yamanaka Sadanori, interview by author, Tokyo, December 16, 1992.

67. Considering Hatoyama's past career, he was the best candidate for the post of the subcommittee chairman. LDP's Policy Research Council chairman Watanabe Michio, however, punished him by not appointing him to the post. But in the cabinet reshuffling after the passage of the consumption tax bills, Hatoyama was appointed to the post. Ôi Keisuke, "Yoyatô no Kôbô" [Battle between the LDP and the opposition parties] in *Kokkai Kinô Ron: Kokkai no Shikumi to Un'ei* [Arguments for the functional Diet: The mechanism and operation of the Diet], ed. Fujimoto Kazumi (Tokyo: Hôgaku Shoin, 1990), p. 81.

68. Takeshita and Hirano, *Shôhizei Seido Seiritsu*, pp. 282–85.

69. For the details of the scandal, see Asahi Shimbun Seiji-bu, *Takeshita Seiken no Hôkai: Rikurûto Jiken to Seiji Kaikaku* [The collapse of the Takeshita administration: The Recruit scandal and political reform] (Tokyo: Asahi Shimbun-sha, 1989); and Asahi Journal Henshû-bu, *Rikurûtogêto no Kakushin* [The core of the Recruitgate] (Tokyo: Suzusawa Shoten, 1989).

70. Takeshita and Hirano, *Shôhizei Seido Seiritsu*, pp. 292–95.

71. Ishihara Nobuo, administrative deputy chief cabinet secretary, looks back: "[Ozawa] was hard working, and seldom stayed in his office from the morning. He worked exhaustively on persuading the opposition parties." Ishihara, *Kan Kaku Arubeshi*, p. 91.

72. Hirano Sadao, *Ozawa Ichirô tono Nijûnen* [Twenty years with Ozawa Ichirô] (Tokyo: President-sha, 1996), pp. 206–8. See also, Takeshita and Hirano, *Shôhizei Seido Seiritsu*, pp. 295–96.

73. Takeshita and Hirano, *Shôhizei Seido Seiritsu*, pp. 360–65. Chairman Kanemaru was hesitant to force passage, but the LDP secretary general convinced Kanemaru by telling him that he had confidence to bring in the *Kômeitô* and the DSP in the case of the floor voting. See Asahi Shimbun Seiji-bu, *Takeshita Seiken no Hôkai*, p. 88.

74. See Asahi Journal Henshû-bu, *Rikurûtogêto no kakushin*, pp. 198–204.

75. Yano Junya, *Nijû Kenryoku Yami no Nagare* [Dual power, current in the dark] (Tokyo: Bungei Shunjû, 1994).

76. Miyazawa expressed in front of journalists, "I would like to decide [the timing of] my resignation, considering only how it would benefit the passage of the tax bills." Miyazawa Kiichi, interview by Tahara Sôichirô, *Bungei Shunjû* (March 1989), p. 272. See also his statement of resignation, quoted in Mizuno, *Shuzei Kyokuchô*, pp. 349–50.

77. Takeshita and Hirano, *Shôhizei Seido Seiritsu*, p. 381.

78. Matoba Junzô, former senior assistant for domestic affairs to Prime Ministers

Nakasone Yasuhiro and Takeshita Noboru, interview by author, Tokyo, December 16, 1992. See also Ishihara, *Kan Kaku Arubeshi*, p. 25.

79. Takeshita and Hirano, *Shôhizei Seido Seiritsu*, pp. 383–84.

80. For the conditions between the opposition parties and the LDP, see Takeshita and Hirano, *Shôhizei Seido Seiritsu*, pp. 391–93.

81. Naikaku Sôri Daijin Kanbô, ed., *Takeshita Naikaku Sôri Daijin Enzetsu-shû* [Speeches of Prime Minister Takeshita Noboru] (Tokyo: Nihon Kôhô Kyôkai, 1990), p. 52.

82. Watanabe Michio, who was later to succeed to the leadership position of the Nakasone faction, interview by Fukuda Yukihiro, in Fukuda, *Zeisei Kaikaku e no Ayumi*, p. 634. A Finance Ministry officer, Ozaki Mamoru, however, argues that the process was not necessarily hasty because it took 16 months to introduce the tax reform bills after Prime Minister Nakasone asked the Government Tax Commission to make a proposal on tax reform in September 1985. See Ozaki Mamoru, "Uriagezei Hitori Gatari" [Monologue on the sales tax], *Fainansu* (September 1989): pp. 43–44.

83. Yamanaka recalls: "Many LDP politicians said to their constituents, 'It was Yamanaka who introduced the tax.' I took the responsibility and told my constituents that they were right and that I was the one who introduced the tax. As a result, I lost in the election by 15 votes. Looking back now, it was a bad strategy. I should have said instead, 'Sorry for troubling you voters. But the new tax is better for the future of the Japanese people and society.' " Yamanaka Sadanori, interview by author, Tokyo, December 16, 1992.

Chapter 7

Administrative Reform by Hashimoto

HASHIMOTO INITIATES ADMINISTRATIVE REFORM

Call for Bureaucratic Reform

Ten years after Nakasone's administrative reform, the need for administrative reform reemerged under the Hashimoto Ryûtarô administration. This time, public attention shifted from fiscal reconstruction to reform of the national bureaucracy largely because of government scandals and the *jûsen* problem, which involved seven housing loan companies that had gone bankrupt. In 1996, the *jûsen* crisis sparked heated debates about the need to reform the Ministry of Finance and divide its functions among independent agencies. Critics argued that MOF authority was too strong, and that the ministry's use of fiscal authority for the financial market distorted the government policy, creating problems such as the *jûsen* crisis.

Underlining the need for bureaucratic reform was the filing of a lawsuit over the transfusion of HIV-tainted blood. The Ministry of Health and Welfare was blamed for failing to take appropriate measures when an American authority issued a worldwide alert that all blood should be heated before infusion to kill HIV.

Public distrust against the national bureaucracy was stronger than ever under the Hashimoto's leadership. One of the factors that created such public sentiment was an MOF *jûsen* liquidation scheme that would require the use of taxpayer's money. The public protested, fueled by the Diet releasing documents, against MOF opposition, that identified the top 100 borrowers of housing loans. The information revealed that corporate borrowers were responsible for more than 95 percent of the nonperforming loans, and that many of the borrowers had loans with more than one housing loan company. The Ministry of Finance had been aware of these practices and the size of the bad loans but had done nothing to correct the problems.

The opposition New Frontier Party adamantly criticized the use of public funds to bail out the *jûsen*. Its members began a sit-in, blocking entry to the budget committee room to protest the ruling coalition's budget proposal that contained such a bailout plan. The Economic Planning Agency expressed concerns that a delay in approval of the budget could slow down Japan's economic recovery. Although the public as a whole was critical of the government plan, more and more people expressed their concern for Japan's economy as the sit-in extended into its third week. According to a poll at the same time, more than 70 percent of respondents wanted politicians to pay more attention to prosperity and economic issues.[1] The sit-in ended with a compromise agreement between the ruling coalition and the New Frontier Party, which assured time for a sufficient debate over the budget bills in the Diet. The Hashimoto government managed to resolve the politically difficult *jûsen* problem, but the public continued to expect the prime minister to reform the bureaucracy.

In summer 1996, entering the last year of the lower house's four-year term, election pressure grew among Diet members. One year earlier, under the Murayama administration, Hashimoto had announced his challenge to the incumbent LDP president Kôno Yôhei's bid for reelection. A majority of LDP Diet members, who saw a better chance for reelection under the leadership of Hashimoto with his high popularity among the public, supported his challenge. As a result, Kôno dropped out of the race, leading to an easy victory for Hashimoto. To many LDP members, an upcoming general election was perhaps the most important reason for Hashimoto to be in the premiership. From January 1996 when he succeeded the Socialist prime minister Murayama Tomiichi to head the coalition government of the LDP, the Socialist Party and *Sakigake*, Hashimoto had sought an opportunity to call for an election. Observing the rising popularity of his cabinet in September 1996, Hashimoto dissolved the lower house to call the first election under the new electoral law, which introduced single-seat districts.[2]

During the election campaign virtually all the political parties, including the LDP, pledged to carry out administrative reform, reflecting public distrust of government agencies. Whereas Hashimoto's rival, Ozawa Ichirô of the NFP, proposed the reduction of government agencies from the current 22 to 15 during the campaign, the prime minister pledged that his government would half that number. In the October 20 general election, the LDP gained 239 seats, up from 211, in the 500-seat lower house. The result, generally seen as a victory, strengthened Hashimoto's power base in his party. The LDP, however, still came up short and was not able to form a majority.

Hashimoto approached the two other government parties to maintain the same coalition. However, the election result for these two parties was a disaster—the Socialist Party decreased to 15 seats from a preelection total of 30, and *Sakigake* won only 2 seats, losing 7. Their participation in the coalition government with the LDP might have been the reason liberal voters withdrew their support. The two parties decided to stay out of the cabinet to maintain their independence while agreeing to support the LDP government to form a majority in the lower house. Thus, Hashimoto had to pursue administrative reform with a minority-led cabinet.

Hashimoto Forms the Council

One month after the October 1996 general election, Prime Minister Hashimoto Ryûtarô inaugurated the Council on Administrative Reform. The legal base of the Council was not as strong as Nakasone's *Rinchô*, which had been established with legislation. Hashimoto felt the immediate need to get going on administrative reform efforts and did not go through the process of obtaining legislative approval. Even the ruling LDP did not officially approve of the establishment and membership of the Council, which left room for the ruling party members to freely attack its recommendations. In order to suppress potential opposition, Hashimoto appointed himself chairman of the Council, thus forcing his government to act on its recommendations.

In addition to Hashimoto, there were two representatives of the political community. Minister for the Management and Coordination Agency (MCA) Mutô Kabun was appointed deputy chairman. Former Diet member Mizuno Kiyoshi, whom Hashimoto also personally appointed to the newly created position of assistant to the prime minister for administrative reform, was also asked to be a member of the Council and to head its secretariat. Among the 12 other members, there were three business leaders who had headed the existing government advisory councils on administrative reform–related matters.[3] In addition, there were six scholars, two media representatives, and one labor leader.[4] It was important to note that Hashimoto chose no bureaucratic representative for the Council for bureaucratic reform, considering public sentiment against the bureaucracy.

The Council's Secretariat, headed by Secretary General Mizuno, was located in the Prime Minister's Office or *Sôrifu*. Under Mizuno, one deputy secretary general and three executives represented the national bureaucracy.[5] In addition, half of the 28 researchers were sent by different ministries. Although 12 researchers represented the private sector, they had no experience in administrative affairs.[6] The Council's deputy secretary general and former MCA deputy director general Yagi Toshimichi once said to private-sector researchers, "You cannot understand how the government agencies work."[7] Although the Council itself had no bureaucratic representation, the Secretariat was under the strong control of bureaucrats.

On November 28, 1996, Prime Minister Hashimoto called the first meeting of the Council. He asked the members for recommendations on three issues: "what functions the state should fulfill in the 21st century"; "how the government should be restructured to perform these functions better"; and "how best to strengthen the cabinet's functions." As an example, he introduced the so-called Hashimoto vision. In his vision, the government's policy areas were divided into four goal-driven themes: (1) the nation's survival; (2) the expansion of national wealth; (3) national welfare, and (4) education and culture. Hashimoto also proposed that the number of government agencies be reduced from the current 22 to 10 in accordance with his campaign pledge. The following day, Hashimoto stated in his policy speech before the Diet that "although resistance and difficulties are inevitable, I am fully committed to the cause of administrative reform." As the public saw Hashimoto's determination, his popularity rate in a *Kyodo News* poll rose to 58.3 percent up from 43.4 percent at the beginning of his term.[8]

The policy process, however, for administrative reform seemed complicated to the public. First, Hashimoto initiated reform schemes in five other policy areas: (1) financial system; (2) economic structure; (3) fiscal structure; (4) social welfare, and (5) education. The Hashimoto administration simultaneously dealt with these five reform schemes along with administrative reform. It was so confusing that the average voter could not follow which council was advanced to what stage. Second, two existing committees dealt with administrative reform: The Administrative Reform Committee was concentrated on deregulation, disclosure of administrative information, and the division of labor between the public and private sectors. The Council on Government Decentralization was focused on the division of labor between the national and local governments. These issues were interrelated. Although the chairmen of the two committees became members of the Administrative Reform Council, the two committees continued their own deliberation. Third, reform of "special corporations" or quasi-governmental organizations was separated from other issues and delegated to the discussion by LDP's Headquarters for Promoting Administrative Reform. The plans to reform the deficit-running organizations would be handled without disclosure to the public.

The process of Hashimoto's reform efforts involved so many institutions that former prime minister Nakasone Yasuhiro criticized that they covered too many issues. Nakasone boasted about his administrative reform efforts in the 1980s and tried to maintain political influence by involving himself in Hashimoto's reform process. Nakasone's close associate and chairman of LDP's Headquarters on Administrative Reform, Satô Kôkô, echoed him and said that Hashimoto's reform efforts, too broad and detailed, should be focused on deregulation and fiscal reconstruction.[9]

Despite his criticism, Satô's appointment was strategically important for Hashimoto. Although Satô was elected to the lower house 11 times, he had never experienced a cabinet position. As discussed in Chapter 1, LDP lower house members usually experienced a first cabinet position after six elections. The reason was due to his criminal record stemming back to the highly publicized Lockheed scandal, which involved selection of airplanes for a major Japanese airline. Nakasone asked Hashimoto to appoint Satô to a cabinet position. Hashimoto instead appointed Satô to the position in charge of administrative reform within the ruling party and implied that Satô might get a cabinet position in the next reshuffle. The lack of cabinet experience made Satô a political insider who had built up his influence within the party. Hashimoto wanted Satô's influence to suppress the opposition within the LDP against his administrative reform.

Reform Plans toward the Interim Report

Between January and March 1997 with strong public attention, the Council held a series of hearings with scholars and experts to exchange views on administrative reform. One member explains this process: "None of the members had had experience in the bureaucracy. We did not know exactly where to start reform efforts. We needed to acquire basic knowledge about the problems of the administration by inviting experts."[10]

At the earlier stage of the reform efforts, crisis management was an immediate issue. In addition to the disastrous experience of the 1995 Hanshin earthquake, the ongoing hostage crisis in Peru, which began in December 1996, and the oil spill disaster in the Sea of Japan in January 1997 made crisis management a top priority issue. The Council decided to separate this issue from other issues and by May 1997 to draft proposals that would provide the prime minister greater control over government ministries in emergency cases. According to the government interpretation of the Cabinet Law at that time, the prime minister could never instruct ministries without the unanimous consent of the entire cabinet. On May 1, the Council announced recommendations for setting a package of cabinet decisions that would allow the prime minister to directly instruct ministries in times of crisis and for establishing a new position in the cabinet, the director for crisis management. Although the new director would interfere with the jurisdiction of existing agencies, such as the National Defense Agency, no strong opposition from the bureaucracy was observed. (The new position was created under the Hashimoto administration in April 1998.)

Strong reactions from ministries emerged when the Council held a series of hearings with every ministry and agency between May and June. The Council asked each ministry and agency specifically how it could reform its own organization. The Ministry of Finance, for example, was asked for its opinion on the issues that the ministry had opposed. They included the division of their control over fiscal and financial issues, the transfer of budget-making function to the cabinet and the privatization of government minting and printing office. These inquiries were in line with the Hashimoto plan to categorize the ministry's two major functions into two different categories of policy areas (fiscal policy important to the nation's survival, and financial policy leading to the expansion of national wealth). This might mean that the ministry would be further divided.

The Ministry of Finance argued against such division, and its officials felt threatened. Since there was no bureaucratic representative in the Council, they tried to manipulate the direction of deliberations through the Secretariat.

The Secretariat provided information used as the basis of debate and summary of previous arguments in the Council. The bureaucratic executives of the Secretariat sneakily changed wording in the information. For example, there was an argument for the establishment of "the Economic Advisory Council," which would give the prime minister strong leadership power in outlining the national budget. Although this proposal appeared in the first version of the information on "Reinforcing Cabinet Functions," it was removed from the third version.[11] Obviously, this change reflected the desire of MOF officials not to weaken their budget-making power.

The Ministry of Finance had been the center of public criticism against the national bureaucracy. On June 16 1997, one year after political turmoil over the *jûsen* scandal, the Diet enacted legislation to establish the new Financial Supervisory Agency. As a result, the inspecting and supervising authority over financial institutions would be removed from the Ministry of Finance. MOF officials managed to maintain influence over financial industry by keeping the planning function of financial policy. Proud MOF officials could endure no more erosion of their power and desperately sought influence over administrative reform planning.

Another example was on the establishment of the powerful Cabinet Office, which would be in charge of coordinating different interests among ministries on behalf of the prime minister. It was not desirable for many ministries to have such a powerful new office directly under the prime minister. The bureaucratic officials in the Secretariat listed an alternative plan that would combine the Prime Minister's Office and the MCA without giving it the coordinating power. According to this plan, the new office would only have equal status with other ministries. In an attempt to manipulate the direction of deliberation, the Secretariat leaked news of this plan to the media identifying it as the Council's "original plan."[12] This upset Secretary General Mizuno. At the June 25 meeting, he criticized the Secretariat for the intentional leak and reintroduced his plan to establish the Cabinet Office, which would be headed by the prime minister and above the other ministries. At the July 2 meeting, several members further criticized the Secretariat. One member stated that "the information materials provided by the Secretariat must not show any direction. . . . Otherwise, the Secretariat cannot escape from criticism for manipulation."[13]

The Secretariat's manipulation included the Hashimoto plan with the four policy categories. In order to avoid the discussion of the division of MOF fiscal and financial power, bureaucratic officials put the two functions under the same category of "expansion of the national welfare." At the July 7 meeting, Hashimoto openly criticized the Secretariat for the change.[14] To avoid bureaucratic manipulation, he decided not to use the Secretariat's materials, but to ask members of the Council themselves to provide sources of information.

Between July and August, most of the substantial discussions were moved to two subcommittees. The Subcommittee on Plans and Institutions mainly dealt with plans to reinforce Cabinet functions; whereas the Subcommittee on Organizational Issues dealt with reorganization of the national bureaucracy. Two scholars were appointed to lead the subcommittee discussion: Satô Kôji on plans and institutions and Fujita Tokiyasu on organizational issues. In the subcommittee meetings, these two scholars provided their own sources of information as a basis for deliberation. As the discussion of the Council proceeding was under the strong control of its members, it became more independent of bureaucratic and political influence. Hashimoto asked Satô and Fujita to come up with the original plan for the interim report, saying, "I will take care of all the political sides. Do not bend to political pressure and provide a good proposal based on your conscience as a scholar."[15] "The Economic Advisory Council" and "the Cabinet Office" were back in the proposal for the interim report. Since Hashimoto's leadership in his administrative reform efforts was seen as strong, his popularity rate hit soared to 59.2 percent.[16]

Battles over the Interim Report

On September 3, 1997, after a four-day series of intense meetings, the Council presented an interim report that included rather drastic plans to streamline the bureaucracy. The plan called for reinforcing the cabinet, privatizing postal saving and insurance services, dividing the politically powerful Ministry of Construction, and decreasing the number of government agencies from 22 to 13, including a newly created, powerful support organ for the prime minister, the Cabinet Office. If these plans were realized, Hashimoto's reform could be at least as significant as Nakasone's administrative reform in the 1980s, which privatized the national railways.

The limited bureaucratic and political influence on the Council made it possible to come up with ambitious plans. At the same time, it was a weakness. The plans did not go through the policy approval process of the three ruling parties—the LDP, the SDP, and *Sakigake*.[17] This was completely different from Nakasone's administrative reform efforts. As described in Chapter 5, Nakasone requested the commission to make its proposals "feasible and practical" with prior consent from the related ministries and the ruling party. Also, the legislation required the government to respect the recommendations of Nakasone's commission. Hashimoto, on the other hand, when presenting the Council's interim report to the representatives of the coalition parties, had to bow and ask them to "respect the proposal to the furthest extent possible."

The media and political attention focused mainly on the reorganization of government ministries and not much on reinforcing the cabinet and other proposals. The reduction of the number of agencies would clearly create winners and losers among the government agencies. This was quite different from Nakasone's administrative reform, which forced all the government agencies to feel the same pain. Losers began attacking Hashimoto's plan.

LDP's *zoku* members argued that there was no need to respect the recommendations of the Council because it did not have legislative approval. LDP members seeking to maintain voter support in the postal industry, for example, adamantly opposed the idea of privatizing the postal saving and life insurance services. Special Post Offices, which make up 80 percent of Japan's 24,600 postal outlets, serve as a solid support base for many LDP members in election times. Hashimoto's privatization plan and the absorption of the telecommunication function into the proposed Industry Ministry would effectively dissolve the Ministry of Post and Telecommunication, an unpopular move among those offices. On September 5, the chairman of the LDP Telecommunication Subcommittee, Furuya Keiji, met with LDP secretary general Katô Kôichi and Policy Research Council chairman Yamazaki Taku and told them that they would oppose the privatization scheme of postal services. Yamazaki publicly stated that the LDP would begin talks with the two other coalition parties on postal services, and start from "scratch."

The mass media supported the Council's plan to privatize postal saving and insurance services. These services provided large financial resource for quasi-governmental organizations, which had been criticized by many economists and the public for their inefficient investments. The postal saving service attracted as much as 35 percent of the nation's individual savings by offering a higher interest rate made possible by the injection of tax money.[18] Many economists argued that this created a major distortion in Japan's financial market.

The public, however, did not feel this was a problem and was satisfied with postal savings services. According to an *Asahi Shimbun* survey, 54 percent of those polled said they were against the privatization of these services.[19] The poll showed that people who lived in less-populated areas with no commercial banks desperately needed the services, whereas those who lived in urban areas felt no particular dissatisfaction with them. Public reaction here was completely different from that evident in the national railway situation under Nakasone's administrative reform in which the dissatisfied, angered customers formed a strong political support base for privatization.

The Council, already weak without legal backing, met with trouble when Hashimoto's popularity declined over the appointment of Satô Kôkô to a cabinet post in a cabinet reshuffle. After Satô had served as chairman of LDP Headquarters on Administrative Reform, Hashimoto could no longer reject former prime minister Nakasone's demand to give him a cabinet post. Satô's appointment was also a political gift to the conservative wing of the LDP led by Nakasone. The LDP was split into wings: one that supported the existing coalition with the Socialists and *Sakigake*, and the other that called for a conservative coalition with the New Frontier Party. Hashimoto, without a strong power base within his own party, was running the government on this delicate balance between the two wings. Reappointing the leaders of the procoalition group into

LDP leadership positions, such as Secretary General Katô Kôichi, Hashimoto needed to offer some form of appeasement to win the support of the conservatives. Hashimoto was in effect forced by Nakasone to replace Mutô Kabun with Satô as the MCA director general, a key position for Hashimoto's top priority issue of administrative reform.

Sensitive to public opinion, Hashimoto was hesitant to appoint Satô to a cabinet post because of his criminal record. LDP secretary general Katô revealed Hashimoto's agony, stating in a television discussion program, "Up until the last moment, the prime minister was torn between Mr. Nakasone's pressure and public opinion."[20] Public reaction was much stronger than Hashimoto had expected. According to a *Kyodo News* poll, 74 percent of the respondents said that they were against Satô's appointment. Subsequently Hashimoto's popularity rating dropped dramatically from 60 percent to 28 percent.[21] After a week of political turmoil, Satô "voluntarily" resigned. At a press council Hashimoto bowed deeply and expressed his apology to the public, saying he "had not considered public opinion enough."

This appointment and resignation incident had changed the political environment surrounding Hashimoto's administrative reform. Former MCA director general Mutô Kabun, who served as deputy chairman to the Council, now headed the LDP's Headquarters on Administrative Reform. A delicate political balance existed between Satô and Mutô. They were both subleaders of the former Nakasone faction who sought to succeed to the faction's leadership. Angered with his removal from the cabinet position as a result of Satô's appointment, Mutô began attacking the interim report for which he himself was responsible. Mutô said at a meeting of the Headquarters that the report would not be binding to their discussions. A powerful political insider, Satô was forced to resign from the cabinet post in charge of administrative reform. Mutô changed from a strong supporter to a major opponent of the reform scheme. Hashimoto lost two most strategic political players for his efforts.

As Hashimoto's popularity eroded, LDP's *zoku* members took the opportunity to attack the prime minister's administrative reform. In addition to the postal *zoku* members, other *zoku* members also joined the movement against Hashimoto's reform plan. The powerful construction *zoku* members, for example, publicly opposed the plan to divide the function of the Ministry of Construction into two newly created ministries. Against their campaign pledges for administrative reform, LDP members swarmed to attack Hashimoto's reform plan in order to protect special interests, an old habit the ruling party had developed under the one-party dominance system.

After the interim report was announced, political-level committees on administrative reform were held among the three coalition parties and within the LDP. Virtually all the government agencies asked for help from their patron LDP members to acquire a better deal in the reform scheme. The opinions of these committees were reported at the Council meetings. Besides such political pressure, many interest groups lobbied hard on the members of the Council. The workers at local post offices and construction companies were organized and requested to write to the members. Bureaucratic officials stepped on each other's toes as they struggled to secure appointments with Council members to explain their standpoints.[22] As the Council members began considering their opinions, Hashimoto's administrative efforts were no longer independent from political and bureaucratic influence.

Over controversial issues, such as the privatization of postal savings and life insurance services, and the division of the Ministry of Finance and the Ministry of Construction, there were widening gaps in the opinions of the Council members. At the September 17 meeting, for example, five different members stated their opposition to the privatization plan, and three members questioned the MOC division. As Moroi Ken describes, "That was the birth of '*zoku iin*' [or *zoku* Council members]."[23] On September 27, LDP Headquarters on Administrative Reform presented its proposal to reform the postal services, instead of the privatization plan in the interim report.[24] As political pressures mounted, a major reworking of the interim report seemed more and more inevitable.

Prime Minister Hashimoto's weakness, the lack of power base within the LDP, and his dwindling political courage became more evident by a series of statements and actions in early October. On October 1, the LDP's Policy Subcommittee on Communications and the Policy Research Commission on telecommunications jointly voted for a resolution to maintain the government-run status of all three postal services. Five days later at the LDP Executive Council meeting, opposition to privatization of postal services was overwhelming. One member emphasized that LDP members knew the needs of people much better than did the Council members.[25] At the October 8 Council meeting, a member, Arima Akito, tried to encourage the prime minister, who was fighting against this political opposition, saying, "We totally support you. Please boldly proceed with your reform efforts." Another member, Moroi Ken, also stated that "administrative reform must be done now. Only the Hashimoto administration can achieve this." Hashimoto's reply, however, was not encouraging: "There is a need for the government and the ruling party to achieve this policy together. In this sense, I need some moderation."[26]

Although Hashimoto was ready to compromise on specific issues, he was determined to maintain the framework of 12 ministries and a cabinet office. There was no rational thought behind his stance. His position was purely political. With strong media attention on the reduction plan, any increase in the number would be widely reported as a major defeat.[27]

Economic conditions further eroded Hashimoto's leadership. The consumption tax raised from 3 to 5 percent in April and tax increases and a tight spending policy in the FY 1997 budget slowed down the economy far more than Hashimoto had anticipated. The economic growth rate of the second quarter (April–June) of 1997, which was announced in mid-September, was minus 2.8 percent—nearly a 5 percent drop from the previous quarter. The burden of medical costs that were increased in September 1997 was expected to make economic recovery difficult. The media portrayed the worsening recession as a result of the failure of Hashimoto's policy. This further tilted the power balance in favor of the LDP. Moroi Ken observed: "Prime Minister Hashimoto lost his strong determination, which he had at the beginning of the reform efforts."[28]

On October 14, LDP Headquarters on Administrative Reform chairman Mutô sent the result of his committee's discussion to the prime minister's office. He implicitly declared to the office that the LDP would be the final decision maker. As Hashimoto's leadership eroded, lobbying by interest groups and their patron LDP *zoku* members was so widely reported in the media that nearly 80 percent of polled voters found the lobbying problematic.[29] At the Council meetings, members found Prime Minister Hashimoto, evidently under strong political pressure, avoiding making a decisive statement on controversial issues.[30] His strong determination for drastic reform was no longer apparent.

Between November 17 and 21, the second intensive session of the Council was held to produce its final report. Simultaneously, the three coalition parties held a conference on administrative reform to form their final offer. Much negotiating, compromising, and deal making took place in this final stage. Not only the LDP but also the SDP opposed the postal privatization plan. On November 18, the three parties agreed that the three postal services would remain government-run. This agreement was announced at the Council meeting. Although expected, the decision disappointed members, who delegated authority to Prime Minister Hashimoto to negotiate with the three coalition parties on further reform suggestions. Moroi Ken, a member of the Council, explains, "At the earlier stage, I suggested that the Council leave the final decision on highly political issues, including the privatization of postal services, to the prime minister. I did not think that the Council should nor could make such decisions."[31]

Because LDP, SDP, and *Sakigake* representatives were determined to refuse any privatization plan, Hashimoto proposed compromises: The services would remain government-run, but they would be separate from the ministry and conducted under a new government corporation in five years. The coalition parties hesitated to accept Hashimoto's proposal because the government corporation plan might be a step toward privatization. In order to acquire an agreement with the coalition parties, Hashimoto promised that the government would not privatize the postal services. In return, the coalition parties also agreed to allow private companies to enter the postal services, and none of the three postal services would receive subsidies.

As the most controversial issue of Hashimoto's administrative reform efforts was resolved, the Council introduced its final report. Although Hashimoto managed to keep the framework of 13 agencies and the plan to strengthen the cabinet's function, he had to yield in several areas. As described above, the privatization plan of the postal services was abandoned. The services would be continued as governmental operations under the Postal Service Agency for five years and would later be run by a newly created, government-run corporation. All the functions of the Construction Ministry would be continued under a new

Ministry of National Land and Transportation.[32] In the final report, an agreement was not reached on the separation of MOF fiscal and financial functions among the coalition parties. *Sakigake* strongly pushed for a total separation the LDP was hesitant to support. But later, a political compromise was reached. According to the compromise, the Ministry of Finance would keep its influence over financial policies by maintaining its authority over financial crises.

On December 4, the Hashimoto cabinet made a decision to respect the Administrative Reform Council's final report. Two months later, a bill for the Basic Law for the Reform of Central Government Ministries and Agencies, based on the final report, was approved by the cabinet and submitted to the Diet. The nature of the law, however, was to provide an outline for reforms that must be carried out within five years. Separate legislation revising many existing laws would be required for further details. More than 90 hours were spent for the deliberation of this bill, but there were not many controversial debates. On June 9, 1998, the Hashimoto government successfully passed the legislation in the Diet.

After the passage, Prime Minister Hashimoto formed the Headquarters of Central Government Reform to design the revisions of the existing laws. In order to oversee and check the progress of administrative reform, Hashimoto formed the Advisory Council chaired by *Keidanren* chairman Imai Takashi.[33] Although new institutional settings were organized, Prime Minister Hashimoto could not continue his reform efforts. In the July 1998 upper house election, the voters demonstrated their discontent of Hashimoto's handling of economic policy and his lack of leadership. The LDP lost 17 seats, leaving it 23 seats short of a majority in the 252-seat chamber. This historic loss forced Prime Minister Hashimoto to resign in the midst of administrative reform.

OBUCHI TAKES OVER REFORM

Three LDP Dietmen declared their candidacy to succeed Hashimoto—then foreign minister Obuchi Keizô, former chief cabinet secretary Kajiyama Seiroku, and Minister of Health and Welfare Koizumi Jun'ichiô. Obuchi, who promised to trim down the central government by cutting 20 percent of its employees within ten years, was elected with 225 of the 411 votes cast. In his first policy speech on August 7, 1998, Obuchi stated, "My target is to submit, under political leadership, the necessary legislation to the Diet as early as next April, aiming to launch the transition to the new regime in January 2001. I will not retract this schedule."[34]

Despite verbal commitments, Prime Minister Obuchi showed little personal involvement in administrative reform. Obuchi, for example, attended only five of 14 advisory council meetings on administrative reform during his tenure. The council's minutes showed no record of his strong leadership. Apparently, economic revitalization was a more urgent issue for the prime minister, who attended all the Economic Strategy Council Meetings proposing how to revive the Japanese economy.[35]

In the fall 1998 Diet session, Prime Minister Obuchi had difficulty passing economic revitalization bills with majority control of only the lower house. In order to legislate the Financial Renewal Bills to help the troubled banking industry, the government party reluctantly adopted the Democratic Party's proposal to gain support from the largest opposition party as well as *Kômeitô* and the Socialist Party. In the negotiation process, the LDP made an agreement with the Democratic Party and the *Kômeitô*, against the opposition from within the government and the ruling party, to totally separate authority over financial industry from the Ministry of Finance. As for the bills for an early reconstruction of the financial system, the LDP forwent teaming up with the Democrats and sought cooperation with the Liberal Party. To pass the budget bills, the LDP had to cut a deal with *Kômeitô* by agreeing to issue consumption coupons to children under 16 and the selected elderly.

These tough Diet operations made Prime Minister Obuchi and his cabinet realize the need to form a coalition government to secure the passage of the bills to revise the U.S.–Japan Security Treaty guideline during the 1999 ordinary diet session. Obuchi's choice for a partner was Ozawa Ichirô's Liberal Party. It was surprising and reasonable at the same time—surprising in consideration of the strong animosity against Ozawa among LDP members, and reasonable if considering the Liberal Party's policy line on strengthening the U.S.–Japan security ties.

The Liberal Party set several conditions for participation in the coalition, including the immediate reduction of the number of cabinet ministers, the gradual downsizing of civil servants by 25 percent over ten years, and an end to the government commissioner system that allowed civil servants to answer questions at the Diet. Before the coalition was officially formed, the LDP agreed to reduce the number of cabinet posts from 20 to 18 and to form five project teams between the two parties to further pursue policy arrangements. Two of these project teams were directly involved in administrative reform. One team discussed the abolition of the government commissioner system, which allowed bureaucratic officials to answer questions from the opposition parties in the Diet, and the introduction of deputy ministers to strengthen the position of the parliamentary vice minister. Another team dealt with reorganization of the central government and downsizing of civil servants. After negotiations, the two parties agreed on the detailed scheme on the reduction of government employees by 25 percent over ten years (5 percent higher than Obuchi's original promise), the abolition of the government commissioner system, and the number of deputy ministers to be introduced. These agreements were incorporated in the final administrative reform bills.

Despite Prime Minister Obuchi's limited personal involvement, the establishment of the LDP-LP coalition government in January 1999 accelerated the drive of administrative reform efforts. For the first four months of 1999, the Secretariat of the Headquarters of Central Government Reform was extremely busy preparing legislation for administrative reform bills. As most of the Secretariat officers were sent from the different ministries and agencies, there were concerns that they might fight with each other or sabotage their task in order to protect their home ministries' interests. Except for the new allocation of jurisdiction of the 12 ministries, there were no major interagency conflicts. One of two dozen officers in the Secretariat sent by a private organization stated, "They were competent bureaucrats once their tasks are specified."[36]

The only major lash back from the bureaucracy was made by the Ministry of Finance. MOF officials moved to maintain some of financial function against the October 1998 three-party agreement. The Democratic Party adamantly criticized such move and stressed that any change from the agreement would destroy any trust of the LDP. MOF officials also tried to reverse the decision on the newly assigned Japanese name, *Zaimushô*, to take back their name with a 1,500-year history, *Ôkurashô*, which literally translates as "Ministry of Treasury." Former Prime Minister Hashimoto, who emphasized the symbolic importance of the name change in the bureaucracy streamlining, argued that there was no specific need to maintain its name while other institutions had changed their names. At the end, the Ministry of Finance won in one battle and lost in the other. The Obuchi government decided to break the agreement with the Democratic Party while sticking with the new name, *Zaimushô*, which is a more accurate translation of its English name, the Ministry of Finance. The Democratic Party condemned the decision, but the party's influence was limited because the LDP gained support from the other participant of the three-party agreement: *Kômeitô*.

On the political front, LDP *zoku* members, who had actively resisted against Hashimoto's reform efforts before the December 1997 final report, took little action, as if all the fights were over. MCA director general Ôta Seiichi, a cabinet member in charge of administrative reform in the Obuchi cabinet, stated at an Advisory Council meeting, "The lobbying from peer Diet members has been really limited. Surprisingly limited." Deputy Chief Cabinet Secretary Suzuki Muneo further said, " 'Limited' is not an accurate description. Nothing happened. Never happened."[37]

With unexpectedly limited political battle, the Obuchi cabinet approved 17 related bills on administrative reform. On the following day, the cabinet introduced them to the Diet. After deliberation in both chambers, the bills passed in the Diet on July 8, 1999, bringing about drastic organizational change in the central government agency in January 2001.

SUMMARY

Hashimoto Ryûtarô was elected LDP president in September 1996 not because of his power base within the party but because of his popularity among the public. With limited internal sources of power, Hashimoto actively sought public support. As the public saw Hashimoto's determination, his approval rate rose, strengthening his control over the government and the party.

Because public distrust against the national bureaucracy remained strong, Prime Minister Hashimoto made administrative reform the most important policy issue of his government. During the October 1996 general election campaign, virtually all political parties pledged to carry out administrative reform. Backed by an LDP victory in the general election, Hashimoto inaugurated the Council on Administrative Reform and appointed himself chairman of the Council in order to force his government to act on the recommendations of the Council.

As there was no bureaucratic representation in the Council, bureaucratic officials tried to manipulate the Council through its Secretariat, which was under strong control of bureaucrats. When Hashimoto found this manipulation, he decided to conduct the Council's proceeding based solely on information provided directly by its members. This limited bureaucratic control in the writing of the interim report, which called for reinforcing the cabinet, privatizing postal saving and insurance services, dividing the politically powerful Ministry of Construction, and decreasing the number of government agencies from 22 to 13.

Everything started falling apart after the cabinet reshuffling of September 1997. Hashimoto appointed to the cabinet Satô Kôkô, a man with a criminal record for taking a bribe. The public reaction was much stronger than Hashimoto expected. The public was disappointed by the appointment; but more important, it was disappointed by the fact that Hashimoto ignored the importance of public support for his actions. The public seemed to stop taking Hashimoto seriously after this cabinet reshuffle.

Worsening recession additionally weakened Hashimoto's leadership. The media blamed Hashimoto, who had introduced a tight fiscal policy for slowing down the economy. As Hashimoto's popularity and leadership eroded, the LDP's *zoku* members took the opportunity to attack the prime minister's administrative reform plan. In addition to postal *zoku* members, other *zoku* members joined the movement against Hashimoto's reform plan. As the political opposition grew, Hashimoto began to avoid making decisive statements on controversial issues. Although Hashimoto managed to keep the framework of 13 ministries and agencies in the final report, there were major setbacks, including abandoning the privatization of postal services (see Figure 7.1).

Hashimoto desperately needed public support for his administrative reform, but before the reforms could be approved, he lost that support and his reform effort came up short. Public support became important especially after the breakup of the long-predominant LDP in 1993. No one faction in the ruling party was a dominant power on the political scene, and the prime minister's power base within the ruling party was subsequently weakened. With a weaker power base, a prime minister must attract considerable public and media support. Hashimoto lost that support by making a fatal mistake in the cabinet reshuffling in an attempt to pay a political favor to the conservative wing of the LDP. This

Figure 7.1
Hashimoto and Administrative Reform

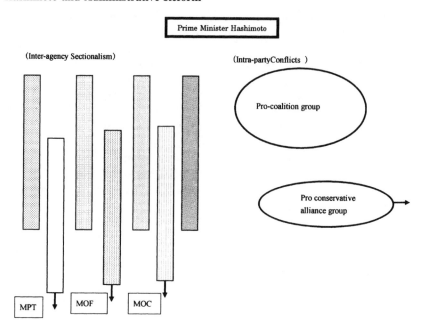

tilted the power balance between his party and himself. Hashimoto's leadership was seen as weak, and LDP members felt free to destroy the reform plan on which Prime Minister Hashimoto had promised to stake his political life. The final report was full of political compromises. Disappointed voters expressed their disapproval of the LDP in the upper house election, forcing Hashimoto to resign and thus leaving his reform efforts incomplete.

The newly elected premier, Obuchi Keizô, took over the reform efforts. Despite his verbal commitments, his involvement was very limited. However, most of the political battles were over by December 1997. The Obuchi government did not confront major political challenges to pass the final administrative bills that brought drastic organizational changes in the central government.

NOTES

1. *Nihon Keizai Shimbun*, March 12, 1996.

2. According to a *Kyodo News* poll of September 28–29, 1996, for example, the approval rate for the Hashimoto cabinet rose to 52.3 percent from 47.0 percent on July 13–14.

3. They were Iida Yôtarô of Mitsubishi Heavy Industry, who chaired the Administrative Reform Committee; Toyota Shôichirô of Toyota Motors, who chaired the Eco-

nomic Policy Council; and Moroi Ken of Chichibu Onoda Cement Company, who chaired the Council on Government Decentralization.

4. The five scholars were Arima Akito of Tokyo University, Inoguchi Kuniko of Sophia University, Kawai Hayao of the International Center for Japanese Culture, Satô Kôji of Kyoto University, Shionoya Yûichi of Hitotsubashi University, and Fujita Tokiyasu of Tohoku University. The two media representatives were Kawaguchi Mikio of NHK and Watanabe Tsuneo of *Yomiuri Shimbun*, and the labor representative was Ashida Jinnosuke of the *Rengô*.

5. Deputy Secretary General Yagi Toshimichi was former deputy director general of the Management and Coordination Agency. Three executive members were Sakano Yasuharu of the Management and Coordination Agency, Koyama Yutaka of the Prime Minister's Office and Ofuji Toshiyuki of the Ministry of Finance.

6. The 12 researchers were from Asahi Beer, Nippon Steel, Toyota Motors, Tokyo Electric Power, Toshiba, Nissan Motors, NEC, Mitsui Company, Mitsubishi Electric, IBM Japan, *Keidanren*, and *Rengô*.

7. One of the researchers at the Council on Administrative Reform (who requested not to be identified) interview by author, December 19, 1997.

8. A poll taken by *Kyodo News Service* on December 7–8, 1996.

9. Mabuchi Masaru, "Shôchô Saihen, Hashimoto Gyôkaku no Owari" [The reorganization of government agencies—the end of Hashimoto administrative reform], *Chûô Kôron*, February 1998, p. 49.

10. Moroi Ken, interview by author, October 22, 1998.

11. Mizuno Kiyoshi, "Gyôkaku Kaigi: Kanryô tono Kôbô" [The Administrative Reform Council: Fights with bureaucrats], *Bungei Shunjû* (October 1997): 105–7.

12. *Nihon Keizai Shimbun*, June 20, 1997.

13. Gyôsei Kaikaku Kaigi Jimukyoku, "Gyôsei Kaikaku Kaigi dai 20kai Giji Gaiyô," July 2, 1997, available at http://kantei.go.jp/jp/gyokaku.

14. Gyôsei Kaikaku Kaigi Jimukyoku, "Gyôsei Kaikaku Kaigi dai 21kai Giji Gaiyô," July 7, 1997.

15. Fujita Tokiyasu, "Gyôkaku Kaigi Iin Zen Uchimaku wo Kataru," *Bungei Shunjû*, February 1998, p. 389.

16. A poll taken by *Kyodo News Service* on July 12–13, 1997.

17. Although Hashimoto held several meetings between the government and the LDP on administrative reform between January and July 1997, the ruling party had limited influence over the interim report.

18. The total postal saving amounted 225 trillion yen at the end of 1996.

19. A poll taken by *Asahi Shimbun* on September 7–8, 1997; *Asahi Shimbun*, September 10, 1997.

20. Katô Kôichi's statement, "Hôdô 2001," on Fuji Television, September 14, 1997.

21. *Tokyo Shimbun*, September 17, 1997.

22. Fujita Tokiyasu, pp. 390–91.

23. Moroi Ken, interview by author, October 22, 1998.

24. Instead of the privatization, it suggested that (1) funds from the postal saving would not be used for Fiscal Loan and Investment Programs; (2) a part of funds would finance the government deficit; (3) the interest rate of postal savings would be lower than that of private banks; and (4) the number of employees of post offices would be significantly reduced. *Nihon Keizai Shimbun*, September 28, 1997.

25. *Asahi Shimbun*, October 10, 1997.

26. Gyôsei Kaikaku Kaigi Jimukyoku, "Gyôsei Kaikaku Kaigi dai 31kai Giji Gaiyô," October 8, 1997.

27. Fujita Tokiyasu, pp. 390–91.

28. Moroi Ken, interview by author, October 22, 1998.

29. They raised reasons that intimate relations between politicians and specific industry were not desirable and that the interests of industry and ministries were considered over national interests. The opinion poll was conducted on October 25–26, 1997, with 1952 samples. *Yomiuri Shimbun*, November 4, 1997.

30. *Nihon Keizai Shimbun*, October 19, 1997. Also, Gyôsei Kaikaku Kaigi Jimukyoku, "Gyôsei Kaikaku Kaigi dai 32kai Giji Gaiyô," October 15, 1997.

31. Moroi Ken, interview by author, October 22, 1998.

32. The new Ministry of National Land and Transportation would be a merger of the Ministries of Construction and Transportation with the Agencies of National Land, Hokkaido Development and Okinawa Development.

33. The other members included two scholar members from the Administrative Reform Council, Satô Kôji and Fujita Tokiyasu, and six new members, former deputy chief cabinet secretary Ishihara Nobuo, Koike Tadao of *Mainichi Shimbun*, former Economic Planning Agency chief Takahara Sumiko, Emoto Teruhito of *Rengô*, Yamaguchi Nobuo of the Tokyo Chamber of Commerce, and Nishizaki Tetsurô.

34. Policy speech by Prime Minister Obuchi to the 143rd session of the Diet, August 7, 1998.

35. About the proceedings of the Economic Strategy Council, see Takenaka Heizô, *Keisei Zaimin: Keizai Senryaku Kaigi no 180 nichi* [Governing the world to rescue people: 180 days of the Economic Strategy Council] (Tokyo: Daiyamondo-sha, 1999). The minutes of the advisory council on administrative reform can be found at http://www.kantei.go.jp/jp/komon.

36. Asakura Kôji, interview by author, Tokyo, April 26, 1999.

37. "Chûô Shôchô Suishin Honbu/Komon Kaigi (dai 9 kai) Gijiroku," December 17, 1998, available at http://www.kantei.go.jp/jp/komon.

Conclusion

Is the Japanese prime minister effective as a national leader? This study centers on this question. The leadership of the prime minister is indeed limited. Why? The conventional answer is that political constraints limit his vast legal authority, leaving his role in the policy process relatively passive and unimportant.

This study, however, provides a different answer. Even though the legal authority of the prime minister is very limited, he has at his disposal various sources of power with which he can play an imperative role in policy making. Because prime ministers must rely on informal sources of power to effectively utilize institutional sources of power, their effectiveness varies depending on their background, experience, political skills, and personality.

SOURCES OF POWER

The Constitution vests executive power in the cabinet, not in the prime minister. The prime minister has the authority to represent and head the cabinet, but this legal authority is ambiguous. The authority over administrative operations is divided among the various ministers. The prime minister does not have direct authority over government agencies. To influence administrative operations, he must, theoretically, go through the cabinet, which requires unanimous consent to approve any cabinet decision. The prime minister's control over the cabinet, therefore, determines his influence over the government. Although he has constitutional authority to appoint and dismiss cabinet members, the political reality is that he does not have a free hand in forming his cabinet.

The long-time ruling Liberal Democratic Party was a coalition of several different groups with different political goals. This has also been the situation with the Hata Tsutomu government. To become prime minister, a candidate had first to form a coalition of factions that would support him, and then to maintain that support to be an effective leader. The appointment of cabinet members from each of inner groups of the government party was the minimum condition necessary to gain support from the entire party organization. Powerful prime ministers have enjoyed relative freedom over appointments, but even they have not been able to ignore totally the wishes of the other factions. Ignoring the factional balance can create a severe split within the party. If this happens, the prime minister no longer has support from a majority in the Diet, which can lead to a vote of no-confidence forcing him out of office. The appointment of cabinet members is a tool whereby the prime minister can hold the party together to pursue his policies.

Among the legal authorities of the prime minister, the appointment and dismissal authority is the only one given to him independent of the cabinet. Factionalism within the party, however, has meant that a prime minister cannot freely exercise his sole appointive power. Cabinet members, though formally appointed by the prime minister, maintain strong loyalty to their faction leaders and have often acted as representatives of their groups to the administration. This factionalism has weakened the prime minister's leadership in the cabinet.

The prime minister must deal with another kind of fraction within the party and the government in addition to factionalism: the issue-specific sectionalism among various *zoku* members and related government agencies. Each section of the bureaucracy has its own interest and client industry to protect. Career bureaucrats spend their entire careers in a single ministry and resist policy changes that negatively affect their clients. LDP *zoku* members, who have increased their power in the issue-specific policy-making process, often allied with the related ministries to protect their client industries. In return for such protection, the client industries provided them with financial and other assistance. Such sectionalism has continued to strengthen since the 1970s and has been an issue facing successive prime ministers.

The major issues that the prime minister handles are so complicated and intertwined that they involve the jurisdiction of more than one ministry and thus different *zoku* groups. A number of issues also require international consideration. The prime minister must coordinate among conflicting interests within the government and the ruling party or coalition to pursue his policies. The strong sectionalism of bureaucrats and LDP *zoku* members was a major obstacle confronting the prime ministers during the long LDP-led government. The leadership of the prime minister depends on his will and his ability to crush the walls of such sectionalism.

Recent prime ministers have faced these two types of fractions: intraparty factionalism and issue-specific sectionalism. Leaders who have successfully contained the fractions within the ruling party and the government have been effective, whereas prime ministers who have lost control over the party and the government and allowed the fractions to stop their policies have proved ineffective leaders.

The prime minister's effectiveness in pursuing his policies depends in part on various informal sources of power. His leadership style is determined by the political resources available to him and by how he utilizes them. Two categories of informal sources were introduced in Chapter 4—resources as a political insider and support from outside political circles.

Among the most important "internal" political resources under the LDP government was the prime minister's status as leader of the ruling party. Obviously, a prime minister with a strong support base within the party has a strong administration. LDP factions would form a coalition that made up more than a majority of the LDP Diet members to choose the president—thus the prime minister—because no faction was large enough to single-handedly appoint their leader. If the prime minister's faction formed a majority within the coalition, he was able to take the initiative in deciding policies. If the unity of the coalition was strong, the prime minister held considerable control over the policy-making process in the party. Prime Ministers Satô Eisaku, Tanaka Kakuei, and Takeshita Noboru enjoyed their status as leaders of the largest LDP factions. The size of their factions and the unity of their interfactional coalitions were important sources of power for these national leaders.

The size of his faction and the unity of the coalition became more important in the 1970s because the prime minister's control over the party has weakened. From the mid-1950s to the end of the Tanaka administration in 1974, prime ministers usually appointed one of their faction members as LDP secretary general, the number-two party post that handles the day-to-day party affairs. Since 1974, in an attempt to avoid too much concentration of power, the party divided the presidency and the post of secretary general between two factions. The prime minister had to delegate most of the authority over party affairs to a senior LDP member of a different faction. With his weaker direct control over the party, maintaining party unity became a prime minister's primary concern.

Whereas support from within the ruling party helps the prime minister exercise his leadership, staff support from the bureaucracy is essential for him to execute any policy decision. Diet members and the cabinet, who have a limited number of personal staffers, have long relied on the bureaucracy for drafting bills, supervising the implementation of policies, and interpreting existing laws for administrative operations. As discussed earlier, the prime minister does not have direct authority over the bureaucracy, and bureaucrats tend to protect their sectional interests. Opposition from the bureaucracy often becomes a major obstacle in the prime minister's pursuit of his policies.

Powerful prime ministers find a way to reach and then effectively control the bureaucracy. Prime Minister Tanaka Kakuei built extensive personal connections with many bureaucrats in various agencies, which he utilized to pursue his policies. Prime Minister Takeshita Noboru, who served as the finance minister for four consecutive terms under the Nakasone administration, used his personal ties with finance ministry officials in his efforts to introduce a new consumption tax. Prime Minister Nakasone Yasuhiro, who did not have strong ties with the bureaucracy, appointed Gotôda Masaharu as chief cabinet secretary. Gotôda's long experience in the bureaucracy more than supplemented the shortcomings of the prime minister in achieving administrative reform.

After a policy decision is made within the government and the ruling party, most major policies go through the legislative process. Here, relations with the opposition parties can be a determining factor in the enactment of the prime minister's policies. The prime minister's ability to persuade the opposition parties is often crucial in legislative actions. Prime Minister Nakasone failed to pass his tax reform bills when the strongly united opposition parties opposed them. Prime Minister Takeshita Noboru, in contrast, successfully passed his tax reform in the Diet by accommodating the requests from two opposition parties; Takeshita utilized channels to the opposition parties that he had built before becoming prime minister.

Informal sources of power are not limited to political circles. "External" support is also important. Popularity, for example, plays an increasingly important role in Japanese politics. Although popularity alone cannot bring a politician to the post of prime minister, it can significantly affect his leadership within the party and the cabinet. High popularity, for example, helped Prime Minister Nakasone Yasuhiro pursue administrative reforms and maintain his administration for five years, the third-longest term for a postwar prime minister. Low popularity, conversely, was a factor in forcing Prime Ministers Yoshida Shigeru, Kishi Nobusuke, Tanaka Kakuei, Uno Sôsuke, and Takeshita Noboru out of office.

Because public support plays an important role, many prime ministers have emphasized public relations activities. In the television age, a major part of one's public image is formulated by appearance and eloquence on the air. Prime Minister Miki Takeo, Nakasone Yasuhiro, and Kaifu Toshiki used their eloquence to their advantage. Hosokawa Morihiro took extensive advantage of this medium, using television in much in the same way as would an American president. At the same time, however, the prime minister's high visibility can work against him. The most extreme example of this is Yoshida Shigeru, who called an opposition party member an "idiot," which forced the prime minister to dissolve the lower house.

Support from the business community and the United States often plays an important role in helping the prime minister maintain stability in his administration. Their disapproval may lead to his resignation. Yoshida Shigeru, Hatoyama Ichirô, Tanaka Kakuei, and Miki Takeo left office soon after the business community requested their resignations. Suzuki Zenkô's poor handling of relations with the United States led to the anti-Suzuki movement within his party, which resulted in his resignation. Prime Ministers Nakasone Yasuhiro and Kaifu Toshiki had friendly relations with American presidents, which contributed to their popularity at home.

These informal sources of power, both internal and external, help the prime minister exercise his institutional power in pursuing his policies. His effectiveness as a national leader, therefore, depends on the informal sources of power he as an individual can muster and his ability to utilize them. These sources are not consistent with each administration but vary depending on the political climate, the issues at hand, and the individual who is the prime minister.

FOUR STYLES OF LEADERSHIP

The case studies in Chapters 5, 6, and 7 show that when the variations of sources of power are grouped, four different leadership styles emerge: the political insider, the grandstander, the kamikaze fighter; and the peace lover. The political insider is a leader with abundant internal sources of power who enjoys stable support within the ruling party and close ties with the bureaucracy and the opposition parties. The other three leadership styles lack internal resources. The grandstander directly seeks external support from the public and the media for his policy goals to supplement his lack of internal sources of power. The kamikaze fighter tries to achieve an unpopular policy by sacrificing his political leadership role. The peace lover is an indecisive leader who fails to achieve a controversial policy goal because he tries to please all the actors.

The Political Insider

Of the three prime ministers observed in the case studies, Takeshita Noboru exemplifies the typical "political insider." In his tax reform attempts of 1988, he vigorously took advantage of his status as leader of the largest LDP faction. His stable power base within the party stemmed from his successful formation of a strong majority coalition within the party with two other factions. His faction also boasted the largest number of LDP *zoku* members, who were effective in their specific policy fields. For example, once Takeshita decided on the no-exemption principle for his consumption tax, senior members of the Takeshita faction played an important role in achieving party consensus by persuading other *zoku* members, their client industries, and the related ministries to support the tax reform efforts. Takeshita's status as a faction leader helped contain both sectionalism and factionalism.

Further, Takeshita had strong control over the bureaucracy. Takeshita, who was taught by Prime Minister Satô Eisaku to establish personal ties with individual bureaucrats, had a personal network in the Ministry of Finance, where he had been a minister for four consecutive terms under the Nakasone administration. Takeshita successfully mobilized the entire ministry and even drew cooperation from the Ministry of International Trade and Industry in the process of introducing a consumption tax. Takeshita, in short, had abundant political resources to avoid fractions.

In recent LDP history, Satô Eisaku and Tanaka Kakuei and possibly Obuchi Keizô, are prime ministers who effectively used their resources as political insiders. All were the leaders of the largest LDP faction. At the same time, Satô and Tanaka had strong ties with bureaucrats. It is interesting that the three prime ministers who enjoyed stable support from within the party—Satô, Tanaka, and Takeshita—could not maintain external support. During the last days of his administration, Satô's popularity fell, and pro-China business leaders openly requested the resignation of the prime minister, who maintained his pro-Taiwan stance. After Satô achieved his top priority, the reversion of the Okinawa Islands in 1972, he announced his resignation.

Tanaka Kakuei succeeded Satô as premier and faction leader. He had strong control over the party and the bureaucracy and close ties with the opposition parties. He successfully normalized relations with China. However, Tanaka was forced to resign in 1974 when the media and the public strongly criticized his financial wrongdoings. Similarly, the revelation of the Recruit scandal created intense resentment against the Takeshita cabinet and lowered its public support to a record low. Takeshita thus had no choice but to resign. These prime ministers who had strong internal sources of power drastically lost their external support.

The Grandstander

A prime minister with less internal support must be a "grandstander" to seek external support from the public and the media. Prime Minister Nakasone Yasuhiro, whose faction was the second smallest of the five LDP factions, was well aware of the importance of public support. Nakasone once compared his efforts in administrative reform to a glider, saying, "As long as the wind of public and mass media support continues to blow, the glider can fly. If the wind of support diminishes, it will stall and crash."

With limited inner-party and bureaucratic support, Nakasone enthusiastically sought public support for his policy. He openly expressed his desire to become a "top-down presidential leader" in Japan's bottom-up society. In his attempt to do so, he became the first prime minister who extensively used his advisory councils. Advisory councils for Nakasone were tools to identify current problems and to gain public support to deal with issues. One of Nakasone's advisors recalls: "Nakasone faced the electorate directly with a showy performance. He made every effort to steer Japan in new directions as the leader of the electorate."[1]

Prime Minister Nakasone formed private advisory councils in various policy areas, including culture and education, security, the Yasukuni Shrine issue, economic policy, education, and international harmonization. The most successful and dynamic of these councils was the Second Ad Hoc Committee on Administrative Reform, or *Rinchô*, which he formed when he was the director general of the Administrative Management Agency in the Suzuki Zenkô cabinet. Nakasone appointed an elderly, charismatic business leader, former *Keidanren* chairman Dokô Toshio, to head the committee. Nakasone recognized the importance of the business leader as a symbol of the reform efforts. Under the leadership of Dokô, administrative reform became a national movement supported by the media and the public, which the other LDP factions and the opposition parties had difficulty opposing.

Media and public support suppressed sectionalism within the government and the ruling party. Because the public recognized the government deficit as a serious problem, LDP *zoku* members could not openly oppose the general direction of the administrative reform efforts. Nakasone successfully contained sectionalism by imposing the zero and minus ceilings over the budget of each ministry as described in Chapter 5. The so-called starve-out strategy forced government agencies to come up with their own solutions. Since every agency was starved out by budget cuts, no single agency or its patron LDP *zoku* members could complain of being "hungry." In similar fashion, the politically difficult privatization of the Japan National Railways was conducted after the privatization of Japan's other two public corporations. This made it difficult for the railways to maintain an anti-privatization position.

Public support was essential to prime ministers who faced internal conflict within the ruling party. For example, Yoshida Shigeru, who was asked to lead the Liberal Party by Hatoyama Ichirô in 1946, did not have strong control over the party. However, his image as a charismatic leader and hard negotiator with the American Occupation authority attracted public support and allowed him to become an effective leader in reconstructing the Japanese economy and concluding the 1951 San Francisco Peace Treaty.

Ikeda Hayato was another prime minister who effectively took advantage of public support. In an attempt to change the gloomy mood created by the turmoil over the revision of the U.S.–Japan Security Treaty in 1960, Ikeda introduced an optimistic economic policy. His "income-doubling plan" was attractive to a public, who desired a higher standard of living. The public's enthusiastic support of his administration helped Ikeda to be elected to the LDP presidency and thus to be the prime minister for three consecutive times. Yoshida and Ikeda as well as Nakasone had a clear political vision and directly sought public support to suppress potentially volatile opposition within the ruling party and the opposition parties.

Prime Minister Hosokawa Morihiro may belong to this category, at least for his achievement of political reform. From the beginning of his term in August 1993, he publicly declared that political reform to introduce a single-seat electoral system would be his top priority and he declared that he would stake his political career on achieving this objective. The public, who had been disappointed by the failure of LDP prime ministers Kaifu Toshiki and Miyazawa Kiichi to deliver a similar reform because of intraparty conflicts, strongly supported Hosokawa. He received an unprecedented 70 percent of public support.

Even with this enormous popularity, it was not easy for Hosokawa to pass the political reform bills, which were controversial within the political community. On January 21, 1994, the leftist faction of the Japan Socialist Party effectively killed the political reform bills by voting against them in the upper house, thereby breaking the agreement reached among the party leaders in the coalition government. Negotiations in the joint committee between the upper and lower house representatives broke up. This meant that Hosokawa had only two more days to achieve political reform in the 128th extraordinary session.

Prime Minister Hosokawa publicly restated his willingness to sacrifice his post for political reform, and he called for a meeting with LDP president Kôno Yôhei. In his negotiations with the LDP leader, Hosokawa accepted the LDP's requests to change the number of electoral districts and to ease the reporting requirements for political finance. An agreement was reached. Although many LDP members opposed the political reform, they did not want to be blamed for blocking bills popular with the public. This compromise enabled the Hosokawa coalition government to pass the political reform bills in the upper and lower houses on January 29, 1994.

The Kamikaze Fighter

In his last year as prime minister, Nakasone Yasuhiro became less sensitive to public reaction and turned into a "kamikaze fighter," one who sacrifices public support and his political career to pursue a politically unpopular policy—in Nakasone's case, tax reform. His statement that his administration would not introduce a large-scale indirect tax was taken as his campaign pledge for the 1986 double election, and many LDP candidates echoed the prime minister in their own election campaigns. This statement became a major constraint on Nakasone's efforts to reform the tax system. The public and the media as well as interest groups felt that he had lied to them, and they strongly objected to the tax reform proposal.

The public and the media also felt that the government was attempting to introduce a drastic change in the tax system without discussing the issue thoroughly. The lack of information accelerated the anti–sales tax movement. The opposition of interest groups such as retailers and the textile industry mobilized both LDP and opposition party members to oppose the tax reform. Especially for first-term LDP Diet members who had been elected in the 1986 election, adhering to the campaign pledge against the indirect tax was vital to sustain their support base for reelection. It is ironic that the 1986 election victory, which secured seats for many new LDP members, hurt Nakasone's tax reform effort by weakening party unity and eventually caused his support base, the public, to desert him.

In short, for a prime minister with limited internal political resources, failure to attract external support can be detrimental to his fight against fractions within the government and the ruling party. When Hatoyama Ichirô tried to normalize relations with the Soviet Union, he met strong opposition from business leaders. This accelerated an anti-Hatoyama movement within the LDP. To suppress the opposition within the party, Hatoyama had to promise he would resign so that Soviet-Japan diplomatic relations could be restored.

Hatoyama was not the only prime minister who, lacking external support, had to sacrifice his premiership for policy achievement. Kishi Nobusuke did not spend much effort on public relations when he introduced his top priority issue, the revision of the U.S.–Japan Security Treaty, in 1960. As a result, massive student groups began protest movements against revision of the treaty, which would assure Japan's security commitment with the United States. Reflecting such reactions, an anti-Kishi movement rose within the LDP. After the treaty revision passed the Diet, Kishi had to resign as prime minister. Prime ministers with less internal political resources, like Hatoyama, Kishi, and Nakasone, are more likely to invite fierce interfactional struggles without receiving strong external support.

The Peace Lover

Whereas kamikaze fighters sacrifice their post for a policy goal, others are not willing to take chances. These are the "peace lovers." Suzuki Zenkô, who was known for his emphasis on party harmony, was a typical peace lover. After the fierce interfactional conflicts in the 1970s, especially between the factions of Tanaka Kakuei and Fukuda Takeo, the party wanted a president who had a wider support base within the party in order to avoid serious conflicts. Suzuki knew exactly why he was chosen for the post and repeatedly emphasized his role in keeping party harmony.

Emphasizing party harmony as the top priority, however, is no way to handle politically difficult tasks like administrative reform, which the Suzuki administration initiated. Suzuki was unwilling to take the necessary risk to achieve administrative reform because he thought that such a risk would invite discord within the ruling party. For example, the prime minister's advisory council, the *Rinchô*, recommended an across-the-board freeze on government spending, including the subsidy for rice prices. In the rice pricing of July 1982, Suzuki chose not to intervene in the price-setting process in order not to disturb party harmony. The prime minister was unwilling to stand up to agricultural interests and their patron *zoku* members. As a result, the rice price increased two years in a row, in 1982 by 1.1 percent. This decision not only disappointed the *Rinchô* officials but also damaged the momentum for reform efforts to cut governmental spending. The public, the media, and business leaders criticized Suzuki, and political pressure began to mount against him. As economic conditions worsened the budget deficit, it became obvious that the Japanese government would have a 6-trillion-yen revenue shortage in FY1982. This negated Suzuki's pledge of "No deficit-financing bonds in FY1985" and exacerbated the anti-Suzuki movement. Suzuki believed that if he remained as prime minister, he would create party disharmony, so he decided to resign in the midst of administrative reform efforts.

Prime ministers with limited internal resources must seek support from the public, the media, and the business groups to pursue their major policies. Without such support, prime ministers likely face dissent from the ruling party and the government by those who emphasize factional or sectional interests over national interests. Some prime ministers with strong determination sacrificed their internal support to promote their policy objectives.

Others, like Suzuki, lacked this determination, and they failed to achieve their policy goals. When Kaifu Toshiki's top priority issue, the political reform proposal, died in the Diet in 1991, Kaifu wanted to dissolve the lower house to gain public support for the reform effort. However, he could not turn a deaf ear to opposition of the largest LDP faction led by Takeshita Noboru. This underscored Kaifu's weakness, accelerated an anti-Kaifu movement already brewing within the party, and led to his resignation. More recently, Miyazawa Kiichi's lack of determination in political reform allowed the party secretary general to kill the political reform in 1993. Disappointed reformists within the LDP broke off from the ruling party and joined the opposition parties to show their disapproval of the Miyazawa cabinet. This leadership failure even brought an end to the LDP's 38-year reign.

An ambitious leader who seeks to be a "grandstander" may end up being a "peace lover." Hashimoto Ryûtarô was elected LDP president in September 1996 not because of his power base within the party but because of his popularity among the public. Hashimoto was often described as the lone wolf. He had very few enthusiastic followers within the party, even in the Obuchi faction to which he belonged. While Hashimoto had expertise in some policy areas and many admirers in the bureaucracy, his ties with the opposition parties were limited. Therefore, it is not appropriate to classify him as a political insider.

With the limited internal sources of power, Hashimoto actively sought public support. After Hashimoto managed to pass the politically difficult *jûsen* bills, he was rewarded by the public when the LDP gained more seats in the October 1996 lower house election. Without losing the momentum from the election victory, he formed the Council on Administrative Reform and named himself chairman. In his policy speech, he expressed his commitment to the reform efforts. As the public saw Hashimoto's determination, his approval rate rose, strengthening his control over the government and the party.

During the first two years, Hashimoto showed direction, and backed by public support his policies moved forward. Over a revision of the land-lease law for American bases in Okinawa in spring 1997, Hashimoto successfully acquired the support from the opposition New Frontier Party when the government failed to make an agreement with the Social Democratic Party. In September 1997, Hashimoto won his second term as LDP president without a contest. At his political peak, Hashimoto's Council introduced an interim report that contained many difficult reorganization proposals to streamline the national government agencies. At this point, he could be classified as "grandstander," taking advantage of public support to supplement his weak power base inside of the political circle.

Everything fell apart after the cabinet reshuffling of September 1997. Hashimoto appointed to the cabinet Sato Kôkô, a man with a criminal record for taking a bribe. This appointment was made in order to win the support of the conservatives for the success of the administrative reforms on which he staked his political life, as a kamikaze fighter would. He decided to sacrifice public support in order to gain internal support. At this point, Hashimoto was no longer a grandstander.

Public reaction was much stronger than Hashimoto expected, and his popularity rating dropped dramatically. As Hashimoto's popularity eroded, LDP's *zoku* members took the opportunity to attack the prime minister's administrative reform. After his failure to maintain public support, the prime minister became more like a peace lover as he scrambled to keep political support for his reform efforts. Although Hashimoto managed to maintain the framework of 13 ministries, he made many political compromises. The final report for Hashimoto's administrative reform was a major setback from the interim report.

With limited legal authority, the prime minister must depend on informal sources of power to shape his leadership style and to determine the effectiveness of his effort. The political insider employs his abundant power within the ruling party, the bureaucracy, and the opposition parties to influence policy. Having fewer internal resources, the grandstander relies on his ability to attract considerable support from the public and the media. The kamikaze fighter sacrifices his political career. The peace lover tries to avoid serious confrontations at all costs.

CHANGES FOR STRONGER LEADERSHIP

The lack of leadership became a focal issue for Japanese politics especially in the 1990s. One of the major themes for Hashimoto's administrative reform was reinforcing the power of the cabinet and the prime minister. During the 1990s, three major political changes were created to shape the leadership of the future prime ministers: the 1994 electoral system; the Diet and government reform of 1999, and Hashimoto's administrative reform efforts effective in January 2001. This section will analyze the possible impact of these changes on the institutional and informal power of the prime minister.

The 1994 Electoral Changes

Political reform became a major issue under the Hosokawa Morihiro cabinet (1993–94). The new electoral rules were introduced as described in Chapter 2. One of the objectives of reform was to weaken the power of factions. The old "middle-size" electoral system of the lower house with three to five seats encouraged multiple candidates from the LDP. The competition among candidates from different LDP factions was much fiercer than with the opposition parties because they shared a similar support base. LDP candidates, therefore, had to rely not on the party organization but on their faction for financial and other campaign support. This strengthened the power of factions and decentralized the power of the LDP leadership and the prime minister. In addition, the old electoral system was considered a cause of political corruption, since LDP factions had to actively seek financial resources in order to compete among them. The new single-seat system was introduced in 1994 in order to weaken some functions of the LDP factions and eliminate factional competition in the general election.

Another objective of the 1994 revision was to strengthen voters' control over the government. Throughout the postwar period, Japanese voters became so accustomed to single-party dominance by the LDP that they did not feel they had a choice in government. The 1993–94 political changes that brought the establishment of non-LDP government under Hosokawa Morihiro and the LDP-*Sakigake*-Socialist coalition government under Murayama Tomiichi came about because of the realigning of coalitions among political parties. Voters still did not have direct control over them. Under the new electoral law, which introduced a single-seat electoral district, voters' frustration and distrust of politics can be expressed through votes against the party at issue.

In the first general election under the new law in 1996, voters did express their dissatisfaction, but their frustration did not reflect actual representation in the Diet. The LDP received only 38.6 percent of total votes in single-seat districts and 32.7 percent in proportional representation district. But with these numbers of votes, the LDP was still able to capture 239 seats of the 500 lower house seats (47.8 percent), enabling the party to form a single-party minority government. In many single-seat districts too many non-LDP candidates were put forth, and anti-LDP votes were split among the opposition parties such as the New Frontier Party, the Democratic Party, the Communist Party, and the Socialist Party. Unfortunately, Japanese voters missed the opportunity to feel that they had the power to choose the government and turned out in record low vote turnout.

For the coming elections, it is likely that some party realignment will take place. It could happen as the reorganization of the opposition parties or as a major realignment involving the LDP. Whatever adjustment is made, the number of candidates in each district is likely to decrease, providing voters with simpler options between pro- and anti–status quo. In such a situation, opposition parties may appeal to the public by clearly stating policy difference from the ruling party. If voters strongly feel that they can transfer the power of the government and choose policy goals, more of them will go to the polls.

In the 1996 election, many candidates, especially those of the LDP and the NFP, ran their election campaigns pretty much as they had under the old multiseat district system. They continued to rely on organized votes of many politically oriented groups and did not spend enough time and energy appealing to the general public. With a higher voter turnout, however, candidates cannot continue their traditional way of campaigning. They must appeal to "the silent majority."

As many critics quickly pointed out, the 1996 election was not as policy-oriented as the supporters of political reform hoped it to be. There were very few policy differences among major political parties. The general election, however, was probably the most party-oriented one in many years. In many single-seat districts, the candidates from the ruling LDP and the largest opposition party, New Frontier Party, fought fiercely. In proportional representative districts, the New Frontier Party received 28.2 percent, only 4.5 percent less than the LDP (32.7 percent).

Under the more party-oriented election, major parties realized the image of the party leader was important. The LDP, the New Frontier Party, and the Socialist Party chose new party leaders for the election. The newly created Democratic Party appointed a popular minister of health and welfare, Kan Naoto, co-leader of the party right before the election.

There are several factors that may strengthen this tendency of party-oriented elections in the future. First, with fewer parties represented in the race, as described earlier, policy difference between parties will be clearer. Second, the party headquarters may develop stronger control over the list of candidates, especially in proportional representation districts. Third, government subsidies are given to the party, not to individual politicians. This will probably give the party leadership stronger control over election campaigns.

These factors likely will contribute to stronger party leadership between elections, thus leading to a more centralized power structure within political parties. If the leader of the ruling party, thus the prime minister, has stronger control over his own party, he will have better control over his cabinet. With a more united cabinet, the national leader can better achieve his policy goals as promised to the public during the election. If the national leader fails to deliver a policy goal the voters desire, under the new electoral system he and his party can more easily lose control over the government.

This does not mean that the electoral change only positively affects the LDP leadership. Although it has weakened some functions of LDP factions, it has not eliminated them. Factions still exist within the LDP, and they remain decisive for the stability of the government and the selection of the prime minister. However, because of the new electoral system, LDP candidates, even powerful incumbents, have found themselves playing a completely different game. In order to win their seat, they need to win a higher percentage of the total votes. To many, the election pressure has been much greater than ever. The increased competition for the single seat has made them more sensitive to election pressures than to national interests, and thus often more enthusiastic to please their constituencies and client industries than to support the prime minister. This may well remain a major obstacle for the national leader.

The Diet and Government Reform of 1999

In January 1999, as discussed in the previous chapter, the LDP formed a coalition government with Ozawa Ichirô's Liberal Party. As a condition to join the coalition, the Liberal Party demanded a set of institutional changes to strengthen the role of the cabinet and politicians and to curb the influence of the bureaucracy.

One condition Ozawa presented was the immediate reduction of cabinet ministers from 20 to 15. In Ozawa's view, a large-sized cabinet was difficult to keep united, making a unanimous decision difficult to reach. The large size also opened the door for incompetent politicians. Less prestigious and junior cabinet positions, such as directors general of the Okinawa and Hokkaido Development Agencies, could be consolidated. By reducing the size, Ozawa believed, the cabinet would become more unified, more selective, and more efficient. When the LDP agreed to reduce cabinet posts from 20 to 18 immediately and then to 14–17 in January 2001, Ozawa compromised.[2]

To further pursue other policy arrangements, the LDP and the Liberal Party formed project teams between the two parties. One of the teams discussed the Diet and government reform plan. Ozawa wanted to abolish "the government commissioner system," which allowed bureaucratic officials to answer questions from the opposition parties in the Diet. This practice perpetuated politicians' dependency on the bureaucracy and allowed incompetent politicians to serve cabinet positions. The project team decided to abolish the government commissioner system, starting with the 146th Diet session (fall 1999). Bureaucratic assistance would be limited to the "government witness," who would answer questions on only highly technical matters and only upon the request of the Diet committee. The abolition would force the prime minister to appoint to his cabinet those politicians with deeper policy knowledge and expertise. The second Obuchi Keizô cabinet became the first government formed under the new rule in October 1999. As Prime Minister Obuchi carefully picked cabinet and sub-cabinet members his appointments received a good reputation. However, one cabinet member and one vice minister were forced to resign because of their careless comments. If the cabinet is composed of more knowledgeable and efficient politicians, the power balance with the bureaucracy eventually shifts toward the cabinet.

Another proposal by Ozawa was the introduction of deputy ministers to upgrade the position of the parliamentary vice ministers. The position was the only other political position in the bureaucracy besides that of minister. Although it was supposed to be the number two position in the ministry, the parliamentary vice minister played a limited role in policy making and was often referred to as an "appendix" of the ministry. Actual power rested in the hands of the administrative vice minister, a top ministry bureaucrat. To increase the government party's control over the bureaucracy, Ozawa wanted to increase the power and number of the politicians, modeled after British junior ministers.

After discussions, the project team between the LDP and the Liberal Party came to an agreement. In January 2001, the old 24 vice ministerial positions will be eliminated with the reorganization of the central government. In their place, a total of 22 deputy ministers and 26 political affairs officers will be appointed. Meanwhile, in fall 1999 the number of vice ministers or "state sec-retaries" for the entire central government was to be temporarily increased from 24 to 32. This step was introduced to strengthen assistance to ministers in the Diet on the occasion of the abolition of the government commissioner system. Deputy ministers will be expected to play a more active and influential role in policy-making processes in each ministry. Political affairs officers will also assist the minister in order to strengthen his control over his ministry.

In addition to these changes, another revision was introduced to further im-prove Diet operations. The project team decided to establish as a standing com-mittee, the National Basic Policy Committee, in both houses of the Diet, starting in the 2000 ordinary Diet session (January 2000). The committees hold weekly meetings for about 40 minutes throughout the session. At the meeting, the prime minister and the party leaders of the opposition parties and coalition partners can debate freely, modeled after the British "question time" system. The prime minister is expected to rely less on notes prepared by bureaucrats and more on his own policy knowledge and political beliefs. Whereas the prime minister is required to attend this weekly meeting, his attendance for other Diet committees and floor meetings will be significantly reduced. This will increase the spotlight on the prime minister, making his leadership and his ability to convey messages to the Diet and to the public much more important than before.

The above three changes were introduced to the Diet as the Bill to Enhance Diet Operation and the Politician-Led Policy Making System. This bill passed on July 26, 1999, with support from the LDP, the Liberal Party, the Democratic Party, and *Kômeitô*. Abolition of the government commissioner system will force the prime minister to select competent cabinet members, thus strengthening the cabinet. Introduction of deputy ministers will increase cabinet control over the bureaucracy. And establishment of the new National Basic Policy Commit-tees will require the prime minister's policy involvement and make his stand on issues more transparent. These changes should help strengthen the leadership of the national leader.

Changes from Hashimoto's Administrative Reform

Enhancing the power of the prime minister and cabinet was a central objective in administrative reform efforts under the Hashimoto Ryûtarô cabinet. One Ad-ministrative Reform Council member told the author, "Strengthening the cabinet function was a much more important achievement for the Council than reor-ganizing the ministries, which attracted the media's attention."[3] The administra-tive reform–related bills, passed on July 8, 1999, have put in motion significant institutional changes to strengthen the power of the prime minister and the cab-inet.

The Cabinet Law was revised to improve the policy initiative of the prime minister. Whereas the national leader's authority at a cabinet meeting was unclear under the old law, the revised Article 4 clarifies his authority to propose important, basic policies at such meetings. Technically, under the old law, it was possible for the prime minister to propose a policy as a member of the cabinet. But cabinet members, including the prime minister, rarely took such initiative. The cabinet dealt with policy issues that had been discussed and preapproved at the vice-ministerial meeting. This practice strengthened the bottom-up style of Japanese government decision making and weakened the political initiative of the prime minister. With the revision, institutional arrangements are clearly set for the national leader to initiate policies at the top.

The authority and function of the Cabinet Secretariat will be also reinforced. The revised Cabinet Law provides it the authority to plan and draft important national policies. This was one of the changes the bureaucrats strongly resisted during the deliberation of Hashimoto's Administrative Reform Council. The existing ministries did not want the Cabinet Secretariat to plan and draft bills that cover their own jurisdiction. The revised law allows the Cabinet Secretariat to develop concrete plans under the direction of the cabinet and prime minister. Theoretically, the prime minister and the cabinet can now initiate and proceed with the policy processes independently of the relevant ministry.

The number and size of the supporting body at the Cabinet Secretariat will be enlarged. The prime minister will be allowed to appoint up to five assistants, increased from three. To assist the chief cabinet secretary and his three deputies, three assistant positions were newly created as special career officers above the bureau-chief level. At this career ranking, the revised law also lists the cabinet public relations officer and the newly created cabinet information officer. In addition, with an executive order the prime minister can also increase the number of secretaries from the current five. This expanded body is expected to strengthen the function of the Cabinet Secretariat as a supporting organ of the prime minister.

Further improving the supporting organ is the establishment of the Cabinet Office. This office will be headed by the prime minister, and administered by the chief cabinet secretary and his deputies. It will be located in the cabinet and therefore ranked higher than other ministries. Its main task is to assist the cabinet and its Secretariat in planning and drafting policy proposals and in coordinating among other ministries.

This new office will be a significant weapon for the prime minister to pursue his policy objectives in several ways. First, the prime minister's authority as head of the Cabinet Office is powerful indeed. He can directly control administrative affairs once the Cabinet Office takes on a policy issue by coordinating among different ministries. Article 7 of the Cabinet Office Establishment Law gives the prime minister authority to direct related ministries and their officers. It also allows the national leader to order the head of the relevant ministries to submit necessary information and provide appropriate explanation. He can also express his opinion to the relevant ministry. This is completely different from the old institutional setting under which the prime minister had no legal authority to supervise each ministry without first receiving cabinet approval.

Second, the Cabinet Office will provide significant administrative support for the prime minister. It will merge a large part of the current Prime Minister's Office and the Economic Planning Agency. Although the total number of officers in the new office is unclear at the time of writing, it will have five bureaus and 20 divisions according to the Obuchi government plan.[4] In addition to 5 bureau chiefs and 20 division directors, there will be 7 bureau-chief-level and 51 director-level officers, and 17 *shingikan* (ranked between bureau chief and director) in charge of different policy issues. This means that nearly 100 executive officers will be working to assist the prime minister in policy areas.

Third, the authority of these officers will be enforced by new institutional arrangements in the National Administrative Organization Law, which was revised as a part of the administrative reform bills of 1999. Article 2 of the revised law facilitates interagency coordination by giving heads of ministries and agencies authority to request other ministries to supply administrative information and explanation and provide their opinion. It also requires each ministry and agency to coordinate with the Cabinet Office as well as with other ministries. This gives the Cabinet Office a legal base to coordinate the interests of different ministries to pursue the prime minister's policy objectives. In addition, the Cabinet Secretariat is designated to conduct "highest-level and final policy coordination."[5] Thus, the new institutional settings provide three levels of policy coordination: among ministries, under the guidance of the Cabinet Office, and finally by the Cabinet Secretariat.

How will these new institutional arrangements change the policy process within the national government? A good and important example will be the budget process. The traditional budget process was typically bottom-up decision making. Initial proposals were drafted by each division of the ministries, and gathered by the ministries' Secretariat. Based on the government's economic forecast, the Ministry of Finance calculated government revenue and set the budget spending ceiling. With the ceiling, the Ministry of Finance examined the initial proposals from the ministries. After this examination, political pressures were taken into consideration in negotiations between the government and the ruling party. Under the old budget process, the prime minister and cabinet had limited roles.

Under the new Cabinet Office Establishment Law, fiscal and budget policies are identified as important national issues. The law also authorizes the prime minister to form the Council on Economic and Fiscal Policy as an advisory organ independent of the bureaucracy. The Council will advise the prime minister on macroeconomic and fiscal policy issues. The new Cabinet Office, which is to merge the functions of current Economic Planning Agency over macroeconomic policy, will provide administrative assistance to the Council and the prime minister. Based on the recommendation of the Council, the prime minister will initiate the budget process by proposing the total size of the budget and prioritizing major spending items. According to former deputy chief cabinet secretary Ishihara Nobuo, this change will "shift the essential function of budget formation from the Ministry of Finance to the Cabinet Secretariat."[6]

The above changes will create new institutional settings for the prime minister. The 1994 electoral changes will eventually make future elections more party-oriented. This will contribute to strengthening the prime minister's control over his own party, and thus over his cabinet. The 1999 diet and government reform will increase the power of the cabinet vis-à-vis the bureaucracy. The introduction of deputy ministers will increase cabinet control over the bureaucracy, and the abolition of the government commissioner system will force the prime minister to form a more competent cabinet. The 2001 administrative reform will provide the prime minister with clear legitimacy to take stronger policy initiatives and empower supporting organs to carry out his policy objectives.

These institutional changes will make it much easier for the prime minister to exercise his leadership. However, they do not automatically guarantee stronger leadership. Such leadership depends on the individual prime minister and his ability to take advantage of the new institutional arrangements. With a weak power base within the ruling party, the new electoral rule may end up strengthening the power of the secretary general and not that of the prime minister. If the prime minister cannot resist factional pressure to choose incompetent cabinet members unable to answer questions in the Diet, the abolition of the government commissioner system may lead to chaotic deliberation. Although the new National Basic Policy Committee is a good forum for the national leader to advertise his policy objectives, it may also reveal that his policy commitment is superficial. Thus, the prime minister may face severe repercussion from the public, the media, the opposition parties, and the business and international communities. Without the prime minister's policy involvement and clear objective, the three-level policy coordination system may pursue a policy outcome different from his original intent. Even with more favorable institutional environments, the fact remains that the prime minister still needs to depend on his informal sources of power to gain support within the government and the ruling party, and from the public, the opposition parties, and the business community.

The prime minister can make a difference in the outcome by utilizing his political resources. For example, although Hosokawa Morihiro was leader of a fragile coalition government, he successfully passed the politically controversial political reform bills that LDP prime ministers Kaifu Toshiki and Miyazawa Kiichi had been unable to enact under a single-majority government. As Hosokawa's political performance demonstrates, the prime minister plays an important role in determining policy.

Japan has undergone a series of tremendous political changes in the postwar period. Contrary to Karel van Wolferen's view of Japan as lacking a political center, there has been a center throughout that period—namely, the prime minister: Yoshida Shigeru's conclusion of the 1951 San Francisco Peace Treaty;

Hatoyama Ichirô's normalization of relations with the Soviet Union in 1955; Kishi Nobusuke's revision of the U.S.–Japan Security Treaty in 1960; Ikeda Hayato's introduction of the 1960 income-doubling plan; Satô Eisaku's successful negotiation of the 1971 reversion of the Okinawa Islands; Tanaka Kakuei's normalization of China-Japan relations in 1972; Miki Takeo's pursuit of the Lockheed scandal in 1976; Nakasone Yasuhiro's administrative reform efforts in 1982–86; Takeshita Noboru's introduction of the 1988 consumption tax; and Hosokawa Morihiro's 1994 political reform. These prime ministers' initiative of policies and their commitment to achieving them are undeniable, and their role has been imperative to the successful outcome of each policy.

NOTES

1. Raisuke Miyawaki, "Difference in the Governing Style between Nakasone and Takeshita" (paper presented at the Johns Hopkins University's Paul Nitze School of Advanced International Studies, December 3, 1992), p. 3.

2. Article 2 of the Cabinet Law to be revised in January 2001 limits the number of cabinet members to 14, but it allows appointment of up to three additional members if necessary.

3. Moroi Ken, interview by author, Tokyo, October 22, 1998.

4. "Kanbô Kyoku oyobi Kashitu no Seiri narabini Bunshôshoku no Katsuyô ni tuite" (Secretariat of the Headquarters of Promoting Central Government Reform, July 15, 1999).

5. "Aratana Shôkan Chôsei Shisutemu ni tuite" (information material no. 10, presented at the 12th Advisory Council Meeting of the Headquarters of Promoting Central Government Reform, March 26, 1999).

6. Ishihara Nobuo, *Kan Kaku Arubeshi* [How the bureaucrats should be] (Tokyo: Shôgakukan Bunko, 1998), p. 189.

Bibliography

ENGLISH LANGUAGE SOURCES

Aberbach, Joel D., Robert D. Putnam, and Bert A. Rockman. *Bureaucrats and Politicians in Western Democracies*. Cambridge: Harvard University Press, 1981.

Allison, Graham T. *Essence of Decision: Explaining the Cuban Missile Crisis*. Boston: Little, Brown, 1971.

Angel, Robert C. *Explaining Economic Policy Failure: Japan in the 1969–1971 International Monetary Crisis*. New York: Columbia University Press, 1991.

———. "Prime Ministerial Leadership in Japan: Recent Changes in Personal Style and Administrative Organization." *Pacific Affairs* 61 (winter 1988/89): 583–602.

Armacost, Michael H. *Friends or Rivals*. New York: Columbia University Press, 1996.

Bagehot, Walter. *The English Constitution*. New York: Dolphin Books, 1964.

Belloni, Frank P. "Factionalism, the Party System and Italian Politics." In *Faction Politics: Political Parties and Factionalism in Comparative Perspective*, ed. Frank P. Belloni and Dennis C. Beller, pp. 73–108. Santa Barbara: ABC Clio, 1978.

Belloni, Frank P, and Dennis C. Beller, eds. *Faction Politics: Political Parties and Factionalism in Comparative Perspective*. Santa Barbara, California: ABC Clio, 1978.

Blustein, Paul. "Japanese Leader Forced to Retreat on Taxes." *Washington Post*, February 5, 1994.

Bryce, James. *Modern Democracy*. New York: Macmillan Company, 1921.

Budge, Ian, and Hans Keman. *Parties and Democracy: Coalition Formation and Government Functioning in Twenty States*. Oxford: Oxford University Press, 1990.

Burch, Martin, and Ian Holliday. *The British Cabinet System*. Hertfordshire: Prentice Hall/Harvester Wheatsheaf, 1996.

Burns, James MacGregor. *Leadership*. New York: Harper Torchbooks, 1978.

Calder, Kent E. *Crisis and Compensation: Public Policy and Political Stability in Japan, 1944–86*. Princeton: Princeton University Press, 1988.

———. "Japan in 1990: Limits to Change." *Asian Survey* 31, no. 1 (January 1991): 21–35.

————. "Kanryô vs. Shomin: Contrasting Dynamics of Conservative Leadership in Post-war Japan." In *Michigan Papers in Japanese Studies No. 1: Political Leadership in Contemporary Japan*, ed. Terry Edward MacDougall, pp. 1–28. Ann Arbor: Center for Japanese Studies, University of Michigan, 1982.

Campbell, Colin. *Governments under Stress: Political Executives and Key Bureaucrats in Washington, London, and Ottawa*. Toronto: University of Toronto Press, 1983.

Campbell, John Creighton. *Contemporary Japanese Budget Politics*. Berkeley: University of California Press, 1977.

Cassese, Sabino. "Is There a Government in Italy? Politics and Administration at the Top." In *Presidents and Prime Ministers*, ed. Richard Rose and Ezra N. Suleiman, pp. 171–202. Washington, D.C.: American Enterprise Institute, 1980.

Cheng, Peter P. "Japanese Interest Group Politics: An Institutional Framework." *Asian Survey* 30, no. 3 (March 1990): 251–65.

Chubb, John E., and Paul E. Peterson, eds. *The New Direction in American Politics*. Washington, D.C.: Brookings Institution, 1985.

Cigler, Allan J., and Burdett A. Loomis, eds. *Interest Group Politics*. Washington, D.C.: Congressional Quarterly Press, 1983.

Crabb, Cecil V., Jr., and Pat M. Holt. *Invitation to Struggle: Congress, the President, and Foreign Policy*. 3d ed. Washington, D.C.: Congressional Quarterly, 1989.

Crossman, R.H.S. "Prime Ministerial Government." In *The British Prime Minister*, ed. Anthony King, pp. 175–94. Durham, North Carolina: Duke University Press, 1985.

Curtis, Gerald. "Big Business and Political Influence." In *Modern Japanese Organization and Decision-Making*, ed. Ezra F. Vogel, pp. 33–70. Berkeley and Los Angeles: University of California Press, 1975.

————. *The Japanese Way of Politics*. New York: Columbia University Press, 1988.

————. *The Logic of Japanese Politics*. New York: Columbia University Press, 1999.

Dalleck, Robert. *Franklin D. Roosevelt and American Foreign Policy, 1932–45*. New York: Oxford University Press, 1979.

Destler, I. M. *American Trade Politics*. 3d ed. Washington, D.C.: Institute for International Economics, 1992.

————. *Presidents, Bureaucrats, and Foreign Policy: The Politics of Organizational Reform*. Princeton: Princeton University Press, 1972.

Destler, I. M., Leslie H. Gelb, and Anthony Lake. *Our Own Worst Enemy: The Unmaking of American Foreign Policy*. New York: Simon & Schuster, 1984.

Destler, I. M., Hideo Sato, Priscilla Clapp, and Haruhiko Fukui. *Managing Alliance: The Politics of U.S.–Japanese Relations*. Washington, D.C.: Brookings Institution, 1976.

Franck, Thomas M., and Edward Weisband. *Foreign Policy by Congress*. New York: Oxford University Press, 1979.

Fukui, Haruhiro. "Japan: Factionalism in a Dominant Party System." In *Faction Politics: Political Parties and Factionalism in Comparative Perspective*, ed., Frank P. Belloni and Dennis C. Beller, pp. 43–72. Santa Barbara, California: ABC Clio, 1978.

————. "The Liberal Democratic Party Revisited: Continuity and Change in the Party's Structure and Performance." *Journal of Japanese Studies* 10, no. 3 (summer 1984): 385–435.

———. *Party in Power*. Berkeley: University of California Press, 1970.

———. "Studies in Policymaking: Review of the Literature." In *Policymaking in Contemporary Japan*, ed. T. J. Pempel, pp. 22–59. Ithaca: Cornell University Press, 1977.

———. "Tanaka Goes to Peking." In *Policymaking in Contemporary Japan*, ed. T. J. Pempel, pp. 60–102. Ithaca: Cornell University Press, 1977.

———. "Too Many Captains in Japan's Internationalization: Travails at the Foreign Ministry." *Journal of Japanese Studies* 13 no. 2 (summer 1987): 359–81.

Government Section, Supreme Commander for the Allied Powers. *Political Reorientation of Japan*. Washington, D.C.: U.S. Government Printing Office, 1949.

Haley, John O. "Consensual Governance." In *The Political Economy of Japan*. Vol. 3, *Cultural and Social Dynamics*, ed. Shumpei Kumon and Henry Rosovsky, pp. 32–62. Stanford, California: Stanford University Press, 1992.

———. "Governance by Negotiation: A Reappraisal of Bureaucratic Power in Japan." *Journal of Japanese Studies* 13, no. 2 (summer 1987): 343–57.

Halperin, Morton H. *Bureaucratic Politics and Foreign Policy*. Washington, D.C.: Brookings Institution, 1974.

Hayao, Kenji. "The Japanese Prime Minister and Public Policy." Ph.D. dissertation, University of Michigan, 1990.

———. *The Japanese Prime Minister and Public Policy*. Pittsburgh: University of Pittsburgh Press, 1993.

Hayes, Louis D. *Introduction to Japanese Politics*. New York: Paragon House, 1992.

Higa, Mikio. "The Role of Bureaucracy in Contemporary Japanese Politics." Ph.D. dissertation, University of California, Berkeley, 1968.

Hine, David, and Renato Finocchi. "The Italian Prime Minister." *West European Politics* 14 (April 1991): 79–96.

Hosoya, Chihiro, and Tomohito Shinoda. eds. *Redefining the Partnership: The United States and Japan in East Asia*. Lanham: Maryland University Press of America, 1998.

Igarashi, Takeshi. "Peace-Making and Party Politics: The Formation of Domestic Foreign-Policy System in Postwar Japan." *Journal of Japanese Studies* 11, no. 2 (summer 1985): 323–356.

Inoguchi, Takashi. "Japan's Response to the Gulf Crisis: An Analytic Overview." *Journal of Japanese Studies* 17, no. 2 (summer 1991): 257–73.

Jain, Purnendra, and Takashi Inoguchi. *Japanese Politics Today: Beyond Karaoke Democracy*. New York: St. Martin's Press, 1997.

Japan Economic Institute. *JEI Report*.

Johnson, Chalmers. "Japan: Who Governs? An Essay on Official Bureaucracy." *Journal of Japanese Studies* no. 2 (autumn 1975): 1–28.

———. *MITI and the Japanese Miracle*. Stanford, California: Stanford University Press, 1982.

Jones, George W. "The Prime Minister's Power." In *The British Prime Minister*, ed. Anthony King, pp. 195–220. Durham, North Carolina: Duke University Press, 1985.

———. "West European Prime Ministers in Perspective." *West European Politics* 14 (April 1991): 163–78.

Kabashima, Ikuo, and Jeffrey Broadbent. "Preference Pluralism: Mass Media and Politics in Japan." *Journal of Japanese Studies* 12, no. 2 (summer 1986): 329–361.

Kaplan, Eugene J. *Japan: The Government-Business Relationship*. Washington, D.C.: Department of Commerce, 1972.

Kato, Junko. *The Problem of Bureaucratic Rationality: Tax Politics in Japan*. Princeton: Princeton University Press, 1994.

Kawasaki, Tsuyoshi. *The Politics of Contemporary Japanese Budget Making: Its Structure and Historical Origins*. Working Paper Series No. 58. Toronto: Joint Centre for Asia Pacific Studies, 1993.

Kernell, Samuel, ed. *Parallel Politics: Economic Policymaking in Japan and the United States*. Washington, D.C.: Brookings Institution, 1991.

King, Anthony. "The British Prime Ministership in the Age of the Career Politician." *West European Politics* 14, no. 2 (April 1991): 25–47.

King, Anthony, ed. *The British Prime Minister*. 2d ed. Durham, North Carolina: Duke University Press, 1985.

Kissinger, Henry, *White House Years*. Boston: Little, Brown,1979.

———. *Years of Upheaval*. Boston: Little, Brown, 1982.

Kohno, Masaru. *Japan's Postwar Party Politics*. Princeton: Princeton University Press, 1997.

Kosai, Yutaka. "The Politics of Economic Management." In *The Political Economy of Japan*. Vol. 1, *The Domestic Transformation*, ed. Kozo Yamamura and Yasukichi Yasuba, pp. 555–92. Stanford, California Stanford University Press, 1987.

Kumon, Shumpei. "Japan Faces Its Future: The Political-Economics and Administrative Reform." *Journal of Japanese Studies* 10, no. 1 (winter 1984): 143–65.

Kumon, Shumpei, and Henry Rosovsky, eds. *The Political Economy of Japan*. Vol. 3, *Cultural and Social Dynamics*. Stanford, California: Stanford University Press, 1992.

Lincoln, Edward. *Japan's Unequal Trade*. Washington, D.C.: Brookings Institution, 1990.

MacDougall, Terry Edward, ed. *Political Leadership in Contemporary Japan*. Michigan Papers in Japanese Studies no. 1. Ann Arbor: Center for Japanese Studies, 1982.

Mackintosh, John P. *The British Cabinet*. 3d ed. London: Stevens, 1974.

Maki, John, ed. and trans. *Japan's Commission on the Constitution: The Final Report*. Seattle: University of Washington Press, 1980.

Mann, Thomas E., ed. *A Question of Balance: The President, the Congress and Foreign Policy*. Washington, D.C.: Brookings Institution, 1990.

McFarland, Andrew S. *Power and Leadership in Pluralist Systems*. Stanford, California: Stanford University Press, 1969.

McNelly, Theodore. *Politics and Government in Japan*. 3d ed. Lanham, Maryland: University Press of America, 1972.

Mény, Yves. *Government and Politics in Western Europe: Britain, France, Italy, Germany*. 2d ed. Oxford: Oxford University Press, 1993.

Miyawaki, Raisuke. "Difference in the Governing Style between Nakasone and Takeshita." Paper presented at the Johns Hopkins University's School of Advanced International Studies, December 3, 1992.

———. " 'Naikaku-Kohokan': Public Relations Advisor to the Prime Minister." Paper presented at the Johns Hopkins University's School of Advanced International Studies, December 3, 1992.

McNelly, Theodore. *Politics and Government in Japan*. 2d ed. Boston: Houghton Mifflin Company, 1972.

Mochizuki, Mike Masato. "Managing and Influencing the Japanese Legislative Process: The Role of Parties and the National Diet." Ph.D. dissertation, Harvard University, 1981.

Murakami, Yasusuke. "The Age of New Middle Mass Politics: The Case of Japan." *Journal of Japanese Studies* 8, no. 1 (winter 1982): 29–72.

Muramatsu, Michio. "In Search of National Identity: The Politics and Policies of the Nakasone Administration." *Journal of Japanese Studies* 13, no. 2 (summer 1987): 271–306.

Muramatsu, Michio, and Ellis Krauss. "The Conservative Policy Line and the Development of Patterned Pluralism." In *The Political Economy of Japan*. Vol. 1, *The Domestic Transformation*, ed. Kozo Yamamura and Yasukichi Yasuba, pp. 516–54. Stanford, California: Stanford University Press, 1987.

Muramatsu, Michio, and Masaru Mabuchi. "Introducing a New Tax in Japan." In *Parallel Politics: Economic Policymaking in Japan and the United States*, ed. Samuel Kernell, pp. 184–207. Washington, D.C.: Brookings Institution, 1991.

Nakamoto, Michiyo. "Hosokawa Plan Has Pleased Few and Made Many Unhappy." *Financial Times*, February 4, 1994.

Nakane Chie. *Human Relations in Japan: Summary Translation of "Tate Shakai no Ningen Kankei."* Tokyo: Ministry of Foreign Affairs, 1972.

Neustadt, Richard E. *Presidential Power and the Modern Presidents: The Politics of Leadership from Roosevelt to Reagan.* New York: Free Press, 1960; revised in 1990.

Norton, Philip. *The British Polity.* 2d ed. New York: Longman, 1991.

Packard, George R. *Protest in Tokyo: The Security Treaty Crisis of 1960.* Princeton: Princeton University Press, 1966.

Page, Glenn D., ed. *Political Leadership: Readings for an Emerging Field.* New York: Free Press, 1972.

Park, Yung H. *Bureaucrats and Ministers in Contemporary Japanese Government.* Berkeley: Institute of East Asian Studies, University of California, 1986.

Paster, Robert A. *Congress and the Politics of U.S. Foreign Economic Policy, 1929–1976.* Berkeley and Los Angeles: University of California Press, 1980.

Patrick, Hugh, and Henry Rovosvky. *Asia's New Giant.* Washington, D.C.: Brookings Institution, 1976.

Pempel, T. J. "The Bureaucratization of Policy Making in Postwar Japan." *American Journal of Political Science* 18 (November 1987): 271–306.

———. "Organizing for Efficiency: The Higher Civil Service in Japan." In *Bureaucrats and Policy Making: A Comparative Overview.* ed. Ezra N. Suleiman, pp. 72–106. New York: Holms and Meier, 1984.

———. "The Unbundling of 'Japan, Inc.': The Changing Dynamics of Japanese Policy Formation." *Journal of Japanese Studies* 13, no. 2 (summer 1987): 271–306.

———, ed. *Policymaking in Contemporary Japan.* Ithaca: Cornell University Press, 1977.

Pempel, T. J., and Keiichi Tsunekawa. "Corporatism without Labor?: The Japanese Anomaly." In *Trend toward Corporatist Intermediation*, ed. Phillippe C. and Lehmbruch Schumitter, pp. 231–69. London: Sage Publications, 1979.

Pyle, Kenneth B. "In Pursuit of a Grand Design: Nakasone betwixt the Past and the Future." *Journal of Japanese Studies* 13, no. 2 (summer 1987): 243–70.

Reischauer, Edwin O. *My Life between Japan and America.* New York: Harper and Row, 1986.

Richardson, Bradley M., and Scott C. Flanagan. *Politics in Japan*. Boston: Little, Brown, 1984.

Rose, Richard. "British Government: The Job at the Top." In *Presidents and Prime Ministers*, ed. Richard Rose and Ezra N. Suleiman, pp. 1–49. Washington, D.C.: American Enterprise Institute, 1980.

———. "The Political Status of Higher Civil Servants in Britain." In *Bureaucrats and Policy Making: A Comparative Overview*, ed. Ezra N. Suleiman, pp. 136–73. New York: Holms and Meier, 1984.

———. "Prime Ministers in Parliamentary Democracies." *West European Politics* 14 (April 1991): 9–24.

Rosenbluth, Frances McCall. *Financial Politics in Contemporary Japan*. Ithaca: Cornell University Press, 1989.

Sartori, Giovanni. *Parties and Party Systems: A Framework for Analysis*. Cambridge: Cambridge University Press, 1976.

Scalapino, Robert A. *Democracy and the Party Movement in Prewar Japan*. Berkeley: University of California Press, 1953.

Scalapino, Robert A, and Masumi Junnosuke. *Parties and Politics in Contemporary Japan*. Berkeley: University of California Press, 1962.

Schlesinger, Arthur M. Jr. *The Imperial Presidency*. Boston: Houghton Mifflin, 1973.

Schlesinger, Jacob M. *Shadow Shoguns: The Rise and Fall of Japan's Postwar Political Machine*. New York: Simon & Schuster, 1997.

Schoppa, Leonard J. *Bargaining with Japan: What American Pressure Can and Cannot Do*. New York: Columbia University Press, 1997.

———. "Zoku Power and LDP Power: Case Study of the Zoku Role in Education Policy." *Journal of Japanese Studies* 17, no. 1 (winter 1991): 79–106.

Schwartz, Frank J. *Advice & Consent: The Politics of Consultation in Japan*. New York: Cambridge University Press, 1998.

Shinoda, Tomohito. "Japan." In *Party Politics and Democratic Development in East and Southeast Asia*, Vol. 2, ed. Wolfgang Sachsenroder. Brookfield: Ashgate Publishing Company, 1998.

———. "Japan's Decision Making under the Coalition Governments." *Asian Survey*, July 1998: 703–723.

———. "Japan's Political Changes and Their Impact on U.S.–Japan Relations." In *Redefining the Partnership: The United States and Japan in East Asia*, ed. Chihiro Hosoya and Tomohito Shinoda. Lanham, Maryland: University Press of America, 1998.

———. "Japan's Political Leadership: The Prime Minister's Power, Style and Conduct: Reform." In *Asian Economic and Political Issues*, Vol. 2, ed. Frank Columbus. Commack, New York: Nova Science Publishers, Inc, 1999: 1–31.

———. "LDP Factions: Their Power and Culture." *Bulletin, The Japan-American Society of Washington* 25, no. 2 (February 1990): 4–7.

———. "Truth behind LDP's Loss." *Washington Japan Journal* 2 (fall 1993): 26–28.

Shoup, Carl S. "The Tax Mission to Japan, 1949–50." In *Lessons from Fundamental Tax Reform in Developing Countries*, ed. Gillis Malcolm. Durham, North Carolina: Duke University Press, 1989.

Spotts, Frederick, and Theodore Wieser. *Italy: A Difficult Democracy*. New York: Cambridge University Press, 1986.

Sundquist, James L. *The Decline and Resurgence of Congress*. Washington, D.C.: Brookings Institution, 1981.

Thayer, Nathaniel B. *How the Conservatives Rule Japan*. Princeton: Princeton University Press, 1969.

Tsurutani, Taketsugu, and Jack B. Gabbert. *Chief Executives: National Political Leadership in the United States, Mexico, Great Britain, Germany, and Japan*. Pullman: Washington State University Press, 1992.

Tucker, Robert C. *Political Leadership*. Columbia: University of Missouri Press, 1981.

Willner, Ann Ruth. *The Spellbinder: Charismatic Political Leadership*. New Haven, Connecticut: Yale University Press, 1984.

van Wolferen, Karel G. *The Enigma of Japanese Power*. New York: Alfred A. Knopf, 1989.

———. "The Japan Problem." *Foreign Affairs* 65 (winter 1987): 288–303.

Young, Jeffrey D. *Japan's Prime Minister Selection Process, 1991 Candidates, and Implications for the United States*. CRS Report 91–695 F. Congressional Research Service, Library of Congress, September 24, 1991.

JAPANESE LANGUAGE SOURCES

Abe Hitoshi, Shindô Muneyuki, and Kawahito Tadashi. *Gaisetsu Gendai Nihon no Seiji* [Introduction to contemporary Japanese politics]. Tokyo: Tokyo Daigaku Shuppan-kai, 1990.

Andô Hiroshi. *Sekinin to Genkai: Akaji Zaisei no Kiseki* [Responsibility and limitation: Tracing fiscal deficit]. Tokyo: Kin'yû Zaisei Kenkyû-sho, 1987.

Aoki Shigeru. *Nagata-chô Makase no Zeisei ga Nihon wo Horobosu* [The tax system made in Nagata-chô to destroy Japan]. Tokyo: Shufu no Tomo-Sha, 1990.

Arai Shunzô and Morita Hajime. *Bunjin Saishô Ôhira Masayoshi* [The intellectual Prime Minister Ôhira Masayoshi]. Tokyo: Shunjû-sha, 1982.

Aruga Tadashi and others, eds. *Kôza Kokusai Seiji 4: Nihon no Gaikô* [Lectures on international politics volume 4: Japan's diplomacy]. Tokyo: Tokyo Daigaku Shuppan-kai, 1989.

Asahi Journal Henshû-bu. *Rikurûtogêto no Kakushin* [The core of the Recruitgate]. Tokyo: Suzusawa Shoten, 1989.

Asahi Shimbun Seiji-bu. *Takeshita-ha Shihai* [The control by the Takeshita faction]. Tokyo: Asahi Shimbun-sha, 1992.

———. *Takeshita Seiken no Hôkai: Rikurûto Jiken to Seiji Kaikaku* [The collapse of the Takeshita administration: The Recruit scandal and political reform]. Tokyo: Asahi Shimbun-sha, 1989.

Asahi Shimbun-sha Seronchôsa-shitu. *Naikaku Shijiritsu Seitô Shijiritsu* [The approval rate for cabinets and political parties]. Tokyo: Asahi Shimbun-sha, April 1996.

Doi Takako. "Watashi no Rirekisho" [My personal history]. *Nihon Keizai Shimbun* (September 1992).

Dokô Toshio. *Watashi no Rirekisho* [My personal history]. Tokyo: Nihon Keizai Shimbun, 1983.

Dokô Toshio, Hosokawa Ryûgen, and Katô Hiroshi. *Dokô-san Yarô* [Let's do it, Mr. Dokô]. Tokyo: Yamate Shobô, 1982.

Ewado Tetsuo. "Ôkurashô: Seikô Tôtei to Zaisei Hatan" [Ministry of Finance: High politic with low bureaucracy and financial crisis]. *Seiron*, April 1986: 172–84.

Fujimoto Kazumi, ed. *Kokkai Kinô Ron: Kokkai no Shikumi to Un'ei* [Arguments for the functional Diet: The mechanism and operation of the Diet]. Tokyo: Hôgaku Shoin, 1990.

Fujimoto Takao. *Fujimoto Takao no Daijin Hôkoku* [Report from Minister Fujimoto Takao]. Tokyo: Planet Shuppan, 1989.

Fukuda Takeo. Interview. "Waga Shushô Jidai" [My time as the prime minister] *Chûô Kôron*, October 1980: 291–95.

———. *Kaiko 90 nen* [Memoir of 90 years]. Tokyo: Iwanami Shoten, 1995.

———. "Watashi no Rirekishol" [My personal history]. *Nihon Keizai Shimbun*, January 26, 1993.

Fukuda Yukihiro. *Zei to Demokuarashî.* [Tax and democracy]. Tokyo: Tôyô Keizai Shinpô-sha, 1984.

———. *Zeisei Kaikaku e no Ayumi* [Steps toward tax reform]. Tokyo: Zeimu Keiri Kyôkai, 1987.

———. *Zoku Zeisei Kaikaku e no Ayumi* [Steps toward tax reform Part II]. Tokyo: Zeimu Keiri Kyôkai, 1988.

Funabashi Yôichi. *Dômei Hyôryu* [Alliance Drift]. Tokyo: Iwanami Shoten, 1997.

Furui Yoshimi. *Shushô no Shokumu Kengen* [The official authority of the prime minister]. Tokyo: Makino Shuppan, 1983.

Furusawa Ken'ichi. *Nicchû Heiwa Yûkô Jôyaku* [China-Japan Peace and Friendship Treaty]. Tokyo: Kôdan-sha, 1988.

Gotôda Masaharu. *Naikaku Kanbô Chôkan* [Chief cabinet secretary]. Tokyo: Kôdan-sha, 1989.

———. *Jô to Ri* [Emotion and logics]. Tokyo: Kôdansha, 1998.

———. *Sasaeru Ugokasu.* [To support and mobilize]. Tokyo: Nihon Keizai Shimbun-sha, 1991.

———. *Sei to Kan* [Politics and bureaucracy]. Tokyo: Kôdan-sha, 1994.

———. *Seiji towa Nanika* [What is politics?]. Tokyo: Kôdan-sha, 1988.

Hanamura Nihachirô. *Seizaikai Paipu Yaku Hanseiki* [My life as a channel between the political and business worlds]. Tokyo: Tokyo Shimbun, 1990.

Hara Yoshihisa. *Kishi Nobusuke: Kensei no Seijika* [Kishi Nobusuke: The politician of power]. Tokyo: Iwanami Shinsho, 1995.

Hasegawa Kazutoshi. "Moto Hishokan Nakasone Yasuhiro wo Kataru III-2" [Former secretary's words on Nakasone Yasuhiro]. *Yatchan's* (May 1990).

Hashimoto Ryûtarô. *Seiken Dakkairon* [To regain power]. Tokyo: Kôdansha, 1994.

Hata Yasuko. *Shushô Kotei* [The prime minister's official residence]. Tokyo: Tokyo Shimbun-sha, 1996.

Hayashi Shigeru and Tsuji Kiyoaki. eds. *Nihon Naikaku Shiroku* [The history of the Japanese cabinet]. Tokyo: Dai-ichi Hôki, 1981.

Hirano Sadao. *Jiyuto no Chôsen* [Challenge of the Liberal Party]. Tokyo: President-sha, 1998.

———. *Ozawa Ichirô tono Nijûnen* [Twenty years with Ozawa Ichirô]. Tokyo: President-sha, 1996.

Hironaka Yoshimichi. *Miyazawa Seiken 644 nichi* [The Miyazawa administration: 644 days]. Tokyo: Gyosei, 1998.

Hirose Michisada. "Gyôsei Kaikaku to Jimintô" [Administrative reform and the LDP], *Sekai*, August 1981: 245–57.

———. *Hojokin to Seikentô* [Subsidies and the government party]. Tokyo: Asahi Shimbun-sha, 1981.

Honzawa Jirô. *Jimintô Habatsu* [LDP factions]. Tokyo: Pîpuru-sha, 1990.

Hori Shigeru. *Sengo Seiji no Oboegaki* [Memorandum of postwar politics]. Tokyo: Mainichi Shimbun, 1975.

Hosokawa Morihiro and Iwakuni Tetsundo. *Hina no Ronri* [The logic of the local community]. Tokyo: Kôbunsha, 1991.

Hosoya Chihiro and Shinoda Tomohito. *Shin Jidai no Nichibei Kankei* [A new era of U.S.–Japan relations]. Tokyo: Yûhikaku, 1998.

Ichikawa Taichi. *"Seshû" Daigishi no Kenkyû* [The study on hereditary Diet members]. Tokyo: Nihon Keizai Shimbun-sha, 1990.

Igarashi Kôzô. *Kantei no Rasen Kaidan* [The spiral staircase of the prime minister's office]. Tokyo: Gyôsei, 1977.

Iio Jun. *Min'eika no Seiji Katei: Rinchô-gata Kaikaku no Seika to Genkai* [Political process of privatization: The achievement and limitation of the Rinchô-style reform]. Tokyo: Tokyo Daigaku Shuppan-kai, 1993.

Ikeda Hayato. *Kinkô Zaisei* [Balanced budget]. Tokyo: Jitsugyô no Nihon-sha, 1952.

Imai Takeru. *Giin Naikaku-sei* [Parliamentary system]. Tokyo: Burên Shuppan, 1991.

Inoguchi Takashi. *Gendai Nihon Seiji Keizai no Kôzu* [The composition of contemporary Japanese political economy]. Tokyo: Tôyô Keizai Shinpô, 1983.

———. *Kokka to Shakai* [The nation and the society]. Tokyo: Tokyo Daigaku Shuppan-kai, 1988.

Inoguchi Takashi and Iwai Tomoaki. *"Zoku Giin" no Kenkyû* [Study on *zoku* members"]. Tokyo: Nihon Keizai Shimbun-sha, 1987.

Ishida Hirohide. *Ishibashi Seiken 71 nichi* [The Ishibashi administration: 71 days]. Tokyo: Gyôsei Mondai Kenkyû-sho, 1985.

Ishihara Nobuo. *Kan Kaku Arubeshi* [How the bureaucrats should be]. Tokyo: Shôgakukan Bunko, 1998.

———. *Kantei 2668 nichi: Seisaku Kettei no Butaiura* [Twenty-six hundred sixty-eight days at the prime minister's office: Behind the scene of decision making]. Tokyo: NHK Shuppan, 1995.

———. *Shushô Kantei no Ketsudan* [The decisions of the prime minister's office]. Tokyo: Chûô Kôron-sha, 1997.

Ishikawa Masumi. *Dêta Sengo Seijishi* [Data on postwar political history]. Tokyo: Iwanami Shoten, 1984.

Ishikawa Masumi and Hirose Michisada. *Jimintô* [The LDP]. Tokyo: Iwanami Shoten, 1989.

Itô Masaya. *Ikeda Hayato Sono Sei to Shi* [Ikeda Hayato: His life and death]. Tokyo: Shiseidô, 1966.

Itô Mitsuharu. "Zeisei Kaikaku wa Dôarubekika" [How tax reform should be]. *Sekai*, October, 1988: 72–87.

Iwai Tomoaki. *Rippô Katei* [The legislative process]. Tokyo Daigaku Shuppan-kai, 1988.

———. *"Seiji Shikin" no Kenkyû* [The study on the political fund]. Tokyo: Nihon Keizai Shimbun, 1990.

Iwai Tomoaki and Inoguchi Takashi. "Zeisei-zoku no Seiji Rikigaku" [Political dynamics of tax *zoku*.] *Chûô Kôron* (March 1987): 96–106.

Kabashima Ikuo. *Seiji Sanka* [Political participation.] Tokyo: Tokyo Daigaku Shuppan-kai, 1988.

Kaizuka Keimei and others. eds. *Zeisei Kaikaku no Chôryû* [The trend for the tax reform.] Tokyo: Yûhikaku, 1990.

Kaminishi Akio. *GNP 1% Waku* [GNP 1% ceiling]. Tokyo: Kadokawa Bunko, 1986.

Kaminogô Toshiaki. *Sôri wo Shikaru Otoko: Dokô Toshio no Tatakai* [The man who scolded the prime minister: The fight of Dokô Toshio.] Tokyo: Kôdan-sha, 1983.

Kan Naoto. *Daijin* [The minister.] Tokyo: Iwanami Shinsho, 1998.

Kanamori Hisao. ed. *Sengo Keizai no Kiseki: Sairon Keizai Hakusho* [Trace of postwar economy: Reexamining the Economic White Papers.] Tokyo: Chûô Keizai-sha, 1990.

Kanemaru Shin. *Tachiwaza Newaza* [Fighting in various ways.] Tokyo: Nihon Keizai Shimbun-sha, 1988.

Kataoka Hiromitsu. *Naikaku no Kinô to Hosa Kikô* [The function of the cabinet and the supporting organizations.] Tokyo: Seibun-dô, 1982.

Katô Hiroshi. *Gyôkaku wa Nihon wo Kaeru* [Administrative reform to change Japan]: Tokyo: Shunjû-sha, 1982.

———. *Nihon Keizai Jiko Henkaku no Toki* [Time for Japan to change.] Tokyo: PHP Kenkyû-sho, 1991.

———. *Taikenteki "Nihon Kaikaku" Ron* ["How to reform Japan" based on my experience.] Tokyo: PHP Brightest, 1990.

Katô Hiroshi and Sandô Yôichi. *Dokô san to tomo ni 730 nichi* [Seven hundred thirty days with Mr. Dokô]. Tokyo: Keizai Ôraisha, 1983.

Katô Junko. *Zeisei Kaikaku to Kanryôsei* [Tax reform and the bureaucracy]. Tokyo: Tokyo Daigaku Shuppankai, 1997.

Kawaguchi Hiroyuki. *Kanryô Shihai no Kôzô* [The mechanism of bureaucratic control]. Tokyo: Kôdan-sha, 1987.

Kawakita Takao. *Ôkurasho: Kanryô Kikô no Chôten* [The Ministry of Finance: The top of the bureaucracy]. Tokyo: Kôdan-sha, 1989.

Kawauchi Issei. *Ôhira Seiken 554 nichi* [The Ôhira administration: 554 Days]. Tokyo: Gyôsei Mondai Kenkyû-sho, 1982.

Kinoshita Kazuo. *Zeisei Chôsa-kai: Sengo Zeisei Kaikaku no Kiseki* [The Tax System Research Council: Trace of postwar tax reforms]. Tokyo: Zeimu Keiri Kyôkai, 1992.

Kishi Nobuhito. *Zei no Kôbô: Ôkura Kanryô Shihanseiki no Sensô* [Battles over tax: A quarter century of war for MOF bureaucrats]. Tokyo: Bungei Shunjû, 1998.

Kishi Nobusuke. *Kishi Nobusuke Kaisô-roku* [Memoirs of Kishi Nobusuke]. Tokyo: Kô-saido, 1983.

Kishi Nobusuke, Yatsugi Kazuo, and Itô Takashi. *Kishi Nobusuke no Kaisô* [Memories of Kishi Nobusuke]. Tokyo: Bungei Shunjû, 1981.

Kishimoto Kôichi. *Gendai Seiji Kenkyû: "Nagata-chô" no Ayumi to Mekanizumu* [Study on contemporary politics. Development and mechanism of Nagata-chô]. Tokyo: Gyôken, 1988.

Kishiro Yasuyuki. *Jimintô Zeisei Chôsa-kai* [The LDP Tax System Research Council]. Tokyo: Tôyô Keizai Shinpô-sha, 1985.

Kitanishi Makoto and Yamada Hiroshi. *Gendai Nihon no Seiji* [Contemporary Japanese politics]. Tokyo: Hôritsu Bunka-sha, 1983.

Kiyomiya Ryû. *Fukuda Seiken 714 nichi* [The Fukuda administration: 714 days]. Tokyo: Gyôsei Mondai Kenkyû-sho, 1984.

Kobayashi Yoshiaki. *Gendai Nihon no Senkyo* [Contemporary Japanese elections]. Tokyo: Tokyo Daigaku Shuppan-kai, 1991.

Kôsaka Masataka. *Saishô Yoshida Shigeru* [Prime Minister Yoshida Shigeru]. Tokyo: Chûô Kôron-sha, 1968.

Kubo Wataru. *Renritsu Seiken no Shinjitsu* [The truth of the coalition governments]. Tokyo: Yomiuri Shimbun-sha, 1998.

Kuribayashi Yoshimitsu. *Ôkurashô Shuzei-kyoku* [Finance Ministry's Tax Bureau]. Tokyo: Kôdan-sha, 1987.

———. *Ôkurashô Shuzei-kyoku* [Finance Ministry's Tax Bureau]. Tokyo: Kôdansha Bunko, 1991.

Kurihara Yûkô. *Ôhira Moto Sôri to Watashi* [Former prime minister Ôhira and me]. Tokyo: Kôsai-dô, 1990.

Kuriyama Takakazu. *Nichibei Dômei: Hyôryu kara no Dakkyaku* [The Japan–U.S. alliance: From drift to revitalization]. Tokyo: Nihon Keizai Shimbunsha, 1997.

Kusano Atsushi. *Kokutetsu Kaikaku: Seisaku Kettei Gêmu no Shuyakutachi* [JNR reform: Main actors in policymaking]. Tokyo: Chûkô Shinsho, 1989.

———. *Shôwa 40 nen 5 gatsu 28 nichi* [May 28, 1965]. Tokyo: Nihon Keizai Shimbun, 1986.

Kusuda Minoru. *Shuseki Hishokan: Satô Sôri tono Jûnenkan* [Chief secretary: Ten years with Prime Minister Satô]. Tokyo: Bungei Shunjû, 1975.

Kusuda, Minoru, ed. *Satô Seiken: 2797 nichi* [The Satô administration: 2,797 days]. Vols. 1 and 2. Tokyo: Gyôsei Mondai Kenkyû-sho, 1983.

Mainichi Shimbun Seiji-bu, ed. *Kenshô Shushô Kantei* [Inspecting the Prime Minister's Office]. Tokyo: Asahi Sonorama, 1988.

———, ed. *Kenshô Kaifu Naikaku* [Inspecting the Kaifu cabinet]. Tokyo: Kadokawa Shoten, 1991.

Maki Tarô. *Nakasone Seiken 1806 nichi* [The Nakasone administration: 1,806 days]. Vols. 1 and 2. Tokyo: Gyôsei Mondai Kenkyûsho, 1988.

———. *Nakasone to wa Nandattanoka* [What was Nakasone?] Tokyo: Sôshi-sha, 1988.

Maruyama Yasuo. *Shôgen Dainiji Rinchô* [Testimony on the second Rinchô]. Tokyo: Shin'ichi Shobô, 1984.

Masumi Junnosuke. *Gendai Seiji 1955 nen igo* [Contemporary politics after 1955]. Tokyo: Tokyo Daigaku Shuppan, 1985.

———. *Sengo Seiji 1945–55 nen* [Postwar politics, 1945–55]. Tokyo: Tokyo Daigaku Shuppan, 1983.

Matsuoka Hideo. *Rengô Seiken ga Hôkai shita Hi: Shakaitô Katayama Naikaku Kara no Kyôkun* [The day the coalition government collapsed: A lesson from the Katayama Socialist cabinet]. Tokyo: Kyôiku Shiryô Shuppan-kai, 1990.

Matsushita Keiichi. *Seiji Gyôsei no Kangaekata* [How to think about politics and government]. Tokyo: Iwanami Shinsho, 1998.

Matsuzaki Tetsuhisa. *Jidai ni totte Soshite Wareware ni totte Nihon Shinto towa Nande Attanoka* [What the Japan New Party was to the time and to us]. Tokyo: Free Press, 1995.

Miki Mutsuko. *Shin Nakuba Tatazu: Otto Miki Takeo to no Gojûnen* [No rising without his belief: Fifty years with my husband, Miki Takeo]. Tokyo: Kôdan-sha, 1989.

Mineyama Akinori. *Kaitai Shinsho Zeisei Kaikakushi* [Explanations: History of tax reforms]. Tokyo, Keibun-sha, 1991.

Minkan Seiji Rinchô. *Nihon Henkaku no Bijon* [Grand vision of political reform]. Tokyo: Kôdan-sha, 1993.

Mitsuzuka Hiroshi. Interview. *Jiyû Minshu*, July 1981: 94–101.

Miyachi Sôshichi. *Shôhizei wo Kenshô suru* [Examining the consumption tax]. Tokyo: Chuô Keizai-sha, 1988.

Miyake Ichirô and others. *Nihon Seiji no Zahyô: Sengo Yonjûnen no Ayumi* [Charts of Japan's politics: Forty years of steps in the postwar]. Tokyo: Yûhikaku, 1985.

Miyamoto Ken'ichi, ed. *Hojokin no Seiji Keizai Gaku* [Political economy of subsidies]. Tokyo: Asahi Shimbun-sha, 1990.

Miyazawa Kiichi. *Sengo Seiji no Shôgen* [Testimony on postwar politics]. Tokyo: Yomiuri Shimbun-sha, 1991.

———. *Shin Goken Sengen* [New declaration to protect the Constitution]. Tokyo: Asahi Shinbun, 1995.

———. *Tokyo-Washington no Mitsudan* [The secret conversations between Tokyo and Washington]. Tokyo: Chûkô Bunko, 1999.

Miyazawa Toshiyoshi. *Nihonkoku Kenpô* [The Japanese Constitution]. Tokyo: Nihon Hyôron-sha, 1955; revised in 1978.

Mizuno Kiyoshi. "Gyôkaku Kaigi: Kanryô tono Kôbô." [The Administrative Reform Council: Unite with bureaucrats]. *Bungei Shunjû*, October 1997: 104–112.

Mizuno Masaichi. *Zaisei Saiken to Zeisei Kaikaku* [Financial reconstruction and tax reform]. Nagoya: Nagoya Daigaku Shuppan kai, 1988.

Mizuno Masaru, *Shuzei Kyokuchô no Sensanbyaku-nichi: Zeisei Bappon Kaikaku eno Ayumi* [Thirteen hundred days as the director general of the Tax Bureau: Steps toward drastic tax reform]. Tokyo: Ôkura Zaimu Kyôkai, 1993.

———. "Yugami no nai Anteishita Zeisei wo Mezashite" [Aiming for undistorted, stable tax system]. *Fainansu*, April 1987: 6–17.

Mori Kishio. *Shushô Kantei no Himitsu* [Secrets of the Prime Minister's Office]. Tokyo: Chôbunsha, 1981.

Morita Minoru. *Seihen: Jimintô Sôsaisen Uramen Antô-shi* [Political upheaval: History of the behind-the-scene battles for the LDP presidency]. Tokyo: Tokuma Shoten, 1991.

Murakami Yasusuke. *Shin Chûkan Taishû no Jidai* [The era of new middle mass]. Tokyo: Chûô Kôron, 1983.

Murakawa Ichirô. *Jimintô no Seisaku Kettei Shisutemu* [The policymaking system of the LDP]. Tokyo: Kyôiku-sha, 1989.

———. *Nihon no Seisaku Kettei Katei* [Japan's policy-making process]. Tokyo: Gyôsei, 1985.

Muramatsu Michio. *Sengo Nihon no Kanryôsei* [Postwar Japan's bureaucratic system]. Tokyo: Tôyô Keizai Shinpô-sha, 1981.

Muramatsu Michio, Itô Mitsutoshi, and Tsujinaka Yutaka. *Nihon no Seiji* [Japan's politics]. Tokyo: Yûhikaku, 1992.

Murayama Chôsa-kai. *Zeisei Kaikaku ni Mukete* [Toward tax reform] (Interim Report). October 8, 1985.

Murayama Tomiichi. *Murayama Tomiichi ga Kataru Tenmei no 561 nichi* [Destined 561 days told by Murayama Tomiichi]. Tokyo: K. K. Best Sellers, 1996.

————. *Sôjanô: Murayama Tomiichi 'Shusho Taiken' no Subete wo Kataru* [Murayama Tomiichi reveals everything about his premier experience]. Tokyo: Daisan Shobô, 1998.

————. "Watashi no Rirekisho" [My personal history]. *Nihon Keizai Shinbun*, June 27, 1996.

Nagai Yônosuke. "Atsuryoku Dantai no Nihonteki Kôzô" [Japanese structure of interest groups]. *Nenpô Seijigaku: Nihon no Atsuryoku Dantai*, 1960.

Nagatomi Yûichirô. *Kindai wo Koete: Ko Ôhira Sôri no Nokosareta mono* [Beyond the contemporary era: What late prime minister Ôhira left for us]. Tokyo: Ôkura Zaimu Kyôkai, 1983.

Naikaku Sôri Daijin Kanbô, ed. *Takeshita Naikaku Sôri Daijin Enzetsu-shû* [Speeches of Prime Minister Takeshita Noboru]. Tokyo: Nihon Kôhô Kyôkai, 1990.

Nakagawa Hidenao. *Shushô Hosa* [Assistant to the prime minister]. Tokyo: PHP Kenkyû-sho, 1996.

Nakamura Akira and Takeshita Yuzuru, eds. *Nihon no Seisaku Katei: Jimintô, Yatô, Kanryô* [Japanese policy making: The LDP, the opposition parties, and the bureaucrats]. Tokyo: Azusa Shuppan-sha, 1984.

Nakamura Keiichirô. *Miki Seiken 747 days* [The Miki administration: 747 days]. Tokyo: Gyôsei Mondai Kenkyû-sho, 1981.

————. *Sôri no Utsuwa* [Caliber for the prime minister]. Tokyo: Kôbun-sha, 1996.

Nakano Shirô. *Tanaka Seiken 886 nichi* [The Tanaka administration: 886 days]. Tokyo: Gyôsei Mondai Kenkyû-sho, 1982.

Nakasone Yasuhiro. "Kokumin Rinchô to Jiritsu Jijo no Gyôkaku" [*Rinchô* for the people and administrative reform for self-reliance]. *Jiyû Minshu*, June 1981: 15–19.

————. *Seiji to Jinsei* [Politics and life]. Tokyo: Kôdan-sha, 1992.

————. *Tenchi Ujô* [Affection in heaven and on earth]. Tokyo: Bungei Shunjû, 1996.

Nakayama Sohei. Interview. *Shûkan Asahi*, May 4 and 11, 1973: 142–46.

Namikawa Shino. *Gyôsei Kaikaku no Shikumi* [The mechanism of administrative reform]. Tokyo: Tokyo Keizai Shinpô-sha, 1997.

Nihon Gyôsei Gakkai, ed. *Naikakuseido no Kenkyû* [The study on the cabinet system]. Tokyo: Gyôsei, 1987.

————, ed. *Gyôsei Kaikakuno Suishin to Teikô* [The promotion for resistance against the administrative reforms]. The Annuals of the Japanese Society for Public Administration, Vol. 5, 1966.

Nihon Keizai Shimbun-sha, ed. *Dokyumento Seiken Tanjô* [Documentary, the birth of an administration]. Tokyo: Nihon Keizai Shimbun-sha, 1991.

————, ed. *Ôkurasho no Yûutsu* [Headache of the Finance Ministry]. Tokyo: Nihon Keizai Shimbun-sha, 1992.

————, ed. *"Renritsu Seiken" no Kenkyû* [Study of coalition governments]. Tokyo: Nihon Keizai Shimbun-sha, 1994.

————, ed. *Seifu to wa Nanika* [What is the government]. Tokyo: Nihon Keizai Shimbun-sha, 1981.

Nonaka Hiromu. *Watashi wa Tatakau* [I fight]. Tokyo: Bungei Shunjû, 1996.

Nosaka Kôken. *Seiken: Henkaku eno Michi* [The administration: Road toward change]. Tokyo: Suzusawa Shoten, 1996.

Ogura Takekazu. *Sankenjin Zeisei Mondô* [Three people's dialogue on Tax Politics]. Tokyo: Nôbunkyo, 1988.

Ôhinata Ichirô. *Kishi Seiken 1241 nichi* [The Kishi administration: 1,241 Days]. Tokyo: Gyôsei Mondai Kenkyû-sho, 1985.

Ôhira Masayoshi. *Watashi no Rirekisho* [My personal history]. Tokyo: Nihon Keizai Shimbun-sha, 1978.

Ôhira Masayoshi Kaisôroku Kankô-kai. *Ôhira Masayoshi Kaisô-roku: Tsuisô hen and Denki-hen* [Memoirs of Ôhira Masayoshi: Vol. 1, Reminiscence; and Vol. 2, Biography]. Tokyo: Ôhira Masayoshi Kaisôroku Kankô-kai, 1982.

Okano Kaoru, ed. *Naikaku Sôri Daijin* [The prime minister]. Tokyo: Gendai Hyôron-sha, 1985.

Okazawa Norio. *Seitô* [Political parties]. Tokyo: Tokyo Daigaku Shuppan-kai, 1988.

Ôkita Saburô. *Ekonomisuto Gaishô no 252 nichi: Takyokuka Jidai no Nihon Gaikô wo Kangaeru* [Two hundred fifty-two days of an economist foreign minister: Talks on the Japanese diplomacy in the multipolar era]. Tokyo: Tôyô Keizai Shinpô-sha, 1980.

Ôkubo Shôzô. *Hadaka no Seikai* [Political world as naked]. Tokyo: Simul Shuppan-kai, 1975.

Ôsuga Mizuo. *Shushô Kantei Konjaku Monogatari* [The prime minister's residence: The past and the present]. Tokyo: Asahi Sonorama, 1995.

Ôtake Hideo. *Gendai Nihon no Seiji Kenryoku Keizai Kenryoku* [Political power and economic power in contemporary Japan]. Tokyo: San'ichi Shobô, 1979.

Ozaki Mamoru. "Kôhei Hiroigaki" [Notes on Equality]. *Fainansu*, February 1989: 10–16.

———. "Uriagezei Hitori Gatari" [Monologue on the sales tax]. *Fainansu*, September 1989: 43–52; (October 1989): pp. 55–65; and (November 1989): 66–74.

———., ed. *Shôhizei Hô Shôkai* [Detailed explanation on consumption tax]. Tokyo: Zaisei Keiri Kyôkai, 1990.

Ozawa Ichirô. *Kataru* [Talk]. Tokyo: Bungei Shunjû, 1996.

———. *Nippon Kaizô Keikaku* [Japan reform plan]. Tokyo: Kôdan-sha, 1993.

Sakurada Takeshi and Shikanai Nobutaka. *Ima Akasu Sengo Hishi* [The secret postwar history revealed now]. Tokyo: Sankei Shuppan, 1983.

Sataka Makoto. *Nihon Kanryô Hakusho* [White paper on Japanese bureaucracy]. Tokyo: Kôdan-sha, 1989.

Sassa Atsuyuki. *Kiki Kanri Saishôron* [On leadership in crisis management]. Tokyo: Bungei Shunjû, 1995.

———. *Shin Kiki Kanri no Nouhau* [New know-hows for crisis management]. Tokyo: Bungei Shunjû, 1991.

Satô Akiko. *Watashi no Tanaka Kakuei Nikki* [My diary on Tanaka Kakuei]. Tokyo: Shinchô-sha, 1994.

Satô Seizaburô and Matsuzaki Tetsuhisa. *Jimintô Seiken* [The LDP administrations]. Tokyo: Chûô Kôron, 1986.

Sekai Heiwa Kenkyusho, ed. *Nakasone Naikakushi* [The history of the Nakasone cabinet]. Vols. 1 and 3 Tokyo: Sekai Heiwa Kenkyûsho, 1995.

Shindô Muneyuki. *Gyôsei Kaikaku to Gendai Seiji* [Administrative reform and contemporary politics]. Tokyo: Iwanami Shoten, 1986.

———. *Zaisei Hatan to Zeisei Kaikaku* [Financial breakdown and tax reform]. Tokyo: Iwanami Shoten, 1989.

Shinkôsô Forum, ed. "Nakayama Sohei shi Nihon no 'Kiki Kanri' wo Kataru" [Mr. Nakayama Sohei talks on "Japan's crisis management"]. *Shinkôsô Booklet* no. 1 (September 20, 1991).

Shinoda Tomohito. *Kantei no Kenryoku* [The power of the Prime Minister's Office]. Tokyo: Chikuma Shinsho, 1994.

———. *Sôri Daijin no Kenryoku to Shidôryoku*. [The power and leadership of the prime minister]. Tokyo: Tokyo Keizai Shinpô-sha, 1994.

Shiota Ushio. *Kishi Nobusuke*. Tokyo: Kodansha, 1996.

Shiratori Rei, ed. *Nihon no Naikaku* [The Japanese cabinet]. Tokyo: Shin Hyôron-sha, 1981.

Sômu-chô Gyôsei Kanri-kyoku. *Gyôsei Kikôzu* [Administrative organizational charts]. 1991.

Sugizaki Shigemitsu. "Zeisei Kaikaku no Gaiyô" [Outline of tax reform]. *Fainansu*, February 1989: 17–59.

Suzuki Kenji. *Rekidai Sôri Sokkin no Kokuhaku* [Confessions by close associates of the prime ministers]. Tokyo: Mainichi Shimbun-sha, 1991.

Suzuki Yukio. *Keizai Kanryô: Shin Sangyô Kokka no Prodyûsâ* [The economic bureaucrats: The producers of a new industrial nation]. Tokyo: Nihon Keizai Shimbun-sha, 1969.

Tachibana Takashi. "Kensatsu no Kakumo Nagaki Nemuri" [Such a long sleep for the Prosecutor's Office]. *Bungei Shunjû*, December 1992: 94–109.

Tagawa Seiichi. *Nicchû Kôshô Hiroku* [Secret record of Sino-Japanese negotiation]. Tokyo: Mainichi Shimbun-sha, 1973.

Tahara Sôichirô *Atama no Nai Kujira: Seijigeki no Shinjitsu* [Headless whale: The truth of political plays]. Tokyo: Asahi Shimbun-sha, 1997.

———. "Gyôji ga Yokozuna ni natte shimatta Suzuki Zenkô Sôri Daijin." [Prime Minister Suzuki Zenkô: A referee who became *yokozuna*]. *Chûô Kôron*, October 1980: 266–90.

———. *Kyodaina Rakujitsu: Ôkura Kanryô Haisô no 850 nichi*. [Huge sunset: the retreat of MOF bureaucrats for 850 days]. Tokyo: Bungei Shunjû, 1998.

———. *Nihon no Kanryô 1980* [Japan's bureaucrats 1980]. Tokyo: Bungei Shunjû, 1979.

———. *Sôri wo Ayatsutta Otokotachi* [Men who controlled prime ministers]. Tokyo: Kôdan-sha, 1989.

Takemura Masayoshi. "Renritsu Seikenka no ano 'Fukushizei' tekkai wa Nani wo Monogataruka" [What does the withdrawal of the welfare tax under the coalition government mean]. *Bungei Shunjû*, July 1997.

Takenaka Heizô. *Keisei Zaimin: Keizai Senryaku Kaigi no 180 nichi* [Governing the world to rescue people: 180 days of the Economic Strategy Council]. Tokyo: Daiyamondo-sha, 1999.

Takeshita Noboru. *Shôgen Hoshu Seiken* [Testimony on conservative administrations]. Tokyo: Yomiuri Shimbun-sha, 1991.

Takeshita Noboru and Hirano Sadao, eds. *Shôhizei Seido Seiritsu no Enkaku*. [Development toward the introduction of the consumption tax system]. Tokyo: Gyôsei, 1993.

Tanaka Kakuei Kinenkan, ed. *Watashi no naka no Tanaka Kakuei* [Tanaka Kakuei in my memory]. Niigata: Tanaka Kakuei Kinenkan, 1998.

Tanaka, Rokusuke. *Futatabi Ôhira Masayoshi no Hito to Seiji* [Again on the personality and politics of Ôhira Masayoshi]. Tokyo: Asahi Sonorama, 1981.

Tanaka Shûsei. *Sakigake to Seiken Kôtai* [Sakigake and political change]. Tokyo: Toyo Keizai Shinpo, 1994.

Tomita Nobuo. *Ashida Seiken 223 nichi* [The Ashida administration 223 days]. Tokyo: Gyôken, 1992.

Tsuda Tatsuo. *Zaikai-Nihon no Shihaisha Tachi* [The business community: The people who rule Japan]. Tokyo: Gakushû no Tomo-sha, 1990.

Tsuji Kiyoaki. *Shinban Nihon Kanryôsei no Kenkyû* [New edition, study on the Japanese bureaucracy system]. Tokyo: Tokyo Daigaku Shuppan-kai, 1969.

Tsujinaka Yutaka. *Rieki Shûdan* [Interest groups]. Tokyo: Tokyo Daigaku Shuppan-kai, 1988.

Tsutsui Kiyotada. *Ishibashi Tanzan: Ichi Jiyû Shugi Seijika no Kiseki* [Ishibashi Tanzan: Trace of one liberal politician]. Tokyo: Chûô Kôron-sha, 1986.

Uchida Kenzô. *Sengo Nihon no Hoshu Seiji* [Conservative politics in postwar Japan]. Tokyo: Iwanami Shoten, 1969.

Uchida Kenzô and others, eds. *Zeisei Kaikaku wo meguru Seiji Rikigaku: Jimin Yûika no Seiji Katei* [Political dynamics of the tax reform: The political process under the LDP predominance]. Tokyo: Chûô Kôron-sha, 1988.

Ueda Kôichirô. *Shôhizei, Seiji Taiketsu no Bunseki* [Analysis on political confrontation over the consumption tax]. Tokyo: Shin Nihon Shuppan-sha, 1989.

Uji Toshihiko. *Suzuki Seiken 863 nichi* [The Suzuki administration: 863 days]. Tokyo: Gyôsei Mondai Kenkyû-sho, 1983.

Usui Nobuaki. *Kansetsuzei no Genjô* [Current status of indirect taxes]. Tokyo: Ôkura Zaimu Kyôkai, 1987.

Wada Yatsuka. *Nihon no Zeisei* [The Japanese tax system]. Tokyo: Yûhikaku, 1988; revised, 1990.

Wakaizumi Kei. *Tasaku Nakarishi wo Shinzemu to Hossu* [Wish to believe that there was no option]. Tokyo: Bungei Shunjû, 1994.

Watanabe Akio, ed. *Sengo Nihon no Saishô tachi* [The prime ministers of postwar Japan]. Tokyo: Chûô Kôron-sha, 1995.

Watanabe Tsuneo. *Habatsu to Tatôka Jidai* [Factions and the multiparty era]. Tokyo: Sekka-sha, 1967.

———. *Nagata-chô Kenbunroku* [Observation on Nagata-chô]. Tokyo: Sekka-sha, 1980.

———. *Tôshu to Seitô: Sono Rîdâshippu no Kenkyû* [Party leaders and political parties: Study on their leadership]. Tokyo: Kôbun-sha, 1961.

Yajima Kôichi. *Kokkai* [The Diet]. Tokyo: Gyôken, 1987.

Yamada Eizô. *Shôden Satô Eisaku* [True story of Satô Eisaku]. Tokyo: Shinchô-sha, 1988.

Yamaguchi Jirô. *Igirisu no Seiji Nihon no Seiji* [British politics, Japanese politics]. Tokyo: Chikuma Shinsho, 1998.

———. *Ittô Shihai Taisei no Hôkai* [The collapse of the one-party-dominance system]. Tokyo: Iwanami Shoten, 1989.

———. *Ôkura Kanryô Shihai no Shûen* [The end of the domination by Finance Ministry bureaucrats]. Tokyo: Iwanami Shoten, 1987.

———. *Seiji Kaikaku* [Political reform]. Tokyo: Iwanami Shinsho, 1993. Yamaguchi Kimio, ed. *Nihon no Zaisei* [Japan's budget]. Tôyô Keizai Shinpô-sha, 1992.

Yamaguchi Yasushi. *Seiji Taisei* [Political system]. Tokyo: Tokyo Daigaku Shuppan-kai, 1989.

Yamamoto Shichihei. *Habatsu no Kenkyû* [Study on factions]. Tokyo: Bungei Shunjû, 1989.

Yan Jiaqi. *Shunôron* [Theory of national leaders]. Translated from Chinese to Japanese language. Tokyo: Gakusei-sha, 1992.

Yanagisawa Hakuo. *Akaji Zaisei no Jûnen to Yonin no Sôri tachi* [Ten years of fiscal deficit and four prime ministers]. Tokyo: Nihon Seisansei Honbu, 1985.

Yano Junya. *Nijû Kenryoku Yami no Nagare* [Dual-power, current in the dark]. Tokyo: Bungei Shunjû, 1994.

Yayama Tarô. "Kokutetsu Rôshi Kokuzoku-ron" [Argument that JNR employers and employees are both traitors to the nation]. *Bungei Shunjû*, April 1982: 92–112.

Yomiuri Shimbun Chôsa Kenkyû Honbu, ed. *Nihon no Kokkai* [The Japanese Parliament]. Tokyo: Yomiuri Shimbun-sha, 1988.

Yomiuri Shimbun Seiji-bu, ed. *Sôri Daijin Nakasone Yasuhiro* [Prime Minister Nakasone Yasuhiro]. Tokyo: Gendai Shuppan-sha, 1987.

———, ed. *Sôri Daijin* [The prime minister]. Tokyo: Yomiuri Shimbun-sha, 1971; revised in 1972.

Yoshida Shigeru. *Kaisô Jûnen* [Memoir of ten years]. Tokyo: Tokyo Shirakawa Shoin, 1957; reprinted in 1982.

Yoshida Taroichi. Interview. "Zaisei Shin Jidai" [New era for fiscal policy]. *Ekonomisuto*, January 25, 1983: 84–91.

Yoshimura Katsumi. *Ikeda Seiken 1575 nichi* [The Ikeda administration: 1,575 days]. Tokyo: Gyôsei Mondai Kenkyû-sho, 1985.

PERSONAL INTERVIEWS

Asakura Kôji, assistant manager, Secretariate for the Preparatory Committee for Central Government Reform. Tokyo, November 5, 1998, and April 26, 1999.

Fukuda Yasuo, member of the House of Representative and former chief secretary to Prime Minister Fukuda Takeo. Tokyo, December 15, 1992.

Gotôda Masaharu, justice minister and former administrative deputy chief cabinet secretary under the Tanaka Kakuei administration and former chief cabinet secretary under the Nakasone Yasuhiro administration. Tokyo, December 18, 1992, and August 27, 1998.

Hagiwara Seiji, deputy director, Corporate Behavior Division, Industrial Policy Bureau, the Ministry of International Trade and Industry. Tokyo, December 22, 1992.

Hamaoka Takashi, research officer, Executive Office of the Administrative Reform Council. Tokyo, December 19, 1997.

Handa Yoshihiro, former senior assistant for public relations to Prime Ministers Murayama Tomiichi and Hashimoto Ryûtarô. Tokyo, July 17, 1996.

Hirose Katsusada, secretary to Prime Minister Miyazawa Kiichi and former director of the Corporate Behavior Division, Ministry of International Trade and Industry. Tokyo, December 15, 1992.

Hosokawa Morihiro, former prime minister. Tokyo, November 15, 1996.

Kannari Yôji, former director of planning, Japan New Party. Tokyo, September 13, 1996.

Katô Hiroshi, professor at Keiô University and chairman of the Government Tax Commission. Tokyo, August 6, 1992.

Kitazawa Hideo, former assistant to Prime Minister Hata Tsutomu. Tokyo, September 2, 1996.

Konaga Keiichi, president of Arabia Oil Company, former assistant to Prime Minister

Tanaka Kakuei, and former vice minister of the Ministry of International Trade and Industry. Tokyo, December 14, 1992.

Kumon Shumpei, professor at the International University of Japan and a former member of the Government Tax Commission. Tokyo, December 15, 1992.

Kuribayashi Yoshimitsu, journalist and author of *Ôkura Shuzei-kyoku* [Finance Ministry's Tax Bureau]. Tokyo, August 6, 1992.

Matoba Junzô, former senior assistant for domestic affairs to Prime Ministers Nakasone Yasuhiro and Takeshita Noboru. Tokyo, December 16, 1992.

Miyawaki Raisuke, former senior assistant for public relations to Prime Ministers Nakasone Yasuhiro and Takeshita Noboru. Washington, D.C., December 9, 1992, and March 10, 1993.

Mizuno Masaru, vice chairman of the Japan Life Insurance Association, former director general of the Tax Agency, and former director general of the Tax Bureau of the Ministry of Finance. Tokyo, August 7, 1992.

Moroi Ken, advisor of Taiheiyo Cement K. K. and member of the Administrative Reform Council under the Hashimoto administration. Tokyo, October 22, 1998.

Murayama Tatsuo, member of the House of Representative and former finance minister. Tokyo, August 10, 1992.

Murayama Tomiichi, former prime minister. Tokyo, September 13, 1996.

Nagatomi Yûichirô, chairman of QUICK Research Institute and former senior assistant to Prime Minister Ôhira Masayoshi. Tokyo, December 17, 1992.

Nakamura Keiichirô, former assistant to Prime Minister Miki Takeo. Tokyo, December 17, 1992.

Nakao Yasuhisa, deputy director, Retail Sales Division, the Agency of Small Business, the Ministry of International Trade and Industry. Tokyo, August 5, 1992.

Nakayama Sohei, special advisor, The Industrial Bank of Japan. Tokyo, August 4 and December 15, 1992, and October 24, 1996.

Namikawa Shino, former assistant to Dokô Toshio and Secretary General of Kokumin Gyôkaku Kaigi. Tokyo, December 19, 1997.

Okano Tadashi, staff, *Keizai Dôyûkai*, December 15, 1998.

Saka Atsuo, budget examiner for the Prime Minister's Office, Budget Bureau, the Ministry of Finance, and assistant to Prime Minister Hashimoto Ryûtarô. Tokyo, August 6, 1992, and July 12, 1996 (on the telephone).

Suzuki Kenji, editorial writer of the Mainichi newspaper and author of *Rekidai Sôri Daijin Sokkin no Kokuhaku*. Tokyo, December 17, 1992.

Tanaka Shigeru, assistant to Nakasone Yasuhiro. Tokyo, December 22, 1992.

Uchimura Yoshihide, former vice minister of agriculture, forestry, and fishery. Tokyo, April 1989.

Watanabe Hiroshi, director, Third Tax System Division, Tax Bureau, Ministry of Finance. Tokyo, August 5, 1992.

Yamanaka Sadanori, former chairman of the LDP's Tax System Research Council and former minister of International Trade and Industry. Tokyo, December 16, 1992.

Index

About the Author

TOMOHITO SHINODA is Associate Professor at the International University of Japan. He formerly served as Tokyo Representative of the Edwin O. Reischauer Center for East Asian Studies. He is the author or coeditor of numerous studies of Japanese politics and government and U.S.-Japanese relations.

ISBN 0-275-96994-0

90000>